Mass Customization Information Systems in Business

Thorsten Blecker
Hamburg University of Technology (TUHH), Germany

Gerhard Friedrich
University of Klagenfurt, Austria

INFORMATION SCIENCE REFERENCE

Hershey · New York

Acquisitions Editor:	Kristin Klinger
Development Editor:	Kristin Roth
Senior Managing Editor:	Jennifer Neidig
Managing Editor:	Sara Reed
Assistant Managing Editor:	Sharon Berger
Copy Editor:	Susanna Svidunovich
Typesetter:	Jamie Snavely
Cover Design:	Lisa Tosheff
Printed at:	Yurchak Printing Inc.

Published in the United States of America by
Information Science Reference (an imprint of IGI Global)
701 E. Chocolate Avenue, Suite 200
Hershey PA 17033
Tel: 717-533-8845
Fax: 717-533-8661
E-mail: cust@idea-group.com
Web site: http://www.info-sci-ref.com

and in the United Kingdom by
Information Science Reference (an imprint of IGI Global)
3 Henrietta Street
Covent Garden
London WC2E 8LU
Tel: 44 20 7240 0856
Fax: 44 20 7379 0609
Web site: http://www.eurospanonline.com

Library of Congress Cataloging-in-Publication Data

Mass customization information systems in business / Thorsten Blecker and Gerhard Friedrich, editors.

p. cm.

Summary: "This book describes original, innovative works on IT systems for mass customization, and provides a multitude of solutions, tools, concepts and successful realizations of IT systems for mass customization. It discusses state-of-the-art mass customization while depicting the importance of IT in making the strategy function efficiently in order to support the business processes required for manufacturing individualized products"--Provided by publisher.

Includes bibliographical references and index.

ISBN 978-1-59904-039-4 (hardcover) -- ISBN 978-1-59904-041-7 (ebook)

1. Flexible manufacturing systems. 2. Product management. 3. Customer relations. 4. Consumers' preferences. I. Blecker, Thorsten. II. Friedrich, Gerhard.

TS155.65.M38 2007

658.4'038011--dc22

2006039660

British Cataloguing in Publication Data
A Cataloguing in Publication record for this book is available from the British Library.

Table of Contents

Section I
Theory of Information Technology for Mass Customization

Section II
Frameworks for Mass Customization

Section III
Innovative Information Technology Approaches for Mass Customization

Detailed Table of Contents

Section I
Theory of Information Technology for Mass Customization

Chapter I

Chapter I provides a systematic review of literature on how mass customization with configurable products and use of configurators affect companies. It focuses on benefits that can be gained and challenges which companies may face. A supplier can move to mass customization and configuration from mass production or from full customization. The chapter also reviews benefits and challenges from the customer perspective. Finally, the future research directions, open challenges, and problems are identified.

Chapter II

Chapter II attempts to present an alternative for product modeling based on applied research activities. The model proposed is based on a concept supported by different views: functional, technological, and physical. With the aim of making the model learner-friendly, the chapter also presents an industrial case applied in the lift industry. The specific problems, the model used, the implementation carried out, and the results obtained are described in detail. The objective is to make a contribution based on the industrial practice to one of the basic enablers for product configuration. The final aim is to speed up the supply-chain process in mass customization scenarios.

Chapter III reviews how mass customization and product configuration can benefit engineer-to-order companies. The relevant main literature in the area is reviewed to identify the benefits. Furthermore, the challenges of implementing product configuration in an engineer-to-order company are described. Finally, a number of suggestions for meeting these challenges are presented. In addition, a case description is introduced which supports that product configuration can benefit engineer-to-order companies even though there are a number of challenges to be met. The chapter concludes that engineer-to-order companies can certainly benefit from product configuration by improving business process efficiency as well as information quality and ultimately improving the company's competitive advantage.

Chapter IV will elaborate on complexity in supply chains and the implications on supply chain design. It investigates the specific requirements of supply chain processes in terms of flexibility versus standardization, evaluating the feasibility of designing, customizing, assessing, and improving logistics processes within a framework provided by process reference models. Mass customization and, in particular, a configuration approach for financial services will be discussed for their applicability for reducing complexity in a process environment. Process reference frameworks will be used as elements of an "open variant process model". The Supply Chain Operations Reference model defined by the Supply Chain Council as the major cross-industry standard for supply chain management will be discussed for its usefulness and shortcomings in "process mass customization", with a focus on systems implementation.

Section II
Frameworks for Mass Customization

Chapter V presents an associative classification-based recommendation system to support online customer decision-making when facing a huge amount of choices. Recommendation systems have been recently introduced to e-commerce sites in order to solve the information overload and mass confusion problem. This chapter applies knowledge discovery techniques to overcome the drawback of conventional recommendation systems approaches. The framework of the associative classification-based recommendation system has been addressed in this chapter. The system analysis, design, and implementation issues in an Internet programming environment are also presented. Taking the advantage of accumulative knowledge from historical data, the efficiency and effectiveness of B2C e-commerce applications are improved.

Chapter VI

Chapter VI presents the knowledge-based recommender environment Koba4MS (Knowledge-based Advisors for Marketing and Sales) which allows a flexible mapping of product, marketing, and sales knowledge to the representation of a recommender knowledge-base. In Koba4MS diagnosis, personalization and knowledge acquisition techniques are integrated to provide an infrastructure for the interactive selling of financial services. Those require deep knowledge about the product domain as well as about potential wishes and needs of customers. In this context, sales representatives can differ significantly in their expertise and level of sales knowledge. Therefore, financial service providers ask for tools supporting sales representatives in the dialog with the customer.

Chapter VII

Chapter VII proposes a standard-based framework to assist industrial organizations develop interoperability in mass customization information systems. After identifying the major challenges for business and information systems in mass customization, the authors propose an innovative standard-based conceptual architecture for a combined model-driven and services-oriented platform. The chapter concludes describing a global methodology for integration of models and applications, to enhance an enterprise's interoperability in the support of mass customization practices, keeping the same organization's technical and operational environment, improving its methods of work and the usability of the installed technology through harmonization, and integration of the enterprise models in use by customers, manufacturers, and suppliers.

Chapter VIII

Chapter VIII presents a Web-enabled, agent-based information system model to support mass customized markets. Furthermore, a distributed, real-time, Java-based, mobile intelligent information system is presented. The system introduces four general-purpose intelligent agents to support the entire mass customization process. The adoption of this approach by a semiconductor manufacturing firm resulted in reductions in product lead time (by half), buffer inventory (from five to two weeks), and manual transactions (by 80%). Similarly, the adoption by a leading automotive manufacturer resulted in a 51% total inventory reduction while increasing plant utilization by 30%. These results verify that the successful adoption of this system can reduce inventory and logistic costs, improve delivery performance, increase manufacturing facilities utilization, and provide a higher overall profitability.

Chapter IX concentrates on the role of the supply chain decoupling point. Therefore, this chapter introduces different levels of customization and mass operations as well as three types of mass customization. It argues that in each mass customization type, information systems in upstream and downstream of the decoupling point can be varied. Consequently, information flows in different types of mass customization have been examined. This analysis is an endeavor to organize mass customization information systems across the supply chain; it can also be a useful structure for future researches in this area as well.

Section III
Innovative Information Technology Approaches for Mass Customization

Chapter X presents a set of scenario-based methods and techniques to support the development of system architectures that are more future-proof, and are also advantageous for mass customization. These methods and techniques have originally been developed for highly-customized professional systems, in particular medical imaging equipment. The chapter introduces mass customization as a business strategy that aims at satisfying, in a timely and cost-effective manner, the various needs of different customers. For that purpose, a system architecture is needed that supports two different kinds of variability: Variability in space provides a range of different products where each addresses the specific needs of an individual customer; and variability in time allows the products to evolve and thus meet new requirements. In defining such an architecture, two issues should be considered. One is how to anticipate the most likely changes in the external business environment, and hence in the customers' future needs. The other is whether the architecture can address these changes effectively

Chapter XI gives an overview on the current research issues in the domain of knowledge-based configuration technology. Knowledge-based configuration systems have made their way into industrial practice. Nowadays, all major vendors of configuration systems rely on some form of declarative knowledge representation and intelligent search techniques for solving the core configuration problem. As the development has not come to an end as, in a world that becomes increasingly automated and wired together, constantly new challenges for the development of intelligent configuration systems arise, this chapter provides a view on future research issues. Finally, this chapter summarizes the state of the art, recent achievements, novel approaches, and open challenges in the field of knowledge-based configuration technology.

Chapter XII draws on the theory of fuzzy cognitive maps to propose a modeling approach for mass customization of services. The proposed model integrates concepts from service quality and customer preferences with business process and IT capabilities models. The model presented in this chapter is, to the best of our knowledge, the only fuzzy service model for mass customization that provides the means to consider the business objectives for service customization, associates them with specific business areas, and suggests opportunities for mass customization. In contrast to other service design and management approaches, the proposed model is dynamic, exhibits flexibility and responsiveness to environmental changes and customizability to specific organizational contexts, and allows the development of planning scenarios.

Chapter XIII introduces a new concept, value customization, to increase the level of customer satisfaction. It presents methodologies and practice for designers to customize value in a service-in-industrial-operation based on the discipline of service engineering. Service engineering aims at creating more value largely by knowledge and service contents rather than just materialistic contents. This chapter addresses the importance of identifying value to be provided with specific customers based on their particular requirements, which has only briefly been discussed in researches of mass customization. In addition, both service activities and physical products can be crucial to realize value. Several further research issues such as general design methods for value customization were also identified.

Foreword

When Henry Ford announced the introduction of the "Model T" in 1908, he remarked that "any customer can have a car painted any color that he wants, as long as it is black" and still had the vision of a cheaper product fulfilling quality and user requirements in his mind. As an outcome, the moving assembly belts were introduced in Ford's plants in 1913, which led to an increase in production and a cheaper product. Ford's invention of producing standardized products on production lines makes mass production work and is now in use at almost every production plant over the world. However, the mass production, in most cases, is inflexible because of the fixed production line after the processes and designs are finished. Moreover, the obtained products are identical or very similar and difficult to adapt to satisfy the user's needs.

Although, the flexibility of production lines have been increased due to the use of more flexible hardware, for example, programmable devices and software, there is still space for improvement where mass customization comes in. The objective of mass customization is to provide goods and products that are adapted according to the users' needs and requirements but can be produced almost as cheaply as mass products. Hence, mass customization can be the next step in production which combines specialized orders and mass production. The idea behind mass customization would be impossible without computers and information systems which help to design and configure products and production processes from user requirements. Moreover, modern recommender systems support the user in selecting appropriate requirements and constraints which represent the customer's wishes in order to maximize their satisfaction. Information and communication technology is the driver for mass customization. It reduces the customizing costs during the product modeling process and provides tools for supporting the required user interaction.

This book provides the latest research in mass customization research and has been written not only for researchers or graduate students but also for practitioners interested in mass customization and its practical implementation. In particular, the book provides insights in product configuration and modeling for mass customization as well as frameworks for mass customization and a discussion of new approaches. The second part of the book is devoted especially to practical applications. In this part, recommender systems are presented as well as agent-based systems which allow for integrate mass customization systems into the companies' existing IT infrastructure. Moreover, knowledge-based configuration systems are introduced and discussed in the last part of the book. Such configuration systems are flexible and provide a solid foundation for successful applications in mass customization. There is also a growing interest in industry to use such configuration systems in order to reduce costs, manage complexity of designs, and improve sales support.

The content of the book comes from several renowned international authors actively working in the area of mass customization. The book provides both an overview of the research area as well as details about the methodologies and techniques. This book is a must for everyone who is interested in the latest developments of information systems for mass customization and its application.

Franz Wotawa
Full Professor in Software Engineering
Graz University of Technology
Austria

Franz Wotawa received an MSc in computer science in 1994, and a PhD in 1996, both from the Vienna University of Technology. He is currently a professor of software engineering and head of the Institute for Software Technology (IST) at the Graz University of Technology. His research interests include model-based and qualitative reasoning, configuration, planning, theorem proving, intelligent agents, mobile robots, verification and validation, and software engineering. Currently, Franz Wotawa works on applying model-based diagnosis to software debugging. He has written many papers for journals, conferences, and workshops, and has been a member of the program committees for several workshops and conferences. He has organized workshops and special issues on model-based reasoning for the journal, *AI Communications*. He is a member of the IEEE Computer Society, ACM, AAAI, the Austrian Computer Society (OCG), and the Austrian Society for Artificial Intelligence.

Preface

Nowadays, the competitive situation of companies is characterized by a very strong orientation towards product individualization. The change from a seller to a buyer market has led to a saturation situation within the industrial goods' markets where the offer by far exceeds the demand. Companies have to struggle to gain new customers. This major change has increased the customer's power, which has driven companies to differentiate their products from those of competitors by offering individualized problem solutions (Nilles, 2002). The customer's expectations with respect to services and physical products have also dramatically risen. Therefore, companies tend to increasingly fragment the markets, sometimes to an extreme level, to where each market is occupied by only one customer ("markets of one").

The individualization trend is mainly ascribed to social changes. The high growth of population was a key factor for the emergence of the mass production system, one century ago. But nowadays, especially in the industrial nations, the demographic development shows the population to be steadily decreasing. Simultaneously, wealth and the demand for luxury continuously increase. Psychologists know that in the postmodern era, the need for change and novelty is becoming as important as survival for human beings. The human behavior is essentially determined by the individual principles and is rarely oriented on the behavior of the others (self-determination). It is also well known that if more and more people possess the same object, then the possession of this object is no longer interesting and loses its attractiveness (Piller, 1998). All of these reasons have contributed to a need for individualization and the demand for products that exactly meet the individual expectations of customers.

Another important trend in the business world is the continuous decreasing of the product life cycles. Consequently, the timeframes for product amortization are considerably reduced. At the same time, the costs of research and development steadily increase because of higher technological complexity of products (Nilles, 2002). In addition, the ability of fulfilling individual customer needs necessitates the capability of producing a large number of product variants, which induces high costs at both operations- and manufacturing-related tasks. In effect, in contrast to the mass production system, in which the economies of scale can be fully utilized, the individualization of customer requirements usually involves a loss of efficiency. On the other hand, globalization and deregulation of markets as well as the rapid diffusion of e-commerce and e-business over the Internet has led to more intensive and aggressive competition. This has also forced companies to develop strategies in order to resist strong price pressures, especially from those companies that are producing in low-wage countries.

The challenge that manufacturing companies have to face is to provide individualized products and services while maintaining a high cost efficiency. To be successful, companies have to address both of these perspectives, which are necessary for gaining a competitive advantage. The manufacturing of products according to individual customer needs is referred to as product customization. Whereas customization does not necessarily imply a focus on the cost perspective, in this book we will concentrate on both product customization and cost efficiency, namely mass customization, which is a new business paradigm that is very challenging for manufacturing companies.

Mass customization is a business strategy that aims at fulfilling individual customer needs with near mass production efficiency (Pine, 1993). Whereas the literature includes many contributions that discuss the strategic benefits of mass customization, there are large deficits concerning its implementation in practice. Companies that want to pursue this strategy need a set of practical tools in order to make mass customization work efficiently. The main problem is about how to be able to produce a large number of customer-oriented product variants by simultaneously providing prices that do not considerably differ from those of mass products.

Providing customers with individualized products at affordable prices is the main goal of mass customization. However, customers generally accept paying premium prices compared to standard products because they honor the additional benefits of customized products. Therefore, if mass customization fails in providing customers with an optimal or a better solution than any mass products, then the product resulting from the customization process will have, from the customer's perspective, no more additional value than any other standard product. As a result, an optimal understanding of customer needs is a necessary requirement for the success of the strategy. In fact, the focus on customers is not new and not only specific to mass customization. Concepts such as "customer orientation", "close to the customer", "customer segmentation", "niche marketing" and "customer relationship management" reveal the importance of the customer. However, during the pursuit of mass customization, customers have to be seen as partners in the value creation, which implies a deeper customer-supplier relationship. The customer provides a valuable input in the production process and is considered to be a "prosumer" as coined by Toffler (1980).

Unfortunately, although the focus on the customer's perspective is a well-known issue, the customer in the specific context of mass customization is still misunderstood. Customers are provided with a high number of product variants and are generally supposed to have the capability of making a rational decision. But this is not true because customers are not able to make optimal choices in extensive choice environments. Thus, models for a better conception of customer needs and preferences are required because the customer is a key factor that considerably determines the success or failure of the strategy. Furthermore, a customer orientation through customization tends to trigger increasing costs because of variety and complexity requirements (Blecker, Friedrich, Kaluza, Abdelkafi, & Kreutler, 2005).

Due to the fact that it is necessary to satisfy the customer, the only chance to meet this challenge is to reduce the customizing costs during the product modeling process. The universal remedy for this is to design, implement, and use a supporting computer system. A computer system is, once implemented, the best way to cope with the problem, because it automates main parts of product designing and producing. This reduces complexity and human efforts, which in the end lead to lower costs. Even if the additional investment for creating such systems is taken into account, the cost-cutting effect of mass-customization supporting systems will exceed this by far.

Furthermore, the advances realized in information technology are critical enablers, which make this strategy function efficiently. Information systems can be implemented to support diverse activities in the mass-customization value chain. They assist customers during the product specification phase in order to lead them in a fast-paced manner to the product variants corresponding to their individual requirements. Modern information systems, which support open innovation, even enable customers to participate actively in the product design. In addition, mass customization information systems contribute to helping companies mitigate excessive product variety and increase cost efficiency on the shop floor and logistics through optimal product modeling, production planning, and scheduling.

Another upcoming logistical challenge is caused by the companies' ambitions of focusing on core competences and therefore reducing the level of vertical integration. Increasing efforts for coordinating the product's supply chain are an inevitable consequence. Logistical issues like planning deliveries of raw materials as well as semi-finished goods become more important. Information systems can support companies in their supply chain management and furthermore promote the automation in the company (Blecker & Friedrich, 2006).

Although the need for supporting information systems becomes obvious, suitable tools for addressing this relevant issue in the specific case of mass customization are missing. Therefore, the intention of this book is to bridge the gap between demand and supply in order to provide information and managerial tools that aim at coping with all of the depicted problems.

This book is divided into three sections. The first section (Chapter I-IV) deals with the ways of product configuration and modeling for mass customization as well as the existing benefits and challenges for mass customization, especially in engineer-to-order companies. Furthermore, the functionality and features of the

Supply Chain Operations Reference Model in terms of scope and modularity to support an "open variant process model" are investigated.

The second section (Chapter V-IX) starts with a presentation of frameworks in the course of mass customization. Afterwards, mass customization information systems are organized across the supply chain.

Finally, this book's last part (Chapter X-XIII) examines several new approaches for mass customization like Scenario-based, Knowledge-based and Fuzzy Cognitive Maps and gives an outlook on future developments in the field of information technology for mass customization.

More detailed, this book includes the following:

Section I - Theory of Information Technology for Mass Customization

Chapter I (*Mass Customization with Configurable Products and Configurators: A Review of Benefits and Challenges*) provides a systematic review of literature on how mass customization with configurable products and the use of configurators affect companies. Configurable products are an important way to achieve mass customization. A configurable product is designed once, and this design is used repetitively in the sales-delivery process to produce specifications of product individuals meeting customer requirements. Configurators are information systems that support the specification of product individuals and the creation and management of configuration knowledge, therefore being prime examples of information systems supporting mass customization. However, to the best of our knowledge, there is no systematic review of literature on how mass customization with configurable products and the use of configurators affects companies. This chapter focuses on benefits that can be gained and challenges that companies may face. A supplier can move to mass customization and configuration from mass production or from full customization. The chapter also reviews benefits and challenges from the customer perspective. Finally, the future research directions, open challenges, and problems are identified.

Chapter II (*Product Modeling and Configuration Experiences*) attempts to present an alternative for product modeling based on applied research activities. The model proposed is based on a concept supported by different views: functional, technological, and physical. With the aim of making the model learner-friendly, the chapter also presents an industrial case applied in the lift industry. The specific problems, the model used, the implementation carried out, and the results obtained are described in detail. The objective is to make a contribution based on the industrial practice to one of the basic enablers for product configuration. The final aim is to speed up the supply-chain process in mass customization scenarios.

Chapter III (*Product Configuration in ETO Companies*) reviews how mass customization and product configuration can benefit engineer-to-order companies. The relevant main literature in the area is reviewed to identify the benefits. Furthermore, the challenges of implementing product configuration in an engineer-to-order company are described. Finally, a number of suggestions for meeting these challenges are presented. In addition, a case description is introduced which supports that product configuration can benefit engineer-to-order companies even though there are a number of challenges to be met. The chapter concludes that engineer-to-order companies can certainly benefit from product configuration by improving business process efficiency as well as information quality and ultimately improving the company's competitive advantage.

Chapter IV (*Open Variant Process Models in Supply Chains*) will elaborate on complexity in supply chains and the implications on supply chain design. It investigates the specific requirements of supply chain processes in terms of flexibility versus standardization, evaluating the feasibility of designing, customizing, assessing, and improving logistics processes within a framework provided by process reference models. Mass customization and, in particular, a configuration approach for financial services will be discussed for their applicability for reducing complexity in a process environment. Process reference frameworks will be used as elements of an "open variant process model". The Supply Chain Operations Reference model defined by the Supply Chain Council as the major cross-industry standard for supply chain management will be discussed for its usefulness and shortcomings in "process mass customization", with a focus on systems implementation.

Section II - Frameworks for Mass Customization

Chapter V (*An Associative Classification-Based Recommendation System for Personalization in B2C E-Commerce Applications*) presents an associative classification-based recommendation system to support online customer decision-making when facing a huge amount of choices. Recommendation systems have been recently introduced to e-commerce sites in order to solve the information overload and mass confusion problem. This chapter applies knowledge discovery techniques to overcome the drawback of conventional recommendation systems approaches. The framework of the associative classification-based recommendation system has been addressed in this chapter. The system analysis, design, and implementation issues in an Internet programming environment are also presented. Taking the advantage of accumulative knowledge from historical data, the efficiency and effectiveness of B2C e-commerce applications are improved.

Chapter VI (*Knowledge-Based Recommender Technologies Supporting the Interactive Selling of Financial Services*) presents the knowledge-based recommender environment Koba4MS (Knowledge-based Advisors for Marketing and Sales) which allows a flexible mapping of product, marketing, and sales knowledge to the representation of a recommender knowledge-base. In Koba4MS diagnosis, personalization and knowledge acquisition techniques are integrated to provide an infrastructure for the interactive selling of financial services. Those require deep knowledge about the product domain as well as about potential wishes and needs of customers. In this context, sales representatives can differ significantly in their expertise and level of sales knowledge. Therefore, financial service providers ask for tools supporting sales representatives in the dialog with the customer.

Chapter VII (*Developing Interoperability in Mass Customisation Information Systems*) proposes a standard-based framework to assist industrial organizations to develop interoperability in mass customization information systems. After identifying the major challenges for business and information systems in mass customization, the authors propose an innovative standard-based conceptual architecture for a combined model-driven and services-oriented platform. The chapter concludes by describing a global methodology for integration of models and applications, to enhance an enterprise's interoperability in the support of mass customization practices, keeping the same organization's technical and operational environment, improving its methods of work and the usability of the installed technology through harmonization, and integration of the enterprise models in use by customers, manufacturers, and suppliers.

Chapter VIII (*An Agent-Based Information Technology Architecture for Mass Customized Markets*) presents a Web-enabled, agent-based information system model to support mass-customized markets. Furthermore, a distributed, real-time, Java-based, mobile intelligent information system is presented. This interfaces with firms' existing IT infrastructures, follows a build-to-order production strategy, and integrates order-entry with supply chain, manufacturing, and product delivery systems. The model provides end-to-end visibility across the entire supply chain, allows for a collaborative and synchronized production system, and supports an event-based manufacturing environment. The system introduces four general purpose intelligent agents to support the entire mass-customization process. The adoption of this approach by a semiconductor manufacturing firm resulted in reductions in product lead time (by half), buffer inventory (from five to two weeks), and manual transactions (by 80%). Similarly, the adoption by a leading automotive manufacturer resulted in a 51% total inventory reduction while increasing plant utilization by 30%. These results verify that the successful adoption of this system can reduce inventory and logistic costs, improve delivery performance, increase manufacturing facilities utilization, and provide a higher overall profitability.

Chapter IX (*Critical Role of Supply Chain Decoupling Point in Mass Customisation from its Upstream and Downstream Information Systems Point of View*) concentrates on the role of supply chain decoupling point. Therefore, this chapter introduces different levels of customization and mass operations as well as three types of mass customization. It argues that in each mass customization type, information systems in upstream and downstream of the decoupling point can be varied. Consequently, information flows in different types of mass customization have been examined. This analysis is an endeavor to organize mass customization information systems across the supply chain; it can also be a useful structure for future researches in this area as well.

Section III – Innovative Information Technology Approaches for Mass Customization

Chapter X (*From Strategy Definition to Product Derivation Using a Scenario-Based Architecting Approach*) presents a set of scenario-based methods and techniques to support the development of system architectures that are more future-proof, and are also advantageous for mass customization. These methods and techniques have originally been developed for highly-customized professional systems, in particular medical imaging equipment. The chapter introduces mass customization as a business strategy that aims at satisfying, in a timely and cost-effective manner, the various needs of different customers. For that purpose, a system architecture is needed that supports two different kinds of variability: Variability in space provides a range of different products where each addresses the specific needs of an individual customer; and variability in time allows the products to evolve and thus meet new requirements. In defining such an architecture, two issues should be considered. One is how to anticipate the most likely changes in the external business environment, and hence in the customers' future needs. The other is whether the architecture can address these changes effectively.

Chapter XI (*Research Issues in Knowledge-Based Configuration*) gives an overview on the current research issues in the domain of knowledge-based configuration technology. Knowledge-based configuration systems have made their way into industrial practice. Nowadays, all major vendors of configuration systems rely on some form of declarative knowledge representation and intelligent search techniques for solving the core configuration problem, due to the inherent advantages of that technology: On the one hand, changes in the business logic (configuration rules) can be accomplished more easily because of the declarative and modular nature of the knowledge bases, while on the other hand highly-optimized, domain-independent problem-solving algorithms are available for the task of constructing valid configurations.

As the development has not come to an end as, in a world that becomes increasingly automated and wired together, constantly new challenges for the development of intelligent configuration systems arise, this chapter provides a view on future research issues: Web-based configurators are being made available for large heterogeneous user groups, the provision of mass-customized products requires the integration of companies along a supply chain, and configuration and reconfiguration of services becomes an increasingly important issue, just to name a few. Finally, this chapter summarizes the state of the art, recent achievements, novel approaches, and open challenges in the field of knowledge-based configuration technology.

Chapter XII (*Mass Customisation of Services and Processes Based on Fuzzy Cognitive Maps*) draws on the theory of Fuzzy Cognitive Maps to propose a modeling approach for mass customization of services. The proposed model integrates concepts from service quality, and customer preferences with business process and IT capabilities models. The model presented in this chapter is, to the best of our knowledge, the only fuzzy service model for mass customization that provides the means to consider the business objectives for service customization, associates them with specific business areas, and suggests opportunities for mass customization. In contrast to other service design and management approaches, the proposed model is dynamic, exhibits flexibility and responsiveness to environmental changes and customizability to specific organizational contexts, and allows the development of planning scenarios.

Chapter XIII (*Applying Service CAD System to Value Customization*) introduces a new concept, value customization, to increase the level of customer satisfaction. It presents methodologies and practice for designers to customize value in a service in industrial operation based on the discipline of Service Engineering. Service Engineering aims at creating more value largely by knowledge and service contents rather than just materialistic contents. Specifically, an information system named Service Explorer, an implementation of the methodologies, is applied to an Italian accommodation industry. After the application, five redesign options such as introducing a new service system with cash-back and a system of renting various goods were generated. Through this, the effectiveness of Service Engineering for value customization is suggested. This chapter addresses the importance of identifying value to be provided with specific customers based on their particular requirements, which has only briefly been discussed in researches of mass customization. In addition, both service activities and physical products can be crucial to realize value. Several further research issues such as general design methods for value customization were also identified.

This book provides the latest research results in the field of information systems for mass customization. This book describes the state-of-the-art, innovative theoretical frameworks, advanced and successful implementations as well as the latest empirical research findings in the area of mass customization information technology. Furthermore, new concepts and methods for successful mass customization are presented (like Scenario- and Knowledge-based approaches). The main objective is to bridge theory and practice, on the one hand, and to fill research gaps and answer open questions, on the other hand. The book improves the understanding of the problems that are encountered during the conception of information systems for mass customization. Furthermore, it provides solution approaches for the mitigation of these problems and simultaneously highlights new directions for future research. Therefore, it is not only a must for researchers and graduate students but also provides practitioners with the latest application-oriented results.

REFERENCES

Blecker, T., Friedrich, G., Kaluza, B., Abdelkafi, N., & Kreutler, G. (2005). *Information and management systems for product customization*. New York: Springer Science+Business Media, Inc.

Blecker, T., & Friedrich, G. (Eds.). (2006). *Mass customization – Challenges and solutions*. New York: Springer Science+Business Media, Inc.

Nilles, V. (2002). *Effiziente Gestaltung von Produktordnungssystemen – Eine theoretische und empirische Untersuchung*. Ph.D. dissertation, University Munich, Munich.

Piller, F. T. (1998). *Kundenindividuelle Massenproduktion – Die Wettbewerbsstrategie der Zukunft*. Munich: Wien, Hanse.

Pine II, B. J. (1993). *Mass customization: The new frontier in business competition*. Boston: Harvard Business School Press.

Toffler, A. (1980). *The third wave*. New York: William Morrow & Co., Inc.

Section I
Theory of Information Technology for Mass Customization

Chapter I
Mass Customization with Configurable Products and Configurators:
A Review of Benefits and Challenges

Mikko Heiskala
Helsinki University of Technology, Finland

Juha Tihonen
Helsinki University of Technology, Finland

Kaija-Stiina Paloheimo
Helsinki University of Technology, Finland

Timo Soininen
Helsinki University of Technology, Finland

ABSTRACT

Configurable products are an important way to achieve mass customization. A configurable product is designed once, and this design is used repetitively in the sales-delivery process to produce specifications of product individuals meeting customer requirements. Configurators are information systems that support the specification of product individuals and the creation and management of configuration knowledge, therefore being prime examples of information systems supporting mass customization. However, to the best of our knowledge, there is no systematic review of literature on how mass customization with configurable products and use of configurators affect companies. In this chapter, we provide such a review. We focus on benefits that can be gained and challenges which companies may face. A supplier can move to mass customization and configuration from mass production or from full customization; we keep the concerns separate. We also review benefits and challenges from the customer perspective. Finally, we identify future research directions and open challenges and problems.

INTRODUCTION

Today, customers are demanding products that will better meet their increasingly diverse needs. *Mass customization* (MC) has been proposed (Pine, 1993a) as a more cost-efficient solution to this challenge than *full customization* (FC), a term we use in this chapter for craft production of one-of-a-kind, bespoke products. MC is the ability to provide products tailored to individual customer needs on a large scale at, or close to, mass production (MP) efficiency, using flexible processes (Da Silveira, Borenstein, & Fogliatto, 2001; Hart, 1995; Pine, 1993a). One way to implement MC is through *configurable products* (CP). The design of a configurable product specifies a set of pre-designed elements and rules on how these can be combined into valid product individuals (Salvador & Forza, 2004; Tiihonen & Soininen, 1997). Such knowledge is called *configuration knowledge*. The design of a configurable product is used repetitively, in a routine manner without creative design, in the sales-delivery process to produce specifications of product individuals that meet the requirements of particular customers. Defining a valid, error-free (sales) specification of a customer-specific product individual can be difficult because the product elements often manifest complex interdependencies and incompatibilities. Some companies have addressed this difficulty by employing information systems called *product configurators* (or configurators, for short) as support in the task of defining a sales specification (Barker & O'Connor, 1990; Forza & Salvador, 2002a, 2002b). A *configurator* is an information system that supports the creation and management of configuration knowledge and the specification of product individuals (Sabin & Weigel, 1998; Tiihonen & Soininen, 1997).

However, to the best of our knowledge, there is no systematic review of literature on how configurators affect the operations and business of companies pursuing mass customization with configurable products. The majority of papers de-

scribe the introduction and use of a configurator in a single-case company. A significant set of papers describes issues of MC, CP, and configurators. This review aims to provide a summary.

The rest of this chapter is structured as follows. Next, the overall framework of the literature review is described. The following section then contemplates the benefits and challenges of MC and CP for the supplier and customer, first compared with MP and then compared with FC.

This section is followed by a discussion of configurator benefits, how they may overcome or alleviate the MC and CP challenges, and then moves on to configurator challenges. Also in this section, the supplier perspective is discussed before the customer perspective. Before suggestions for future research directions, discussion, and conclusions end this chapter, the rationale for a company to move to MC are briefly discussed.

LITERATURE REVIEW METHODS AND FRAMEWORK

For the literature review, we first identified the benefits and challenges attributed to MC, configurable products, and configurators. Second, we studied how configurators have been used to meet the challenges related to MC with configurable products. Third, we identified unmet challenges and remaining problems in configurator-supported MC and derived suggestions for future work. The framework for our literature review reflects this process and illustrates our viewpoints (see Figure 1). We classified benefits and challenges according to whom they concern (supplier or customer) and the direction of a move to MC. A supplier can move to MC (Duray, 2002; Lampel & Mintzberg, 1996; Svensson & Barfod, 2002) and CP (Tiihonen & Soininen, 1997) from either the direction of MP or FC. The latter classification is not visible in Figure 1.

We used electronic scientific databases with search terms such as mass customization, customization, product configuration, configurator, configurable products, benefits, challenges, opportunities, threats, limitations, problems, and drawbacks. From the yield of hundreds of articles, books, and conference papers, we browsed the abstracts and selected about 75 publications for closer examination. Further selection left some of them out of this chapter. For readability, we omit a full list of references to a benefit or challenge from the text. All references are shown in tables at the end of each subsection. The tables also show whether a reference belongs to MC or CP literature, when applicable.

MASS CUSTOMIZATION AND CONFIGURABLE PRODUCTS

Supplier Benefits Compared with Mass Production

In this section, we discuss the benefits for a supplier from MC or CP compared with MP. The benefits and references are summarized in Table 1.

In general, MC refers to the ability to effectively fulfill a wider range of customer needs than with MP (Pine, 1993a), an idea often incorporated into definitions of MC.

Perhaps the most cited benefit of MC and CP is the reduction in inventories of finished goods

and work-in-progress, tying less capital compared to build-to-forecast MP (Pine, 1993a). Less inventory handling and management is necessary (Broekhuizen & Alsem, 2002) and improvements in inventory turnover are implied (Beaty, 1996). Similarly, MC can eliminate or reduce the need to sell aging models and seasonal products by discount as MC products are less subject to product obsolescence and fashion risk (Kotha, 1995). MC often involves modular products. An inventory of modules is less subject to fashion and technological obsolescence than differentiated inventory (Berman, 2002). As a result, the supplier does not have to include markdowns or high inventory accumulation in its pricing (Berman, 2002).

In MC and also with CP, the customer participates in the specification of the product. Customers may enjoy the participation in design and it can increase customer satisfaction in the finished good as well (Huffman & Kahn, 1998). Further, the effort spent and information accumulated and stored in the specification process can become a switching cost for the customer (Pine, Peppers, & Rogers, 1995). Switching to competition would mean spending the effort again. However, this benefit can be realized fully only if the interactions or repurchases with the customers are frequent enough (Broekhuizen & Alsem, 2002; Pine et al., 1995). As customers need to express

Figure 1. Framework for literature review

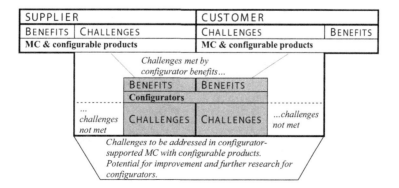

their needs, the supplier has an opportunity to gather more accurate customer information (Pine et al., 1995) and develop a deep understanding of the customer's needs (Berman, 2002). This and engaging the customer in a continuous dialog (Berman, 2002) and learning relationship (Pine et al., 1995) makes it more difficult for competitors to accumulate the same depth of customer knowledge and entice customers away. Moreover, information on actual orders directly reflects current market information (Berman, 2002). This may enable quicker product development response to changes in overall customer needs (Berman, 2002; Slywotzky, 2000). However, Kakati (2002) argues that all customer needs cannot be captured with tracking choices on physical product elements. The customers must also be willing to share their preferences and purchase patterns with the sup-plier on an ongoing basis if the supplier is to be able to use them for their own purposes (Wind & Rangaswamy, 2001).

MC can enable premium pricing (Kotha, 1995) due to the better fit of the product to customer needs and due to the difficulty of comparison-shopping of customized products (Agrawal, Kumaresh, & Mercer, 2001, see Table 8). Ability to participate in design may also increase willingness to pay for the self-designed, customized final product (Franke & Piller, 2004).

Supplier Challenges Compared with Mass Production

In the following, we discuss the supplier challenges from MC or CP compared with MP from a number of viewpoints.

Table 1. Summary of supplier benefits compared with mass production

Benefit	References	MC/CP
Efficient way to fulfill a wider range of customer needs	Pine, 1993a; Hart, 1995; Da Silveira et al., 2001 (*MC has been usually defined in a similar vein.*)	MC
	Tiihonen, Soininen, Männistö, and Sulonen, 1996; Tiihonen and Soininen, 1997; Tiihonen,, Soininen, Männistö, and Sulonen, 1998; Bonehill and Slee-Smith, 1998	CP
Reduction in inventories	Pine 1993a; Kay, 1993; Kotha, 1995; Ross, 1996; Beaty, 1996; Gilmore and Pine, 1997; Radder and Louw, 1999; Slywotzky, 2000; Zipkin, 2001; Agrawal et al., 2001; Wind and Rangaswamy, 2001; Berman, 2002; Broekhuizen and Alsem, 2002; Svensson and Barfod 2002; Piller, Moeslein, and Stotko, 2004; Piller and Müller, 2004	MC
	Tiihonen and Soininen, 1997; Tiihonen et al., 1998	CP
Reduction in product model obsolescence, fashion risk	Kotha, 1995; Agrawal et al., 2001; Zipkin, 2001; Berman, 2002; Piller et al., 2004; Piller and Müller, 2004	MC
Customer participation in design: satisfaction, effort spent, and switching cost	*Satisfaction*: Huffman and Kahn, 1998; Wind and Rangaswamy, 2001; Bardacki and Whitelock, 2003. *Switching costs*: Pine et al., 1995; Broekhuizen and Alsem, 2002; Bardacki and Whitelock, 2003; Piller et al., 2004; Piller and Müller, 2004	MC
More accurate customer information	Pine et al., 1995; Hart, 1995; Åhlström and Westbrook, 1999; Slywotzky, 2000; Agrawal et al., 2001; Kakati, 2002; Broekhuizen and Alsem, 2002; Berman, 2002; Brown and Bessant, 2003; Bardacki and Whitelock, 2003; Piller et al., 2004; Franke and Piller, 2004	MC
Potential for premium pricing	Kotha, 1995; Ross, 1996; Agrawal et al., 2001; Berman, 2002; Broekhuizen and Alsem, 2002; MacCarthy and Brabazon, 2003; Piller and Müller, 2004; Piller et al., 2004; Franke and Piller, 2004	MC

Business

See Table 2 for a summary of the supplier business challenges which we discuss in this section.

MP products have to be developed or adjusted to be suitable for MC. MC tends to be more costly than MP (Kotha, 1995). One of the key challenges for MC with CP for the supplier is to find the right amount of customization to offer that balances the costs of added complexity and increased customer value (Beaty, 1996). The offered customization range has to be matched to customer needs of the targeted segment(s). A mismatch reduces sales potential and can lead to excessive one-of-a-kind design (Tiihonen & Soininen, 1997; Tiihonen et al., 1998). Excessive customization increases the specification complexity both for the supplier and the customer, and may strain the production process too far (Berman, 2002). Further, development of a product to be easy to configure ("design for configuration") can be a significant effort (Tiihonen & Soininen, 1997; Tiihonen et al., 1998).

MC products often are modular and possibly share components across product lines or families. Component sharing may cause customers to see the products as overly similar (Pine, 1993b) and create confusion over the "true" customiza-tion level of the product (Berman, 2002; Kakati, 2002).

MC may cause channel conflicts (Broekhuizen & Alsem, 2002; Wind & Rangaswamy, 2001) as retailers may be unwilling to participate in fear of the supplier bypassing them in the future, and they may also be reluctant to take on more specification tasks. Difficulties of eliciting customer needs and creating sales specifications (discussed in section Specification Process below) can cause severe challenges. These include loss of confidence from customers (Fohn, Liau, Greef, Young, & O'Grady, 1995), lost sales, customers, and repeat business (Fohn et al., 1995; Heatley, Agraval, & Tanniru, 1995), and decreased customer satisfaction (Forza & Salvador, 2002a; Heatley et al., 1995). Further, the problems and complexity of specifying a product individual, and dissatisfaction in the shop-ping process are often attributed to the retailer (Huffman & Kahn, 1998). Elicitation difficulties, resulting order errors, and delays may also lower dealer loyalty (Yu & Skovgaard, 1998).

Organization and Operations

The organizational and operational challenges for the supplier which we contemplate here are summarized in Table 3. The extent of operational

Table 2. Summary of supplier business challenges compared with mass production

Challenge	References	MC/CP
Producing customized products often costs more than MP	Kotha, 1995; Åhlström and Westbrook, 1999; Zipkin, 2001; Berman, 2002; Broekhuizen and Alsem, 2002; Kakati, 2002; Bardacki and Whitelock, 2003; Piller et al., 2004; Piller and Müller, 2004	MC
Finding right amount, balance of offered customization	Beaty, 1996; Svensson and Barfod, 2002; Berman, 2002; MacCarthy and Brabazon, 2003; Piller and Müller, 2004	MC
	Tiihonen and Soininen, 1997; Tiihonen et al., 1998	CP
Component sharing across product lines may cause customer to see the products as overly similar	Pine, 1993b; Berman, 2002; Kakati, 2002	MC
Possible channel conflicts with retailers	Wind and Rangaswamy, 2001; Broekhuizen and Alsem, 2002	MC
Elicitation difficulties can cause lost business, image, and lower customer and dealer loyalty and satisfaction.	Huffman and Kahn, 1998	MC
	Fohn et al., 1995; Heatley et al., 1995; Yu and Skovgaard, 1998; Forza and Salvador, 2002a	CP

changes required is large (Pine et al., 1993). Sales and marketing has to increase interaction with the customers (Kakati, 2002) and learn new specification tasks (Tiihonen & Soininen, 1997). MC requires more manufacturing and logistics flexibility (discussed in section Manufacturing below).

A commonly-cited challenge in MC is that it increases the need for information management (Åhlström & Westbrook, 1999). What an MC supplier basically does is that it takes the customer requirements, that is, information, and translates them to a manufactured product (Da Silveira et al., 2001). The information about the customer requirements flows through the supplier organization from sales to manufacturing and distribution, crossing organizational boundaries, until the customer-specific product is finally delivered to the customer. This increases both the amount of information transferred and the information flows (or paths) in the supplier organization. Both operations flow information, and customer information need to be managed by the supplier (Broekhuizen & Alsem, 2002). MC also increases the need for product data and variant handling (Comstock, Johansen, & Winroth, 2004).

The extent of required organizational and cultural changes is large (Pine et al., 1993).

Functional silos are a hindrance to MC (Pine et al., 1993). It can be difficult to create company-wide understanding of the benefits of MC with CP. Effort spent and effects felt may occur at different places. Developing well-managed and documented configuration knowledge takes effort in the product process but helps sales. Producing error-free and complete sales specifications takes extra effort at sales but helps to reduce fire-fighting in manufacturing (Tiihonen & Soininen, 1997). Highly-skilled, more costly sales staff and increased training may be required for eliciting customer needs, specification tasks, and verification of specifications (Berman, 2002). Achieving the required skills is more difficult if the supplier does not own the sales companies (Broekhuizen & Alsem, 2002; Tiihonen et al., 1996) or if the turnover in sales is high (Berman, 2002).

Specification Process

In this section, we discuss the supplier challenges related to the specification process; for a summary, see Table 4. The most-often cited challenge with MC and CP is the difficulty of customer needs elicitation and defining corresponding valid sales specifications (Ross, 1996) as customization increases both the complexity and amount of re-

Table 3. Summary of supplier organizational and operational challenges compared with mass production

Challenge	References	MC/CP
Extent of operational changes large	Pine et al., 1993; Hart, 1995; Kotha, 1995; Ross, 1996; Agrawal et al., 2001; Zipkin, 2001; Berman, 2002; Broekhuizen and Alsem, 2002	MC
	Tiihonen & Soininen, 1997	CP
Increased information management	Åhlström and Westbrook, 1999; Da Silveira et al., 2001; Zipkin, 2001; Berman, 2002; Broekhuizen and Alsem, 2002; Kakati, 2002; MacCarthy and Brabazon, 2003; Brown and Bessant, 2003; Piller et al., 2004; Comstock et al., 2004	MC
	Forza and Salvador, 2002a; Salvador and Forza, 2004	CP
Extent of organizational and cultural changes large	Pine et al., 1993; Kay, 1993; Ross, 1996; Åhlström and Westbrook, 1999; Slywotzky, 2000; Agrawal et al., 2001; Kakati, 2002; Berman, 2002	MC
	Tiihonen and Soininen, 1997	CP

quired information. Sales often have incomplete or out-of-date configuration knowledge, which is one contributing factor to the specification errors. This issue is discussed in detail in section Long-Term Management of Configuration Knowledge below.

Several specification error types have been identified. (1) The specified product individual cannot be produced at all or it would not work properly (Aldanondo, Véron, & Fargier, 1999; 2000). Such errors cause iterations in the sales-delivery process (Wright, Weixelbaum, Vesonder, Brown, Palmer, Berman, & Moore, 1993) between the customer and supplier or sales and manufacturing because specifications have to be reconsidered. (2) The specification might not meet customer

needs optimally (Aldanondo et al., 1999; Forza & Salvador, 2002a). One reason may be the different terminology or level of abstraction in expressing customer requirements and technical specifications (Tiihonen & Soininen, 1997; Tiihonen et al., 1998). Communicating customization possibilities of a very flexible product to the customer may also be hard (Tiihonen & Soininen, 1997). Technical experts consulted for specification feasibility may not communicate with the customer at all, which may be a cause for mismatch as well (Tiihonen & Soininen, 1997). Further, it is difficult to identify intangible preferences like the preferred fit of a shoe (tight/loose) (Wind & Rangaswamy, 2001). (3) Pricing errors: for example, a specification might define a smaller price than the effective

Table 4. Summary of the supplier challenges in the specification process compared with mass production

Challenge	References	MC/CP
Difficulty of customer needs elicitation and definition of a corresponding, complete, and error-free sales specification	Ross, 1996; Huffman and Kahn, 1998; Åhlström and Westbrook, 1999; Zipkin, 2001; Wind and Rangaswamy, 2001; Berman, 2002; MacCarthy and Brabazon, 2003; Piller et al., 2004; Comstock et al., 2004	MC
	Sviokla, 1990; Wright et al., 1993; Heatley et al., 1995; Fohn et al., 1995; Tiihonen et al., 1996; Tiihonen and Soininen, 1997; Tiihonen et al., 1998; McGuinness and Wright, 1998; Sabin and Weigel, 1998; Yu and Skovgaard, 1998; Vanwelkenheysen, 1998; Aldanondo et al., 1999; Aldanondo et al., 2000; Forza and Salvador, 2002a, 2002b; Salvador and Forza, 2004	CP
Can specified product individual be produced/manufactured, and will it work properly?	Aldanondo et al., 1999; Aldanondo et al., 2000	CP
Errors noticed after sales specification phase lead to iterations in sales-delivery process	Wright et al., 1993; Heatley et al., 1995; Fohn et al., 1995; Tiihonen and Soininen, 1997; Tiihonen et al., 1998; Sabin and Weigel, 1998; Aldanondo et al., 2000	CP
Does the specified product individual fit customer needs optimally?	Aldanondo et al., 1999; Forza and Salvador, 2002a	CP
Erroneous, smaller price than effective cost for the specified product individual.	Wright et al., 1993; Fohn et al., 1995; Aldanondo et al., 1999; Aldanondo et al., 2000; Salvador and Forza, 2004	CP
Erroneous delivery time	Salvador and Forza, 2004	CP
Sales staff create repertoires of typical specifications, valid but not optimal in fit with customer needs	Sviokla, 1990; Heatley et al., 1995; Salvador and Forza, 2004	CP
Two sales persons may produce different specifications for identical customer orders	Sviokla, 1990	CP
Technical experts deeply involved in verifying specifications	Tiihonen et al., 1998; Forza and Salvador, 2002a; Salvador and Forza, 2004	CP

cost of producing the product individual (Wright et al., 1993). If pricing information is not available during the specification task, the sales staff is not able to "guide" the customer to more profitable options, nor inform the customer of costly options (Salvador & Forza, 2004). (4) An erroneous delivery time could also be specified (Salvador & Forza, 2004).

To avoid difficulties of specification, sales staff may create repertoires of typical sales specifications that are valid but not necessarily optimal in fit with customer needs (Sviokla, 1990). Therefore, the full customization potential of the product is not offered to the customer (Salvador & Forza, 2004). Specification task complexity may also cause sales persons to produce different specifications for identical orders (Sviokla, 1990). To counter the difficulties of sales staff, technical experts are often deeply involved in verifying specification validity (Tiihonen et al., 1998), which detracts them from other tasks like product development (Forza & Salvador, 2002a), and also increases the lead-times in order processing (Wright et al., 1993). The validity checks are often bypassed under time pressure, which results in more errors (Forza & Salvador, 2002a; 2002b).

Manufacturing

The manufacturing challenges for the supplier are summarized in Table 5. The manufacturing of customer-specific products requires more manufacturing and logistics flexibility, which can be difficult to achieve (Kotha, 1995). It is difficult to reach lead times (Åhlström & Westbrook, 1999; Comstock et al., 2004; Svensson & Barfod, 2002) and consistent quality (Svensson & Barfod, 2002) comparable to MP. Further, the supplier has to handle variable costs instead of fixed costs (Hart, 1995). To operate efficiently, an MC supplier needs to produce, sort, ship, and deliver small quantities of highly-differentiated products (Berman, 2002), which increases the complexity of production planning and quality control (Piller et al., 2004). Achieving the flexibility can require investments in expensive flexible machinery (Piller & Müller, 2004) and hiring and training highly skilled staff (Kotha, 1995).

Specification errors that reach manufacturing cause fire-fighting activities (Heatley et al., 1995) that can take up to even 80% of the order-processing time (Tiihonen et al., 1996) to manage incorrect bills-of-materials (BOMs) and production orders, missing parts, rush deliveries from part suppliers at an extra cost, and missed delivery dates (Forza & Salvador, 2002a).

Long-Term Management of Configuration Knowledge

For a summary of the challenges we discuss here, see Table 6. MC based on CP requires up-to-date

Table 5. Summary of supplier manufacturing challenges compared with mass production

Challenge	References	MC/CP
Difficulties in achieving the required production process flexibility	Kotha, 1995; Åhlström and Westbrook 1999; Slywotzky, 2000; Zipkin, 2001; Kakati 2002; Berman 2002; Piller et al. 2004	MC
	Tiihonen and Soininen, 1997; Tiihonen et al., 1998; Forza and Salvador, 2002a	CP
May require expensive investments in flexible machinery and acquiring highly-skilled staff.	*Machinery:* Piller and Müller, 2004 *Staff:* Kotha, 1995	MC
Fire-fighting in manufacturing from sales specification errors	Heatley et al., 1995; Tiihonen et al., 1996; Yu and Skovgaard, 1998; Forza and Salvador, 2002a; Salvador and Forza, 2004	CP

configuration knowledge, stressing the importance of its management. The long-term management and maintenance of configuration knowledge is a major task and its level in companies often poor (Wright et al., 1993). This contributes to the sales specification errors discussed earlier. Sales may not know the variation possibilities because configuration knowledge is not systematically documented (Tiihonen et al., 1996; Tiihonen et al., 1998). Product development rarely creates configuration knowledge and if it does, extracting the knowledge to sales is problematic and the transfer rarely systemized (Tiihonen et al., 1996; Wright et al., 1993). Knowledge transfer to retailers is even more challenging (Tiihonen et al., 1996). A compounding factor is that the configuration knowledge is often dispersed among a variety of sources across the supplier organization, like manufacturing, assembly, and marketing (Haag, 1998; McGuinness & Wright, 1998; Wright et al., 1993). This impedes knowledge acquisition in maintenance and update situations (McGuinness & Wright, 1998).

A further problem is that the configuration knowledge often changes frequently (Tiihonen & Soininen, 1997), which together with the transfer problems means that the configuration knowledge used in sales is often not up-to-date (Wright et al., 1993). The workarounds that sales staff sometimes invent to curb the elicitation complexity, like the aforementioned repertoires of typical specifications, are especially easily outdated (McGuinness & Wright, 1998). Reasons for configuration knowledge changes can be shifts in customer requirements and marketing strategies (Fleischanderl et al., 1998; Tiihonen & Soininen, 1997), product and component evolvement (Tiihonen et al., 1996), and added or removed product functionalities (Tiihonen & Soininen, 1997).

Long-term management of delivered product individuals (Tiihonen et al., 1996) is a related challenge. Information on the product type and product individual is needed when changes have to be made to an existing product individual for maintenance and servicing reasons, or when new or better functionality is added (Sabin & Weigel, 1998; Tiihonen & Soininen, 1997). This reconfiguration is problematic and prone to errors as it involves adding and removing components that may have complex interdependencies (Sabin & Weigel, 1998; Tiihonen & Soininen, 1997) and the required configuration knowledge may have to be retrieved from various sources and has to bridge temporally-different versions of the configuration knowledge base (Tiihonen & Soininen, 1997; Tiihonen et al., 1996, 1998).

Table 6. Summary of supplier challenges in long-term management of configuration knowledge compared with mass production

Challenge	References	MC/CP
Long-term management of configuration knowledge	Wright et al., 1993; Tiihonen et al., 1996; Tiihonen and Soininen, 1997; Tiihonen et al., 1998; Yu and Skovgaard, 1998; McGuinness and Wright, 1998; Haag, 1998; Fleischhanderl et al., 1998	CP
Transferring updated configuration knowledge to sales force	Wright et al., 1993; Tiihonen et al., 1996	CP
Configuration knowledge changes frequently	Tiihonen and Soininen, 1997; Fleischanderl et al., 1998; McGuinness and Wright, 1998	CP
Long-term management of delivered product individuals and reconfiguration	Tiihonen et al., 1996; Tiihonen and Soininen, 1997; Tiihonen et al., 1998; Yu and Skovgaard, 1998; Sabin and Weigel, 1998	CP

Customer Benefits Compared with Mass Production

This section presents the customer benefits as compared with MP; see Table 7 for a summary. The customer viewpoint has received relatively little attention in literature.

The main benefit from MC is the better product fit with customer needs (Pine, 1993a) which applies to CP as well. Customers may also find participation in the design and specification enjoyable in itself (Huffman & Kahn, 1998), and it can also increase satisfaction in the final product (Bardacki & Whitelock, 2003).

Customer Challenges Compared with Mass Production

Next, the customer challenges from MC and CP compared with MP are discussed; a summary can be seen in Table 8. As for benefits, the customer viewpoint of the challenges appears to have received little attention in CP literature.

In MC, customers have to express their preferences for the product and may suffer from the complexity of the specification (Pine, 1993a). They may be overwhelmed by the number of options, sometimes referred to as "mass confusion" (Huffman & Kahn, 1998). Customers can

Table 7. Summary of customer benefits compared with mass production

Benefit	References	MC/CP
Improved fit with customer needs	Pine, 1993a; Kotha, 1995; Radder and Louw, 1999; Agrawal et al., 2001; Wind and Rangaswamy, 2001; Berman, 2002; Broekhuizen and Alsem, 2002; Bardacki and Whitelock, 2003; MacCarthy and Brabazon, 2003	MC
Enjoyable participation in specification and design	Huffman and Kahn, 1998; Wind and Rangaswamy, 2001; Bardacki and Whitelock, 2003; Piller and Müller, 2004; Franke and Piller, 2004	MC

Table 8. Summary of customer challenges compared with mass production

Challenge	References	MC/CP
Complexity of design and specification	Pine, 1993a; Pine et al., 1993; Pine et al., 1995; Beaty, 1996; Gilmore and Pine, 1997; Huffman and Kahn, 1998; Berman, 2002; Wind and Rangaswamy, 2001; Zipkin, 2001; Svensson and Barfod, 2002; Broekhuizen and Alsem, 2002; Piller et al., 2004; Dellaert and Stremersch, 2005	MC
	Forza and Salvador, 2002a	CP
Time and effort spent in design and specification	Gilmore and Pine, 1997; Berman, 2002; Broekhuizen and Alsem, 2002; Kakati, 2002; Bardacki and Whitelock, 2003	MC
Feeling of invaded privacy	Pine, 1993a; Pine et al., 1995; Wind and Rangaswamy, 2001; Broekhuizen and Alsem, 2002	MC
Waiting for the finished product	Radder and Louw, 1999; Agrawal et al., 2001; Zipkin, 2001; Svensson and Barfod, 2002; Bardacki and Whitelock, 2003; MacCarthy and Brabazon, 2003	MC
Need to trust supplier to deliver exactly as specified	Berman, 2002; Broekhuizen and Alsem, 2002	MC
Increased price of products	Hart, 1995; Radder and Louw, 1999; Wind and Rangaswamy, 2001; Zipkin, 2001; Agrawal et al., 2001; Broekhuizen and Alsem, 2002; Kakati, 2002; Svensson and Barfod, 2002; Bardacki and Whitelock, 2003; Piller and Müller, 2004	MC
More difficult comparison-shopping, limited transparency of product	Wind and Rangaswamy, 2001; Broekhuizen and Alsem, 2002; Piller et al., 2004	MC

be unsure of their needs and have trouble both in deciding what they want and in communicating their decisions precisely (Gilmore & Pine, 1997; Zipkin, 2001). Further, some needs are unarticulated (Gilmore & Pine, 1997). Customers may also feel uncertainty about whether they have been exposed to all alternatives and have complete information about the options (Huffman & Kahn, 1998). Specification difficulties are compounded if the customers lack sufficient product expertise (Huffman & Kahn, 1998). Moreover, due to the time and effort customers have to spend in specification, expressing preferences is an added drawback (Gilmore & Pine, 1997) compared to picking a product "off-the-shelf" as in MP. Some customers may feel that expressing preferences invades their privacy (Pine, 1993a), especially in Internet (Wind & Rangaswamy, 2001).

In MC, the customers usually have to wait for the finished product (Radder & Louw, 1999) as it is produced for order. Moreover, customers must trust the supplier to deliver exactly according to the specification (Berman, 2002; Broekhuizen

& Alsem, 2002). Customized products tend to be more expensive (Hart, 1995). The limited transparency of products, their complexity, and the uniqueness of individual products make comparison-shopping and judging whether the product is good value for money more difficult (Wind & Rangaswamy, 2001). On the other hand, customization raises customer expectations, which can backfire as more severe disappointment if the end product does not meet the higher expectations (Berman, 2002). Further, customers may fear that the customized products have more inconsistent quality (Svensson & Barfod, 2002).

Supplier Benefits Compared with Full Customization

This section discusses the supplier benefits (summarized in Table 9) from MC or CP compared with FC. Literature on moving to MC from FC and on associated benefits and challenges is limited to Svensson and Barfod (2002) while CP literature gives a bit more attention.

Table 9. Summary of supplier benefits compared with full customization

Benefit	References	MC/CP
Increased efficiency, more controlled production	Svensson and Barfod, 2002	MC
	Tiihonen et al., 1996; Tiihonen and Soininen, 1997; Tiihonen et al., 1998	CP
Improved, more uniform quality	Svensson and Barfod, 2002	MC
	Tiihonen et al., 1996; Tiihonen and Soininen, 1997; Tiihonen et al., 1998; Bonehill and Slee-Smith, 1998; Salvador and Forza, 2004	CP
Shorter lead-times, more accurate on-time delivery	Svensson and Barfod, 2002	MC
	Tiihonen et al., 1996; Tiihonen and Soininen, 1997; Tiihonen et al., 1998	CP
Lower costs	Svensson and Barfod, 2002	MC
	Bonehill and Slee-Smith, 1998	CP
Reduced design effort… …which freed expert engineering to other tasks like R&D	Tiihonen et al., 1998; Bonehill and Slee-Smith, 1998; Salvador and Forza, 2004	CP
Easier to do specifications, even by customers or retailers themselves, easier selling	Tiihonen et al., 1998; Salvador and Forza, 2004	CP
Easier pricing	Tiihonen et al., 1998	CP

Svensson and Barfod (2002) mention several benefits that a FC supplier can gain from switching to MC. They all seem to stem from increased standardization. The benefits are increased efficiency and more controlled production, improved and more uniform product quality, shorter lead-times, and lower costs. These benefits are mentioned in CP literature as well. A reason for improved control of production is the use of a relatively small number of components to produce a large variety of end products (Tiihonen et al., 1996). A cause for quality improvements can be the use of a standard, modular design, which reduces incorrect assemblies (Bonehill & Slee-Smith, 1998). Lead-time reductions can result from quality improvements, and from the reduced need for customer-specific design of components or end products (Tiihonen et al., 1998). This also may free expert engineering resources to other tasks like product development (Tiihonen et al., 1998). Reduced effort also contributes to lower costs.

Lead-times may also be reduced by easier selling. For a configurable product, the sales options have been defined in advance. Choosing from existing options rather than beginning from scratch brings two benefits: it is easier to arrive at a sales specification and to price the product (Tiihonen et al., 1998). This may allow retailers or even customers to do specification themselves (Salvador & Forza, 2004). Customers who are engaged in the specification process may accept more responsibility for the product's fit to their needs (Salvador & Forza, 2004).

Supplier Challenges Compared with Full Customization

Next, the supplier challenges from MC or CP compared with full customization are contemplated. The challenges are summarized in Table 10. It seems that MC has not been compared with FC in terms of benefits and challenges as often as with MP.

Compared to FC, MC with CP requires changes in operations and organization that can be significant (Tiihonen & Soininen, 1997). Achieving more uniform quality and repeatable production may be a difficult challenge (Svensson & Barfod, 2002). For FC suppliers, the main challenge in MC is the shift from managing the product and processing materials (which they master) to systematically managing and processing information involved in customer-specific orders, product documentation, and so forth, according to Svensson and Barfod (2002). This requires a cultural change that can be difficult to achieve. Finding the right amount

Table 10. Summary of supplier challenges compared with full customization

Challenge	References	MC/CP
Requires changes in operations and organization	Tiihonen and Soininen, 1997; Tiihonen et al., 1998	CP
Achieving uniform quality	Svensson and Barfod, 2002	MC
Systemizing information management	Svensson and Barfod, 2002	MC
Finding right amount and balance of offered customization	Beaty, 1996; Berman, 2002; Svensson and Barfod, 2002; MacCarthy and Brabazon, 2003	MC
	Tiihonen and Soininen, 1997; Tiihonen et al., 1998	CP
Customer needs elicitation, specification	Svensson and Barfod, 2002	MC
Sales staff must not offer changes outside pre-designed customization possibilities	Tiihonen and Soininen, 1997; Tiihonen et al., 1998	CP
Systemizing product design from configuration viewpoint a big effort	Tiihonen and Soininen, 1997; Tiihonen et al., 1998	CP
Reverse engineering of modular designs	Pine, 1993a, 1993b	MC

of offered customization is equally important (Beaty, 1996), as when compared with MP. A balance must be found between the added standardization, uniform quality, and lowered costs, and compromising the optimal fit of a fully-customized product.

Customer needs elicitation and error-free specification is still a challenge (Svensson & Barfod, 2002). Sales specification errors cause similar problems in manufacturing, as when compared to MP. The sales force must learn not to offer changes to the product that would require customer-specific design (Tiihonen & Soininen, 1997).

For product development, it is a challenge and a big effort to develop a design for the configurable product, with a modular structure of reusable, replicable product components (Tiihonen & Soininen, 1997) and clearly-defined module interfaces. On the other hand, Pine (1993a; 1993b) has expressed the fear that modular designs are easier to reverse engineer and copy than unique designs.

Customer Benefits Compared with Full Customization

Here, the customer benefits compared with full customization are contemplated. However, the literature is scant. Nevertheless, the benefits for the supplier (see Table 9) could also generate benefits for the customers like shorter delivery times, more predictable deliveries, better serviceability, more communicable product specifications, improved spare part stock management, better and more consistent quality, more affordable products, better accessibility to products, and the like. Further, customers may prefer the easier specification by choosing from existing options and receive better product documentation than for an FC product.

Customer Challenges Compared with Full Customization

The literature we studied seems not to have examined the customer challenges compared with full customization. However, it is probable that explicit specification is difficult for customers, as it is a complex task nevertheless. Customers may also have to compromise on the optimal fit of the product, and the customer service experience may not feel personal enough, as with FC the customers are used to get exactly what they want.

CONFIGURATORS

Overview

A configurator checks the specification of a product individual, that is, a *configuration*, for *completeness* (i.e., that all the necessary selections are made) and *consistency* (i.e., that no rules are violated) with respect to the configuration knowledge, stored in configuration models in configurators (Tiihonen & Soininen, 1997). Configurators also support the user in specifying a product individual, called a configuration task. Depending on the configurator, additional functionality such as price and delivery time calculation, layout drawing and document generation, and so forth, may be provided. Configurators are also used to create and manage the configuration models and configuration knowledge embedded in them.

In the rest of this section, the benefits and challenges related to configurators are discussed. The discussion is divided into supplier and customer viewpoints. The supplier perspective is further divided to issues concerning the business, organization, specification process, manufacturing, product development, and long-term management of configuration knowledge perspectives. The benefits are related to configurator use compared with MC with CP prior to configurator introduction. Challenges relate to configurator use. The benefits are also discussed in terms of whether they alleviate or overcome some challenges related to MC with CP.

Supplier Benefits

This section discusses the benefits configurators can bring to the supplier and if they overcome challenges related to MC with CP. The benefits are summarized in Tables 11-17.

Business

In this section, we review the business benefits of configurators for the supplier. They are summarized in Table 11. In some circumstances configurators can enable premium pricing. Heatley et al. (1995) document a case where a sixfold shortening of the order throughput cycle brought a competitive advantage that enabled premium pricing. They also observed that configurator-

supported sales engineers sold more complex products, often commanding a high premium. In a similar vein, Yu and Skovgaard (1998) claim increased sales due to (partially) configurator induced shorter delivery times and product flexibility. Heatley et al. (1995) report that products that were at the borderline of profitability prior to the configurator because of order delays, pricing errors, and rework costs became attractive as the configurator reduced these costly problems. Overall, avoidance of errors, related rework, and production problems seem to reduce costs. Fleischanderl et al. (1998) report of a case where configuration-related costs were reduced 60% over the product life cycle.

Barker and O'Connor (1989) and Heatley et al. (1995) argue that customer satisfaction increases as many of the configurator-induced benefits affect customers' perceptions positively. Giving the configurator to customers to use had the effect of "tying" customers to the company in the case reported by Forza and Salvador (2002b). The configurator reduced the time that customers needed for defining product specifications. Dealer and retailer loyalty may be improved by configura-

Table 11. Summary of business benefits for the supplier

Benefit	References	Challenges met?
Better price from products, in some situations	Heatley et al., 1995	Higher costs of producing customized products
Increased sales from shorter delivery times and product flexibility.	Yu and Skovgaard, 1998	Higher costs of producing customized products
Products at borderline of profitability can become more attractive	Heatley et al., 1995	Higher costs of producing customized products
Reduction of costs in many areas	Fleischanderl et al., 1998	Higher costs of producing customized products
Improved customers' satisfaction, perception	Barker and O'Connor, 1989; Heatley et al., 1995	Low customer satisfaction, lost image from elicitation difficulties
Customer "lock-in" from configurator usage; dealer and retailer loyalty	*Lock-in:* Forza and Salvador, 2002b. *Loyalty:* Heatley et al., 1995; Yu and Skovgaard, 1998	Low dealer and customer loyalty from elicitation difficulties
Improve tracking of purchases and sales; mining of customer orders and preferences from configurator for future strategy	McGuinness and Wright, 1998; Bramham and MacCarthy, 2004	

tors (Heatley et al., 1995; Yu & Skovgaard, 1998) due to less errors and subsequent hassles, and as configurators can enable selling products with a higher premium. Further, configurators can boost customer relationship management by enabling storage and mining of customer orders and preferences for cues to future strategy, forecasting, and supply chain management (Bramham & MacCarthy, 2004) and improve tracking of purchases and sales (McGuinness & Wright, 1998). This can be an enabling factor for realizing a benefit of MC, getting access to real-time, more accurate customer information (Table 10).

Organization

Next, we discuss the benefits from configurators to the organization; for a summary, see Table 12. As configurators ensure the consistency of configurations and reduce manufacturing problems, they allow for the use of less skilled workers in sales (Bramham & MacCarthy, 2004) and in production (Sviokla, 1990). This probably lowers employment costs, as skilled labor tends to be more expensive. In a similar vein, customers (Forza & Salvador, 2002b) or retailers (Yu & Skovgaard, 1998) may do the specification themselves with configurators. Further, technical experts are no

longer needed for consistency checks or technical consulting during sales (McGuinness & Wright, 1998), or preparing customer-specific documentation (Forza & Salvador 2002a); see also Table 4. This frees them to other tasks like new product development (Bonehill & Slee-Smith, 1998; Forza & Salvador 2002a) or, less personnel may be necessary in general (Barker & O'Connor, 1989; Sviokla, 1990). Work satisfaction increases as configurators obviate the need to working with mundane details, like verifying specifications, and more time may be devoted to intellectually challenging cases (Heatley et al., 1995).

Specification Process

For a summary of the benefits, see Table 13 and Table 14. The ability of configurators to ensure the consistency and completeness of sales specifications by managing the complex interdependencies and incompatibilities between choices brings a number of benefits to the specification process. Configurators can reduce or even eliminate the errors in sales specifications (Barker & O'Connor, 1989) meaning also that the specified product individuals can be manufactured. Further, configurators also help to eradicate the errors noticed after sales, thus reducing or eliminating the itera-

Table 12. Summary of supplier benefits in organization

Benefit	References for benefit	Challenges met?
Allows for less-skilled workers in sales and production	*Sales:* Bramham and MacCarthy, 2004; Salvador and Forza, 2004. *Production:* Sviokla, 1990	Higher costs of producing customized products.
Allows for specification by retailers or even customers themselves	*Retailers:* Yu and Skovgaard, 1998. *Customers:* Forza and Salvador, 2002b	Technical experts deeply involved in verifying specifications
Technical experts needed less in specification → freed to other tasks, like R&D	Barker and O'Connor, 1989; Sviokla, 1990; McGuinness and Wright, 1998; Bonehill and Slee-Smith, 1998; Forza and Salvador, 2002a	Technical experts deeply involved in verifying specifications
Configurators eliminate some tasks, even parts of organization related to consistency checks	McGuinness and Wright, 1998; Forza and Salvador, 2002b	
Work satisfaction increases as configurators reduce working with mundane details, and more time may be devoted to challenging cases	Heatley et al., 1995; Tiihonen and Soininen, 1997	

tions between sales and manufacturing (Wright et al., 1993), and help sales staff to promptly give either correct or good estimates of delivery times (Vanwelkenheysen, 1998) and prices (Barker & O'Connor, 1989). As configurators ensure the specifications are error-free, sales staff can devote more time to actual selling instead of doing consistency checks (Heatley et al., 1995) and technical staff need not do consistency checks anymore either (McGuinness & Wright, 1998).

The support configurators lend to the specification process, making it less difficult and complex. Therefore, the sales staff can more freely and efficiently explore the alternatives, which can help to optimize the specification to customer needs (Tiihonen & Soininen, 1997). This also enables the sales staff to sell more complex products that often are more expensive as well (Heatley et al., 1995). Configurators also reduce the effort needed in the specification (Wright et al., 1993) by taking care of consistency checks and supporting the specification task, and often automatically generating documents that previously had to be

produced manually. All this also results in shorter lead-times in order-processing before manufacturing (Barker & O'Connor, 1989) and in an increase in the volume of processed quotations and orders without increasing sales staff (Sviokla, 1990).

With configurator support, the repertoires of typical specifications sales staff invented to workaround the specification process complexity should become unnecessary. Further, as configuration knowledge and therefore the customization range of configurable products are "built-in" to configurators, they standardize specification results: It is not possible to specify product individuals outside the customization range or to specify different product individuals for identical customer orders.

Overall, configurators improve the productivity of sales, quoting, and engineering for the aforementioned reasons. Moreover, customers may perceive the quality of operations to be higher, as a single contact produces a manufacturable specification, often with a price and delivery time (or estimate), and in a prompt manner. Further,

Table 13. Summary of supplier benefits in the sales specification process (Part 1)

Benefit	References for benefit	Challenges met?
Reduce or eliminate errors in sales specifications	Barker and O'Connor, 1989; Sviokla, 1990; Fohn et al., 1995; Heatley et al., 1995; Ariano and Dagnino, 1996; Tiihonen and Soininen, 1997; Bonehill and Slee-Smith, 1998; Fleischhanderl et al., 1998; Vanwelkenheysen, 1998; Günter and Kühn, 1999; Yu and Skovgaard, 1998; Aldanondo et al., 1999; Aldanondo et al., 2000; Forza and Salvador, 2002a; Pedersen and Edwards, 2004	Difficulty and complexity of specification; repertoires of typical specifications; specified individuals that cannot be manufactured
Reduce or eliminate iterations between sales and manufacturing	Wright et al., 1993; Heatley et al., 1995; Tiihonen and Soininen, 1997; Vanwelkenheysen, 1998; Aldanondo et al., 1999; Aldanondo et al., 2000	Errors noticed after sales lead to iterations in the sales-delivery process
Correct delivery time, or good estimate	Vanwelkenheysen, 1998; Forza and Salvador, 2002a	Incorrect delivery time
Correct price, or good estimate	Barker and O'Connor, 1989; Heatley et al., 1995; Ariano and Dagnino, 1996; Vanwelkenheysen, 1998; Forza and Salvador, 2002a	Incorrect, smaller price than effective cost
Sales can devote more time to selling	Heatley et al., 1995; Tiihonen and Soininen, 1997; Vanwelkenheysen, 1998	Difficulty and complexity of specification
Technical staff need not check consistency	McGuinness and Wright, 1998; Yu and Skovgaard, 1998; Forza and Salvador, 2002a, 2002b	Technical experts deeply involved in verifying specifications

configurators lower the costs due to less effort required in specification, and the reduced rework and iterations due to elimination of specification errors (Wright et al., 1993; Vanwelkenheysen, 1998).

Manufacturing

This section discusses the benefits configurators can bring to manufacturing. Summary of the benefits can be found in Table 15. The main benefits for manufacturing stem from the error-free,

Table 14. Summary of supplier benefits in the sales specification process (Part 2)

Benefit	References for benefit	Challenges met?
More free exploration or product alternatives; helps to optimize to customer needs	Tiihonen and Soininen, 1997; Bonehill and Slee-Smith, 1998; McGuinness and Wright, 1998; Hvam, Malis, Hansen, & Riis, 2004; Pedersen and Edwards, 2004	Does specified product individual meet customer needs optimally?
Reduce specification effort	Wright et al., 1993; Heatley et al., 1995; Ariano and Dagnino, 1996; McGuinness and Wright, 1998; Yu and Skovgaard, 1998; Aldanondo et al., 1999; Aldanondo et al., 2000; Forza and Salvador, 2002a; Hvam et al., 2004; Pedersen and Edwards, 2004	Customer has to spend time in specification and wait for the finished product.
Shorter lead-times in order-processing	Barker and O'Connor, 1989; Sviokla, 1990; Wright et al., 1993; Heatley et al., 1995; Fohn et al., 1995; Ariano and Dagnino, 1996; Tiihonen and Soininen, 1997; Bonehill and Slee-Smith, 1998; Günter and Kühn, 1999; Vanwelkenheysen, 1998; Aldanondo et al., 1999; Aldanondo et al., 2000; Forza and Salvador, 2002a, 2002b; Hvam et al., 2004; Pedersen and Edwards, 2004	Customer has to spend time in specification and wait for the finished product.
Increases volume of quotations and orders processed, without increasing staff	Sviokla, 1990; Tiihonen and Soininen, 1997; Vanwelkenheysen, 1998; Pedersen and Edwards, 2004	
Standardize specification results	Sviokla, 1990; Tiihonen et al., 1996; Vanwelkenheysen, 1998; Forza and Salvador, 2002b	Sales force must not offer changes outside pre-designed customization options. Different specifications for identical customer order

Table 15. Summary of supplier benefits in manufacturing

Benefit	References for benefit	Challenges met?
Ordered products can be manufactured; less production problems, stoppages, fire-fighting	Heatley et al., 1995; McGuinness and Wright, 1998; Forza and Salvador, 2002a, 2002b	Fire-fighting in manufacturing from specification errors Achieving uniform quality
More reliable and on-time delivery	Forza and Salvador, 2002a; Pedersen and Edwards, 2004	
More accurate planning and scheduling of production	Heatley et al., 1995; Bonehill and Slee-Smith, 1998; Yu and Skovgaard, 1998; McGuinness and Wright, 1998; Forza and Salvador, 2002a	
Configurators guide to more standard solutions → easier production	McGuinness and Wright, 1998; Forza and Salvador, 2002b; Pedersen and Edwards, 2004	
Lower (buffer) inventories	Barker and O'Connor, 1989; Yu and Skovgaard, 1998; McGuinness and Wright, 1998; Forza and Salvador, 2002a	Higher costs of producing customized products

manufacturable sales specifications (Heatley et al., 1995). Without errors there are less production problems, stoppages, and firefighting due to, for example, missing or wrong parts. Consequently, the reliability of deliveries improves (Forza & Salvador, 2002a) and planning and scheduling of production become more accurate (Heatley et al., 1995). Moreover, as configurators guide customers to ordering within the supplier's normal product range there is less variation to handle, making production easier overall (McGuinness & Wright, 1998). The aforementioned manufacturing benefits meet or alleviate the challenges of firefighting in manufacturing and help in achieving uniform quality. Finally, improved predictability of production and reduced order-processing time also allow reduction of buffer inventories at the factory (Barker & O'Connor, 1989).

Product Development

The benefits from configurators to product development, summarized in Table 16, are discussed next. As configurators improve the complexity-handling capabilities of the supplier in sales and production, more complex products with competitive features can be developed (Heatley et al., 1995) and increased variety can be offered (Sviokla, 1990).

Configurators require explicit definition, that is, modeling, of the configuration knowledge. This can initiate a better understanding of company's products (Ariano & Dagnino, 1996) or redefinition of the products to better suit the market and reduce unnecessary complexity, according to Forza and Salvador (2002a). Forza and Salvador (2002a) also argue that configuration modeling may provide ways to describe architectural product knowledge. Further, more resources may be available for product development because configurators free the technical experts from doing consistency checks (Barker & O'Connor) and ongoing management of configuration knowledge (Yu & Skovgaard, 1998).

Long-Term Management of Configuration Knowledge

For a summary of the configurator benefits discussed here, see Table 17. Configurators support centralized configuration knowledge maintenance and management (Sviokla, 1990). Without a configurator, configuration knowledge can be dispersed in the supplier organization, and transferring up-to-date configuration knowledge within it can be problematic. With configurators, up-to-date configuration knowledge is easily available in the organization (Barker & O'Connor, 1989), in sales and for customers as well.

Table 16. Summary of supplier benefits in product development

Benefit	References
Increased complexity handling capability → products with a wider customization range can be developed	Sviokla, 1990; Heatley et al., 1995
Explicit configuration modeling may initiate better understanding of the products, or redefining them to meet markets better	Ariano and Dagnino, 1996; Forza and Salvador, 2002a
Configuration modeling may provide a way to represent architectural product knowledge	Forza and Salvador, 2002a
Configurators free resources to product development from consistency checks and ongoing management of configuration knowledge	*Checks:* Barker and O'Connor, 1989; Sviokla, 1990; McGuinness and Wright, 1998; Bonehill and Slee-Smith, 1998; Forza and Salvador, 2002a *Management:* Yu and Skovgaard, 1998

Having systematic configuration knowledge embedded in the configurator may help in training new employees to become productive (Fleischanderl et al., 1998). Further, configuration knowledge managed centrally in a configurator helps to turn individual knowledge into organizational knowledge, reducing the need of the organization to rely on (few) knowledgeable individuals (Günter & Kühn, 1999) and supports systematic management of information.

Supplier Challenges

Business

The business challenges of the supplier, discussed next, are summarized in Table 18. Taking a configurator into use is a significant investment, as developing, deploying, and maintaining a configurator represents a significant cost, requires a significant effort, can take a considerable time, and can widely affect the organization and its functions. The cost may include software licenses,

software development and integration, hardware, consultation, product modeling, and long-term maintenance (Tiihonen at al., 1997). Case experiences of costly configurator implementation and deployment projects taking a lot of effort and time have been reported in Aldanondo et al. (2000); Forza and Salvador (2002a, 2002b); Hvam et al. (2004); and Pedersen and Edwards (2004). Investment into a configurator must be paid back in its repetitive use. Thus, a high enough volume is needed to justify the costs (Pedersen & Edwards, 2004).

Problems related to configurator introduction or long-term management might delay new product introductions or product improvements (Barker & O'Connor, 1989; Tiihonen et al., 1996). The supplier may end up being over-dependent of the configurator and the knowledge embedded in it (Sviokla, 1990). Thus the configurator becomes a mission-critical application.

A major challenge in configurator implementation is aligning the business needs and processes of the supplier and the configurator. It is necessary

Table 17. Summary of supplier benefits from configurator in long term maintenance of configuration knowledge

Benefit	References for benefit	Challenges met?
Support to maintain configuration knowledge, centrally	Sviokla, 1990; Tiihonen and Soininen, 1997; Yu and Skovgaard, 1998; McGuinness and Wright, 1998; Fleischhanderl et al., 1998; Forza and Salvador, 2002a	Long-term management of configuration knowledge; systemizing information management; dispersed configuration knowledge in the organization
Correct, up-to-date configuration knowledge available in the organization	Barker and O'Connor, 1989; Sviokla, 1990, Wright et al., 1993; Tiihonen et al., 1996; Tiihonen and Soininen, 1997; Fleischanderl et al., 1998; Bonehill and Slee-Smith, 1998; McGuinness and Wright, 1998; Vanwelkenheysen, 1998; Yu and Skovgaard, 1998	Transferring updated configuration knowledge to sales force
Availability of systematic configuration knowledge helps in training new employees to become productive	Fleischanderl et al., 1998; Bonehill and Slee-Smith, 1998; Salvador and Forza, 2004; Pedersen and Edwards, 2004	
Centralized configuration knowledge in a configurator helps to turn individual knowledge into organizational	Günter and Kühn, 1999; Forza and Salvador, 2002a; Bramham and MacCarthy, 2004; Pedersen and Edwards, 2004	Systemizing information management.

and challenging to integrate the configurator to the company's business processes (Bramham & MacCarthy, 2004). Business, not technologists, should guide the implementation (Barker & O'Connor, 1989). The scope of support provided by a configurator must be determined according to business needs. It may be feasible to leave the most complex products out to reduce the complexity of systemizing and managing configuration knowledge, as was done due to limited volume in a case reported by Forza and Salvador (2002a).

Aligning the processes with the configurator may require business process re-engineering to achieve full benefits (Tiihonen & Soininen, 1997). The sales process, especially, may have to be systemized or streamlined. The need for different sales-delivery processes after the deployment of a configurator should be determined. For example, separate processes may be needed for mass-produced products, configurable products, and products that require case-specific engineering in addition to configurable parts (Tiihonen et al., 1996). A manual configuration process may have to be retained even when a configurator is deployed. For example, in less-developed areas, the availability or price of computers and data communications or the computer illiteracy of sales-persons may limit the use of a configurator (Tiihonen et al., 1996). Further, multiple sales channels may have to be supported, for example, in-shop "off-line" configuration, and online self-service in Web (Reichwald, Piller, & Mueller, 2004).

Effective distribution of the configurator to the entire sales force, especially to retailers, may be problematic (Heatley et al., 1995). When the supplier does not own or control the sales channel, configurator use cannot be enforced (Tiihonen et al., 1996). Retailers, possibly having low volumes, may be unwilling to adopt a configurator due to the cost of the system or training (Tiihonen & Soininen 1997).

Organization

Next, the supplier challenges involving the organization are reviewed. The challenges are outlined in Table 19.

Introducing a configurator can significantly change an organization (Barker & O'Connor, 1989), making it harder to implement than anticipated (Ariano & Dagnino, 1996). Configurators can reduce or eliminate the need for consistency checks, consulting technical staff during sales,

Table 18. Summary of business challenges of the supplier

Challenge	References
Configurator development and maintenance takes considerable time and represents significant cost and effort.	*Cost:* Tiihonen at al., 1997; Pedersen and Edwards, 2004. *Effort:* Barker and O'Connor, 1989; Sviokla, 1990; Aldanondo et al., 2000; Forza and Salvador, 2002b. *Time:* Forza and Salvador, 2002a; Hvam et al., 2004
Challenges of long-term management may delay product introductions or improvements	Barker and O'Connor, 1989; Tiihonen et al., 1996
Risk of becoming over-dependent of configurator and knowledge in it	Sviokla, 1990
The necessary alignment of business needs and processes, and scope of configurator-support is challenging.	Barker and O'Connor, 1989; Tiihonen et al., 1996; Forza and Salvador, 2002a; Bramham and MacCarthy, 2004; Hvam et al., 2004; Pedersen and Edwards, 2004
Business process re-engineering may be required	Tiihonen and Soininen, 1997; Tiihonen et al., 1998; Hvam et al., 2004
Multiple sales processes and channels may have to be supported	*Processes:* Tiihonen et al.1996; Tiihonen and Soininen, 1997; Reichwald et al., 2004. *Channels:* Reichwald et al., 2004
Effective distribution of the configurator to the sales force	Heatley et al., 1995; Tiihonen et al., 1996; Tiihonen and Soininen, 1997

part-list creation, and other tasks related to creating specifications. This changes personnel roles (Barker & O'Connor, 1989) and may make organizational units involved in the tasks redundant (Barker & O'Connor, 1989).

Cooperation between different parts of the organization is required to align the configurator with business needs (Barker & O'Connor, 1989), as well as for configuration knowledge acquisition and modeling (Sviokla, 1990). Configuration knowledge can be dispersed in the organization between different units and personnel. Some modeling decisions are business decisions. It can be challenging to have prompt access to individuals who have the necessary authority and knowledge to make these decisions (Vanwelkenheysen, 1998). The required work in implementing and maintaining a configurator and the challenges it alleviates may touch different parts of the organization (Tiihonen & Soininen, 1997), which may hamper cooperation and cause resistance towards the configurator.

Resistance in the organization towards the configurator can also be caused by changes in personnel roles (Bonehill & Slee-Smith, 1998) and organization (Forza & Salvador, 2002a). Further, personnel may see the configurator as a menace to their position (Forza & Salvador, 2002a) or

be unwilling to trust the decisions made by an automatic system (Tiihonen et al., 1996). In a case described in Heatley et al. (1995), achieving 100% usage had required an enforcing policy.

A new function responsible for configurator development and maintenance may be introduced (Ariano & Dagnino, 1996; Sviokla, 1990) as continuity in development and maintenance of the knowledge bases needs to be ensured (Vanwelkenheysen, 1998). This can cause subtle challenges. Configurator maintenance can be very critical (Sviokla, 1990) with configurator experts becoming vital to the company (Ariano & Dagnino, 1996; Forza & Salvador, 2002b). Expertise on configuration knowledge may shift to the configurator development and maintenance organization, whose people may not be good enough product experts (Sviokla, 1990). Management challenge may move from keeping staff up-to-date to keeping configurator software up-to-date (Sviokla, 1990).

Specification Process

In this section, the challenges related to the specification process are discussed. The challenges are summarized in Table 20.

Table 19. Summary of organizational challenges of the supplier

Challenge	References
Significant organizational changes may be necessary and harder to implement than anticipated.	Barker and O'Connor, 1989; Ariano and Dagnino, 1996; Aldanondo et al., 2000; Forza and Salvador, 2002b
Roles of individuals change, and some people delegate part of their tasks to configurator.	Barker and O'Connor, 1989; Bonehill and Slee-Smith, 1998; Forza and Salvador, 2002a
Organizational cooperation required to align configurator with business needs, and in configuration knowledge acquisition	Barker and O'Connor, 1989; Sviokla, 1990; Wright et al., 1993; Vanwelkenheysen, 1998; Forza and Salvador, 2002b
Benefits and challenges of the configurator and required work may touch different parts of the organization.	Tiihonen and Soininen, 1997
Potential for resistance towards configurator.	Heatley et al., 1995; Tiihonen et al., 1996; Bonehill and Slee-Smith, 1998; Forza and Salvador, 2002a
Configurator development and maintenance organization may be introduced and can become critical for company and individuals leaving a risk	Sviokla, 1990; Ariano and Dagnino, 1996; Vanwelkenheysen, 1998; Forza and Salvador, 2002b; Hvam et al., 2004.

Even with configurators, eliciting and understanding real customer needs may be difficult. It is possible that customers do not know their real needs (Blecker, Abdelkafi, Kreutler, & Friedrich, 2004; Franke & Piller, 2003), cannot express them (Blecker et al., 2004), or that the supplier may misinterpret customer requirements (Blecker et al., 2003; Tiihonen & Soininen, 1997). Customers may not want to part with all types of needed information (e.g., personal information affecting needs) during the specification task (Bramham & MacCarthy, 2004). These issues may be more serious in self-service settings where personal interaction with sales staff is not available. In some cases customers may prefer consultative selling where sales employees operate the configurator over self-service with Web-based configurator (Reichwald et al., 2004).

Configurators may fix interaction with the customer in general (Bramham & MacCarthy, 2004) or at the level of fixing the order of selections (Fohn et al., 1995). The customer interaction which the configurator enables is easily imitated and may yield the same offering as competitors (Bramham & MacCarthy, 2004). Franke and Piller (2003) discussed the need to support creative product specification during the configuration task instead of simply choosing from pre-designed options. Configurators support partially-configurable products that still involve some custom design, but they do it poorly (Tiihonen et al., 1998).

It may be difficult to modify created configurations (Sviokla, 1990). Most often reconfiguration is managed on a case-by-case basis, which cannot be efficiently supported by configurators (Männistö, Soininen, Tiihonen, & Sulonen, 1999).

Long-Term Management of Configuration Knowledge

In the following, we review the challenges related to configurators in long-term management of configuration knowledge. For a summary of the challenges, see Table 21.

Configuration knowledge often changes frequently due to product changes and for business related reasons like shifting customer needs and marketing strategies (Fleischanderl et al., 1998) and pricing changes. If the sales rely on configuration support, fast updating of configuration knowledge is important, even business-critical (Barker & O'Connor, 1989). Over time, configuration models grow and new ones are added to the configurator increasing the complexity of management (Barker & O'Connor, 1989; Bramham & MacCarthy, 2004). More complexity arises from regional differences in products and prices (Tiihonen & Soininen, 1997) and if reconfiguration needs to be supported (Männistö et al., 1999).

There must be means for deploying the updated configurator and/or configuration knowledge bases to the entire sales force and/or to customers (Tiihonen et al., 1998). The related challenges are different in different architectural scenarios. Configurators based on a centralized, for example, Web-based architecture require updates only

Table 20. Summary of supplier challenges in the specification process

Challenge	References
Obtaining and understanding real customer needs	Tiihonen and Soininen, 1997; Franke and Piller, 2003; Blecker et al., 2004
Personal service may remain preferable to self-service with a configurator.	Reichwald et al., 2004
Configurators may fix interaction with the customer	Fohn et al., 1995; Bramham and MacCarthy, 2004
Support for creative product specification	Franke and Piller, 2003
It may be difficult to modify created configurations	Sviokla, 1990; Männistö et al., 1999

to the centralized system and knowledge base. Stand-alone configurators require either a synchronization mechanism (e.g., a docking station with appropriate software) or actions by the user and cannot therefore guarantee that configuration knowledge updates will be taken into use. Ensuring the correctness of the configurator knowledge may be challenging after updates (Tiihonen & Soininen, 1997).

The challenges of dispersed configuration knowledge and diverse expertise possibly required in implementing configurators play their role in long-term management as well. To reduce these burdens, Fohn et al. (1995) and Tiihonen and Soininen (1997) propose that configuration modeling and maintaining the configurator knowledge-base should not require any configurator expertise. Rather, updates should be performable by product experts.

It can be concluded that long-term management of configurators is both mission-critical and challenging (Tiihonen & Soininen, 1997). Its failure may be a reason for many failed configurator projects. However, empirical evidence has not been published.

Development and Initial Introduction of a Configurator

Here we discuss the challenges related to the development and initial introduction of a configurator. For a summary, see Table 22.

Fleischanderl et al. (1998) point out that the development and introduction of a configurator is a demanding task. Configuration modeling requires knowledge acquisition from different parts of the company, which is not always easy or frictionless (Wright et al., 1993). The people with the required knowledge may be different individuals, located in different parts of the organization, also geographically (Barker & O'Connor, 1989). The gathered configuration knowledge must be systemized and formalized (Tiihonen et al 1998) to make it coherent and usable in the configurator. Thus, taking a configurator into use requires expertise both in the domain (products and industry) and in configurators (e.g., modeling, possibly programming) and related IT. However, validation and testing of configuration models is a challenge due to combinatorial nature of configurable products (Barker & O'Connor, 1989). Regional differences increase the complexity of configuration models

Table 21. Summary of supplier challenges in long term management of configuration knowledge

Challenge	References
Fast updating and creating of configuration knowledge bases and configuration models	Barker and O'Connor, 1989; Wright et al., 1993; Tiihonen et al., 1996; Fleischanderl et al., 1998; Forza and Salvador, 2002b; Bramham and MacCarthy, 2004
Configuration models grow and new ones are introduced, increasing complexity	Barker and O'Connor, 1989; Bramham and MacCarthy, 2004
There must be mechanisms that distribute and take configurator and/or knowledge base updates to use in entire sales force and/or customers.	Tiihonen et al., 1998
Ensuring correctness of the configurator knowledge base may be challenging after updates	Tiihonen and Soininen, 1997; Felfernig, Friedrich, Jannach, and Stumptner, 2004
Updates can require both product and configurator expertise (*should need only product expertise*).	Fohn et al., 1995; Tiihonen and Soininen, 1997
Long-term management of configurators is both mission-critical and challenging.	Tiihonen and Soininen, 1997; Tiihonen et al., 1998

and related information systems. Often all product options are not available everywhere, prices differ from one area to another, and there may be several language versions to maintain (Tiihonen & Soininen, 1996).

It may be necessary to improve product modularization to enable configuring (Hvam et al., 2004). Tiihonen and Soininen (1997) argue that good long-term results in using a configurator can be expected only when the product has been designed to be easily configurable as it simplifies the configuration models.

Integration of a configurator to other systems may be necessary (Barker & O'Connor, 1989). Integration can facilitate efficient and error-free transfer of configurations (e.g., parts lists, drawings, connection information, etc.), price, delivery time or capacity, and product model information. Systems that could be integrated include sales and CRM tools, ERP, PDM, and CAD. However, the high cost and complexity of integrations calls for judgment. Integration to IT systems of retailers or customers may also be desirable (Tiihonen et al., 1998).

Developing an efficient, learnable user interface for a configurator can be difficult. Determining "the best and most logical" sequence of user prompts can be challenging (Aldanondo et al., 2000). Additional concerns are the ability of the user interface to provide a satisfactory customer experience, which also provides integration into the company brand, and whether the configurator supports creative innovation by the customers (Franke & Piller, 2003).

Customer Benefits

Next, we discuss the customer benefits from configurators, summarized in Table 23. Because configurators check the consistency and enable rapid specification, it is possible to explore the alternatives and their impacts in a more thorough and free manner during sales (McGuinness & Wright, 1998). This increases the possibility to find a good match with needs and probably lessens the complexity of specification to some extent. Moreover, as sales staff need not worry about consistency checks, they can devote more time to the customer (Vanwelkenheysen, 1998). This increased advice available to customers should help alleviate the complexity of specification in customers' mind and increase the possibility of finding a suitable product. Some configurators can help to explain the incompatibilities and dependencies between product options to the customer (Aldanondo et al., 1999), alleviating the complexity in specification. Forza and Salvador (2002b) argue that communication may become easier

Table 22. Summary of supplier challenges in configurator introduction

Challenge	References
Configuration knowledge acquisition	Wright et al., 1993, Tiihonen and Soininen, 1997; Forza and Salvador, 2002a
Configuration knowledge systemization and formalization	Tiihonen et al., 1998; Forza and Salvador, 2002a
Expertise in products and industry, in configurators, modeling, and IT required	Barker and O'Connor, 1989; Fleischanderl et al., 1998; Aldanondo et al., 2000
Validation and testing of configuration models	Barker and O'Connor, 1989; Heatley et al., 1995; Tiihonen and Soininen, 1997; Felfernig et al., 2004
Integration to other IT systems	Barker and O'Connor, 1989; Tiihonen et al., 1996; Tiihonen and Soininen, 1997; Tiihonen et al., 1998; Franke and Piller, 2003
Developing a good and suitable user interface	Aldanondo et al., 2000, Franke and Piller, 2003

as a configurator makes the company language available to customers. The differences in terms used by the customer and supplier to describe the preferred product could be reduced, alleviating the difficulty of finding an optimal product to customer needs.

A configurator can enable the customers to do the specification task themselves (Salvador & Forza, 2004) whenever they want (Forza & Salvador, 2002b) if the configurator is available on the Web or distributed to the customers. In general, configurators can save customer time during specification (Forza & Salvador, 2002b). Some configurators allow using existing configurations as a basis for specification, which also saves customer time (McGuinness & Wright, 1998). The price and delivery time (or estimates) may be available immediately (Vanwelkenheysen, 1998).

Customer Challenges

The challenges from the customer point-of-view have not been discussed much in literature. The challenges caused by configurators mostly relate to self-service configurators.

All customers may not want to use a self-service configurator. Selecting a suitable configurable product from the set of available products can be difficult, especially for non-expert customers typical to consumer e-commerce (Heiskala, Anderson, Huhtinen, Tiihonen, & Martio, 2003; Pargamin, 2002). Special product selection support may be needed (Heiskala et al., 2003). However, trusting recommendation(s) of a system can be a problem (Tiihonen et al., 1996). Self-service customers may find configurator user interfaces difficult, especially if the needs are not clear, or if there is a mismatch between configurator and customer logic for preferences. A configurator may also restrain the interaction, making it too rigid for customers' liking.

Several customer challenges discussed for MC and CP probably apply, even with configurator support. The number of options may overwhelm the customer (Huffman & Kahn, 1998), who may not be able accept the risk of making wrong decisions (Berman, 2002). Additionally, the documentation of the customer's explicit preferences and personal information in the product specification process may feel as an invasion of privacy (Broekhuizen & Alsem, 2002). Even with a configurator, it may be

Table 23. Summary of customer benefits from configurators

Benefit	References for benefit	Challenges met?
More product alternatives and their impact can be more freely inspected during specification → increase possibility to find a good product fit.	McGuinness and Wright, 1998; Forza and Salvador, 2002b; Salvador and Forza, 2004	Optimal product individual fit to customer needs; complexity of specification
Sales can devote more time for customer	Vanwelkenheysen, 1998	Complexity of specification; optimal product individual fit to customer needs
Configurator can help to explain to the customer why some alternative choices are not compatible	Aldanondo et al., 1999	Complexity of specification
Configurator makes company product language available to customer, which may make communication easier	Forza and Salvador, 2002b	Optimal product individual fit to customer needs
Customers can do the specification themselves, when they want (over the Web)	Forza and Salvador, 2002b; Salvador and Forza, 2004	
Save customer time in specification	Forza and Salvador, 2002b	Time and effort spent in specification
Possibility to use existing specifications as basis saves customer time	McGuinness and Wright, 1998	Time and effort spent in specification
Price and delivery time immediately	Vanwelkenheysen, 1998	

difficult to judge whether the end product presents good value (Broekhuizen & Alsem 2002). Price in e-commerce is also an issue; it is difficult to know if personal contact could provide a better price. The challenges related to modifying created configurations, reconfiguration, and creative product specification are probably relevant as well.

RATIONALE FOR INTRODUCING MASS CUSTOMIZATION

In this section, we briefly discuss under what kind of conditions it does make sense to introduce an MC strategy to the company and when it does not. Naturally, the benefits we have listed provide motivation for a company to introduce MC. Further, the company probably should have capabilities in place to overcome or alleviate the challenges we have listed, at least to an extent that ensures that the benefits gained from MC outweigh the additional sacrifices, for both the company and its customers.

The necessary conditions and capabilities for MC have been discussed by several authors, again dominantly from an MP viewpoint (Bardacki & Whitelock, 2003; Berman, 2002; Broekhuizen & Alsem, 2002; Da Silveira et al., 2001; Hart, 1995; Kotha, 1995; Pine, 1993a, 1995; Radder & Louw, 1999; Zipkin, 2001). Berman (2002) and Radder and Louw (1999) provide checklists for practitioners to assess the soundness of an MC switch. An integrative overview of the conditions is given by Blecker et al. (2005, pp. 23-41), which we summarize here.

Blecker et al. (2005) categorize the conditions to ones relevant before and after moving to MC. Before the move, the company should assess the market conditions on a macro (demand and structural factors) and micro (customer demand for customization) levels. On the demand and structural factors, Blecker et al. (2005, p. 31) follow Pine's (1993a) market turbulence indicators, like unstable, unpredictable, and heterogeneous de-

mand, uncertain and quickly-changing customer needs, low-price consciousness, but high quality and fashion/style consciousness and high level of pre- and post-sale service. Customer demand for customization must truly exist, and it is likely to be so only for a limited group of products (Blecker et al., 2005, p. 32; Svensson & Barfod, 2002). For luxury products (Pine, 1993a, p. 56) and business-to-business customers that arguably, in many markets, are more knowledgeable and demanding than consumers (MacCarthy & Brabazon, 2003), this might be more probable. The value of customization to customers must also overcome the challenges of possible higher prices, time to wait for the final product, effort spent in specification, and privacy concerns (Bardacki & Whitelock, 2003; Broekhuizen & Alsem, 2002). Blecker et al. (2005, p. 33) also state that possible first-mover advantages have to be taken into account. Pine et al. (1995) argue that frequent enough repeat business and interactions with the customer are positive conditions for MC to be a viable option. On the other hand, Spring and Dalrymple (2000) argue that on occasions that the price premium does not lead to increased profitability, there are still valid reasons to customize products: (1) to keep competition out, (2) to force the organization to learn and develop new capabilities, and (3) to enhance the company's standing/brand in the industry.

In addition to the external conditions, before moving to MC the company must assess whether it has or can acquire the capabilities necessary to customize its products (Blecker et al. 2005, p. 33). The company's value chain must be responsive and flexible and willing and able to meet the added challenges of MC (Blecker et al., 2005), and connected with an efficiently-linked information network (Da Silveira et al., 2001). The production processes of the company must be flexible to be able to produce a variety of products, and the products themselves must be customizable (Blecker et al., 2005, p. 35). A key ingredient for MC is customer needs elicitation capability of the company (Blecker et al., 2005, p. 35). MC with CP requires significant investment in product design, information management, and the like. Payback requires a high enough volume to cover the costs (Tiihonen & Soininen, 1997). This can be a challenge especially for those companies whose background is in FC with limited volumes.

When pursuing MC on a continuous basis, the company must maintain and improve its MC capabilities. These include the aforementioned customer needs elicitation, process flexibility, supply chain agility, and customer-oriented product design. Blecker et al. (2005, p.38) also emphasize the importance of having capabilities to manage the increased complexity and variety in products and production processes and of efficient knowledge-sharing throughout the company.

SUGGESTIONS FOR FUTURE RESEARCH DIRECTIONS

The customer view on mass customization, configurable products, and configurators is thin in the literature. Moving to MC with CP has been mainly documented from the direction of MP, especially in the MC literature. We call for research, especially empirical, on the customer benefits and challenges of MC with CP and on the move to MC from the direction of FC.

This review makes the same observation as Da Silveira et al. (2001) and Paloheimo, Miettinen, and Brax (2004) that services have received little attention in MC literature, at least as regards to the benefits and challenges. Literature on configurable service products and configurators is even scarcer. We therefore call for future research on MC, CP, and configurators in service settings. We also observed, as Franke and Piller (2003), that empirical findings on MC are limited.

Research on ways to overcome or alleviate the challenges, a collection of best practices, would probably be of interest to practitioners. A specific viewpoint could be avoiding the pitfalls in the

initial move to MC with CP and in configurator introductions. The reviews of Broekhuizen and Alsem (2002) and Da Silveira et al. (2001) provide a good starting point. We would expect to find different necessary conditions, success factors, enablers, and best practices when switching from MP versus switching from FC. In literature, the configurator benefits are dominantly discussed with relation to the company not having a configurator. Comparative studies on what kinds of configurators are best for a given situation would be of interest.

Research on configurator introductions could benefit from literature on information system implementations and account for relevant differences. Is configuration knowledge acquisition different for technical knowledge and knowledge related to identifying optimal fit to customer needs? How tacit are these types of configuration knowledge? Is a configurator sufficient to transfer knowledge to sales? What are the challenges? In our view, especially empirical knowledge management research could provide interesting insights for MC and CP suppliers and configurator research. Further, empirical research on long-term management of modern configurators would be most welcome. How much effort is needed? What are the challenges? Can product experts do it? What are the costs versus the benefits?

We echo the notion of Franke and Piller (2003) that future research is needed on user interaction with configurators. This includes user interaction process patterns with configurators, user perception of "mass confusion", user satisfaction drivers with configurators, and how configurators affect customers' valuation of individualization. We would like to extend the perspective from self-service configurator use over the Web in consumer markets towards business-to-business (B2B) environments. In some B2B scenarios, the need to support consultative selling may be more important than self-service.

Configurators presently fail to provide support for ensuring that the created configuration models correspond to the real customization possibilities of the configurable product. Configurator vendors, for example, SAP (Haag, 2005) and Tacton (Orsvärn, 2005) call for research on methods and techniques to debug and diagnose configuration models. Significant steps towards diagnosis have been provided, for example, by Felfernig et al. (2004), who present a method that applies knowledge-based diagnosis techniques with configuration test cases for locating errors in configuration models. On a more basic level, using capabilities of inference engines could provide semantic level configuration model checking without writing test cases. For example, it could be possible to check if, any discrete configuration variable value can be present in a consistent configuration, or if any individual requirement that can be expressed can be satisfied. Future work on empirical evaluation on benefits versus sacrifices is required after such tools are in widespread use.

Another source of potential improvement is in user interfaces of configuration modeling tools that could apply ideas from Integrated Development Environments that are common in software development tools. This could provide model overview and navigation as well as immediate experimentation with the configuration model (Haag, 2005).

Although configurators do alleviate the complexity of specification, there is still room for improvement and future research. Configurators are not well-equipped to find optimal product fit with customer needs (Blecker et al., 2005, p. 92). Recommender or advisory system functionality could be included in configurators, or they could be integrated with such systems. Reconfiguration is also still a challenge (Manhart, 2005, Männistö et al., 1999).

DISCUSSION AND CONCLUSION

MC literature has been reviewed from a general perspective (Da Silveira et al., 2001), with the aim of recognizing the necessary conditions for successful MC (Blecker et al., 2005, p. 23; Broekhuizen & Alsem, 2002), and from the angle of customer sacrifices of MC (Bardacki & Whitelock, 2003). Franke and Piller (2003) have identified empirical research in the field of MC and discuss configurators among other user design toolkits for MC. The approaches to describe, model, and formalize configuration knowledge in configurators have been reviewed earlier (Günter & Kühn, 1999; Stumptner, 1997). Blecker et al. (2005, p. 80) have classified configurators to different categories. Our review has a different perspective and also synthesizes findings from MC, CP, and configurator literature. However, the scientific quality of the articles which we have reviewed varies. We chose to aim for broad identification of issues instead of concentrating only on the papers of highest scientific quality. The amount of references discussing an issue may be an indicator of the level of its importance.

Judging from the benefits that configurators can bring and the challenges that their use can overcome or alleviate, configurators truly are key enablers for mass customization with configurable products. However, only individual cases with more efficient and streamlined business processes have been reported, and conclusive evidence on realized configurator benefits and whether the benefits outweigh the required sacrifices in a given situation is still lacking.

Configurator challenges remain. We believe our review, although by no means exhaustive, has been able to identify most of them, providing practitioners a useful checklist of issues that have to be taken into account when contemplating configurator-supported mass customization with configurable products.

Long-term management of configurators is claimed as one of the most significant challenges. The literature we examined does not provide a comprehensive answer on how difficult long-term management of configurators really is and to what extent it is easier with current configurators that do not require programming in configuration knowledge maintenance. Also, configurator introduction remains as a challenge, and configurators represent significant cost over the whole life cycle. Future opportunities and challenges remain in supporting customers in self-service settings; selecting a suitable product and appropriate technical specifications is a challenge, especially for customers who configure their products or services infrequently.

Applicability of the configurable products paradigm and configurators to services has received relatively little attention and remains a subject for future research.

REFERENCES

Agrawal, M., Kumaresh, T. V., & Mercer, G. A. (2001). The false promise of mass customization. *The McKinsey Quarterly, 3,* 62-71.

Åhlström, P. & Westbrook, R. (1999). Implications of mass customization for operations management: An exploratory survey. *International Journal of Operations & Production Management, 19*(3), 262-274.

Aldanondo, M., Véron, M., & Fargier, H. (1999). Configuration in manufacturing industry, requirements, problems, and definitions.In *Proceedings of the IEEE International Conference on Systems, Man, and Cybernetics: Vol. 6* (pp. 1009-1014).

Aldanondo, M., Rougé, S., & Vérnon, M. (2000). Expert configurator for concurrent engineering: Caméléon software and model. J*ournal of Intelligent Manufacturing, 11,* 127-134.

Ariano, M., & Dagnino, A. (1996). An intelligent order entry and dynamic bill of materials system for manufacturing customized furniture. *Computers in Electrical Engineering, 22*(1), 45-60.

Bardacki, A., & Whitelock, J. (2003). Mass-customisation in marketing: The consumer perspective. *Journal of Consumer Marketing, 20*(5), 463-479.

Barker, V. E., & O'Connor, D. E. (1989). Expert systems for configuration at Digital: XCON and beyond. *Communications of the ACM, 32*(3), 298-318.

Beaty, R. T. (1996). Mass customisation. *IEE Manufacturing Engineer, 75*(5), 217-220.

Berman, B. (2002). Should your firm adopt a mass customization strategy? *Business Horizons, 45*(4), 51-60.

Blecker, T., Abdelkafi, N., Kreutler, G., & Friedrich, G. (2004). Product configuration systems: State of the art, conceptualization, and extensions, In A. B. Hamadou, F. Gargouri, & M. Jmaiel (Eds.), *Proceedings of the Eighth Maghrebian Conference on Software Engineering and Artificial Intelligence (MCSEAI 2004)* (pp. 25-36).

Blecker, T., Friedrich, G., Kaluza, B., Abdelkafi, N., & Kreutler, G. (2005). *Information and management systems for product customization.* New York: Springer.

Bonehill, E., & Slee-Smith, P. (1998). Product configurator. *IEE Workshop on Responsiveness in Manufacturing (Digest No.1998/213),* 9/1-9/4.

Bramham, J., & MacCarthy, B. (2004). The demand-driven chain. *IEE Manufacturing Engineer, 83*(3), 30-33.

Broekhuizen, T. L. J., & Alsem, K. J. (2002). Success factors for mass customization: A conceptual model. *Journal of Market-Focused Management, 5*(4), 309-330.

Brown, S., & Bessant, J. (2003). The manufacturing strategy-capabilities links in mass customisation and agile manufacturing - An exploratory study. *International Journal of Operations & Production Management, 23*(7), 707-730.

Comstock, M., Johansen, K., & Winroth, M. (2004). From mass production to mass customization: Enabling perspectives from the Swedish mobile telephone industry. *Production Planning & Control, 15*(4), 362-372.

Da Silveira, G., Borenstein, D., & Fogliatto, F. S. (2001). Mass customization: Literature review and research directions. *International Journal of Production Economics, 72,* 1-13.

Dellaert, B. G. C., & Stremersch, S. (2005). Marketing mass-customized products: Striking a balance between utility and complexity. *Journal of Marketing Research, 42*(2), 219-227.

Duray, R. (2002). Mass customization origins: Mass or custom manufacturing? *International Journal of Operations & Production Management, 22*(3), 314-328.

Felfernig, A., Friedrich, G., Jannach, D., & Stumptner, M. (2004). Consistency-based diagnosis of configuration knowledge bases. *Artificial Intelligence, 152*(2), 213-234.

Fleischanderl, G., Friedrich, G., Haselböck, A., Schreiner, H., & Stumptner, M. (1998). Configuring large-scale systems with generative constraint satisfaction. *IEEE Intelligent System- Special issue on Configuration, 13* (7), 59-68.

Fohn, S. M., Liau, J. S., Greef, A. R., Young, R. E., & O'Grady, P. J. (1995). Configuring computer systems through constraint-based modeling and interactive constraint satisfaction. *Computers in Industry, 27,* 3-21.

Forza, C., & Salvador, F. (2002a). Managing for variety in the order acquisition and fulfilment process: The contribution of product configuration systems. *International Journal of Production Economics, 76,* 87-98.

Forza, C., & Salvador, F. (2002b.) Product configuration and inter-firm co-ordination: An innovative solution from a small manufacturing enterprise. *Computers in Industry, 49,* 37-56.

Franke, N., & Piller, F. (2004). Value creation by toolkits for user innovation and design: The case of the watch market. *Journal of Product Innovation Management, 21,* 401-415.

Franke, N., & Piller, F. T. (2003). Key research issues in user interaction with user toolkits in a mass customisation system. *International Journal of Technology Management, 26*(5/6), 578-599.

Gilmore, J. H., & Pine II, B. J. (1997). The four faces of customization. *Harvard Business Review, 75*(1), 91-101.

Günter, A. & Kühn, C. (1999). Knowledge-Based Configuration: Survey and future directions. *In XPS-99: Knowledge Based Systems, Proceedings of the 5th Biannual German Conference on Knowledege Based Systems. Springer Leture Notes in Artifical Intelligence 1570.*

Haag, A. (1998). Sales configuration in business processes. *IEEE Intelligent Systems, 13*(4), 78-85.

Haag, A. (2005). "Dealing" with configurable products in the SAP business suite. *Workshop on Configuration, International Conference on Artificial Intelligence (IJCAI 2005), Edinburgh, Scotland* (pp. 68-71).

Hart, C. W. L. (1995). Mass customization: Conceptual underpinnings, opportunities, and limits. *International Journal of Service Industry Management, 6*(2), 36-45.

Heatley, J., Agraval, R., & Tanniru, M. (1995). An evaluation of an innovative information technology - The case of carrier EXPERT. *Journal of Strategic Information Systems, 4*(3), 255-277.

Heiskala, M., Anderson, A., Huhtinen, V., Tiihonen, J., & Martio, A. (2003). A tool for comparing configurable products. *Workshop on Configuration, International Conference on Artificial Intelligence (IJCAI 2005), Acapulco, Mexico* (pp. 64-69).

Hvam, L., Malis, M., Hansen, B., & Riis, J. (2004). Reengineering of the quotation process: Application of knowledge-based systems. *Business Process Management Journal, 10*(2), 200-213.

Huffman, C., & Kahn, B. E. (1998). Variety for sale: Mass customization or mass confusion? *Journal of Retailing, 74*(4), 491-513.

Kakati, M. (2002). Mass customization - Needs to go beyond technology. *Human Systems Management, 21,* 85-93.

Kay, M. J. (1993). Making mass customization happen: Lessons for implementation. *Strategy & Leadership, 21*(4), 14-18.

Kotha, S. (1995). Mass customization: Implementing the emerging paradigm for competitive advantage. *Strategic Management Journal, 16,* 21-42.

Lampel, J. & Mintzberg, H. (1996). Customizing Customization. *Sloan Management Review, 38*(1), 21-30.

MacCarthy, B., & Brabazon, P. (2003). In the business of mass customisation. *IEE Manufacturing Engineer, 82*(4), 30-33.

Manhart, P. (2005). Reconfiguration – A problem in search of solutions. In D. Jannach & A. Felfernig (Eds.), *Configuration – Papers from the Configuration Workshop at IJCAI'05* (pp. 68-71).

McGuinness, D. L., & Wright, J. R. (1998). An industrial-strength description logic-based configurator platform. *IEEE Intelligent Systems, 13*(4), 69-77.

Männistö, T., Soininen, T., Tiihonen, J., & Sulonen, R. (1999). Framework and conceptual model for reconfiguration. *Configuration Papers from the AAAI Workshop* (AAAI Technical Report WS-99-05) (pp. 59-64). AAAI Press.

Orsvärn, K. (2005). Tacton configurator - Research directions. *Workshop on Configuration, International Conference on Artificial Intelligence (IJCAI 2005), Edinburgh, Scotland.*

Paloheimo, K. -S., Miettinen, I., & Brax, S. (2004). *Customer-oriented industrial services.* Espoo, Finland: Report Series –Helsinki University of Technology BIT Research Centre.

Pargamin, B. (2002). Vehicle sales configuration: The cluster tree approach. *ECAI 2002 Workshop on Configuration* (pp. 35-40).

Pedersen, J. L., & Edwards, K. (2004). Product configuration systems and productivity. In *Proceedings of International Conference on Economic, Technical and Organisational Aspects of Product Configuration Systems (PETO) 2004.*

Piller, F. T., Moeslein, K., & Stotko, C. M. (2004). Does mass customization pay? An economic approach to evaluate customer integration. *Production Planning & Control, 15*(4), 435-444.

Piller, F. T., & Müller, M. (2004). A new marketing approach to mass customisation. *International Journal of Computer Integrated Manufacturing, 17*(7), 583-593.

Pine, B. J. II (1993a). *Mass customization: The new frontier in business competition.* Boston: Harvard School Business Press.

Pine, B. J. II (1993b). Mass customizing products and services. *Strategy & Leadership, 21*(4), 6-13, 55.

Pine, B. J. II, Peppers, D., & Rogers, M. (1995). Do you want to keep your customers forever? *Harvard Business Review, 73*(2), 103-114.

Pine, B. J. II, Victor, B., & Boynton, A. C. (1993). Making mass customization work. *Harvard Business Review, 71*(5), 108-119.

Radder, L., & Louw, L. (1999). Research and concepts: Mass customization and mass production. *The TQM Magazine, 11*(1), 35-40.

Reichwald, R., Piller, F., & Mueller, M. (2004). A multi-channel interaction platform for mass customization – Concept and empirical investigation. *Workshop on Information Systems for Mass Customization (ISMC 2004), Fourth International ICSC Symposium on Engineering of Intelligent Systems (EIS 2004)*.

Ross, A. (1996). Selling uniqueness. *IEE Manufacturing Engineer, 75*(6), 260-263.

Sabin, D., & Weigel, R. (1998). Product configuration frameworks – A survey. *IEEE Intelligent Systems & Their Applications, 13*(4), 42-49.

Salvador, F., & Forza, C. (2004). Configuring products to address the customization-responsiveness squeeze: A survey of management issues and opportunities. *International Journal of Production Economics, 91*(3), 273-291.

Slywotzky, A. J. (2000). The age of the choiceboard. *Harvard Business Review, 78*(1), 40-41.

Spring, M., & Dalrymple, J. F. (2000) Product customisation and manufacturing strategy. *International Journal of Operations & Production Management, 20*(4), 441-467.

Svensson, C., & Barfod, A. (2002). Limits and opportunities in mass customization for "build to order" SMEs. *Computers in Industry, 49*, 77-89.

Sviokla, J.J. (1990). An examination of the impact of expert systems on the firm: The case of XCON. *MIS Quarterly, 14*(2), 127-140.

Tiihonen, J., & Soininen, T. (1997). *Product configurators – Information system support for configurable products* (Tech. Rep. TKO-B137).

Helsinki University of Technology, Laboratory of Information Processing Science. Also published in Richardson, T. (Ed.). (1997), *Using information technology during the sales visit*. Cambridge, UK: Hewson Group.

Tiihonen, J., Soininen, T., Männistö, T. & Sulonen, R. (1996). State-of-the-practice in product configuration—A survey of 10 cases in the Finnish industry. In T. Tomiyama, M. Mäntylä, & S. Finger (Eds.), *Knowledge Intensive CAD. Vol. 1* (pp. 95-114). Chapman & Hall.

Tiihonen, J., Soininen, T., Männistö, T. & Sulonen, R. (1998). Configurable products - Lessons learned from the Finnish industry. In *Proceedings of 2nd International Conference on Engineering Design and Automation (ED&A '98)*. Integrated Technology Systems, Inc.

Vanwelkenheysen, J. (1998). The tender support system. *Knowledge-Based Systems, 11*, 363-372.

Wind, J., & Rangaswamy, A. (2001). Customerization: The next revolution in mass customization. *Journal of Interactive Marketing, 15*(1), 13-32.

Wright, J. R., Weixelbaum, E. S., Vesonder, G. T., Brown, K. E., Palmer, S. R., Berman, J. I., & Moore, H. H. (1993). A knowledge-based configurator that supports sales, engineering, and manufacturing at AT&T network systems. *AI Magazine, 14*(3), 69-80.

Yu, B., & Skovgaard, H. J. (1998). A configuration tool to increase product competitiveness. *IEEE Intelligent Systems, 13*(4), 34-41.

Zipkin, P. (2001). The limits of mass customization. *MIT Sloan Management Review, 42*(3), 81-87.

Chapter II
Product Modeling and Configuration Experiences

Joseba Arana
IKERLAN Technological Research Centre, Spain

María Elejoste
IKERLAN Technological Research Centre, Spain

José Ángel Lakunza
IKERLAN Technological Research Centre, Spain

Jone Uribetxebarria
IKERLAN Technological Research Centre, Spain

Martín Zangitu
IKERLAN Technological Research Centre, Spain

ABSTRACT

This chapter attempts to present an alternative for product modeling based on applied research activities. The model proposed is based on a concept supported by different views: functional, technological, and physical. With the aim of making the model learner-friendly, the chapter also presents an industrial case applied in the lift industry. The specific problems, the model used, the implementation carried out, and the results obtained are described in detail. The objective is to make a contribution based on the industrial practice to one of the basic enablers for product configuration. The final aim is to speed up the supply-chain process in Mass customization scenarios.

INTRODUCTION

The environment in which our companies now conduct business is radically different from that in which they operated only a few years ago (Arana, Lakunza, & Astiazaran, 2005). Ever-increasing demands, both from markets and customers, constant technological evolution, and greater competitiveness from developed and developing countries, means new organizational paradigms and approaches to business must be created.

Among such paradigms, special mention should be made of mass customization (Davis, 1987; Toffler, 1970). Mass customization could be defined as the path taken by organizations leading to the supply of customized and personalized products and services, with efficiency ratios similar to those for mass production. The development of the concept of mass customization, together with the concept of continuous innovation, should enable companies to maintain their competitiveness by establishing differentiation factors that are based on tailoring products closer to customers' needs.

Arriving at the concept of mass customization is, however, different depending on the point of departure: mass production or engineering-to-order (ETO). On the one hand, companies focusing on Mass Production will need to adapt their products and services so that their catalogues will feature options that are more closely tailored to the real needs of the different target markets. At the same time, companies of this type will need to make production processes more flexible to adapt to a varied output without compromising efficiency. On the other hand, companies focusing on engineering-to-order will have to make a major effort to streamline their products and processes in order to uphold their offer differential, furthermore including efficiency and productivity aspects that surpass current ones.

Whichever the approach, the implementation of the concept of mass customization requires actions in almost every business area and process (Broekhuizen & Alsem, 2002; Hsuan & Skjoett-Larsen, 2003): strategy, new product development, attracting orders, supply-chain, after-sales services, and product end of life.

Besides a suitable development of the strategic approach and the new product development process, one of the main challenges is to achieve the dynamic performance of the supply-chain, both in catering to customer requirements, and in the engineering-production-logistics process.

In short, the challenge is to uphold the service with high levels of efficiency.

With this aim, product configuration is one of the key technologies for a more effective response under the paradigm of mass customization. The aim of product configuration is the development of design software tools and methods that enable swift generation of the technical documentation required for producing the products and services tendered, based on a generic model and the customer's specific requirements.

Regardless of the area in which it is to be used, product configuration depends on two major factors. On the one hand, there is the actual architecture designed for the product itself and, on the other, there is the model that allows the generic product and the rules, norms, and constraints that define it to be represented.

The purpose of this chapter is to delve further into the latter of these requirements. The aim is to outline the various alternatives required for modeling the product from the perspective of different business activities, and stress is placed on the need to consider multi-view modeling.

The chapter also contains some of the more significant requirements of the different configuration systems, and the relationship between them and all the other legacy systems providing product information.

Finally, with a view to facilitating an understanding of the model being addressed, a real case in Basque industry, the configuration of lifts, is presented.

BACKGROUND

Since the 1980's, there have been numerous approaches to product modeling from various fields: Computer Aided Design, Design Theory, Production, Configuration, and so forth.

Some of the leading theories that have underpinned the development of an advanced view on product modeling have been covered by Riis, Hansen, and Hvam (2003) in their definition of a framework for product knowledge that supports product modeling. Some of the theories that the authors highlight are: axiomatic design theory (Suh, 1988), technical systems theory (Hubka & Eder, 1988), theory of domains (Andreasen, 1980) and their version transformed by Mortensen (1999), theory of structuring (Andreasen, Hansen, & Mortensen, 1997), theory of properties (Jensen, 1999).

At the end of the 1980's, Mittal and Frayman (1989) introduced the notion of functional architecture in order to explicitly design functional structures, which were relevant to the specification of customer requirements. The authors proposed the integration of functional architecture into the product model by defining the relationship between functions and key components, to be included in the configurations for function provision.

In the 1990's, the need to address the product model from different perspectives has been propounded by numerous authors and has served as the basis for the development of schemes in the different fields of business activity. Along these lines, mention should be made of the work carried out within the Deklare European project (Forster, Fothergill, Lakunza, & Arana, 1995). The methodologies and tools developed in Deklare specifically focus on redesign in ETO applications and propose a concept of product model based on several views: design process, technology, physical structure, and geometric structure (Vargas, 1995).

In turn, Jiao, Tseng, Duffy, and Lin (1998) adopt a conceptual approach to propose the use of a model based on three views for describing the family of products within the field of mass customization: Functional view, Behavioral view, and Structural view.

From a more general point of view, Hvam (1999) describes a procedure for the building of product models. This is an eminently practi-cal approach that describes the seven steps for building a configuration system based on product analysis and running through to implementation and maintenance.

The multiplicity of views regarding a product is also upheld by Mortensen and Hansen (1999) when they affirm: "*A composite product does not exhibit one structure, but hides in its structure of parts several different structuring principles, which fit the production, service, transport, etc.*" The authors identify four key factors that have a bearing on the structure of a product model: genetics, functionality/property, product life, and product assortment.

Recently, Jørgensen and Petersen (2004), analyzing the challenge posed by product modeling in Engineering-to-Order companies, propose a new approach for the modeling of product families in multiple levels of abstraction. The result is a top-down approach through the definition of purpose, function, form, content, and structure. The aim pursued is to use the models built as the basis for the design of configurators.

PRODUCT MODEL

Definition and Need

The concept of the product model has been widely addressed in the literature. The aim in all cases is to depict digitally the information associated with a product in a structured manner.

According to different authors, a product model may be defined as a model that describes the structure, its function, and other properties related to the product's life cycle, for example, manufacturing, assembly, transportation, and service (Hvam, 1999; Krause, 1993; Mortensen, Yu, Skovgaard, & Harlou, 2000)

In this case, and from the viewpoint of configuration, the concept addressed in this chapter is the one that may be referred to as the generic product model. What sets it apart from other existing concepts of product model is the fact that the generic product model does not depict a single end product, but rather a whole family of products that may be derived (configured) on the basis of that generic product model. This approach is mirrored in the literature in papers by Tseng and Jiao (1998) (product family architecture (PFA)), Andreasen (1992) (Chromosome model), and others.

In order to distinguish them from this generic model, this chapter will use the expression "product variant" for those information models (instances) that constitute specific performances of a product on the part of the company.

In order to support customization, this information model (generic product model) contains all the knowledge on the product family in the form of the deployment of features, rules, norms, and constraints. Based on this knowledge, and assisted by a software tool (configurator), a user may configure, as automatically as possible, a specific product variant.

Accordingly, the generic product model will depict the information model that will be used by the product configurator for the configuration of product variants that meet the customer's requirements.

Product Model and Views

The fact that the product model is the feature that should grant access to knowledge on the product from different contexts throughout its life cycle implies that it should be described differently according to the context in which it is to be used. A product view is defined as each one of the product descriptions used in each one of the different contexts throughout its life cycle.

Figure 1 portrays the notion that the generic product model consists of three basic views: the Functional view that depicts the product's functionality, the Technological view that depicts the design solution, and the Physical view that depicts the product's structure. This same notion is supported by other authors, such as Tseng and Jiao (1999) and Riis, Hansen, and Hvam (2003).

Although it is possible to consider the existence of other further views, for example, those cor-

Figure 1. Different product views

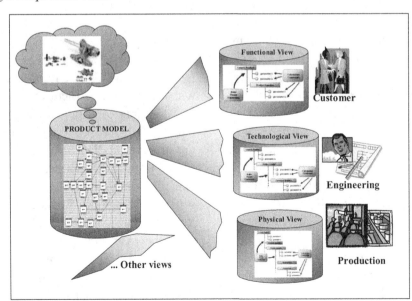

responding to the different production stages in the life of the product (assembly, manufacturing, purchases, distribution, maintenance, etc.), these views are not addressed by this chapter, which will focus on the specific circumstances surrounding the product models required for assisting the user at the design and definition stages.

Functional View

The Functional view more closely represents the customer's requirements. Functions, identified by means of standard functional analysis techniques, act as liaising elements between the product configurator and the customer when establishing product's requirements.

This Functional view, as can be seen in Figure 2, comprises the following elements:

- **Product Function:** Functionality identified in a product to be defined by functional parameters.
- **Functional Parameters:** Requirements to which the customer must respond in order to define the function.

In addition to these entities, building the model requires establishing the relationship between them. These relationships basically consist of decomposition aspects (generic product-function, Function-Parameter) and of dependence (Function-Function, Parameter-Parameter) (Pahl & Beitz, 1996). In turn, these relationships may be conditioned by rules and constraints.

In order to help a user select functions, it is important to relate the functional structure to a costing model, timeframe, or any other attribute that might help in the selection. This information will also allow for the commercial configuration of products based on the optimization of any of the attributes (cost, timeframe, etc.).

Technological View

The Technological view focuses on design users and shows how to resolve the product from a design viewpoint.

The Technological view reflects the company's know-how and also relates the customer's requirements to technical specifications.

From the technological point of view, the product would be arranged as a tree of Design Concepts, which represent the problems that have to be solved by design in order to respond to the functionalities provided for in the product, and Technical Solutions of possible application, which represent the different ways that the company has established for solving the problems posed

Figure 2. Functional view

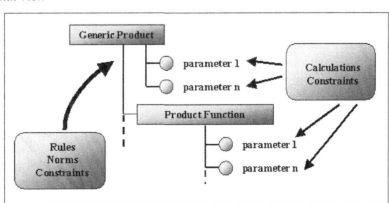

with the Design Concepts (Forster, Fothergill, Lakunza, & Arana, 1995).

As may be observed in Figure 3, the structure of this Technological view is portrayed as an and/or tree of Design Concepts and Technical Solutions. The entities that comprise this Technological view are:

- **Design Concepts:** Representing the problems to be solved in order to provide a specific functionality with the product, and which will be defined by parameters.
- **Technical Solutions:** Representing the different designs defined by the company to solve the problem posed by a Design Concept, and which are also defined by parameters.

In this model, besides the aggregate relationships (AND) between the product and the Design Concepts, and the option relationships (OR) between a Design Concept and its Technical Solutions, identification may be made of other dependency relationships between Design concepts, and between Technical solutions.

The different relationships between the model's entities, as well as between the parameters that define them, are to be well governed by means of the rules and constraints that allow the user to instance the product's specific variant.

Physical View

The Physical view would be the nearest to the product structure such as it is normally envisaged in engineering departments. It corresponds to a hierarchy of modules, assemblies, sub-assemblies, and parts that in many cases are related with aspects of assembly process and supply. It is the structure nearest to the concept of "bill of materials".

As may be seen in the figure, this Physical view consists of the following entities:

- **End components:** Represented on the tree by those physical elements of the product that are indivisible and which normally correspond to the product's component parts.
- **Aggregate components:** Representing groups of end components, which tend to be referred to as assemblies and which may be performed according to different criteria, such as assembly, modularity, and so forth.

Figure 3. Technological view

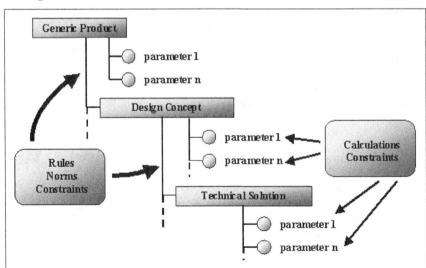

Each one of these entities constituting the Physical view may be typified as:

- **Standard:** If they represent a single component; and
- **Parametric:** When in reality they represent a family of components; in such cases, they tend to be defined by parameters.

The main relationship between the entities in this Physical view is that of composition or aggregation, although other dependence relationships may be defined between the components. In any case, and as in previous views, these relationships may be governed by rules and constraints, which are to be resolved in the configuration process.

Most of the technical configurators are based on this point of view for modeling the generic product. Accordingly, the generic product will be a structure of elements established hierarchically and with given composition relations (see Figure 4).

In the majority of the cases, a close integration exists between the structure according to this point of view and the item master supported by the ERP system.

In certain cases, and with a view to simplifying the complexity of variant management and improving response time, the company may decide to apply a criterion of modularity when defining the Physical view (product made of modules which are in turn made up of parts). At first glance, a physical structure of sub-assemblies/parts and a physical modular structure appear to be similar. However, the scope of a modular structure in the following stages in a product's life cycle may be much greater, simplifying its management.

In certain cases, and depending on the type of product/application, it is very difficult to define a priori a complete product structure. In this case, the definition of the model goes as far as the components level and their rules of composition, but it does not define a higher structure that defines the product architecture.

Figure 4. Physical view

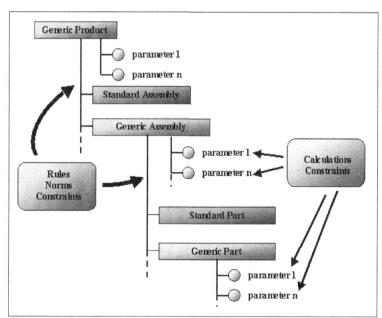

Integration of the Views

In order for the views of a product to make up a single product model, they are to be integrated with each other. Regarding the product model proposed, two integrations should be highlighted between the different views of the model: integration between the Functional and Technological views and integration between the Technological and Physical views (see Figure 5).

The first relationship that can be defined between the different model views is that existing between the Functional and Technological views. In this case, the relationship is established between a function in the Functional view and one or several Design Concepts in the Technological view. The response to the series of requirements brought together in a Function of the Functional view raises a series of technological problems that we have denominated Design Concepts in the Technological view. The Technical Solution selected to cover the Design Concept will correspond to the real implementation of the function from the technological point of view.

This relationship between both views may be directly determined between the entities of both views through the parameters that define the func-

tions (requirements) and the parameters that define the Design Concepts (technical specifications).

A further integration between the views of the model is that addressed between the Technological view and the Physical view. The customization of a given Technical Solution to respond to a Design Concept will unfold via part of the physical structure of the product, selecting the appropriate components and customizing the parameters of these components that respond to the specific specifications of the order.

We should bear in mind that a Technical Solution will customize only the parts of the components that are related to it and not others. In general, a component will be completely customizable when all the Technical Solutions that affect it are so.

With this in mind, a new entity is required in order to integrate both views (Technological and Physical). We shall refer to this new item as "Design Feature", and it depicts that part of the component that is instanced by a Technical Solution.

We could say that a given component consists of the sum of Design Features and that a Technical Solution customizes different Design Features of different components. When all the Design Fea-

Figure 5. Product views' relationship

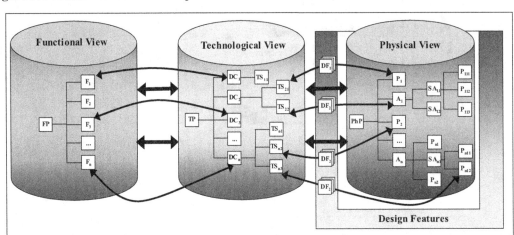

tures of a component have been customized, we can consider the component to be customized.

Integration between the Functional view and the Physical view is established through the Technological view.

In those cases in which the Technological view is not required (product simplicity through standardization, etc.), the relationship is established directly between the Functional view and the Physical view of the product, linking the product's functions to modules or components of the Physical view.

CONFIGURATION SYSTEM

As has been mentioned before, the product configurator is one of the more important systems for streamlining the response to customers within a mass customization environment.

There are various aspects according to which we can classify configurators. Blecker, Abdelkafi, Kreutler, and Friedrich (2004) use what they refer to as a morphological box to describe some of the criteria to be applied, as well as the possibilities present in each one of them. Other authors (Günter & Kühn, 1999; Pargamin, 2002; Sabin & Weigel,

1998; Skjevdal & Idsoe, 2005; Soininen, 2002; Strom & Axworthy, 2000) also use similar classifications within their contributions. From the viewpoint of the use of the product model and its views, the most noteworthy criteria from among those mentioned in literature is that corresponding to what may be referred to as the *sphere of application*.

Through this approach, the chapter will set out to delve further into the information system by laying down the more salient characteristics, both from the point of view of the use of different product model views and from the demands made by the various models that make up the system's architecture (see Figure 6).

From the viewpoint of the sphere of application and within the supply chain to the customer, an initial classification enables us to distinguish between the configurators that provide a response to the process of tendering (sales configurators) and those that provide a response to the engineering and production processes (order-fulfillment configurators).

Sales Configurators

The aim of sales configurators is to support the customer or the company's sales staff in the process of selecting alternatives and generating the tender.

With this aim, the product model view used as a basis for the development of sales configurators is essentially the Functional view, as this is the one closest to the customer's vision. The configurator is to present the user, customer, or sales representative with the sum of functionalities provided by the product, as well as the different alternatives which are available.

It is important to note on this point that, depending on the degree of integration between function and physical structure or even the level of knowledge regarding the product on the part of the user, the Functional view stated may sometimes be relatively close to other views. Such is the

Figure 6. Configurator architecture

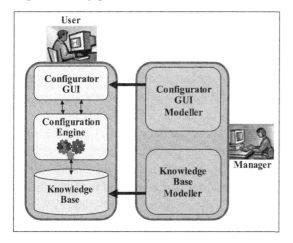

case of certain products in the field of footwear, clothing, or computers.

Besides the Functional view, in the majority of cases the generic product model has to be supported by a pricing and timeframe model that acts as a basis for calculating the price and delivery date of the configured product instance or variant. This model need not necessarily adhere to the costing model and is to take into account other kinds of aspects and constraints stemming from the actual commercial activity itself: localization, customer loyalty, discount policies, and so forth.

The importance of configurators of this kind is growing, and their access via the Internet has spread with a view to bringing customization and purchase competencies closer to the customer's environment.

Order-Fulfillment Configurators

Within the category of order-fulfillment configurators, we include the set of configurators that, on the basis of order information, whether or not achieved through a sales configurator, support the company's technical staff in the generation of the technical documentation required for producing the specific product instance or variant.

Nonetheless, order-fulfillment configurators may come in very different forms depending on the type of production envisaged: engineering-to-order, make-to-order, or assembly-to-order. They all, however, stem from the product variant definition laid down for a specific order and which has been obtained as a result of the execution of a sales configurator.

In engineering-to-order type production, and at the engineering stage, we may encounter what are referred to as engineering configurators. The aim of these configurators is to generate the final definition of the product variant that responds to the customer requirements at the tender stage. Its existence is logical in those cases in which the product is not based solely on standard components and requires design customization.

These kinds of engineering configurators are based mainly on the product model's Technological and Physical views. It is important to bear in mind also that the customer's requirements in configurators of this kind often need to be complemented by technical specifications, which although they might not have been necessary for the definition of the tender, they are indeed required for the full definition of the product variant to be generated.

The output of the engineering configurators will consist of the technical specifications on the product variant from the design point of view. In many cases, obtaining the documentation will require integration between the actual configurator and other business legacy systems within the area of graphic depiction (e.g., CAD) or calculus. This aspect will be particularly necessary in those applications in which the generic model does not contemplate a higher hierarchical level and it is the user who, using the base components, builds the product variant or instance on an interactive basis.

At the production stage, regardless of whether this involves manufacturing or assembly, other kinds of configurators may be found, namely production configurators. Based on the customer requirements and technical specifications set out in the order, the mission of the production configurators is to generate the product information required for manufacturing or assembly, depending on the case.

The production configurators are based mainly on the product's Physical view, and in the majority of the cases the product model is integrated within some other model corresponding to the manufacturing or assembly process.

In many cases, and within an engineering-to-order operation, the coexistence of engineering configurators and production configurators may be advisable. In such a case, the output of the former would act as the input for the latter. In all other cases, the production configurators would receive the input of the order itself or of the output from the sales configurators.

Requirements

From the perspective of implementation, the requirements made of the sales configurators and of the order-fulfillment configurators are different in a number of the aspects related to what could be an overall architecture (see Figure 7).

In the case of sales configurators, proximity to the customer imposes the need for these to behave as user-friendly environments that constantly uphold the customer's decision-making process. Accordingly, the interaction environment (Configurator GUI) should have the following characteristics:

- Be user-friendly, intuitive, and developed in a language that the customer can understand;
- Not present the user with alternatives that may have been inferred or ruled out on the basis of prior decisions;
- Guide the user's decisions at each step, presenting the pros and cons of the alternatives presented;

- Permit both the selection and exclusion of alternatives on the part of the user; and
- Implement the configuration based on alternative optimization criteria.

The configuration engine itself is to meet the user's expectations by providing all the information corresponding to the product instance, including pricing and delivery times, within a timeframe that is compatible with the environment used, whether the Web or any other. It should likewise ensure the proper management of preferences, constraints, and optimization criteria, ensuring the full inference of the variant. In the event of inconsistencies, the engine for this type of configurators should be capable of analyzing them and proposing to the user the minimum changes required for their resolution.

From the point of view of implementation and maintenance, it is important to demand that both the Knowledge Base Modeler, which permits the definition of the generic product model, and the Graphic User Interface Modeler, which permits the definition of the interaction environment, are ready to be used by staff at the company that know the product, but are not necessarily familiar with information technologies. Loading the data

Figure 7. Configurators and views

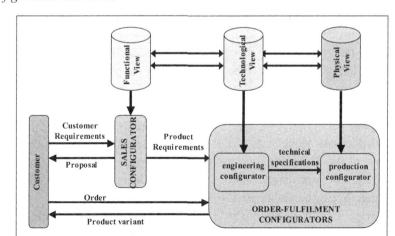

regarding the generic product model and interaction into the configurator's database (Knowledge Base) should be a straightforward process and be rendered possible through the use of visual Integrated Development Environment (IDE) type tools. The actual definition of the model should be easy to perform with the tool, furthermore allowing for the modifications that will almost certainly be required in response to the product's evolution.

The case of order-fulfillment configurators is different. As these are used by in-house staff in the organization, they are to be supported by an interaction environment (Configurator Graphic User Interface) adapted to the language used by the company's technicians and imbued in the business process in which it is used.

In the case of engineering configurators, their use in design will often involve close integration with the design tools, especially with CAD systems. There are times in which the actual CAD system can act as the configurator front-end.

An important characteristic that order-fulfillment configurators should have regarding the actual configuration engine is their perfect adjustment to the elements of the process in which they are used. In many cases, above all in production configurators, the configurator engine itself should work not only with product entities but also with entities belonging to the process models which are involved.

The adjustment of order-fulfillment configurators to each company's specific context hinders the application of visual IDE-type tools in their use in the Configurator Graphic User Interface Modeler, and in many cases requires their customization on the part of staff with expertise in information technologies.

In turn, the Knowledge Base Modeler should allow for the insertion of the different product model views in a straightforward manner and using the actual language used by the technicians. It should also have the required tools for establishing the relationships between the different views

of the model and between these and the entities handled in manufacturing and assembly. As in the case of the sales configurators, it is recommended that the environment should use visual IDEs for facilitating the work of technicians without expertise in information technologies.

Configurators and Legacy Systems

If there is any one characteristic that can be identified with mass customization, it is managing variety. The management of different products and processes in order to respond to the particular needs of market segments and individual customers requires the handling of an enormous amount of product and process data. Moreover, the constant innovation of products and processes in order to adapt to new technological advances and new demands establishes the need to continually update the data and information that support them.

In this respect, the complexity associated with variety must be added to the complexity of handling and managing the information. The application of Product Data Technologies (PDT) is the logical way to offer a solution to the problem associated with the management of mass customization.

It may of course be stated that configurators are one of the PDT tools with the greatest influence on streamlining the supply-chain to the customer. However, they are not the only systems that manage product-related information. Both during the new product development cycle, as in the tender processes, and in the supply-chain itself, there is an intensive use of other systems that support views, generally instanced, of the product throughout its life cycle. Among those that are characteristic of these systems, we might highlight CAD systems, PDM systems, and ERP systems. The implementation of product configuration without taking into account the integration with those other systems may be hazardous.

On the one hand, depending on the field of application, on the problem to be resolved, and on the product itself, the CAD system and configurator relationship may be more or less necessary.

In the case of those products in which the visualization of geometric models is important at the tender stage, the sales configurators are to be integrated with the CAD in one way or another. This is also the case of those configurators that need visualization of results during the course of the configuration process.

Within the supply-chain, the configurators that usually require major interaction with CAD systems are engineering configurators. We may distinguish between two kinds of interaction:

- The CAD system supports a geometric view of the product model that is instanced on the basis of the decomposition of the product model in the configurator; and
- The configurator generates the geometric model of the instanced product through the use of the libraries in the CAD system.

In both cases, communication may be resolved by means of the Application Program Interface (API) provided by the CAD system.

On the other hand, the implementation of Product Data Management systems and configurators in companies has raised significant doubts as to the role each one of the two technologies should play and the degree of possible integration.

The present state of the art of configurators and PDM systems seems to be directed towards the need to select a solution depending on the type of product with which is being dealt:

- The application of solutions based on configurators would be a valid option for mature products with ample formalization possibilities; and
- The PDM option would be the solution for products with formalization difficulties or for managing the product development process in innovative or creative design.

However, experience tells us that in reality, this is not so clear-cut. Some reasons to support this viewpoint are:

- In many companies, the generic product model (supported by the configurator) has to coexist with the information associated with standard structures (supported by the PDM);
- Product structures, whether they are generic or standard, have their own evolution within R&D (configuration management in PDM);
- In some companies, readily-configurable formalized products (configurator) can coexist with less formalized products (managed with the PDM);
- In many cases, and even with a formalized product (which is therefore usable with a configurator), it may be necessary to carry out unexpected customization (modifications in PDM); and
- Even though a product configurator exists, the PDM may be considered by the company as the backbone for information and communication between different activities.

From this point of view, we should therefore consider the coexistence of PDM and order-fulfillment configurators throughout the product life cycle, in accordance with the characteristics of the business activity itself.

Coexistence will necessarily be upheld by means of access on the part of the KB Modeler to the actual database of standard elements in the PDM and through the generation of customized product structures within the PDM system itself on the basis of the decomposition of the configurator (Arana, Lakunza, Elejoste, & Mendizabal, 2005).

Finally, Configurator and ERP coexistence is a necessity that can hardly be avoided.

Firstly, it will be relatively common at the tender stage to find that the sales configurator will be part of a broader environment of ERP applications dedicated to the commercial area.

Moreover, in the area of order-fulfillment configurators, the key to coexistence will be the actual management of product structures. As we have pointed out for the coexistence with PDM systems, the integration approach is to be based on the management of standard references and the personalized structures resulting from the execution of the configurator.

We can summarize all the above by saying that the coexistence of the four systems (Configurator, CAD, PDM and ERP) poses a problem that is hard to resolve. Furthermore, the particular viewpoint of each one of the organization's areas will, in most cases, strive to impose as master that system which supports a structure more in accordance with its specific task.

There is no single solution that can resolve the conflict. In each case, and depending on the peculiarities of the production system, determination will have to be made of the architecture and requirements of integration. Nonetheless, it may indeed be stated that the approach to the system should be determined by assimilating the following:

- The key lies in the management of the views of the product model and the output structures; and
- In many cases, the designation of the master system will not depend solely on the type of production, but will also have to take into account the life cycle of the order in which the specific command is to be found.

INDUSTRIAL CASE

In order to render the use of the different product views in the configuration user-friendly, this section presents a practical case of the implementation of configuration technology in an industrial scenario. The case selected corresponds to a lift-manufacturing firm.

It is important to stress at this point that each lift is to be designed and manufactured according to the customer's specifications and that, in most cases, this is not the end user but rather the contractor or architect in charge of the building project.

The Problem

A lift is a product that has always required an approach based on the concept of customization. The different technical approaches, the multiple options to be chosen by the user, the aesthetic differentiation, and especially the problems of adapting to a given building (shaft, floors, machine room...) make a lift a complex structure that practically demands a unique personalization. This complexity is furthermore heightened by the need to comply with the different regulations in force in each country.

The need to respond to productions of more than three hundred lifts per week, together with the complexity of managing structures with a concept close to that of engineering-to-order within the supply-chain, establishes a bottleneck difficult to deal with without approximation to the concept of mass customization.

Determining that the requirements are adequate, designing the assembly drawings for cabin layout, machine room, pulleys, counterweights, and other elements, obtaining the bill of materials, developing the sheet steel drawings and their corresponding NC programs, and so forth, is an arduous task not exempt from risks and errors that also excessively lengthens the productive cycle and monopolizes technical office and R&D department resources.

The complexity of the problem has meant that since the middle of the 1990's, numerous studies have appeared that are dedicated to finding solutions for lift configuration. Noteworthy are those conducted at Helsinki University of Technology (Männistö, Peltonen, Alho, & Sulonen, 1993, 1994; Peltonen, 2000)

The Solution

In the selected case, the proposed solution to the problem is based on a process of rationalization and formalization of the product that might allow a generic product model to be obtained, supportable by the R&D department and implemented by means of tailor-made configurators, and integrated into the company's IT system.

On the one hand, the solution which was developed centers on the definition of a sales configurator (see Figure 8) that allows for the uptake of client information, the validation of the requirements with regard to product possibilities and authorized regulations, and the generation of a valued tender for the required lift in terms of price and delivery time. The solution has been implemented by means of specific software that manages data corresponding fundamentally to the building and user options. This sales configurator is designed for use by the commercial network.

Furthermore, it should be taken into account that it often occurs during the tender stage that the building's final characteristics are still not known. It is quite common, for example, to know

the number of floors in the building, but not the height of each one. Information might well be available on the numbers to be carried by the lift, but not on the final dimensions of the lift-shaft itself. Accordingly, the sales configurator has been designed whereby, in response to initial requirements, it provides certain elements that may serve as the basis for the development of the project. The configurator generates information on the minimum dimensioning of the shaft, preparation work for the contractor, and other kinds of information based on the feasibility of the solution which is proposed.

The required Functional view of the product is described by means of functional parameters, domains, and constraints, and considers all the possibilities tendered by the product. The functional parameters and their domains are contained in a data dictionary, and constraints are implemented by means of an ad hoc language that provides for conditional and others sentences that enable the definition of rules, norms, and the technical calculations to be made.

In the selected case, nearly 100 functional parameters were grouped into seven different functional groups related to aesthetics, shaft dimensioning, opening and closing of doors, and so forth.

Figure 8. Lift sales configurator

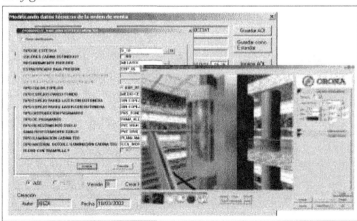

Each one of the functional parameters had associated attributes related to preconditions, local calculations, domains, checking procedures, and execution processes.

Figure 9 illustrates a group of functional parameters and a portion of code used to represent the rules used for that combination.

The combination of attributes and general processes that dynamically regulate the relationships of dependency between parameters complete the functional definition of the lift.

In this case, the problem is compounded due to the fact that the customer's requirements, forthcoming on the basis of the Functional view, albeit essential, do not suffice to ensure an effective assessment of costs, prices, and timeframes. For the same functional requirements from a customer, there are various technological solutions with widely-varying costs and timeframes depending on the configuration of drive systems, counterweight systems, cabin layouts, lift-shaft layouts, and so forth. These circumstances mean that, in order to ensure the suitability of the proposed arrangement and submit a proper valuation, and in addition to the product Functional view, the sales configurator also makes use of the Technological view.

The Technological view is supported by a tree of Design Concepts and Technical Solutions.

Each one of these elements is defined by a series of parameters with relationships established by means of constraints defined in a language similar to that used in the Functional view. In a similar way to the functional case, the parameters of the Technological view are defined by means of a data dictionary.

In the pilot case, the Technological view takes into account the different modules that comprise the lift to a high level of design: cabin, doors, machine, counterweight, sensors, and so forth. This view also takes into consideration different feasible Technical Solutions, and is dependant on the parameters defined in the Functional view and also on the decisions taken by the designer.

The internal relationship between Technical Solutions and between these and functional parameters is established in the same manner as with the Functional view.

Figure 10 illustrates different Technical Solutions for a counterweight concept, and also the "norm" that tells the configuration engine to select a type, based on two functional parameters: load (QTCP) and speed (VR).

Furthermore, the selection of type of counterweight will influence the selection and dimensioning of other Technical Solutions, as is the case for cabin guidance (see Figure 11).

In order to exploit the Functional view and the Technological view in a coordinated manner, the

Figure 9. Example of functional view

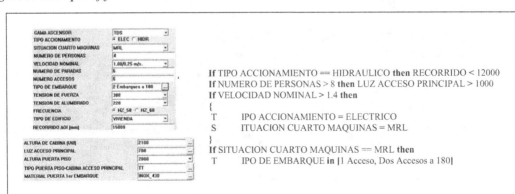

Figure 10. Examples of technical solutions

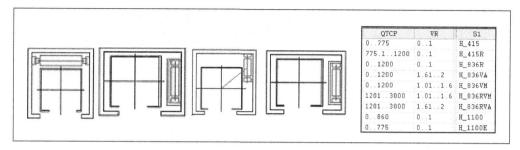

QTCP	VR	S1
0..775	0..1	H_415
775.1..1200	0..1	H_415R
0..1200	0..1	H_836R
0..1200	1.61..2	H_836VA
0..1200	1.01..1.6	H_836VM
1201..3000	1.01..1.6	H_836RVM
1201..3000	1.61..2	H_836RVA
0..860	0..1	H_1100
0..775	0..1	H_1100E

Figure 11. Influence of counterweight on cabin guidance

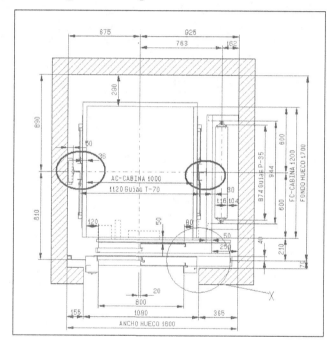

sales configurator uses the involvement relationships between customer requirements and product requirements. This relationship and the necessary rules allow for the automatic generation at the tender stage of product requirements on the basis of customer requirements (see Figure 12).

Furthermore, the Functional and Technological views are completed by means of a price-timeframe model that allows for an assessment of the customer's requirements and the output calculation. In this case, the price-timeframe model is not based on the typical activity-based cost model that would require the full generation of the entire physical structure of the lift, but on a pricing model that relates prices and timeframes to the product's functional and technological characteristics.

Once the tender has been formalized, and if the order is received, that is when the production process begins. In order to generate all the technical information required for the manufacture and assembly of the lift, this obviously requires

Figure 12. Lift sales configurator architecture

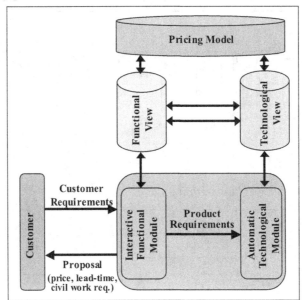

Figure 13. Lift engineering configurator

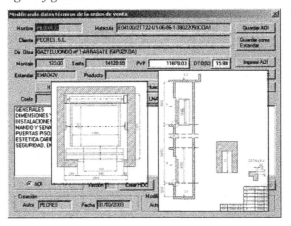

a significant contribution by the engineering department in response to the order. An engineering configurator (see Figure 13) has been included in order to streamline this part of the process.

The first task involves updating the customer's functional requirements (bear in mind that the requirements introduced through the sales configurator were, in many cases, preliminary). The building's final dimensions, the height of the floors, the size of the shaft and well, and other elements are to replace those introduced at the tender stage.

The designer, using the engineering configurator, will subsequently complete the lift's definition taking the necessary decisions on the product's technology view. The need at this stage to perform constant verification of the decisions taken and, above all, of the consequences forth-

Figure 14. Lift engineering configurator architecture

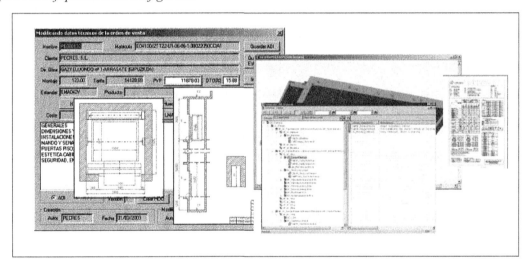

Figure 15. Lift production configurator

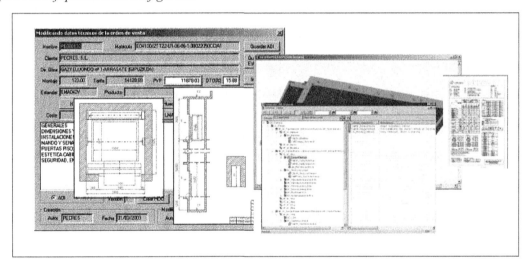

coming from the configurator engine have led to the inclusion of a graphic depiction system in the actual configurator (see Figure 14).

Once this stage has been completed, the definition of the lift is complete and the utilities are now available that use this definition to generate the information corresponding to the layout for on-site assembly and to the installation project to be submitted to the authorities.

The last module used in the process is the production configurator (see Figure 15). Based on the information generated by the engineering configurator, the production configurator, on the basis of the Physical view of the product model, generates the necessary bill of materials, CNC programs, purchase orders, assignment of manufacturing paths, and assignment of dispatches.

The Physical view of the lift is defined by means of standard and configurable items and structures that express the variety of possible combinations. Items and configurable structures have similar attributes that can be used in other views.

Figure 16. Example of physical view

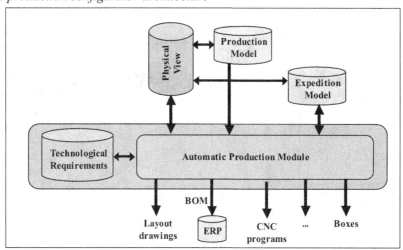

codigo componente	descripcion	cantidad	precondicion
HJ_10_0032.S1 (QTCP)	CHASIS DE CONTRAPESO	1	
910077001	GRUPO FIJACION DE CONT	2	if .....
110103502	CONTRAPESO OXICORTE 38	(TRUNC (NPOX*HJ_53_	
HJ_10_0020.S1 (GUIACP,EGCP)	CONJUNTO ENGRASADOR	2	
HJ_10_0020.S2 (GUIACP,EGCP)	GRUPO DESLIZADERA	4	
910358601	CONJ SUPLEMENTO PLACA	HJ_53_0055.S2 (CHCP	
690099001	PREPARACION DE CONTRAP	1	

GUIACP	EGCP	S1	S2
CP_P_35	EGCP_445	910260101	910368301
CP_P_35	EGCP_615	910260101	910368301
CP_P_35	EGCP_874	910260101	910368101
CP_P_35	EGCP_1150	910260101	910372101
CP_P_35	EGCP_1130, EGCP_1160	910260101	910368301
CP_P_35	EGCP_1230	910260101	910368101
CP_P_35	EGCP_1250	910260101	910372101
CP_P_35	EGCP_1260	910260101	910368301
CP_T_50	EGCP_445	910260001	910368201
CP_T_50	EGCP_615	910260001	910368201

QTCP	S1
0..1030	810312201
1030..1231	810312301

Figure 17. Lift production configurator architecture

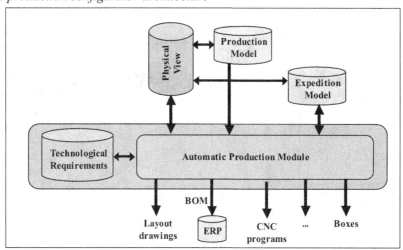

For structures, model implementation allows for a component to be a norm. The norm entity simplifies the implementation of the OR branch. The norm, when executed, returns an item (standard or configurable) depending on the functional or technological parameters entered or calculated previously.

Figure 16 illustrates the structure of the counterweight, defined by its components, each one with the attributes (code, description, quantity, precondition, etc.). Three of the components of the structure are calls to norms (HJ_...), and in the figure one can also observe the definition of such norms.

So that the production configurator may configure the product and generate all these data, it has been necessary to complement all the model views with other views pertaining to the production model and develop the necessary integration utilities with all the other legacy systems upholding manufacturing and assembly information (see Figure 17).

In order to generate the necessary technical documentation, a series of utilities have been designed that are upheld in the Physical view and allow for defining the CNC programs in a parameterized manner. The visual environment designed allows for the definition of programs, the specification of necessary constraints, and the required simulation for their processing. Naturally enough, the link with each numerical control is ensured by means of the development of the respective post-processors.

In order to launch production of over 180 lifts arranged in three days in the most rational and compact way, utilities have also been designed that allow for making the necessary groupings according to the needs of the various activities: purchases, machining, assembly, and so forth.

The system also considers the integration of the Physical view with a model of dispatches required for the logistics of the lift's delivery to the site.

Finally, the overall system is integrated by means of the necessary interfaces with the CAD design systems and the business product data management systems for the management of information, versions, and workflow management.

The Tool

The development of the configurators used in sales, engineering, and production is based on systems developed by the IKERLAN Technological Research Centre. This basis for the development of configurators is the result of European level projects (DEKLARE), research programs in the Basque area (SAIOTEK), and industrial experiences in the application of industrial projects (home appliances, luxury coaches, machining tools, vending machines, pumps, kitchen furniture, presses, etc.).

One of the fundamental requirements that IKERLAN has maintained when developing configurators, both for elevators (as we are dealing with here) and other industrial applications, has

been the need to create a descriptive environment for product models that can be easily maintained by the companies' employees. The product continuously evolves, and it is not easy to find personnel that, in addition to knowing about the product, have the knowledge to maintain a complex structure of entities, rules, and restrictions defined in a manner excessively close to implementation.

Therefore, the system allows the trained user (but not in IT) to move among different editors allowing him/her to define any of the entities supported by the system: types defined by the user, functions, functional parameters, concepts, technical solutions, technological parameters, items, structures, physical parameters, rules, and so forth.

Also, the system permits the definition of any type of restriction and calculation via an interpreted language, defined "ad hoc" and close to the company administrator. The language can be used in specific fields of preconditions and calculations within editors, and even in procedures that can be called from different elements and which enable more complex calculations, rules, and constraints to be tackled.

In any case, product modifications on any of the supported elements do not imply further compilation for the system and allow the administrator to focus on the suitability of the model for further development.

The system also contains a powerful navigation environment that facilitates the modeling of product knowledge (see Figure 18).

RESULTS

In recent years, the company subject to this process of implementation has undergone a spectacular growth in its turnover as a result of new sales, which have risen sixfold.

The two key factors that have made this growth possible are the company's clear commitment to product innovation on the one hand and, on the

Figure 18. Lift knowledge acquisition environment

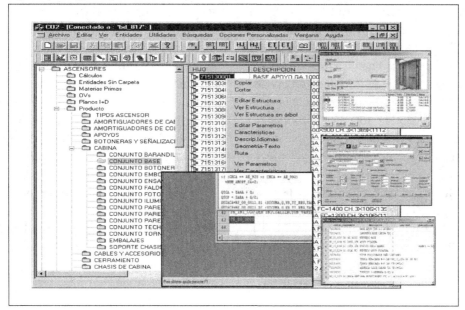

other, the mass customization model which was implemented.

Thanks to this production model, the company has been able to respond to an exponentially increasing demand for lifts that are fully customized to the specifications of each client and project.

The implementation of the new model, together with subsequently-developed support tools, has contributed to achieving the following specific results:

- More accuracy and quality in the tendering phase,
- Drastic reduction in tendering preparation time,
- Large reduction (20 to 1) in the engineering and documentation generation timeframe,
- Important reduction in CNC programs and bill of materials preparation work,
- Release of human resources for R&D tasks,
- Unification and elicitation of enterprise know-how, and

- Reduction in training period for new personnel.

The high level of flexibility and reliability for customized lift design and manufacture provided by the product configurator system has given the company a highly-significant competitive edge.

CONCLUSION

Presentation has been made of a product model consisting of three views of the same: functional, technological, and physical.

Each one of the views is designed to provide a service for a specific activity: commercial activity for the Functional view, that of design for the Technological view, and that of manufacturing for the Physical one.

Yet there is no need for the product model to consider the three views in order to respond to the questions posed by configuration within the scenario of mass customization. Depending on the issues to be resolved, all three views will be required, or only two of them (Functional-Physical, Technological-Physical), or even a single view in certain cases (Physical, Technological, or Functional). This selection will depend on the product's complexity or even on the nature of the configurator (see next section) that one wishes to implement in the mass customization scenario.

Furthermore, the efficacy of the implementation of a supply-chain under the concepts of mass customization depends on numerous factors. A key factor is the implementation of an information system that enables variety to be managed and streamlined.

Product configurators are a vital tool. Depending on the type of operation inherent to the product and to established business processes, the types of configurators and the areas of application may be different, and requirements may vary.

The design of an information systems' architecture that considers the integration of the product data in the different support systems is a key factor for certifying proper operation and ensuring results that are compatible with the targets of the business processes dealing with mass customization.

FUTURE TRENDS

The industrial case presented here in detail, as well as others undertaken in other industrial sectors, stresses the importance that the consideration of multiple views of the product model has in the implementation of mass customization concepts and particularly in the use of product and process configuration techniques.

Product configuration based on a multi-view product model may be a key element for developing and streamlining the supply-chain. This importance is based both on the aim of creating the support for configuration systems and on the establishment of a common language for communication between the organization's different areas.

Nonetheless, in many cases the current offer in configurators does not respond to the integration concept. It seems that an initial challenge for future development lies in the development of configurators that consider the existence of multiple views right from the very start. The architecture of these configurators should also include elements that allow for interaction between the product structure's different support systems.

In addition, the concept of maximizing the process of value creation under extended company approaches imposes the need to consider extended configuration networks that allow for synchronizing customers' and suppliers' product models and configuration systems at different levels.

In this context, configurators must be enhanced to include the sharing of knowledge by means of standardized representation languages as indicated by Felfernig, Friedrich, Jannach, and Zanker (2002).

Not only that, the implementation of mass customization concepts in the performance of the supply-chain and its adaptation to contingencies forthcoming from any one of the system's elements sets out the need to consider dynamic planning elements embedded within the configuration. These elements will enable the supply-chain to react, thereby upholding customer service.

There is no doubt that facing these challenges will require the adaptation of the very technology that upholds the configuration systems. The ways of resolving the configurators should be reviewed and updated in order to include other technological concepts that improve deductive capacities and streamline their use.

Finally, the movement to provide the production system with greater intelligence and autonomy, equipping the infrastructures, the machines, and the products with embedded and intelligent products that enable them to take decisions in real-time, poses the challenge of considering configurators on another scale and developed, bearing in mind the progress made in the following type of technologies: SET (Smart Embedded Tags), SED (Smart Embedded Devices), and DISA (Distributed Intelligent Situated Agents).

REFERENCES

Andreasen, M. M. (1980). *Machine design methods based on a systematic approach – Contribution to a design theory.* Unpublished Ph.D. thesis, Lund Technical University, Sweden.

Andreasen, M. M. (1992). Designing on a designer's workbench (DWB). In *Proceedings of the 9ᵗʰ WDK Workshop*, Rigi, Switzerland.

Andreasen, M. M., Hansen, C. T., & Mortensen, N. H. (1997). *On the identification of product structure laws.* Paper presented at the 3ʳᵈ WDK Workshop on Product Structuring, Delft, The Netherlands.

Arana, J., Lakunza, J. A., & Astiazaran, J. C. (2005). *Product models and mass customization experiences in the Basque country.* Paper presented at the International Mass Customization Meeting, Klagenfurt, Austria.

Arana, J., Lakunza, J. A., Elejoste, M., & Mendizabal, B. (2005). *Configurators and product data management systems: Living together.* Paper presented at the Mass Customization and Personalization Congress, Hong-Kong, China.

Blecker, T., Abdelkafi, N., Kreutler, G., & Friedrich, G. (2004). *Product configuration systems: State of the art, conceptualization, and extensions.* Paper presented at the Eight Maghrebian Conference on Software Engineering and Artificial Intelligence, Sousse, Tunisia.

Broekhuizen, T. L. J., & Alsem, K. J. (2002). Success factors for mass customization: A conceptual model. *Journal of Market-Focused Management, 5,* 309-330.

Davis, S. M. (1987). *Future perfect.* Reading, MA: Addison-Wesley.

Felfernig, A., Friedrich, G., Jannach, D., & Zanker, M. (2002). Configuration knowledge representation using UML/OCL. *Lecture Notes in Computer Science, 2460,* 49–62.

Forster, J., Fothergill, P., Lakunza, J. A., & Arana, I. (1995). *DEKLARE: Knowledge acquisition and support system for re-design.* Paper presented at the Expert Systems Annual Conference, Cambridge, UK.

Günter, A., & Kühn, C. (1999). *Knowledge-based configuration – Survey and future directions.* Paper presented at the XPS-99, Knowledge-Based Systems, Würzburg, Germany.

Hsuan, J., & Skjoett-Larsen, T. (2003). *Mass customisation, postponement, and modularisation strategies in shaping supply chains.* Paper presented at the 12ᵗʰ International Conference on Management of Technology, Nancy, France.

Hubka, V., & Eder, W. E. (1988). *Theory of technical systems.* Berlin: Springer-Verlag.

Hvam, L. (1999). A procedure for building product models. *Robotics and Computer-Integrated Manufacturing, 15,* 77-87.

Jensen, T. (1999). *Functional modelling in a design support system.* Unpublished Ph.D. thesis, Technical University of Denmark, Denmark.

Jiao, J., Tseng, M. M., Duffy, V. G., & Lin, F. (1998). Product family modeling for mass customization. *Computers & Industrial Engineering, 35,* 495-498.

Jørgensen, K. A., & Petersen, T. D. (2005). *Product modelling on multiple abstraction levels.* Paper presented at the International Mass Customization Meeting, Klagenfurt, Austria.

Krause, F. L., Kimura, F., & Kjellberg, T. (1993). Product modelling. *Annals of the CIRP, 42*(2).

Männistö, T, Peltonen, H., Alho, K., & Sulonen, R. (1993). *A framework for long-term information management of product configurations* (Tech. Rep. TKO-B105). Helsinki University of Technology, Laboratory of Information Processing Science.

Männistö, T., Peltonen, H., Alho, K., & Sulonen, R. (1994). *Product configurations - An application for prototype object approach.* In M. Tokoro & R. Pareschi (Eds.), Object-Oriented Programming, 8th European Conference, ECOOP'94 (pp. 513-534). Springer-Verlag.

Mittal, S., & Frayman, F. (1989). *Towards a generic model of configuration tasks.* Paper presented at Eleventh International Joint Conference on Artificial Intelligence, Detroit, MI.

Mortensen, N. H. (1999). *Design modelling in a designers workbench.* Ph.D. project, Department of Control and Engineering Design, DTU.

Mortensen, N. H., & Hansen, C. T. (1999). Structuring as a basis for product modelling. In N. H. Mortensen & J. Sigurjonsson (Ed.), *Some implications in critical enthusiasm in contribution to design science* (pp. 111-128). Trondheim, Norway: P2005 Research Program - Norwegian Research Council.

Mortensen, N. H., Yu, B., Skovgaard, H. J., & Harlou, U. (2000). Conceptual modeling of product families in configuration projects. In *Proceedings of Product Models 2000-SIG PM,* Linköping, Sweden.

Pahl, G., & Beitz, W. (1996). *Engineering design: A systematic approach, 2nd ed.* London: Springer-Verlag, Limited.

Pargamin B. (2002). *Vehicle sales configuration: The clusters tree approach.* Paper presented at the 15th European Conference in Artificial Intelligence, Lyon, France.

Peltonen, H. (2000). *Concepts and an implementation for product data management.* Ph.D. thesis, Helsinki University of Technology, Department of Computer Science and Engineering. Published in Acta Polytechnica Scandinavica, Mathematics, and Computing Series. No. 105, Espoo.

Riis, J., Hansen, B. L., & Hvam, L. (2003). *Framework for product knowledge and product-related knowledge which supports modelling for mass customization.* Paper presented at the 2nd World Congress on Mass Customization and Personalization, Munich, Germany.

Sabin, D., & Weigel, R. (1998). Product configuration frameworks-A survey. *IEEE Intelligent Systems and Their Applications, 13*(4), 42-48.

Skjevdal, R., & Idsoe, E. A. (2005). *The competitive impact of product configurators in mass tailoring and mass customization companies.* Paper presented at the World Congress on Mass Customization and Personalization, Hong-Kong, China.

Soininen, T. (2002). *Configurable products and product configurators.* Helsinki University of Technology.

Strom, U., & Axworthy, A. (2000). *Product configurators: The big picture.* Retrieved from http://www.midrangeERP.com

Suh, N. P. (1988). Basic concepts in design for producibility. *Annals of the CIRP, 37*(2), 559-567

Toffler, A. (1970). *Future shock.* New York: Bantam Books.

Tseng, M. M., & Jiao, J. (1998). Fundamental issues regarding developing product family architecture for mass customisation. In *Proceedings of the 5th International Conference on Industrial Engineering and Engineering Management,* Beijing, China.

Vargas, C. (1995). *Modélisation du processus de conception en ingénierie des systèmes mécaniques. Mise en oeuvre basée sur la propagation de contraintes. Application à la conception d'une culasse automobile.* Unpublished PhD thesis, ENS Cachan, France.

Chapter III
Product Configuration in ETO Companies

Thomas Ditlev Petersen
Aalborg University, Denmark

ABSTRACT

This chapter reviews how mass customisation and product configuration can benefit engineer-to-order companies. The relevant main literature in the area is reviewed to identify the benefits and, subsequently, the challenges in implementing product configuration in an engineer-to-order company are described. Finally, a number of suggestions for meeting these challenges are presented, and a case description is introduced, which supports that product configuration can benefit engineer-to-order companies, even though there are a number of challenges to be met. The chapter concludes that engineer-to-order companies can certainly benefit from product configuration by improving business process efficiency as well as information quality and ultimately improving the company's competitive advantage.

INTRODUCTION

"The customer may have any colour car he wishes, as long as it is black" is the famous quotation by Henry Ford from 1908 on the launch of his new Ford T model. This quote has often been used for illustrating the development in product variety that the consumers have experienced through the 20th century and continuing in the 21st century. This development is a result of many factors; however, one of the single factors that have contributed the most to this development is the introduction of the mass customisation (MC) paradigm. This has been used by various industries for presenting the consumers with an ever larger variety of goods. Much research has been performed on developing methods and techniques as well as new strategies for MC. However, mass customisation has typically been described as companies which have been mass producers moving towards mass customisation, that is, increasing variety.

During the recent years, attention has also been brought to the possibilities in utilising the methods from MC in other industrial environments than what is known as mass customisers. Some engineer-to-order companies have successfully utilised some of these methods, achieving increased competitive advantages. However, the advantages which engineer-to-order companies can achieve are different from traditional MC, as are the applicability of the methods.

This chapter seeks to describe which advantages engineer-to-order companies can achieve through utilising elements from traditional MC, what challenges these companies could be facing in doing that, and finally recommendations to face these challenges.

BACKGROUND

Engineer-to-Order Companies

Since this chapter primarily concerns engineer-to-order (ETO) companies, it is relevant to define precisely what characterises an ETO company. One definition is that ETO companies are companies which, for each order, reengineer the product after getting the order and before starting production (Caron & Fiore, 1995). Furthermore, ETO companies are characterised by time-limited projects related to the supply of complex equipment to third parties, and this process often includes the phases: design, manufacturing, installation, and commissioning (Caron & Fiore, 1995). Also, ETO products are usually physical products, that is, custom-made software is not commonly referred to as an ETO product. Naturally ETO products can contain custom-made software; however, they will always contain custom engineered physical elements. Another characteristic of ETO products is that the number of manufactured products of a given design is very low, in many cases only one. ETO companies may very well (and do in most cases) also manufacture and sell other products

which are not engineer-to-order products apart from the ETO products.

Because the topic of this chapter is product configuration, which is implemented in a product configuration system that should support or improve the business processes in a company, it is relevant to review the business processes in ETO companies. In this context, focus is on the business processes related to the processes from sale to delivery of the product.

According to Hicks, McGovern, and Earl (2000), ETO business processes can be considered as three distinct sequential processes: (i) marketing, or developing a potential customer's awareness of the company's products; (ii) response to an invitation to tender for a particular contract, involving some development of a preliminary concept; and (iii) detailed design, procurement, manufacturing, construction, and commissioning.

Forza and Salvador (2002) describe the case of a voltage transformer producer which has implemented product configuration and which benefits this company had gained from the implementation. Here the business processes are also described briefly: (i) definition of the product variant requested by the customer, including sale and order acquisition; (ii) product variant design and engineering; and (iii) production. Forza and Salvador (2002) describe the business processes somewhat more narrowly than Hicks et al. (2000) by not including marketing and commissioning activities. The case described in Forza and Salvador (2002) can be designated as an ETO case, even though it is one of the lesser complex cases regarding product as well as business process complexity. However, from the two descriptions a number of conclusions can be drawn regarding the characteristics of business processes in ETO companies. In Figure 1, it is illustrated how mass producing, mass customising, and ETO companies differ in their value chain, to show that the business processes in ETO companies are somewhat

Figure 1. The three different simplified value chains for MP, MC, and ETO companies

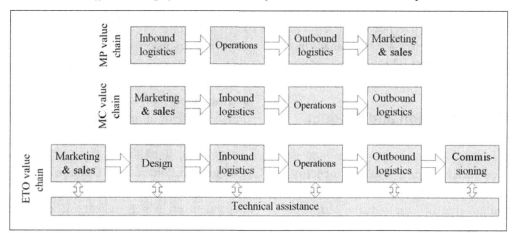

more complex than for mass producers and mass customisers.

As mentioned previously, one of the characteristics of ETO products is that the detailed design of the product is not carried out until an order has been acquired. This is fundamentally different than non-ETO companies, where the design of a product is carried out before it is sold. This again presents a number of challenges for the ETO companies, since a number of uncertainties may exist, both technically and commercially, since not all details about a product are known at the time of sale.

Another common characteristic for ETO business processes is that much technical knowledge is needed to sell the product. This means, in most cases, that the sales personnel are technically educated to be able to fit the product to the customer's needs. Also, it is often necessary in the sales process to query the engineering department for technical feasibility and appropriateness of a given solution as well as price consequences and other details depending on the particular case. The reason for this is that an order for an ETO product is seldom equal to an earlier order, and hence the sales person cannot rely exclusively on experience from previous orders, and must turn to the engineering department for advice.

Sometimes it may even be necessary to develop an initial concept for the product to ensure technical feasibility.

In an ETO business process from customer inquiry to delivery of a product, it is also worth noting that the information obtained through the sales process is controlling the processes in the detailed design phases. This means that if the quality of information is low, there will be a risk of errors in the later phases. Examples of this could be ambiguous specifications of the order or simply missing information. These errors could, worst case, mean that the product which the customer receives does not meet the customer's expectations. Less critical risks include that the information determining the product cost has been insufficient, meaning that the cost of the finished product does not match the budget cost, implying a deviation in contribution margin. Also, low quality or missing information can cause delays in the detailed design phase, since the engineering department may have to contact the customer or sales person to clarify technical details.

Due to the great differences between each order in an ETO company, the information flow associated with an order is much more intensive than for non-ETO companies. This is partly due to the fact that the products are often large complex systems, and partly that parts of the product are often custom designed (Forza & Salvador, 2002). This information, of course, needs to be managed in order to have an efficient workflow in the business processes and is naturally an important issue in relation to product configuration.

Mass Customisation and Product Configuration

When considering which strategic benefits a company can achieve from MC and product configuration, it is difficult to distinguish which advantages come from which element. This is because product configuration is usually a part of a mass MC strategy, and MC strategies often contain product configuration elements. Hence in the following, the main literature addressing MC and product configuration is reviewed together.

Mass Customisation was first foreseen three decades ago by Toffler (1970), who described the sociological tendencies that would create the basis for what would later be widely known as MC (Toffler, 1970). Two decades later it became a research topic with Davis' publication "From Future Perfect: Mass Customization" (Davis, 1989), presenting how products and services could be realised as a one-of-a-kind manufacture on a large scale. Davis also presented the idea that the customisation could be done at various points in the supply chain. In 1993, Pine published a major contribution to the MC literature: "Mass Customization: The New Frontier in Business Competition", which was an extensive study of how American enterprises during the seventies and eighties had been overrun by the efficient Japanese manufacturers, which could produce at lower costs and higher quality (Pine, 1993). This called for a change of paradigm in American manufacturing, and several companies recognised the need for MC; as a result, the related techniques were developed.

Since MC has been a topic for much research since that time, many different definitions have been suggested. However, a commonly-accepted definition was presented in Hart (1995): "*The use of flexible processes and organizational structures to produce varied and often individually-customized products and services at the low cost of a standardized, mass production system.*" Furthermore, MC is often associated with an intensive use of information technology for both sales and manufacturing (Silveira, Borenstein, & Fogliatto, 2001).

The question of how a company may benefit from adapting an MC strategy is naturally dependent on which industry it is in, current manufacturing strategy, and several other factors. Lampel and Mintzberg (1996) suggested that the optimal degree of customisation is dependent on which type of industry of which a company is a part (Lampel & Mintzberg, 1996). The two extremes are "Mass Industries" manufacturing pure standardised goods, and on the other hand, "Thin Industries" or engineer-to-order (ETO) companies, which provide products with a very large degree of customisation. An example of the first could be the process industry, and the latter steam turbines or super computers. In between these two extremes, there is a continuum of other industries, which according to Lampel and Mintzberg (1996) calls for a diversity of MC strategies. Lampel and Mintzberg (1996) classify these strategies by the point of which the customer interacts with the production process from initial design to distribution. Another form of classification is done by Gilmore and Pine (1997), where they are classified by whether the product is customised and if the product representation is customised. As stated above, the benefits that a company can achieve from implementing an MC strategy differ. Generally speaking, companies coming from mass production can diversify their product portfolio and thereby target more markets or market segments at once without an excessive increase in costs. ETO companies are already customising their products, but can use the methods of MC to achieve economies of scale while still customising (Pine, 1993).

There is not a single strategy which can describe how a company successfully can transist to a mass customising company, since it is very dependent on the type of product and company (Pine, Victor, & Boyton, 1993). However, much research has been done in addressing an identification of various success factors for MC. Silveira et al. (2001) have listed which success factors are commonly acknowledged. These include market-related issues, as well as organisational issues. The latter are divided in four distinct categories, which are described by four statements:

- Value chain should be ready
- Knowledge must be shared
- Products should be customisable
- Technology must be available

Due to the subject of this chapter, we shall focus on the last two statements in the following section.

The statement, "Products should be customisable", has been described comprehensively in the literature. In order to achieve MC, a company's products must be ready for customisation (Silveira et al., 2001). Berman (2002) and Pine (1993) proposed that the use of modular product design, combined with postponement of product differentiation, would be an enabler to a successful MC implementation.

Many authors acknowledge that modularisation in most cases is a necessity to achieve MC, by designing product as modules which can be combined in different ways to form a variety of products (Ericsson & Erixon, 1999; Pine, 1993; Tseng & Jiao, 1996; Ulrich & Eppinger, 2000). This was also described by Feitzinger and Lee (1997) using the case of Hewlett-Packard which had greatly reduced the cost of laser and inkjet printers by modularisation and, at the same time, obtained a greater variety (Feitzinger & Lee, 1997).

Many methods exist to design for MC, but among the latest contributions are Hsu and Wang (2004) which describe an algorithm to determine the best form of modularisation to optimize, for example, costs along the value chain. In Robertson and Ulrich (1998), Mikkola and Gassmann (2003), and Martin and Ishii (2002), new contributions are also presented on how to achieve the best trade-off between commonality and differentiation in products. Especially Martin and Ishii (2002) and Mikkola and Gassmann (2003) provide pragmatic approaches to the task of developing new product families based on product platforms, using mathematical methods to calculate the exact costs and benefits from different design choices.

Designing for MC is equally important whether it takes place in a former mass producing or an ETO company; however, the two cases present different challenges. Former MP companies will often try to increase the variety as seen from the customer's viewpoint, while still limiting the internal variety. For ETO companies, it can be beneficial to reduce the variety seen from the customer's viewpoint, in order to reduce the internal variety. However, for both cases it is a matter of optimizing the variety as seen from the customer's viewpoint, that is, having the lowest possible external variety, while still meeting the customers' expectations to flexibility, and at the same time minimizing the internal variety.

Beside that the products should be customisable, manufacturing and information flow also play a great role in MC. In order to control an MC manufacturing system, it has proven necessary to use information technology to a great extent. Much effort has been put into developing configurators which are considered the core of configuration systems. When moving from mass production to MC, the need for obtaining, processing, and distributing information greatly increases (Forza & Salvador, 2002). The increase in information flow results in a greater use of resources during the order processing as well as a greater risk of errors, assuming a traditional order processing system is being used. However, by using a configuration system, the information processing can be automated, reducing the use of resources and the risk of errors (Forza & Salvador, 2002; Steger-Jensen & Svensson, 2003). Furthermore, according to Frutos and Borenstein (2004), the information system, of which the configuration system is a part, must be extended to include both customers and suppliers to successfully implement an MC strategy. This has also been described in the area of build-to-order supply chain management in Gunasekarana and Ngai (2005). However, companies may achieve great advantages from implementing configuration systems only for internal use, but to achieve the full potential of MC the value chain should be integrated.

In order to implement a configuration system, a model describing the product must be defined and implemented, usually in the configurator. An often-used approach is to describe a series of products building a product family model, which describes a product family in one single model. A product family can be viewed as a predefined set of modules, which can be combined in different ways, to form an end product (Jørgensen, 2003). The product family model describes which modules are parts of the product family model, and how they can be combined. Implementing the product family model in a configurator allows the user to select modules to configure products; in some cases, the user can even select the desired properties of the end product, and the configurator selects the corresponding modules (Jørgensen, 2003). Several different methods for defining product models have been constructed during the latest years, each with their own advantages. When selecting a method, the organisation's requirements must be taken into account regarding, for example, ease of use while defining the model, overview of the model, ease of maintenance and implementation in the configurator and, of course, it must describe all feasible products. To meet these requirements, as mentioned above, several

methods have been developed, of which a few are briefly described in the following section.

The task of defining a product family model may be a huge task for ETO companies, because the variety must be larger than for former MP companies. For this reason it can be beneficial to perform a cost benefit analysis regarding which options should be included in the product family model. If an option is seldom used, the cost of implementing it may exceed the benefit, leading to the conclusion that not all options necessarily should be implemented.

A widely-used and acknowledged product modelling method in Denmark is the: "*Procedure for building product models*" described in Hvam (1999) based on Hvam (1994). It is a pragmatic approach with a seven-step procedure, describing how to build a configuration system from process and product analysis to implementation and maintenance. For the product modelling purpose, it uses the Product Variant Master method followed by object-oriented modelling to describe both classification and composition in a product family.

The object-oriented approach is also taken by Felfernig, Friedrich, and Jannach (2001), who use the unified modelling language (UML) to describe a product family. This is done by using a UML metamodel architecture which can be automatically translated into an executable logical architecture. In contrast to Hvam (1999), this method focuses more on formulating the object-oriented product structure, rules, and constraints most efficiently. The method also focuses on how the customers' functional requirements can be translated into a selection of specific modules in the product family.

The mapping of functional requirements to specific modules is also considered in Jiao, Tseng, Duffy, and Lin (1998) and Du, Jiao, and Tseng (2000), where it is proposed to use a triple-view representation scheme to describe a product family. The three views are the functional, the technical, and the structural view. The functional view is used to describe, typically the customers, functional requirements, and the technical view is used to describe the design parameters in the physical domain. The structural view is used for performing the mapping between the functional and technical view as well as describing the rules of how a product may be configured. The description of this modelling approach is, however, rather conceptual, and it does not easily implement in common configuration tools.

Most of the methods which exist for modelling configurable products focus on modelling the solution space of a configuration process. This means that they describe the possible attributes of the products and the product structure as described above. Hence they typically do not focus on information which is not directly used to perform the configuration itself. This information which could include, for example, customer, logistics, and manufacturing information, is, according to Reichwald, Piller, and Möslein (2000), similarly important, since a successful implementation of MC must integrate all information flows in the so-called "Information Cycle of Mass Customization", which is also presented in Reichwald et al. (2000). The information cycle consists of five steps, which represent different activities in relation to MC. The five steps are listed below:

1. Listen to your customers
2. Configuration (existing and new customers)
3. Manufacturing planning
4. Production assembly and supply chain integration
5. Distribution and relationship marketing

Reichwald et al. (2000) emphasise the importance of managing these flows efficiently, which is most likely to be done by building an integrated information flow. In order to do this, the information must be structured in an appropriate way, which can be done by constructing an information model. In this respect, an appropriate structure is a structure which allows an efficient information flow by means of time and resource consumption, while still providing a sufficient amount of high-quality information in the distinct steps in the information cycle. There are, of course, different strategies on how to construct the most appropriate information models, and these naturally also vary between different companies, markets, and products.

But even though there is not a single generic strategy from which the optimal information model can be constructed, the importance of this issue must be emphasised because of the great potential benefits. There is an especially great potential for ETO companies, since an optimisation of information structure and flow can reduce the resources spent on information processing.

GAINS FROM USING MC IN ETO COMPANIES

Since ETO companies are very much different from mass producers, even after the ETOs have transformed their businesses into MC, ETOs will not necessarily achieve the same benefits from implementing MC elements as former mass producers. In the following section, a number of possible benefits for ETOs from using MC elements will be presented.

Generic MC Benefits

As mentioned above, Berman (2002) described four distinct categories of benefits from MC. The identified benefits are shown below, and are subsequently described in detail. Since these identified benefits are generic to MC companies, it is evaluated whether they can be applied to the special case of ETO companies as well as mass producers.

- Improved fit with a customer's unique needs;
- More efficiency due to lower inventory levels throughout the distribution channel;
- Ability to raise the price of a good or a service; and
- Improved ability to analyse opportunities due to continuing dialogue with consumers.

Improved Fit with a Customer's Unique Needs

Berman (2002) states that through MC, a company can achieve an improved fit with the customers' needs. This is done by filling the "sacrifice gaps", which are the gaps between what mass producers make, often with little variety to minimise variable costs, and what customers actually want. By increasing variety, these gaps will be minimised or even removed, because the customers can have exactly what they desire (Berman, 2002). However, this reasoning is based on the assumption that the companies are mass producers moving towards MC. For ETO companies this reason does not apply, since these companies have always made tailored products for their customers, and thereby they have always had a very large variety. Hence there will typically not be any reason for increasing the variety. However, a large variety does not necessarily signify a better fit with the customers' needs. In order to achieve a fit with customer needs, the product variety must be utilised efficiently to fulfil the needs. This is usually obtained by combining certain features in the products, which is usually referred to as a configuration. Hence, in order to achieve the best fit with customers' needs, a company must have both a sufficient variety as well as an ability to supply the customer with the correct variant of the products in the portfolio.

From this it can be concluded that for ETO companies, the greatest challenge in obtaining the best fit with customers' needs is not to increase variety, but to efficiently utilise the current portfolio to meet the customers' demands. In some cases, it may even prove necessary or beneficial to reduce the variety in the product portfolio if the company is an ETO manufacturer. The process of matching specific customer needs with product options is often carried out in a configuration system, which is common to both mass producers and ETO companies; hence, the methods for this configuration system, developed for mass producers, can in many cases be adapted to ETO companies.

More Efficiency due to Lower Inventory Levels throughout the Distribution Channel

According to Berman (2002), a major benefit in MC is a reduction of inventory, that is, raw materials, work in progress, and finished goods. Especially for industries with ever-falling component prices, this is an advantage, since components can be bought just-in-time and the price decline for the reduced time is saved. As an example, when Dell was the only mass customiser in the computer industry, Dell had seven days of sales in inventory, whereas the non-mass customising competitors had 78 days of inventory. Hence, less money is bound in inventory and the purchase prices are lowered; thereby the margins can be increased. Also, less money is bound because the market will pull goods instead of the company pushing products to the retailers. Furthermore, Berman (2002) points out that manufacturers can also save money due to products at retailers becoming obsolete; also, higher margins can be achieved, because payment for the product can be received as soon as the product is ordered.

Like the benefits from improved fit with customers' needs, these conclusions are based on companies traditionally being mass producers. However, for ETO companies the conclusions and arguments are slightly different.

As ETO companies' products are often large, complex, and thereby expensive products, the supplier and customer will often have special payment agreements, usually in the form of contracts, to ensure that neither the supplier nor the customer breaks the sales agreement, with great economical losses as a result. Hence the benefit from earlier payments probably does not apply to all ETO cases. Furthermore, ETO companies usually do not have retailers and finished goods in stock, which are not already ordered. Hence, this benefit does not apply to ETO cases either.

As a result of this, no reduction of inventory can be expected due to elimination of finished goods inventory. However, by using the methods of MC, it is possible for ETO companies to reduce inventory levels regarding raw materials and work in progress. In order to implement MC, modularised products are often a necessity (Pine, 1993); product platforms also are often a part of the strategy for implementing MC. For ETO companies, modularisation will often imply standardising the product programme, which will mean that the variety of the product portfolio, seen from a manufacturing point of view, will be reduced. Assuming a fixed or increasing sales volume while reducing manufacturing variety, the volume per standard component or module will increase. Increasing component volumes usually imply improved opportunities to improve the manufacturing flow and thereby reduce work in progress. Also, the inventory levels for raw materials can be reduced since the variety of required raw materials will also decline as a result of reduced internal variety.

The potential benefit from postponing purchase and thereby saving the purchase price decline can also apply to ETO cases; however, this entirely depends on which industry the company is in, that is, if the purchase prices are constantly declining, as in the computer industry, this benefit applies. Hence, no general conclusion can be drawn for ETO companies.

Ability to Raise the Price of a Good or a Service

Another benefit from MC, stated in Berman (2002), is that the supplier is able to raise the prices for a product or a service due to the better fit with the customers' needs.

The reasoning in Berman (2002) also primarily addresses mass producers for this issue. ETO companies do as a basis provide highly-customised products; hence, they do not necessarily achieve a better fit with customer needs by implementing MC. This is not an argument for raising the price, since this alone does not increase the value added from the customers' point of view. However, there are a number of other ways to add value to the customer, which are not part of the product itself using product configuration.

Since the engineer-to-order products do often require a very high degree of customer interaction in the sales phase to specify the product, approve designs, and so forth, this is a point where the ETO companies have a possibility to add value. By easing the buying process for the customer, and thereby saving the customer time and resources, premium prices can be justified. Depending on the specific business, there may of course be other benefits to the customer which can justify premium sales prices. If, for example, the implementation of MC is done through a standardisation of modules, this can imply lower spare part prices throughout the product life cycle and hence a lower total cost of ownership in the product life cycle.

Improved Ability to Analyse Opportunities due to Continuing Dialogue with Consumers

If a customer purchases a mass-customised product, the customer will choose exactly what the customer wants, as opposed to mass-produced products, where the customer will choose whatever product fits the best with the requirements. Since the customer can choose specific options in an MC setup, statistics can be gathered which tell in detail about the customers' needs. These statistics can be used in various ways, but Berman (2002) states that they can especially be used for two distinct purposes.

The first purpose is identifying frequent combinations in the products, which can be adapted to mass production, if the company has a diverse strategy including both low-cost mass-produced products and differentiated mass-customised products. The second purpose relates to the limitation of options to be chosen by the customer. If statistics on customer choices regarding the product are gathered, it can be identified if some options are rarely used, and thereby are not cost beneficial to have in the product programme. If relating these issues to ETO cases, it can be concluded that the first benefit, identifying products to be mass produced, does obviously not apply to ETO companies, since a greater number of identical ETO products are never produced. However, elements of the products may be used repetitively which can be identified and manufactured with better efficiency. Although the volume will not be the same scale as mass production, this could result in lower manufacturing costs for the ETO companies. In contrast, the second issue is highly relevant to ETO companies. As previously mentioned, it is highly beneficial for ETO companies to limit the variety internally. If variety can be reduced externally, this will in most cases imply a reduction of variety internally also; hence, this is a highly relevant benefit for ETO companies.

Benefits from MC Unique to ETO Companies

In the section above, it was evaluated whether the benefits from traditional, that is, non-ETO, MC, and product configuration also apply to ETO companies. However, there are also a number of benefits from using product configuration in ETO companies, which are not applicable to non-ETO companies. Since ETO companies are as different as their products are, different benefits apply to different companies. However, in this section it is sought to identify benefits which apply to "typical" ETO companies, by evaluating a number of case descriptions. These include Petersen and Jørgensen (2005), which describe a marine boiler producer, Forza and Salvador (2002) describing a

voltage transformer producer, and Hvam, Malis, Hansen, and Riis (2004) a cement plant contractor. All of these case companies have implemented product configuration to some degree, and the argumentation in the following sections are derived from these cases.

Increased Efficiency in Business Processes

In most industries, the area of blue-collar automation has been of great interest during the 20th century. Blue-collar automation refers to the automation of manual, physical work in manufacturing. Much later, the advantages of white-collar automation, which refers to automation of business processes, that is, administrative and engineering processes, were discovered and utilised. However, this type of automation also presents opportunities for great cost savings as well as other benefits such as consistent quality in the business processes, like blue-collar automation provides for the manufacturing processes.

The product configuration element of the MC paradigm can be perceived as white-collar automation, because product configuration systems fully or partially automate the processes of sale, order processing, and in some cases manufacturing. The potential of white-collar automation, of course, varies between companies. However, for ETO companies there will usually be a great potential because the cost of administrative and engineering activities account for a significant share of the total product costs.

The cases referred to above all describe that ETO companies which have implemented product configuration have also increased their business process efficiency. As described above, the sales process in ETO companies is often a significant task which is very resource-consuming. Often the sales process also has a long lead time. Both of these parameters can be addressed using product configuration. Using product configuration, the sales process will be partly automated, thus saving work for the sales organisation. This can be done by embedding technical knowledge in a product configuration system, achieving that the sales organisation can configure an ETO product totally or partly without consulting the technical organisation; also, trivial tasks can be automated. By embedding technical knowledge in a configuration system, it is also ensured that only technically-feasible products are offered to the customer, reducing the need for reviewing the specifications in the quotation to the customer.

All of the factors above help in automating the sales process and thereby in reducing the man-hours spent on making a quotation for a customer; thereby, the cost of making a quotation is also reduced. Furthermore, the lead time for making a quotation can be greatly reduced, meaning that the company becomes more responsive to customer inquiries. In the case described in Hvam et al. (2004), the implementation of product configuration meant a reduction of man-hours spent per quotation to 4% of the hours before the configuration system was implemented. Also, the lead time was reduced greatly from several weeks to just a few days.

In the cases where many resources are put into designing a product for a customer inquiry and making a quotation, the company may have to be selective in which customer inquires should be answered with a quotation because it would be too expensive to make quotations for all inquiries. However, if the product design can be made using a product configuration system, which would use far fewer resources, more quotations can be made since the economical risk is lower as fewer resources are spent per quotation. Assuming that some of these quotations turn into order, this would mean increased sales for the company and thereby direct economical benefit from the product configuration system.

However, it is not only the sales process which can be automated by using product configuration in ETO companies. Also, the processes such as detailed design and procurement can often, to

some degree, be automated. This is done in the case described in Petersen and Jørgensen (2005), where production BOMs are generated partly automatically, as well as production drawings and system diagrams. In this case, the man-hours per order were also reduced as well as the lead time, but equally important the quality of this documentation was also improved, meaning that the consistency between what had been specified to the customer in the sales phase and what was delivered in the later phases of detailed design was improved.

Using a product configuration approach in the sales process in ETOs also presents the possibility to control which information should be determined in the sales process. If information needed in the detailed design phase or procurement has not been determined during the sales phase, it will in these phases be necessary to contact the customer for clarification. This interaction can be avoided if the product configuration system has certain constraints on which information is needed before an order can be placed, leading again to improved efficiency in the processes following a sales order, since the necessary information will be available when needed.

CHALLENGES IN ETO CONFIGURATION

As already mentioned, ETO companies are fundamentally different from traditional companies moving towards MC regarding products as well as business processes. Hence, the challenges for implementing product configuration in ETO companies are also different than for non-ETOs. The challenges which are specific for ETO companies are described in this section in order to present an overview of the problems that ETOs may encounter. It should be noted that the internal organisational impact of implementing product configuration in a company is an issue of great importance. However, this subject is outside the scope of this chapter, but has been described comprehensively elsewhere in the MC literature.

Product Characteristics

The structure of ETO products is often much more complex than the structure of products offered by traditional MC companies. For many traditional MC companies, the process of configuring a product is often a matter of combining a set of different predefined modules, which make up the product in a well-defined structure. This could, for example, be the configuration of a computer by selecting a casing, disk, processor, and so forth, from predefined lists of available components. In the even simpler cases, the customisation is a matter of altering a few options on a standardised product. However, for ETO products this kind of configuration is seldom possible, due to the much more complex product structure and higher variety.

The configuration process in an ETO product configuration system may also be a matter of combining different modules; however, for ETO products modules will often have variety internally as opposed to modules in traditional MC companies. Also, the structure by which the modules can be combined will often be more complex. These circumstances present the ETOs implementing product configuration with a number of problems. First of all, the product family which is to be implemented in the configuration system must be defined. In order to do this, it must be defined which elements, that is, modules, should be possible to combine in order to define an end product. Secondly, it must be defined how the modules should be allowed to be combined, and finally the internal variety for each module and possible links from internal module variety to other modules must be defined. The higher the variety, the more complex this task becomes. Due to the nature of ETO products, this task is indeed very complex. Once the product family has been defined, a product configuration system

can be implemented. However, this implementation is equally complex if the product structure is complex.

The customers' requirements to ETO products are often very diverse and specific. Because of this, when modelling the product family, it may be difficult to predict which options the customers will demand. Hence, once the product configuration system has been implemented and is in use, the customers may demand properties of a product which are not possible to configure in the product configuration system. For this reason, the system must support customer demands, which do not have corresponding options in the configuration system. This is not a functionality which is common in traditional configurations systems, and is therefore an extra challenge when implementing such systems in ETO companies.

Another issue related to the large diversity in customer demands is that even though a customer option has been identified when defining the product family, it may not be cost-beneficial to implement it in the product configuration system. If an option is only very seldom relevant and it has a significant cost to implement, it may have a lower total cost not to implement it and handle this option manually when necessary. In general, when determining which diverse demands the product configuration system should be able to address, it will be a matter of finding an optimal trade-off between automation and flexibility.

In the case described in Hvam et al. (2004), which addresses a product configuration system for making quotations, it has been chosen only to implement the 20% of the product accounting for 80% of the cost, and estimate the remaining 20% of the cost. This is, of course, not possible if the configuration is to be used in the detailed design phase after the order has been placed, since all of the product must be configured in this case; this illustrates the trade-off between automation and flexibility. This solution is very flexible; however, it is not appropriate for automation in the later processes.

Customer Relations

ETOs which implement product configuration may also face a number of challenges related to the interaction with their customers. Since ETO products are often also large projects for the customer, the ETO may communicate with several different organisational units at the customer. Looking at the case from Petersen and Jørgensen (2005), whose customers are primarily shipyards, the case ETO interacts with several different departments at the customer. The first department is the purchasing department with which the overall design of the product is determined. Later, when the order has been placed, the responsibility at the customer changes to a detailed design department. With this department, the case company determines the details of the product. This means that the case ETO actually defines the product in two phases, that is, the sales phase and the detailed design phase. There are a number of technical difficulties in doing this; however, one key issue is that all product properties which are significantly determinant for the product price must be clarified in the sales phase and cannot be altered in the detailed design phase.

Long Time Span

ETO companies often operate with very long lead times for an order from initial customer inquiry to delivery and, if relevant, commissioning, because the orders are often very large projects. This also presents the ETOs which are considering implementing product configuration with a number of challenges. For the cases described in Petersen and Jørgensen (2005) and Hvam et al. (2004), this time can easily span years. This is a challenge when making a product configuration system, since this introduces a number of uncertainties. These uncertainties include currency exchange rates, which are not easily predictable, and are important when calculating a price for a product. However, this should rely on economic

theory which is outside the scope of this chapter. Furthermore, factors such as sourcing capabilities, supplier availability, legal regulations, as well as the ETO's own product portfolio may change. All of these factors may change in the time between when an order is placed and when the corresponding product is delivered. This necessitates changes in the product which was originally agreed upon with the customer and defined in the product configuration system; therefore, the ETO must have procedures for handling this through or bypassing the configuration system.

All of the challenges for product configuration described above are relevant to many ETO companies which consider implementing product configuration. In the following section, recommendations are presented on how to meet these challenges.

MEETING THE CHALLENGES

Since there is little literature describing product configuration in ETO companies, the following recommendations for meeting the challenges described above are not validated in practice but merely suggestions for how these challenges could be handled.

Handling Complex Product Structures

In order to model products which have a complex structure, the elements of the product model must be decoupled from each other. Decoupling the elements means that the interfaces of the elements must be well-defined and specified in such a way that the elements are interchangeable. By structuring the model this way, it becomes possible to configure products in a structure which has not been predefined.

However, it can be difficult to describe the product family in this way, if the existing product structure does not support it. This will typically be the case if the company's products have an integral architecture, which is the opposite of a modularised architecture, where interfaces between modules are typically clearly defined, and modules can be interchanged (Ulrich & Eppinger, 2000). Hence if an ETO company chooses to use product configuration, it should be considered if new product development should be aimed at developing modular products, since this is usually described as an enabler for MC and product configuration (Berman, 2002; Pine, 1993).

It was also pointed out above that it is unlikely that an ETO would deem it possible or even cost-beneficial to implement all customer options in the product configuration system. Hence, these options, if demanded by the customer, should be handled differently than the options which can be configured. This could be done by integrating the information about the options that cannot be configured with the configuration information. This is important since this information is critical for the later use of the configuration for detailed design, for example, and these processes will be faulty if the information about the configuration is incomplete. However, this task can require a significant development effort, since standard systems support this only to a very low degree.

Configuration on Multiple Abstraction Levels

One approach to address the problems regarding the long time span from initial customer contact to final product delivery could be by using functional specifications. This has been described in Jørgensen and Petersen (2005), where it is suggested that products should be modelled and configured on multiple abstraction levels. This means, in practice, that when configuring a product, it should be configured by using mainly functional specifications, that is, describing what the product should be able to do, and not by selecting actual modules or components. By using this approach, the ETO company will have the freedom to select specific components at a later point in the business process, and thereby reducing the effects described above caused by changes over time in supplier, sourcing availability, and so forth.

Modelling the products on multiple abstraction levels will also allow the configuration in multiple steps, which is needed in some ETO cases, when the full specifications cannot be determined at the time of sales agreement. Hence, the product family model as well as the product configuration system implementing the model should support configuration on multiple abstraction levels.

CASE DESCRIPTION: AALBORG INDUSTRIES

The following case describes the company Aalborg Industries A/S (AI), which primarily produces marine boiler for ships. AI has all the characteristics of an ETO company: large complex products which are reengineered after each sale; long order process; and much technical knowledge is needed to sell and design the products. The purpose of this case description is to exemplify the theory presented above and point out how an ETO in practice can benefit from product configuration.

AI has chosen to implement a configuration system to support the sales and order processing of boiler plants for different reasons. First of all, a configuration system can help in meeting the challenges presented above. Also, being the market leader, AI wishes to be trendsetting in the industry. Furthermore, competitive advantages can be gained by achieving faster response to customer inquiries; also, a configuration system can aid a wish to be closer to the customer since knowledge can be embedded in the system, and the technical knowledge can be present in local sales offices close to the customer.

It was chosen to implement the configuration system gradually, by implementing one or two product families at a time. Using this approach,

AI has implemented a configuration system for the boiler families, MISSION™ OS, MISSION™ OL, MISSION™ OC, MISSION™ XW and MISSION™ XS. The MISSION™ product series is a series of boiler families, which is an attempt to standardise the product line. The MISSION™ series replaces a large number of old products, in a smaller number of product families, and presents advantages due to the new modularised product structure and improved technology. One of these advantages is the possibility to implement a configuration system, as well as other advantages such as a stronger purchasing power, benefits to customers, and so forth.

Using the configuration system, sales personnel is able to configure boiler plants, ensuring that only a valid configuration can be made. From the configuration system, it is possible to generate documents such as price calculations, quotation letters, technical data, bill of materials for the ERP system, CAD drawings, and P&I diagrams. The benefits from implementing these functionalities are, among others, reduced lead times for sales and order processing as well as reduced time consumption. However, the configuration system can only contain a limited number of customer options, meaning that some customer requirements are outside of the configurator scope. The reason that not all possible customer options have been implemented in the configuration system is that the implementation in many cases will require more resources spent than doing the sales and order processing without the configurator.

AI has established sales offices near the big ship building centres in the world to ensure competitiveness on the local markets. Since it is often difficult to hire employees with the knowledge needed to design boiler plants from scratch, the configuration system is a valuable tool for sales support in AI's subsidiaries, since it, to a large degree, ensures a consistent system design.

The development of the configuration system has been a process which includes technology assessment of various configuration systems

and a standardisation of the product programme. The reduction of products and standardisation of the product programme had the purpose to minimise the number of modules used in the product families, while sustaining the ability to deliver sufficiently-customised boiler plants to the customers. Also, a great task in these projects has been defining the rules, which delimit the choices that can be made in the configurator. The final configuration system is based on the Danish company 3DFactos VirtuBUILD configurator, which handles the configuration process and thereby the rules for the boiler plants as well as providing the data for generating the documentation.

The AI case demonstrates that there are great potential benefits from implementing product configuration in ETOs. However, the case also verifies that there are a number of hurdles to be overcome when doing so. Still, the AI case shows that it is possible to overcome these challenges and get the advantages of product configuration in ETOs.

FUTURE TRENDS

It seems that more and more ETOs are discovering the opportunities in product configuration, and gaining from them. This hopefully also means that more research will be conducted in this specific area of MC and product configuration, and more practical experiences will be described in literature. It may also mean that the vendors of product configuration systems will begin tailoring their products for ETO companies, which will ease the transition from ETO to ETO product configuration.

If the trends in product configuration in ETO companies follow the trends in general product configuration, a number of expectations to the future can be pointed out.

Many mass customisers, in presenting their product configuration systems to the customers, are starting to use 3D visualisation where applicable. This can be utilised to visualise what the finished product will look like and how it will work before it is manufactured and becomes a physical product. It can thereby help the customer in the buying process by presenting an overview by viewing a realistic model of the product; also, details can be reviewed. These possibilities can also be used in ETO configuration to configure, for example, complex geometric options, as well as presenting an overview of large systems.

More and more traditional mass customisers are beginning to give customers access to their configurators via the Internet, allowing the customers to configure their own products from their home computer. This has been possible for years for relatively simple products such as personal computers; however, more and more complex product configurators are available over the Internet. For example, it is now possible to configure and buy a house on the Internet. As these Internet-based configurators become able to handle more complex products, they may also be able to handle ETO products. If this is the case, ETO customers will also be able to configure their own products themselves. This could be beneficial to the ETO companies because it would save resources in the sales organisation if the customers were able to define, in the configuration system, what the characteristics of their product should be. Possibly this should only be a conceptual configurator, defining the overall properties of the products and presenting an estimated price, since most customers probably would not be able to define all product properties in a more detailed configuration system.

Finally, a trend in general MC which is likely also to be applied to ETOs is the digitalisation of customisation. This means that products are not customised physically but rather digitally, by applying different software to the products. This means that larger volumes can be obtained per component type, and thereby manufacturing or purchase costs can be reduced for a component or product. However, this kind of customisation

will most likely require a complete redesign of the affected part of the product, meaning it would also have a significant cost.

CONCLUSION

When reviewing the literature on general MC and product configuration, and relating these principles to ETO cases, it is evident that MC and product configuration contain elements which can benefit some ETO companies. In many cases, ETOs will be able to reduce the resources needed for making a quotation for a customer; also, the lead time will be reduced. Furthermore, the risk of errors in the order processing can be reduced due to automation of the workflow and embedding of engineering knowledge in a configuration system. Also, by using the principles of modular product architecture, it may be possible to reduce the internal variety, which again can lead to reduced inventory levels.

However, there are a number of challenges in implementing product configuration in an ETO company. These include modelling and implementing the product portfolio, since the variety is very high while the structure is very complex. Furthermore, the customer relations in ETO companies are also more complex than in non-ETOs. ETO companies will often have contact to different organisational units at the customer with different responsibilities. This is also a challenge to support in the configuration system, since the configuration should be able to be performed in different stages. Finally, ETO products are often projects which span over months and even years. This also makes product configuration more difficult since different uncertainties must be taken into account, such as currency exchange rates, supplier availability, and so forth.

These challenges can, in some cases, be met by using modular product architecture, which can be difficult in ETOs due to the very large and complex product structure. However, by decoupling the different modules and components in the structure, the difficulties may be reduced. Also, modelling and configuring products on multiple levels of abstraction may be a means to meet the challenges regarding especially the long time span and different organisational interfaces.

Since not many ETOs have advanced very far using product configuration, the attention on this subject has been sparse in the literature. However, as more and more ETOs discover the possibilities, it is expected that more research will be performed in this area; thereafter, more technologies and products for product configuration will be made available to ETOs, which will then more easily be able to implement product configuration and to benefit from it.

REFERENCES

Berman, B. (2002). Should your firm adopt a mass customization strategy? *Business Horizons, 45*(4), 51-60.

Caron, F., & Fiore, F. (1995). Engineer to order companies: How to integrate manufacturing and innovative processes. *International Journal of Project Management, 13*, 313-319.

Davis, S. (1989). From future perfect: Mass customizing. *Planning Review.*

Du, X., Jiao, J. & Tseng, M. M. (2000). Architecture of product family for mass customization. In *Proceedings of the 2000 IEEE International Conference on Management of Innovation and Technology.*

Ericsson, A., & Erixon, G. (1999). *Controlling design variants: Modular product platforms.* ASME Press.

Feitzinger, E., & Lee, H. (1997). Mass customization at Hewlett-Packard: The power of postponement. *Harvard Business Review, 75*(1), 116-121.

Felfernig, A., Friedrich, G., & Jannach, D. (2001). Conceptual modeling for configuration of mass-customizable products. *Artificial Intelligence in Engineering, 15*, 165-176.

Forza, C., & Salvador, F. (2002). Managing for variety in the order acquisition and fulfilment process: The contribution of product configuration systems. *International Journal of Production Economics, 76*, 87-98.

Frutos, J. D., & Borenstein, D. (2004). A framework to support customer-company interaction in mass customization environments. *Computers in Industry, 54*, 115-135.

Gilmore, J., & Pine, J. (1997). The four faces of mass customization. *Harvard Business Review, 75*(1), 91-101.

Gunasekarana, A., & Ngai, E. (2005). Build-toorder supply chain management: A literature review and framework for development. *Journal of Operations Management, 6*, 223-451.

Hart, C. (1995). Mass customisation: Conceptual underpinnings opportunities and limits. *International Journal of Service Industry Management, 6*(2), 46-45.

Hicks, C., McGovern, T., & Earl, C. F. (2000). Supply chain management: A strategic issue in engineer to order manufacturing. *International Journal of Production Economics, 65*, 179-190.

Hsu, H. -M., & Wang, W. -P. (2004). Dynamic programming for delayed product differentiation. *European Journal of Operational Research, 156*, 183-193.

Hvam, L. (1994). *Anvendelse af produktmodellering, -set ud fra en arbejdsforberedelsessynsvinkel.* PhD thesis, Driftteknisk Institut, DTU.

Hvam, L. (1999). A procedure for building product models. *Robotics and Computer-Integrated Manufacturing, 15*, 77-87.

Hvam, L., Malis, M., Hansen, B., & Riis, J. (2004). Reengineering of the quotation process: Application of knowledge based systems. *Business Process Management Journal, 10*, 200-123.

Jiao, J., Tseng, M. M., Duffy, V. G., & Lin, F. (1998). Product family modeling for mass customization. *Computers & Industrial Engineering, 35*, 495-198.

Jørgensen, K. A. (2003). Information models representing product families. *Product Structuring Workshop, Technical University of Denmark,* January 23-24.

Jørgensen, K. A., & Petersen, T. D. (2005). Product modelling on multiple abstraction levels. In *Mass customization, concepts - Tools - Realization* (pp. 243-254).

Lampel, J., & Mintzberg, H. (1996). Customizing customization. *Sloan Management Review, 38*, 21-30.

Martin, M. V., & Ishii, K. (2002). Design for variety: Developing standardized and modularised product platform architectures. *Research in Engineering Design, 13*, 213-235.

Mikkola, J. H., & Gassmann, O. (2003). Managing modularity of product architectures: Toward an integrated theory. *IEEE Transactions on Engineering Management, 50*, 204-218.

Petersen, T. D., & Jørgensen, K. A. (2005). Product modelling for mass customisation in global ETO companies. In *Mass customization, concepts - Tools - Realization* (pp. 333-344).

Pine, B. J. (1993). *Mass customization: The new frontier in business competition.* Harvard Business School Press.

Pine, J., Victor, B., & Boyton, A. (1993). Making mass customization work. *Harvard Business Review, 71*(5), 108-119.

Reichwald, R., Piller, F. T., & Möslein, K. (2000). Information as a critical success factor or: Why even a customized shoe not always fits. In *Proceedings Administrative Sciences Association of Canada, International Federation of Scholarly Associations of Management 2000 Conference.*

Robertson, D., & Ulrich, K. (1998). Planning for product platforms. *Innovation Driving Product, Process, and Market Change. MIT Sloan Management Review, 39*(4), 19-31.

Silveira, G. D., Borenstein, D., & Fogliatto, F. S. (2001). Mass customization: Literature review and research directions. *International Journal of Production Economics, 72*, 1-13.

Steger-Jensen, K., & Svensson, C. (2003). Issues of mass customisation and supporting IT-solutions. *Computers in Industry, 54*, 83-103.

Toffler, A. (1970). *Future shock.* Bantam.

Tseng, M. M., & Jiao, J. (1996). Design for mass customization. *Annals of the CIRP, 45*(1), 153-156.

Ulrich, K. T., & Eppinger, S. D. (2000). *Product design and development.* McGraw Hill.

Chapter IV
Open Variant Process Models in Supply Chains

Corinna Engelhardt-Nowitzki
University of Leoben, Austria

Helmut Zsifkovits
University of Leoben, Austria

ABSTRACT

The following chapter will elaborate on complexity in supply chains and the implications on supply chain design. It investigates the specific requirements of supply chain processes in terms of flexibility versus standardization, evaluating the feasibility of designing, customizing, assessing, and improving logistics processes within a framework provided by process reference models. Mass customization and, in particular, the configuration approach developed by Winter for financial services will be discussed for their applicability for reducing complexity in a process environment. Process reference frameworks will be used as elements of an "open variant process model". The Supply Chain Operations Reference (SCOR) model defined by the Supply Chain Council as the major cross-industry standard for supply chain management will be discussed for its usefulness and shortcomings in "process mass customization", with a focus on systems implementation.

INTRODUCTION

As a consequence of increasing market volatility and globalization, most companies are facing a rising complexity within their supply chain regarding the supplier and the customer interface as well as their internal procedures. In addition to that, demand individualization at the customer side and shortened market cycles enabled through the latest technological achievements are causing the necessity to not only manage a higher amount of complexity but also to handle upcoming matters within shortening schedule frames, while still providing a high reliability. With the logistics focus moving from micro-level optimization to integrated supply chains and supply chain communities, the difficulty in coordinating the logistics activities within and among firms is expected to increase, with the number of network nodes and interfaces growing as well. Axelrod and Cohen (2000, p. 26) expect: *"systems to exhibit increasingly complex dynamics when changes occur that intensify interactions among the elements"*. Christopher (1998) describes customer service explosion, time compression, globalization of industry, and organizational integration as the major factors in the changing logistics environment and notes that: *"the complexity of the logistics task appears to be increasing exponentially"* (p. 54). A recent study on the factors traditionally influencing supply chain performance by the European Logistics Association / A.T. Kearney Management Consultants (2004) finds dramatic changes driving the complexity of all supply chain activities. The complexity drivers identified are lead time, requirements on delivery reliability, internationality of business partners, product life cycles, and number of stock-keeping units (SKUs).

Being embedded in such a dynamic and complex supply network or, as Adam and Johannwille (1998) are stating it, being caught in the "complexity trap" and as a consequence experiencing disproportionately-increased cost per unit, a company has to meet contradicting targets: a sufficient ability to perform a manifold range of products and services on a high quality and reliability level, in other words, a satisfying stability towards unforeseen changes, failures, and risks, and at the same time an appropriate sensitivity and situation-related flexibility towards individual customer requirements. In order to achieve an adequate balance between the mentioned performance abilities at acceptable economic conditions (effort, cost, return, etc.), implementing mass customization in existing mass or serial production is still a major challenge. Products, services, production organization, and logistics systems typically have evolved individually, often induced by specific customer requirements, creating a high degree of variability and complexity not only re-

garding the product itself, but often also inducing sophisticated procedures for either the company-internal value creation or the services that are accompanying a product. Although theoretical approaches are available (for example, Blecker, Friedrich, Kaluza, Abdelkafi, and Kreutler (2005) have developed a: "comprehensive framework encompassing the main conditions for achieving mass customization" (p. 40) based on an elaborate literature review), the implementation of the mass customization concept in practice still is a major challenge for a high amount of companies.

This chapter discusses the role of complexity in supply chains with increasingly individualized products and services and the conflict between standardization and flexibility requirements. The mass customization paradigm is applied to processes and analyzed for its implications on information systems and interface design. Process reference models and standards are assessed for their potential to reduce complexity and enable open process mass customization.

Furthermore, the authors investigate whether the Supply Chain Operations Reference model (SCOR) provides the functionality and features in terms of scope and modularity to support an "open variant process model", and whether it is flexible enough to build individual, customer-centered processes.

COMPLEXITY IN SUPPLY CHAINS

Supply chains typically consist of a complex network of business units and facilities that source raw materials, transform them into intermediate goods and then final products, and deliver the products to customers through various distribution channels. Technical development has, in many cases, enhanced product and process complexity, whereas price development has made many complex (and formerly expensive) products available also for the mass market far beyond individually-produced volumes. At the same time, current trends like outsourcing and globalization have led to an increased number of parties that are involved in the supply chain (Geimer, 2005 p. 38). Thus, logistics activities have to be coordinated across regional, cultural, and organizational boundaries; goods and information flows have to be managed in a collaborative manner.

Within the economic context, there are a number of systematization approaches trying to address the various manifestations of complexity which show a close coherence with demand individualization, such as:

- **Luczak and Fricker (1997, p. 313):** Consideration of structural and organizational issues in order to systematize complexity, especially taking into account the research work that has been done on synergetics, fractal theory, deterministic chaos theory, and self-organization; or Mainzer (1997) who identifies two complexity drivers: people and systems, further on referring to non-linearity as a *"necessary but not sufficient condition of chaos and self-organization"* (p. 282) and emphasizing on the *"algorithmic complexity"* (p. 283).

- **Kirchhof (2003, pp. 8-16):** Structural complexity (system elements and relations) and functional complexity (situational ability of a system to perform variation); also refer to Gell-Mann (1994) or Heylighen (1992, 1996), who emphasize cognition as a possible adaptation to growing complexity as an inherent principle of any evolutionary development, becoming manifest within the categories of structural and functional complexity.

- **Adam and Johannwille (1998, pp. 5-7, 24):** Complexity is caused by increased individualization and differentiation requirements, being categorized in target complexity, customer complexity, variant and coordination complexity.

- **Eversheim, Schenke, and Warnke (1998, pp. 31):** Product and production system complexity are causing "diseconomies of scope" to be reduced by "variant mode and effects analysis (VMEA)", a method that is mainly based on standardization and modularization. Regarding process management, the authors are recommending decentralized processes and segmentation concepts; (pp. 40, 42).

- **Wildemann (1998, p. 48):** External complexity drivers (customers and customer requirements, globalization, market dynamics, range of products, country specifications, demand fluctuation, supplier variety) and internal complexity drivers (organization and structure, information and communication issues, individual attitudes).

- **Bliss (2000, pp. 133-173):** Target conflict between the static potential of a company that enables an adequate reaction towards environmental changes but at the same time rises complexity. Dynamic complexity is looked at from an opposite perspective: The lower the possible number of alternatives, the less time is needed for adaptation, which leads to a better ability to survive. Bliss defines three complexity categories: the autonomous enterprise complexity (can be reduced without a direct influence on demand variety), the correlated enterprise complexity (weak interdependency with demand variety), and the perceived market complexity (directly connected with demand variety).

A profound discussion of further definitions of complexity can be found in Blecker et al. (2005). Although the majority of general complexity definitions and concepts are also feasible within a supply chain perspective, further systematization is necessary in order to gain deeper insights in the context of logistics. According to Nilsson and Waidringer (2002), *logistics complexity* can be defined as "transportation and logistics systems' complexity that resides in the nature of structure, dynamics, and adaptation. "It is a measure of the possibility of modeling theses properties and their interaction in a way that allows of implementation of control mechanisms, forcing the system under study to meet required service, cost, and environmental demands" (p. 115). Using this definition, they developed a logistics complexity framework in order to classify logistics management activities:

- **Structure:** Related to the infrastructure in the logistics context, covering physical as well as informational and communicational structures.
- **Dynamics:** Related to the processes performed on the supply network, that is, the flow of goods, information, and money within the process structure.
- **Adaptation:** Used to describe the management and control of the process structure and dynamics, that is, the organizational and the decision-making environment in order to realize the process on the network.

Following Bliss (2000, p. 206), who recommends to reduce complexity starting with the autonomous enterprise complexity first, exhausting the correlated enterprise complexity second, and dealing with the direct market complexity as a third step, the challenge is to rank supply chain-related complexity drivers analogue, using Nilsson and Waidringer's categories as a preceeding differentiator.

IMPLICATIONS ON SUPPLY CHAIN DESIGN AND SUPPLY CHAIN OPERATIONS

Structure-Related Complexity Drivers

Analyzing the structure-dimension, the typical supply chain complexity drivers are well known from process optimization approaches and from logistics theory. From the authors' point of view, the Nilsson and Waidringer approach has to be extended and further systematized into three concrete factors that are driving the structural supply chain complexity:

- **Input – "Inbound Flow":** This category includes the number of sourcing markets and regions, suppliers, parts ordered, services achieved, as well as the interdependencies between the mentioned elements and the number of variants to which each element can vary (e.g., the different colors or sizes that a sourced good might have or the individually-varying bundle of services which a company may order according to the situational requirements). This refers to the very first "inbound-interfaces"; that means the "entry points" of a supply network at the raw material level as well as to any other interface that is part of a supplier-customer relationship all over the chain between companies as well as within one company.
- **Process Steps and Activities:** Typically, this category regards the number of process steps, alternative process variants, people/

organizational units/companies/locations or other parties involved, types of involvement (decide, execute, consult, agree, be informed, …), technological devices (such as tools, machines), interfaces, IT systems, documents, and technologies. In addition to that, the connectivity and the number of possible or allowed variants are also increasing the structural supply chain complexity in this category.

- **Output – "Outbound Flow":** This third category is looking at the assortment of goods, the number of markets and regions, customer groups and customers, products sold, deliveries fulfilled, services performed, as well as (again) the interdependencies and the rising number of variants. In analogy to the input aspect, this category covers not only the "outbound interfaces" towards the end-customer or end-user, but also any "outbound-interface" within the supply network.

Apart from process structure and supply chain configuration, Geimer (2005, p. 42) identifies one more driver for supply chain complexity: the supporting management processes and IT systems that are often not harmonized well according to the workflow logic. The typical consequence is decreasing delivery reliability and rising costs.

Looking at the structure dimension, the challenge for a company consists of two issues: The first is to sort out which of the aforementioned issues belongs to which category – autonomous, correlated, or direct complexity. As a second step, as many issues as possible should be moved towards a weaker (or ideally towards none) correlation to the perceived market complexity in order to establish the majority of supply chain factors as independent as possible from the market-driven complexity. As it will be shown below, process reference models comprise a major leverage in this context.

Complexity Drivers Related to Supply Chain Dynamics

The perspective of the dynamic supply chain complexity is partly influenced by the setup provided by the supply chain structure during the preliminary supply chain design phase: For example, will a process structure that shows a lot of process alternatives, decision points, and loops with a high probability cause a complex dynamic process flow? This effect is even stronger if a production order is using the same equipment several times during the manufacturing process, as it is the case, for example, in the semiconductor business (as well as in many other high-technology fields) that is producing up to a hundred and more process steps running through ten or less work centers. In this type of environment, production planning has to pay respect not only to the originally-started volume of production lots, but also to a high amount of interdependencies between the lots caused by the loops to be planned on each work center several times during the production process. Other dynamic process flow performance indicators, such as customer service level and flexibility, are downgraded as well by an ineligible process structure (Geimer, 2005, pp. 38-40), herewith also impairing the adaptiveness of an enterprise.

Furthermore, there are many typical complexity drivers related to process flow dynamics that are at least partly independent from the process structure, therefore being an element of either the autonomous or the correlated enterprise complexity. They can be allocated to the same categories as the structural topics that were introduced above:

- **Input – "Inbound Flow":** This category regards the incoming flow of either goods, information, or services, looking at two main parameters: the volume of incoming pieces and the synchronization of the flow according to the requirements of the following process step. At first, incoming volume has to be adequate in comparison to the possible throughput of the process step, resulting into an acceptable utilization (high enough to be cost efficient, but still low enough to not drive cycle time and work in progress to unwanted amounts). At second, the inbound flow should be as least varying as possible to avoid process disturbances with lot sizes that are cost efficient on the one hand (transportation and delivery cost), and well-synchronized with the throughput rate (just in time/just in sequence, adequate bundles) on the other hand. Typical key performance indicators to be looked at in depth are bundle size and the average time (including the variance) between two deliveries. A further focus should be laid on the complexity of the delivery model: One example is a Kanban cycle or a vendor-managed inventory model which is much less complex regarding forecasting, order processing, and monitoring compared to single-order processing.

- **Process Steps and Activities:** During process execution, the typical aspects to be analyzed from the dynamic perspective are lot size, lot prioritization policies, machine allocation options, throughput, maintenance and setup time-volume and -cycles, yield and rework rates, and shift models. As described already while discussing the structural supply chain complexity category, the complexity is rising with the number of items, the number of interdependencies between single parameters, and the possible variants.
- **Output – "Outbound Flow":** Unless placed directly beneath the current working center after processing and therefore resulting into handling and storage activities, the outbound flow in most cases is not directly influencing the current process step, but does influence the following step: In other words, whatever piece or order is delivered to the following

process step is part of the related incoming flow, therefore, and influences the inbound dynamics as described above.

In addition to the listed items, Blecker et al. (2005, pp. 51-62) have identified mass customization complexity triggers, coming up with a balance between factors that are reducing complexity and factors that are inducing complexity (p. 60). The complexity increasing factors, the "proliferation of product variety" and the "use of flexible manufacturing systems" (p. 60), are related to the supply chain structure, but are as well causing a rising dynamic flow complexity. Blecker et al. explicitly mention planning and scheduling complexity, and other logistics issues which cannot be avoided even with the most precise scheduling procedure, like dynamic process fluctuations, for example, measured on the coefficient of variation (COV) of time periods between lot deliveries or the COV of machine setup and availability timeslots. Apart from the necessity to manage an increased degree of complexity, a company is therefore facing a reduced ability to utilize production equipment and human resources, resulting in higher costs per unit (Engelhardt, 2000, p. 74). In addition to that, traditional PPS systems are focusing on capacity utilization rather than a constant material flow (Westphal, 2000, p. 13), taking into account disadvantageous flow fluctuations.

The above discussion on dynamic supply chain topics shows a variety of phenomena that can be handled separately, but still from a holistic point of view, with logistics best-practice approaches such as the logistics management navigator (Jahns, Gäde, & Langenhan, 2004, p. 367). A quantitative, more accurate approach is the application of formal operations research methods such as queuing models in conjunction with simulation tools and algebraic optimization algorithms (see e.g., Hopp & Spearman, 1996), having the disadvantage of strict modeling prerequisites and normally-huge computation effort.

Applying the scheme that Bliss (2000) has proposed also on the dynamic process flow dimension, a company initially has to identify the appropriate category that an issue belongs to—autonomous, correlated, or direct complexity. Subsequently, a weaker (if possible, none) correlation to the perceived market complexity should be the aim. Again, process reference models are a promising enabler that can provide advantages in this process (see below).

Interdependencies between Adaptation Ability and Supply Chain Complexity

Having spoken about structural and dynamic supply chain complexity, the last aspect to be discussed, according to Nilsson and Waidringer (2002), is adaptation. This first refers to the adaptation requirements that are induced by the market and environmental factors (the "external complexity drivers", see Wildemann, 1998, p. 48). The higher volatility and uncertainty, the more globally-distributed and the higher-connected with each other the market-induced influences are, the better a company has to develop its adaptation abilities. Especially in the context of mass customization, a high product diversity (and therefore complexity) is an essential element of the product strategy rather than an unwanted source of turbulences. Similar considerations are to be undertaken concerning internal complexity drivers, such as capacity flexibility (e.g., applying flexible shift models or employment contracts), planning flexibility, and other topics. Apart from that, future expectations are that improved IT abilities will most probably intensify supply chain integration, leading to a networked supply chain, herewith causing an even higher complexity (Chen & Paulraj, 2004, p. 131). Following Bliss (2000), the challenge does not primarily lie in a lower complexity but in the skill of a company to keep internal issues, preferably such as processes, hierarchical organization, and IT system structure,

as independent from external complexity drivers as possible.

According to a number of authors (refer, e.g., to Bliss, 2000; Liening, 1999; Malik, 2000), constraints are often induced by lacks within current management thinking and paradigms. For example, one common, although not always valid, assumption is that there is a clear correlation between adaptability and complexity. A strong empiric evidence for this phenomenon can be found, for example, in the automotive sector: Customers are demanding automobiles exactly configured to their requests within fast-changing fashion and technology trends. Whereas European manufactures are experiencing a high adaptation restraint that leads into exaggerated complexity, the Japanese manufacturers are able to cope with the given requirements without having to face similarly strong effects (Schlott, 2005).

Additional Supply Chain Inherent Complexity Drivers

As further analysis shows, within the context of supply chain management, Nilsson and Waidringer's considerations have to be extended by three further categories of complexity drivers:

- **"Interface-Induced Complexity":** Each interface within the supply chain, inter-company-related and intra-company-related, is increasing the supply chain complexity; therefore, one approach is to reduce the number of interfaces as far as possible during structural process optimization. The remaining interfaces are still relevant complexity drivers. Therefore, the "interface design" (parties involved, parts, documents, ... to be handed over, forms to be used, supporting IT systems, number of transactions per time...) has to be "designed for low complexity". Approaches herein are, for example, delivery model standardization, IT interface standardization and harmonization, long-term contracts with simple transaction steering routines, and similar.

- **"Consecutive Complexity":** Even if an aspect is not driving complexity itself, it may cause a higher complexity in related fields. This is typically the case if, for example, a company decides to enlarge the product assortment by selling accessories or accompanying services ("consecutive product complexity") or if a process is requiring complex maintenance, control, or support procedures ("consecutive process complexity"). Another source of consecutive complexity is the IT system design ("consecutive IT system complexity"). This effect typically occurs if one sector of the supply chain is simplified and automated by, for example, a workflow system, therewith causing higher complexity at its interfaces or within related processes. Being aware of this effect, a company should not only undertake Total Cost of Ownership considerations, but in analogy to that also establish a consequent "Total Complexity of Ownership" attitude in order to avoid "consecutive complexity" as far as possible. For example, one could think of a service strategy that is not enhancing but lowering product communication. In a concrete case, a product could be delivered to the point of sales in a limited amount of variants (reducing supply chain complexity as a postponement approach would do). A local service provider could then customize the product for each individual order, thereby providing an utmost customer orientation without consequences for supply chain complexity.
- **"Make-or-Buy-Driven Complexity":** A second aspect that is often not taken into consideration with enough care is the complexity resulting out of a make-or-buy decision. Whereas an outsourcing decision is reducing complexity within the company's own processes (regarding structure, dynamics, and

adaptation), it may induce new complexity at the supplier or service provider interface that either has not been thought of at all or that has been underestimated during the decision process. As another consequence, "consecutive complexity" effects may arise that have not been analyzed before.

For all mentioned topics, these principles apply, according to Bliss (2000): The less dependent on direct market complexity they can be configured, the less relevant is the trade-off between complexity reduction and individualization demands.

As shown above, one major source of improvement that is not yet fully exploited in many enterprises is the establishment of concepts increasing the ability to adapt while simultaneously lowering or at least not endangering or even stabilizing complexity. One example is a complexity-reducing process standardization in the human resource area not at all related to the contract contents or which is a high part of product diversity not necessarily enhancing complexity; a reduction of delivery models to a few simple standard types according to part specifications may even reduce complexity without any influence on part variety at all. For example, a highly sophisticated product structure is not necessarily demanding complex management, support, or control procedures. According to situational conditions, any company could continue to, furthermore, look for similar scenarios, herewith resolving the prior presumed positive correlation between adaptability, flexibility, and complexity. Another often assumed but not necessarily compulsive antithesis to be analyzed in the following paragraphs is the correlation between product complexity and supply chain complexity.

Summarizing the considerations on supply chain complexity that have been discussed so far, it can be said that mass customization may, but is not necessarily causing a high supply chain complexity (refer also to the framework provided by Blecker et al., 2005, p. 60 that comes to a similar conclusion). Conversely, a company has to systematically analyze the different complexity causes according to the concrete situation and to implement strategies that are reducing supply chain complexity without at the same time resulting in a limited ability to mass-customize products and services. The following sections, therefore, will concentrate on the question how to successfully use process reference models for that intention.

Reducing Complexity through the Application of Process Reference Models

Complexity reduction approaches are typically based on the application of *system theory* principles (normally referring to early publications like Ashby, 1960, 1961; Beer, 1959, 1966, 1972; Ulrich, 1968) and consequently implemented into approaches within the context of complexity reduction (see, e.g., Bliss, 2000; Kirchhoff, 2003; Ulrich & Probst, 1995) or mass customization (see, e.g., Blecker & Friedrich, 2005; Piller, 2003; Pine, 1993, Pine & Gillmore, 1999) as well as the supply chain design and optimization methods that have already widely proven their applicability also in the practical context. Basic principles that can also be transferred to process reference models are mainly the following:

- **Black Box Principle (see, e.g., Ulrich, 1968, pp. 132) and Modularity (see, e.g., Ulrich & Eppinger, 1995):** The target is to divide a complex issue into smaller units (projects, phases, layers, work packages, activities, etc.) that are fulfilling two conditions: They must have as few interfaces as possible, and the interfaces shall be simple and well-defined. If the inner part of a black box is encapsulated well, the surrounding modules do not need and, most of the time, are not even allowed to look inside, herewith strongly reducing complexity. If a black box, for example, a

software procedure or a sub-process can be reused many times by several applications, the complexity of the whole system is even driven further down. A lot of practical concepts are relying on that principle, for example, in logistics or informatics: Based on the black box principle, modularization concepts are structuring, for example, projects into phases, processes into sub-process-level with growing granularity, IT architectures into layers, software-products into modules, products into part-bundles, or service offers into individually-configurable service packages. Segmentation approaches simplify business processes. Platform concepts are supporting lean product structures or service packages. Reference models are used within informatics to reduce system and software engineering effort (enterprise reference models, application data models) as well within supply chain design and optimization in order to achieve lean and well-performing processes with stable and efficient interfaces. A process reference model is typically designed with a modular structure (e.g., SCOR - see Supply Chain Council, 2005), providing a construction kit of standardized process modules that can be combined according to concrete supply chain requirements.

- **Feedback Principle and Elasticity Analysis (see, e.g., Malik, 1996, pp. 383-389):** Processes or interfaces that are designed according to the feedback principle are much simpler and much less difficult to steer in comparison to those who are not using feedback mechanisms. The elasticity of a system towards impulses (wanted interventions or not appreciated disturbances) is often not only relying on the system element characteristics but also on the impact of a feedback loop. Within the supply chain, this should not only be applied on interface design (e.g., using models such as self-steering Kanban cycles), but also should be consequently integrated into a leadership approach based on management by objectives/management by exception and performance measurement systems that are based on a sensitivity analysis. This is to ensure that not only the supply chain can be steered with a minimum of complexity, but also that the impact of management interventions will be adequately predicted during the decision-taking process. Again a process reference model can support supply chain design a lot, although the process logic is not completely elaborated for most models (e.g., SCOR - see Supply Chain Council, 2005). In order to fully exploit the effectiveness potentials of a process reference-based approach, the used models, if necessary, have to be extended to the specific needs of an industry sector or a concrete company: Not only process modules (structure) but also steering logics and related key performance indicators (dynamics) have to be complemented and customized to requirements.

Informatics and logistics have developed a number of methods that should be further analyzed in upcoming research projects as a potential source of supply chain complexity reduction in an environment that requires a high flexibility, adaptability, and product or service variety. To mention just a few examples from the fields of informatics and logistics:

Informatics:
- Layer models are adding virtual layers to separate the physical view from the logical view of a database or network architecture using standard communication procedures and protocols. Process management and, consecutively also, process reference models can gain huge benefits from the application of such concepts, although this analogy has not yet reached the maturity of a common standard.
⇒ The definition of layers within the process flow in order to manage complexity is a promising approach that is currently in the development process for specific industry applications (e.g., in the automotive sector, the concept of a modular order management that introduces a virtual layer to material flow concepts in order to reduce complexity; see Winkler, 2005).

- Normalization procedures within data warehouse data modeling schemes are designing redundancies to a best possible compromise between performance and data consistency according to individual application requirements in a multi-dimensional environment. ⇒ Workflow-related IT systems have to be able to flexibly represent complex multi-dimensional tasks, herewith combining heterogeneous OLTP sources into an OLAP-based architecture; an overview of current business intelligence applications can be found in Kühner (2005, Appendix A).

- Object-oriented programming methods are applying principles such as encapsulation, information hiding, complex and individual data type and function design, inheritance mechanisms, and others. ⇒ Innovative process reference models will be tailored to these principles and will therefore take the chance to share their inherent advantages (Kirchhoff, 2003, pp. 113), for example, the Supply Chain Council has announced an object-oriented SCOR model version 8.0 (BPT, 2005).

- Latest cognition on customer-oriented interaction systems that enclose an advisory component enables a company to establish IT systems that are able to handle "complexity faced by customers during the interaction process" (Blecker et al., 2005, p. 113). This approach may be extended further by the use of multi-agent systems in order to deal with complexity that is induced within the business processes of a company (pp. 117). Blecker et al. are proposing to assign autonomous rational agents to product module variants for the purpose of variety steering (p. 146). ⇒ From a current point of view, it is not yet possible to predict accurately, to what extent the described concept can be applied on process reference models as well with the intention to steer process variety. Looking at the number of process variants a company might have to face, for example, when customizing the SCOR model to its operations (Level 4 can include up to a four-digit number of sub-processes if applied on major enterprises; for a practical example, refer, for example, to SIEMENS, 2003), it is at least supposable that a need for computational process variety steering will arise.

Logistics:

- Segmentation concepts that are currently mainly used in the manufacturing context could be brought into a wider application. In the context of "variety-engineering" (Beer, 1985, p. 26), Westphal (2000, p. 23) differentiates measures that reduce the need for coordination from measures that meet the need for coordination. He mentions segmentation as an approach that reduces complexity by lessening the number of relations, although his considerations are confined to the material flow and production logistics. ⇒ Process reference models have to provide clearly-defined modules and to packetize them into a suitable construction kit which enables and supports the application of segmentation principles to all kinds of processes (according to process characteristics and environmental conditions).

- According to Zhang and Huang (2005, p. 457) "platform product development is one of the most important means of realizing the mass customization (..) strategy". Platform concepts

that are currently mainly applied to product design could be also applied to processes. ⇒ Process reference models consist of standardized modules that are connected to each other in a hierarchical order (in the case of SCOR, implemented as a three-level concept, Supply Chain Council, 2005), therefore first providing an excellent process configuration platform, and second offering a distinct feasibility for roll-up and drill-down according to situational requirements.

- The postponement principle that has mainly been implemented into manufacturing processes could be used in management, support, and administration processes with a much higher consequence (for a example that systematically applies process postponement, refer to Brown, Lee, & Petrakian, 2000). ⇒ Process reference models should be purposely designed for a late generation of process variants.

- Quick response concepts should be applied not only towards the end customer, but all over the whole supply chain, putting a special emphasis on the critical path. ⇒ This induces the claim to implement a strong process- and interface-steering logic in a process reference model (e.g., applying just-in-time or Kanban principles).

A summarizing reflection of the discussion of complexity within the supply chain and complexity reduction potential through the application of process reference models points out two major issues: At first, existing and well-known approaches of several disciplines should be developed further and implemented with much more consequence within complexity management projects. Above, some approaches have been shown how process reference models could possibly contribute to this claim. The widely-found beliefs such as "product complexity is raising supply chain complexity" or "individualization and customer-orientation are demanding a higher amount of complexity compared to standardized assortments" should be carefully analyzed and tested for their validity and applicability, for example, through the differentiation of autonomous, correlated, and direct complexity that has been proposed by Bliss (2000).

IMPLEMENTATION OF MASS CUSTOMIZATION WITHOUT INCREASING SUPPLY CHAIN COMPLEXITY

Taking a closer look on the subject of mass customization (for details regarding the mass customization concept, see, e.g., Blecker & Friedrich, 2005; Piller, 2003; Pine, 1993), one will find several well-known aspects from former mass production concepts that are still providing valid principles and strategies for uncertain market environments, although the majority of mass production cases that have successfully raised efficiency was based on a stable business environment, mainly exploiting economies of scale provided by, for example, advanced technological possibilities (automation, flexible manufacturing systems), changed working principles (flow orientation, vertical integration, synchronization of factors of production), or productivity enhancement (lean production, reduction of cost per piece, asset and cycle time reduction). What a company, therefore, has to achieve is first to still and at the best utilize potentials resulting from a high production volume within a changed environment that today is less (or not at all) predictable. The second challenge within a saturated market, which is forcing a company to explore heterogeneous market niches, is to additionally exploit potentials resulting from economies of scope. Pine (1993) mentions the following key success factors that are supporting a firm to achieve a customer-oriented variety, flexibility, and celerity within their supply chain activities:

- Huge capacity flexibility (employees, machines, etc.): Process reference models facilitate capacity and resource management through standardized module specifications and key performance indicators; therefore, process standardization is raising the flexibility and the ability to adapt to a changed environment;

- Fast development and product life cycles: Based on standardized process modules, it is much easier to redesign parts of the supply chain, if product or technology changes are desiring other process types;

- Highly-adaptive products (if possible, by using stable processes, and/or by using a low amount of processes for a high number of product variants): Best possible independency between products or services and business processes;

- Independence of products and the flow of goods: This claim corresponds with Bliss (2000) and his three complexity categories (autonomous, correlated, and direct);

- Distinctive flexibility (provided through concepts such as just-in-time, setup time, and tooling time reduction, cycle-time-decrease, order-related manufacturing, small lot sizes, sales-encouraging services): Supported by process reference models that gain benefits from a disciplined module design that consistently applies the black box principle, herewith enabling a flexible supply chain adaptation (respectively re-design).

Furthermore, the mass customization concept tries to compensate fast-changing and heterogeneous customer demands by inducing broadly-varying and fast (eventually fashion-related) product and service alternations in order to meet uncertain and volatile expectations with a better hit rate. The higher the degree of independency between processes and product range, the easier this claim can be reached. For the remaining correlations, the process reference model approach at least opens up a high ability to adapt.

Many authors and publications are hypothesizing that diversity is, at any rate, causing high process complexity. Empiric evidence might initially suggest this assumption, but is this a compulsive correlation? The aspects discussed so far have provided some answer proposals to the main question of how to accomplish two at-first-sight dichotomous alignments: mass production advantages, on the one hand, but instability and diversity on the other hand, therefore purposely raising product and service complexity.

AN OPEN VARIANT PROCESS CONFIGURATION APPROACH

Winter (2003) proposes two approaches to individualization in a financial services context. The *product-oriented approach* adopts configuration methods from mechanical engineering, using an open variant product model. The *process-oriented approach* should be based on an in-depth analysis of consumer processes and integrates corporations with complementary core competencies to form a value-added network. According to Winter's considerations, product variant design should rely on a model-based configuration that regards the product structure itself as the underlying data structure that should be easily adaptable due to the consequent use of parametric variant descriptions. Process configuration is discussed from the consumer's perspective as well as from the provider's perspective and is kept essentially open towards the product or service to be delivered and the configuration of the point of sales.

Concerning the product design, Winter's open variant product configuration proposal could most probably be directly applied in the context of service providing: A company would have to define several product types, to allocate a domain of corresponding attributes (e.g., the attribute

"content" or "duration" or "location" related to a product type "seminar") and to establish rules regarding which attribute values could be combined by the customer when tailoring the service package to individual requirements. In the context of physical goods, the open variant product configuration could be applied in an analogous manner, although in some cases manufacturing-related requirements might set technical limits to the amount of attribute combinations.

Winter is furthermore proposing an *open process configuration* from the consumer's point of view as well as from the provider's point of view, although not taking a closer look at the question of how an open process configuration could be achieved. If one intends to work that idea further out in detail there has to be one initial postulation: Taking into account the implications from the first section of this chapter on complexity, product design and product variant building has to be made independent from the underlying processes in the best possible way. In most cases, this is not a problem regarding management, support, and controlling processes, but might be a challenge for the manufacturing or delivery processes. The better this independence can be realized, the less supply chain complexity will be induced from a high amount of product variants. A second initial requirement concerns the data structures: Workflow data and product data have to be designed within separate dimensions of the data model and have to be kept independent to each other as well; changes within the product data may not cause the need to modify workflow-related data and vice versa. Even if changes within the product data are inducing the necessity to change related algorithms, object-oriented approaches (and other techniques) could limit the modification necessity to the involved entities without touching other procedures and modules as far as possible.

Assuming that both presumptions are fulfilled, the implementation of an open variant process configuration could be realized using process reference models.

PROCESS REFERENCE MODELS AND FRAMEWORKS

Reference models in general are frameworks which describe relevant relationships among the elements of a system. Sheffi (2005, pp. 187-193) proposes common processes for more resilient enterprises, with the modules and interfaces of a system described in a consistent manner. Standardization creates interchangeability, which in turn creates flexibility to respond to disruptions.

Process reference models define standard sets of business processes on different levels of abstraction, a framework of relationships among the standard processes and standard metrics to measure process performance. Reference models help to describe and communicate processes unambiguously, tune them to a specific purpose, measure and control process performance, and implement processes more efficiently. The use of reference models can speed up the development and documentation of business processes for implementation of applications like ERP systems.

Becker (1999, p. 150) lists four applications of reference models in retail: checking applications against reference models for consistency and completeness, developing custom software based on reference models, selecting and comparing COTS applications, and developing software component strategies. This list is entirely focused on software development and implementation, and neglects other applications outside the information systems domain.

The building-block approach used in process reference models opens the possibility to select the appropriate processes and integrate them into a way that best fits the specific organization or supply chain. The process maps built from reference models can be as-is or would-be configurations, describing either the present state of operations or the intended state. Thus, reference models can assist in reengineering current business processes.

Sometimes, reference models also integrate advanced concepts, like best practices, benchmarking, process measurement, and business process reengineering.

The origins and purposes of process reference models are manifold. One or more of the following categories in the table apply to most of the frameworks (adapted from Sheard, 1997). Examples are given for each of the categories.

Table 1. Sources of process reference models (Adapted according to Sheard, 1997)

Source	Example
1. Standards and Guidelines	ISO 9000 series SCOR ECR Processes International Benchmarking Clearinghouse Process Classification Framework Lean Enterprise Manufacturing Model Project Management Process Reference Model
2. Process Improvement Models	CMM relatives
3. Assessment Standards and Internal Appraisal Methods	ISO/IEC 15504 / SPICE ITIL
4. Quality Awards	Malcolm Baldrige National Quality Award Deming Award European Quality Award
5. Software Engineering Life Cycle Models	ISO/IEC 12207 BASEL II Operational Risk Management Process Reference Model

Not all of them are focused on or even include supply chain processes, but the general structure of the frameworks can well serve as a guideline for implementing other types of processes.

Standards and Guidelines

Standards and guidelines are typically used as recommendations in a contractual situation; in general, they can be customized or adapted by both parties. Relevant frameworks include international standards, such as the *ISO 9000 series* for Quality Management, and also commercial and military standards.

In addition, there is a number of frameworks that are not formal standards but rather models developed by industry consortia, such as the *Supply Chain Operations Reference model* (Supply Chain Council, 2005) and the processes defined by the *efficient consumer response* (ECR) initiative, a joint trade and industry body, launched in 1994 to make the grocery and fast-moving consumer goods sector more responsive to consumer demand and to better integrate retailers, wholesalers, manufacturers, suppliers, brokers, and third-party service providers in the supply chain (ECR Europe, 2005).

The *International Benchmarking Clearinghouse Process Classification framework* was developed by APQC, the American Productivity and Quality Center (2005) and by Arthur Andersen. It has about 280 activities. These activities are all cross-referenced to sub-activities of "produce as a business" or its specializations. The Process Classification Framework is a benchmarking tool that allows organizations to measure their activities in an industry-neutral paradigm.

The *Lean Enterprise Manufacturing Model* has a structure of "enabling practices" which help to promote lean processes. It was developed by the Lean Aircraft Initiative consortium led by MIT (Massachusetts Institute of Technology, 2005).

The *Project Management Process Reference model* is based on standards that are approved and licensed by the Project Management Institute, the leading not-for-profit project management professional association with more than 100,000 members worldwide. The tool is a model of the Project Management Body of Knowledge (Project Management Institute, 2005).

We do not include technology standards for collaboration, like CPFR (Continuous Planning Forecasting and Replenishment), ECR (Efficient Consumer Response) or RosettaNet in this context. It has to be noted, though, that they include definitions of processes. A discussion of collaboration technology standards can be found in Ireland (2005).

Process Improvement Models

Process improvement models define the characteristics of good processes; their purpose is to establish a roadmap from an "As-Is" to a "To-Be" scenario. These models include the *Capability Maturity Model* for Software (also known as the CMM and SW-CMM) as a model used by many organizations to identify best practices useful in helping them increase the maturity of their software processes (Carnegie-Mellon Software Engineering Institute, 2005).

The CMM relatives address the software development organization within an enterprise. There are sub-models that apply to an acquisition agency, to organization building systems, and to the product development enterprise, including such groups as marketing, manufacturing, business management, and development organizations.

Assessment Standards and Internal Appraisal Methods

In general, as a first step that an organization performs in a process improvement initiative is an appraisal. Standards and guidelines for assessments are frequently part of other frameworks, like quality management and process improvement.

The *ISO/IEC 15504 standard* (Software Quality Institute, 2005) defines a general framework for process assessment and improvement, containing a process reference model, a process assessment model, and a measurement framework. Although designed for software process assessment, the generic framework can be easily adapted to other areas of application. ISO/IEC 15504 includes a model for process management that was developed in the *SPICE* (Software Process Improvement and Capability dEtermination, 2005) project, an ancillary effort staffed primarily by volunteers from around the world, to document the set of practices fundamental to good software engineering. The model contained in the standard describes processes in five categories (Customer-Supplier, Engineering, Project, Support, and Organization category processes) in terms of base practices, which are its unique software engineering or management activities. The model is based on a three-tier hierarchy of process categories, processes, and base practices. The process model is specific to software engineering, but can be easily adapted to other industries or areas of application.

ITIL (Information Technology Infrastructure Library) is essentially a representation of best practice for IT service management and comprises a series of books which provide guidance on the quality provision of IT-related services. It is now a very widely practiced discipline. Within this arena, the British Standard BS 15000 is the first standard for service management. Its eight sections form the basis for the assessment of a managed IT service and are based upon the ITIL framework (ITIL, 2005).

Quality Awards

Quality awards were established by many national governments to improve businesses' focus on quality and customer satisfaction and to assess an organization's progress along a path to excellence. All these award programs require thorough analysis, documentation, and continuous improvement of business processes; the majority of programs also integrate a specific process framework. Quality awards include the American *Malcolm Baldrige National Quality Award* promoted by the National Institute of Standards and Technology (2005), the Japanese *Deming Award*, and the *European Quality Award* of the European Foundation for Quality Management (2005).

Figure 1. The SPICE process model (Software Quality Institute, 2005)

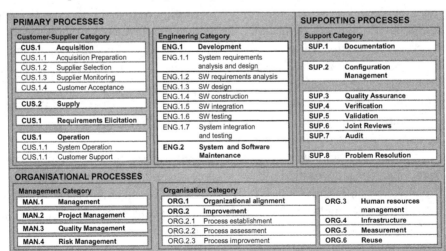

The quality award models are based on a weighted score of categories of performance criteria that can be used to assess management systems and identify major improvement areas. Process management is an important area in all the models, but the framework they provide is a generic one and does not define processes in detail. The "Business Excellence" model of the European Quality Award is split into five "enablers" (leadership, people management, policy and strategy, resources, and processes) and four "results" (people satisfaction, customer satisfaction, impact on society, and business results).

A further initiative to be mentioned is *ISO/CD 9004-8*, a draft standard on Quality Management Principles with categories identical to the seven categories of the Baldrige model (Sheard, 1997).

SOFTWARE ENGINEERING LIFE CYCLE MODELS

ISO/IEC 12207 is an international standard that succeeded and replaced the previous military standards in this field. ISO/IEC 12207 provides a process reference model in accordance with the requirements of ISO/IEC 15504, with definitions of processes described in terms of process purpose and outcomes, with an architecture describing relationships between the processes.

ISO/IEC 12207 is also the basis used for the *BASEL II Operational Risk Management Process Reference Model* (Commission de Surveillance du Secteur Financier, 2005), which has a focus on management processes which a bank can implement to manage the operational risks. The reference model is used to provide a common framework for different models and methods for bank process assessment, ensuring that the result of the assessment can be reported in a common context.

THE FEASIBILITY OF PROCESS REFERENCE FRAMEWORKS FOR OPEN VARIANT CONFIGURATION

The following section will evaluate the feasibility of designing, customizing, assessing, and improving logistics processes within a framework provided by process reference models, specifically the Supply Chain Operations Reference model (SCOR).

The Nature of SCOR

The Supply Chain Operations Reference (SCOR) model defined by the Supply Chain Council, an independent, not-for-profit corporation of more than 800 companies, is the major cross-industry standard for supply chain management (Supply Chain Council, 2005). The process reference model contains standard descriptions of supply chain management processes and integrates the concepts of business process reengineering, benchmarking, and process measurement. Processes are aligned to features and functionality, and can therefore be communicated and coordinated across companies and industries.

The process reference model contains standard descriptions of supply chain management processes and indicates how they are interrelated. Processes are aligned to features and functionality, and can therefore be communicated and coordinated across companies and industries. The first level of SCOR describes the process types in supply chains. The SOURCE – MAKE – DELIVER processes of the companies are linked for successive steps in a supply chain; in addition, there are PLAN and RETURN processes. The SCOR model is built on three levels, with each level refining the previous one and providing optional elements to select for specific configurations.

Levels 4 and below are implementation levels. Those are typically very individually designed for a specific organization or supply chain and therefore outside the scope of SCOR.

The SCOR framework also provides standard metrics to measure process performance and management practices that produce best-in-class performance. The process of measuring performance and using metrics as a benchmark for continuous improvement is one of the less developed features in SCOR, though. There have been a number of international benchmark studies (including Asia and Europe) which give a good overview of best-in-class performance.

Companies could save 10 - 15% of total logistics costs from properly aligning their logistics networks, as some estimates suggest (Hansen Harps, 2002). Optimizing production planning could save another 10 - 15%, and optimizing production scheduling could potentially cut an additional 10% in logistics costs. Optimizing transportation can save a company 10 - 40% in transportation costs.

Approaches to Reference Modeling

General requirements on reference models were defined by Fetter and Loos (2004, pp. 15-17) in the context of retail reference models. The criteria for model quality can be applied to any reference model, though.

- *Syntactics* refers to the modeling language applied to represent reference processes, functions, and structures. Modeling languages include rules and guidelines to improve formal correctness and consistency. For different levels of abstraction, different syntactic frameworks and perspectives are applied. A well-known example is Event-Driven Process Chain (EPC) which is often complemented by Value Chain Diagrams for high-level modeling. Entities represented in reference models can be data, functions, or processes.
- *Semantics* define the model contents, that is, the specific features of a certain enterprise or industry. The semantic quality depends on the adequacy, completeness, and consistency of the functions or processes included in the model. Fetter and Loos give a number of examples for retail models (pp. 17-20).
- *Pragmatics* refers to the model user and the mode of application intended by the user. Highly pragmatic quality criteria include clear language, adaptability, openness, and usability in general.

Applying this classification, SCOR can be described as follows: From a syntactic view, SCOR represents information objects and processes at different levels. The scope of the model (semantic view) is the supply chain as a whole, excluding the design and marketing processes in a value chain.

Figure 2. General requirements on reference models (Fetter & Loos, 2004)

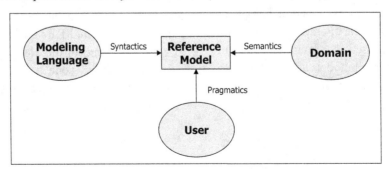

The focus is on process modeling, communication, and improvement rather than application design (pragmatic view).

Reference models differ in their way to partition the process domain according to different criteria (Kitson & Kitson, 1998). Various perspectives are valid and useful, depending on the utility for a specific purpose ("fitness for use").

One approach is to partition the process domain such that each sub-element can itself be regarded and treated as a process. This facilitates improvement initiatives by thinking in terms of increasing process capability. Processes can be treated more or less independently. This is the approach followed by the SCOR reference model.

A different approach is to partition the process domain such that each sub-element (Key Process Area) consists of a set of functionally-related capabilities which constitute a milestone on the evolutionary path to continuous process improvement. Thus, the users can think in terms of increasing process capability for organization.

An Open Variant Process Configuration Example

Winter describes the concept of open variants that underlies state-of-the-art standardized software packages (Winter, 2001). Product variants are specified by certain values for a set of attributes. He shows its applicability for financial services.

Figure 3. Open variant process model

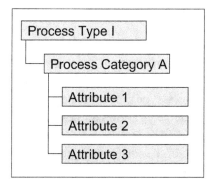

A similar approach could be used in designing processes, resulting in a three-level hierarchy. Like products, processes are composed of standardized building-blocks. In the SCOR Model, these are defined by the process type, process category, and process element hierarchy. In level 1, the general type of process (Plan, Source, Make, Deliver, Return) is selected. In level 2, specific categories of processes are defined (e.g., Deliver Retail Product). Level 3 is not linked with the SCOR process elements level, though. These are steps in a process that have to follow a logical order and cannot be combined in any order. The sequence is more or less stable, with only a few options from which to choose. Therefore, we introduced attributes at the third level which describe the process in more detail. Attributes could be:

- **Process functions** (referring to SCOR level 3 elements, with the possibility to opt out certain elements rather than making a real selection),
- **Process inputs** (documents, data elements),
- **Process outputs** (documents, data elements),
- **Roles** (process owner, sponsor, technical expert, etc.), and
- **Metrics** (these can again be derived from the SCOR set of metrics).

The following is a specific example of supply chain processes modeled in an open variant mode. From the SCOR set of Deliver processes, D2: Deliver Make-to-Order Product, and D4: Deliver Retail Product, are selected.

On the attribute level, the descriptive features of the process are defined. For D4, process functions are comprised of SCOR elements, that is, Generate Stocking Schedule, Receive Product at the Store, Pick Product from Backroom, Fill Shopping Cart, Checkout, and Deliver and/or Install.

Figure 4. Supply chain processes as open variants

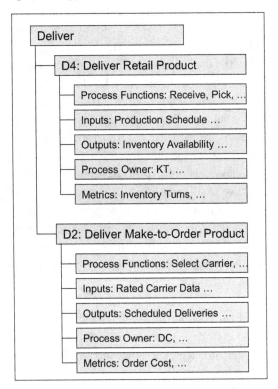

Process inputs include, among others, Scheduled Receipts, Inventory Availability, Production Schedule, and Finished Product Release. Obviously, not all the combinations are feasible or useful.

Piller (2003, p. 154) has discussed the advantage of establishing an individual customer interface: the establishment of "learning relationships". According to this concept, mass customization leads to a close customer contact that results into a permanent optimization process, driven by continuous communication and monitoring activities regarding required specifications of products, services, and delivery procedures. The better the underlying information flows and information systems, the better the herewith retrieved market-, customer-, or product-related information can be exploited for strategic, tactic, and operational planning purposes.

Summarizing, it can be said that mass customization is used as a "generic methodology to individualize products and services while preserving cost-efficient production processes" (Winter, 2001). What applies to products and services can also describe the nature of business processes. Customized processes are the product of experienced managers, skillful designers, and professional software engineers. Traditionally, customization and low cost of implementation have been mutually exclusive. Standard processes provided low cost but at the expense of uniformity. As for products and services, customer centricity and individualization are requirements on processes, too. As shown above, a systematic focus on complexity and its drivers and the consequent application of process reference models that obey the mentioned principles is a promising approach to reduce supply chain complexity in the best possible way without losing customer orientation, and to successfully operate the remaining diversity according to the requirements even within unstable market environments.

SCOR Potentials and Shortcomings in Open Variant Process Configuration

In the next section, the feasibility of process reference models in general and of SCOR in particular as a framework for designing open variant processes will be assessed. We defined a set of criteria, partly derived from the initial postulations, and partly derived from general requirements on mass customization environments.

- **Modular architecture of processes to enable management of process variety:** The simple structure with a three-level hierarchy of process types, process categories, and process elements allows for flexible configuration based on clearly-defined modules. This is one of the major strengths of the SCOR initiative.

- **Independence of product design from the underlying processes:** SCOR addresses all customer interactions, all physical material transactions, and all market interactions in a supply chain perspective. It does not describe business processes or activities in sales and marketing, product development, research and development, and some elements of post-delivery customer support. Most of the product-specific activities are excluded from the reference model. The processes described are independent from specific industries, products, and services.

- **Independence of product data and workflow-related data:** SCOR describes a comprehensive set of input and output information for the individual process elements. This is rather a collection of necessary data elements than a clear data structure. Moreover, there is no visible distinction between product data and workflow-related data. Thus, the requirement to create a consistent data model is not adequately addressed in SCOR, leaving this as an issue for implementation. Object-oriented approaches could ensure independence of product and process data, reducing the necessity of modifications in the process model in case of product changes.

- **Standard interfaces:** Interfaces have to be observed at multiple levels. The functional interaction between the modules, and also the informational relation in terms of input/output is clearly defined. The scheme by which the modules interact and communicate on a technical level is out of the scope of SCOR. This is an issue to handle on the implementation level.

- **Standard design rules:** The rules to which the modules conform are adequately defined in SCOR, with a clear definition of terminology, process attributes, and a consistent process structure. Modeling concrete

processes on an implementation level is outside the scope of SCOR. The modeling language used on level 3 does not seem to be adequate for requirements analysis and software design.

- **Normative nature of reference models:** In order to produce recommendations for process design, implementation, and improvement, SCOR uses a best-practice approach. Still, a major shortcoming is the description of management practices that produce best-in-class performance. SCOR fails to provide the link between metrics and best practices. There are intentions to improve this in future versions of the reference model.

- **Flexible automation of processes:** Modular process design is prerequisite for cost-effective, flexible workflow. Integration should supply fully-automated data transfer. Logistics optimization requires high quantities of data. Thus, SCOR is a suitable basis for process automation but does not provide any links to operational systems, like workflow applications or ERP systems.

In conclusion, it can be stated that SCOR is, while not an intricate model, sufficiently detailed to allow supply chain partners to communicate effectively. It also allows individuals and organizations to go to the level of detail they require. Every process element is, at the same time, supplier/customer to the preceding/consecutive process element.

The structure is clear and allows for future extensions. SCOR uses a pragmatic approach, and was obviously developed by experienced practitioners, making it a valuable tool for process documentation, design, and improvement. There are limitations in scope; the model does not define processes in sales and marketing, development, or post-delivery customer support. This is in line with the Supply Chain Council's mission to create a model for supply chains. There are efforts to develop reference models for certain industries in special-industry groups.

There are some shortcomings and restrictions in SCOR, though. It is not a universal tool that can be readily deployed in a given environment.

The system of metrics seems unstructured. Some are related to each other; some high-level metrics, like total logistics costs, have to be broken down by the user. Consequently, this limits comparability, and reduces the value of SCOR metrics in benchmarking. The hierarchy of metrics is not consistent, and not all the metrics used can be found in the glossary.

Some deficits and inconsistencies in SCOR process definitions make it difficult to standardize. A distinction of "mandatory" and "conditional" process elements would be helpful.

The methods of deploying the framework and implementing SCOR are not easily accessible. It takes learning to be able to apply the elements in a specific configuration, unless the expertise of external consultants is used.

SUPPLY CHAIN INDIVIDUALIZATION AND THE REQUIREMENTS ON INFORMATION SYSTEMS

Today, supply chain managers are confronted with customer-specific service level agreements, new interactive information technologies, the demand for high visibility, short response times and cycle times, and the requirements to provide interfaces between heterogeneous information systems. Thus, the feasibility and usefulness of standard processes and applications can be shortened by a lack in the ability of an IT system to adequately support material and information flow. The call for individual and, at the same time, flexible process flow enabling solutions becomes louder. One often-cited example for dynamic effects within a supply chain that is distributed among several

organizational units or even companies is the bullwhip effect (Chen, Drezner, Ryan, & Simchi-Levi, 1999; Forrester, 1961). Well-designed information flows and interfaces are playing an enormous role to avoid that problem: A fast and reliable vertical supply chain integration regarding forecast and planning data can help to lower or even reduce the bullwhip effect considerably. Other dynamic effects within the supply chain (e.g., regarding capacity balancing or lot allocation policies, to just mention some effects) are profiting from a well-designed and working IT solution in a similar way.

But within a mass customization environment, IT systems have to provide far more than the ability to facilitate the supply chain well: New applications, such as multi-agent-based configuration software (refer to Blecker et al., 2005, regarding latest development approaches), electronic marketplace applications, tracking and tracing solutions, and many others, are providing significant competitive market advantages if applied strategically sufficient, but are on the other side immensely raising IT system complexity within the supply chain. Another aspect that leads to an increased information intensity (and herewith complexity) is the growing data volume that is generated at the customer interface. This is related to the end-customer interface (exploring market requirements or competitive advantages, customer-behavior, etc.), but as well to intra-supply chain interfaces (exploring sourcing markets, technology-related matters, order flow information or transferring experience and knowledge chunks between involved units or persons, etc.).

To add one more complexity driver, not only the information quantity is growing, but also the need to integrate structured and unstructured chunks of information (and the underlying data). New technologies (such as the Semantic Web) are currently in the development stage; the first commercial prototypes and applications are arising, for example, in the field of knowledge management. This is (a sufficient amount of experience and further development up to market maturity presumed) opening huge application opportunities, but is again a step towards rising complexity. Another important issue is the "consecutive IT system complexity" that may affect the processes to a wide extent.

Looking at all those IT-related complexity drivers (that might not even be complete) there is no doubt of the importance of concepts that draw IT systems towards agility on the one side, but that keep complexity treatable at the same time. According to Haberfellner and de Weck (2005), within system engineering the implementation of agility has two dimensions: "*Agile System Engineering*" (p. 129) is putting emphasis on a flexible design process that keeps the system open as long as possible herewith paying respect to existing uncertainties even at the price of minor development cost increases ("piecemeal engineering", see Popper, 1944). Approaches used are, for example, the INCOSE-Approach (p. 133), the Hall-ETH-Approach (p. 133), the spiral model (p. 135), or simultaneous engineering/concurrent engineering (p. 136). Using the mentioned (and possibly also other existing) approaches, flexibility can be installed on dimensions such as changing customer requirements and changing product requirements (that are resulting from unavoidable interdependencies between product variant design and supply chain design), but also on changing technology requirements or process specifications. This dimension becomes especially important if an enterprise intends to develop its own solutions and has to take into account development cycle times that are above reliable forecast horizons.

The second dimension is the "*Engineering of Agile Systems*" (p. 143). Since the physical process flow is monitored and controlled by an underlying information flow, the individualization of processes has, at one hand, consequences for and, at the other hand, is enabled by the information systems design. One presumption to keep a system

tolerant towards varying product specifications was already mentioned above: the consequent encapsulation of product data structures against workflow-related data. Further requirements for an information system design that can enable flexible and adaptive process chains are:

- The *ability to flexibly extend or redesign the system* according to changing requirements with minor efforts (achieved by the application of principles such as modularity, encapsulation and information hiding, etc., Thomas, 1996, pp. 30); all elements and procedures of a system should be designed in a way that enables a sudden and fast exchange or adaptation.

- "*Design to granularity*", which means to provide the ability to drill down to a higher granularity if necessary but, on the other side, to reduce information volumes by rolling up to a summarized level; current data modeling structures are already paying respect to that fact, developing modeling schemes (e.g., OLAP normalization strategies, see Thomson, 1997) that can handle exploding data volumes with an acceptable performance level.

- "*Design to scalability*", allowing the handling of a changing volume of functionalities and transactions by providing a flexible and easy capacity adaptation to current throughput requirements; the objective is to reach an acceptable throughput performance and response time at one hand and an affordable system (investment and investment-related risks, continuous operation cost) at the same time; this requires a sophisticated harmonization concept that includes the hierarchical and procedural aspects of the process reference model (level-concept, process step order) as well as the corresponding parts of the IT-system.

- "*Design to agility*", which means stability towards unwanted changes or risks, receptiveness towards necessary or appreciated changes combined within a proactive development approach and system design, and a resource scenario that grants a certain buffer (quantitative: capacity, qualitative: knowledge, experience, creative potential); again, the fit between supply chain agility and IT-system adaptiveness has to be good; additionally, the supply chain has to be matched with the products (Blecker et al., 2005, p. 39).

These requirements are also of concern in the development and design of process-supporting IT solutions as new solutions are needed for use with an individualized customer (and supplier) interface.

CONCLUSION

With mass customization being a relevant challenge for the majority of companies within an uncertain and complex environment, a number of issues need to be handled in order to become and stay competitive in often saturated buyer-markets. Supply chain effectiveness ("what product or service to deliver to what customer") and efficiency ("how fast", "how cost-intensive", "how reliable and stable", "at what quality level", etc.) are basic requirements. In order to attain a viable performance, it is in addition necessary to:

Figure 5. Supply chain complexity and process reference models

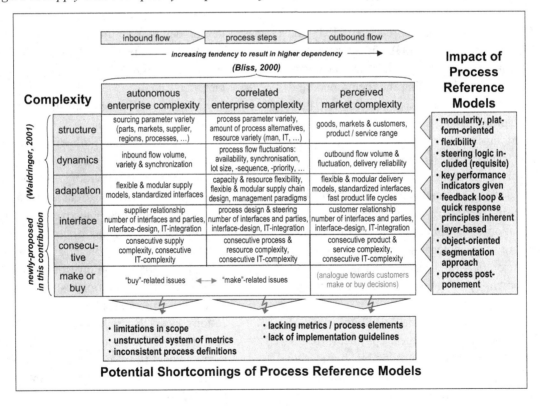

- Construct or configure product and service variants that are best-possible solutions for meeting the "Voice of the Customer" and have the fewest possible interdependencies with the underlying supply chain workflow in order to avoid a transfer from product volatility and complexity into a high supply chain variability and complexity.
- Implement well-built and flexible processes with the minimum level of complexity that is obligatory in order to realize the required output due to customer specifications, herewith using process reference models; and
- dDesign highly-performing and responsive IT systems according to the implications of agility.

Among a lot of additional situational factors that have to be taken into account, there is one strong implication never to be forgotten in order to make an improvement project (e.g., having the objective to introduce mass customization in a company) successful: If an enterprise intends to improve agility and the ability to act properly towards sudden changes, there are only a few elements that can, but also have to provide agility. These are: the employees (no matter on what hierarchical position or geographical location), the machine capacity, other material and immaterial assets which are part of the order fulfillment process, supplier or service provider within the supply net, and customers (or from the inside of a company, customer orders). All methodological approaches will deliver the mentioned promising potentials only if reality proves that those elements can be changed and will change their behavior within the system according to the intended stage. If those base elements cannot (due to technical limits, contradicting contracts, legal restrictions, insufficient qualification, turbulence-driven information flow, etc.) or do not want (due to lack of motivation, fears, contradicting target agreements

or career mechanisms, etc.) to adjust to the proposed principles, any attempt on improvement will fail no matter how well-thought the methodology and theoretical concept have been.

SCOR as a process reference model seems feasible as a framework for supply chain configuration in an open variant process approach. It is very pragmatic in its approach, making it a valuable tool for the purpose. It seems sufficiently detailed to allow supply chain partners to communicate effectively. Limitations in scope do not impact the usefulness for modeling supply chains.

It supports the task of modeling custom processes based on a clear, modular structure, and also supports the efforts to reduce complexity while at the same time ensuring utmost flexibility, allowing users to go to the level of detail they require.

Among the weaknesses of the model is the lack of structure in the hierarchy of metrics, limiting comparability, missing process definitions, and the lack of guidelines on how to assess and implement best practices.

There are some shortcomings, though, specifically in the missing link between configuration and implementation. There is no guidance for the development of operational information systems, leaving a gap between process descriptions on a general level and the functionality of application systems workflow applications or ERP systems.

The benefits of standardization and modular design on the three upper levels could be lost with enterprise-specific design and individual processes on level 4 and below. Therefore, it is critical to follow the building-block approach instead of implementing solutions optimized for a single enterprise or supply chain.

Figure 5 summarizes the complexity factors analyzed in this chapter and their implications for supply chains. Process reference frameworks as an approach to create an "open variant process model" with their impact and potential shortcomings are shown.

REFERENCES

Adam, D. & Johannwille, U. (1998). Die Komplexitätsfalle. In D. Adam et al. (Eds.), *Komplexitätsmanagement* (pp. 5-28). Wiesbaden, Germany: Schriften zur Unternehmensführung, Gabler.

American Productivity and Quality Center (2005). Retrieved December 29, 2005, from http://www.apqc.org/portal/apqc/ksn/APQC_PCF_June_2005.pdf?paf_gear_id=contentgearhome&paf_dm=full&pageselect=contentitem&docid=121388

Ashby, W. R. (1960). *Design for a brain*, (2nd ed.). London.

Ashby, W. R. (1961). *An introduction to cybernetics*, (4th ed.). London: Chapman & Hall.

Axelrod, R., & Cohen, M. D. (2000). *Harnessing complexity – Organizational implications of a scientific frontier.* New York: Basic Books.

Becker, J. (1999). *Branchen-Referenzmodelle, dargestellt am Beispiel des Handels-Referenzmodells.* In J. Becker et al. (Eds.), *Referenzmodellierung – State-of-the-Art und Entwicklungsperspektiven* (pp. 150-165). Heidelberg, Germany: Physica.

Beer, S. (1959). *Cybernetics and management.* London: The English Universities Press.

Beer, S. (1966). *Decision and control – The meaning of operational research and management cybernetics.* London: John Wiley & Sons.

Beer, S. (1972). *Brain of the firm – The managerial cybernetics of organization.* London: Penguin Press.

Beer, S. (1985). *Diagnosing the system for organizations.* Chichester, England: John Wiley & Sons.

Blecker, T. & Friedrich, G. (2005). Mass customization, concepts – Tools - Realization. In *Proceeding of the International Mass Customization Meeting 2005 (IMCM'05),* Gito, Berlin.

Blecker, T., Friedrich, G., Kaluza, B., Abdelkafi, N., & Kreutler, G. (2005). *Information and management systems for product customization.* New York: Springer.

Bliss, C. (2000). *Management von Komplexität. Ein integrierter systemtheoretischer Ansatz zur Komplexitätsreduktion.* Wiesbaden, Germany: Gabler.

BPT (2005). *Supply-chain council partners with proforma to release object-oriented SCOR®-Model.* Retrieved March 11, 2006 from http://www.bptrends.com/news_items.cfm

Brown, A. O., Lee, H. L., & Petrakian, R. (2000). *Xilinx improves its semiconductor supply chain using product and process postponement.* Retrieved March 12, 2006, from http://markov.kaist.ac.kr/scm/refer/Semiconductor-postponement.pdf

Carnegie-Mellon Software Engineering Institute (2005). *Capability Maturity Model for Software (SW-CMM).* Retrieved December 29, 2005, from http://www.sei.cmu.edu/cmm/

Chen, F., Drezner, A., Ryan, J. K., & Simchi-Levi, D. (1999). The bullwhip effect: Managerial insights on the impact of forecasting and information on variability in a supply chain. In S. Tayur, et al. (Eds.), *Quantitative models for supply chain management* (pp. 417-440). New York: Springer.

Chen, I. J., & Paulraj, A. (2004). Understanding supply chain management: Critical research and a theoretical framework. *International Journal of Production Research, 42*(1), 131-163.

Christopher, M. (1998). *Logistics and supply chain management, strategies for reducing cost and improving service* (2nd ed). London: Financial Times Prentice Hall.

Commission de Surveillance du Secteur Financier (2005). *BASEL II Operational Risk Management*

Process Reference Model. Retrieved December 29, 2005, from http://www.cssf.lu/docs/PRM_ORM_BALEII_V01_00.pdf

ECR Europe (2005). *ECR Europe: Organisation and principles*. Retrieved December 29, 2005, from http://www.ecrnet.org/

Engelhardt, C. (2000). *Betriebskennlinien. Produktivität steigern in der Fertigung*. München/Wien, Germany: Hanser.

European Foundation for Quality Management (2005). *The EFQM Excellence Model*. Retrieved December 29, 2005, from http://www.efqm.org/Default.aspx?tabid=35

European Logistics Association/A. T. Kearney Management Consultants (2004). *Differentiation for Performance – Excellence in Logistics 2004*. Hamburg, Germany: Deutscher Verkehrs-Verlag.

Eversheim, W., Schenke, F.-B., & Warnke, U. (1998). Komplexität im Unternehmen verringern und beherrschen – optimale Gestaltung von Produkten und Produktionssystemen. In D. Adam et al. (Eds.), *Komplexitätsmanagement* (pp. 29-45). Wiesbaden, Germany: Schriften zur Unternehmensführung, Gabler.

Fetter, P., & Loos, P. (2004). Referenzmodelle für den Handel. In K. Hildebrand (Ed.), (Hrsg.), IT-Lösungen im Handel, dpunkt. Heidelberg, Germany: Verlag.

Forrester, J. (1961). *Industrial dynamics*. Cambridge, MA: MIT-Press.

Geimer, H. (2005). Komplexitätsmanagement globaler Supply Chains. In K. Hildebrand (Ed.), *Supply chain management* (pp. 38-46). Heidelberg, Germany: HMD-Praxis der Wirtschaftsinformatik, HMD 243.

Gell-Mann, M. (1994). *Das Quark und der Jaguar: Vom Einfachen zum Komplexen*. München, Germany: Piper.

Haberfellner, R., & de Weck, O. (2005). Neuere Entwicklungen im systems engineering. In C. Engelhardt-Nowitzki & J. Wolfbauer, (Eds.), *Gelebtes Netzwerkmanagement* (pp. 129-149). Göttingen, Germany: Cuvillier Verlag.

Hansen Harps, L. (2002). Super-charging your supply chain. Retrieved March 12, 2006, from http://www.inboundlogistics.com/articles

Heylighen, F. (1992). Building a science of complexity. Retrieved March 10, 2006, from http://pespmc1.vub.ac.be/papers/Buildingcomplexity.html

Heylighen, F. (1996). *The growth of structural and functional complexity during evolution*. Retrieved March 10, 2006, from http://pespmc1.vub.ac.be/papers/Complexitygrowth.html.

Hopp, W. J., & Spearmann, M. L. (1996). *Factory physics. Foundations of manufacturing management*. Chicago: Irwin.

Ireland, R. (2005). *How to implement CPFR and other best collaborative practices*. Boca Raton, FL: J. Ross Publishing.

ITIL (2005). *What is ITIL*. Retrieved December 29, 2005, from http://www.itil.org/

Jahns, C., Gäde, C., & Langenhan, F. (2004). Der Management Navigator Logistics. Ein integrierter Managementansatz für die Waren- und Dokumentenlogistik,. In W. Dangelmaier, D. Kaschula, & J. Neumann (Eds.), *Supply chain management in der Automobil und Zulieferindustrie* (pp. 365-374). Paderborn, Germany: ALB-HNI..

Kitson, D. H., & Kitson, L. J. (1998). *ISO/IEC 15504 - Overview and Status*. Software Engineering Institute, Carnegie Mellon University, Pittsburgh, PA, September, 1998. Retrieved March 10, 2006, from http://www.sei.cmu.edu/iso-15504/resources/symp-se-98.pdf

Kirchhof, R. (2003). *Ganzheitliches komplexitätsmanagement*. Wiesbaden, Germany: Gabler.

Kühner, M. (2005). *Ein Verfahren zur Analyse prozessualer Logistikleistung auf Basis der Data Envelopment Analysis.* Dissertation thesis. Retrieved March 11, 2005, from http://elib. uni-stuttgart.de/opus/volltexte/2005/2321/pdf/ Diss_Kuehner.pdf

Liening, A. (1999). *Komplexe Systeme zwischen Ordnung und Chaos. Neuere Entwicklungen in der Theorie nicht-linearer dynamischer Systeme und die Bedeutung für die Wirtschaftswissenschaft und Didaktik.* Lit. Münster etc.

Luczak, H., & Fricker, A. (1997). Komplexitätsmanagement – ein Mittel der strategischen Unternehmensgestaltung. In G. Schuh & H. P. Wiendahl (Eds.), *Komplexität und Agilität. Steckt die Produktion in der Sackgasse?* (pp. 309-323). Berlin: Springer.

Mainzer, K. (1997). *Thinking in complexity* (3rd ed). Berlin: Springer.

Malik, F. (1996). *Strategie des Managements komplexer Systeme* (5th ed). Bern, Germany: Haupt.

Malik, F. (2000). *Systemisches Management, Evolution, Selbstorganisation – Grundprobleme, Funktionsmechanismen und Lösungsansätze für komplexe Systeme.* Bern, Germany: Haupt.

Massachussetts Institute of Technology (2005). *Lean Enterprise Model {LEM}.* Retrieved December 29, 2005, from http://process.mit.edu/Activity. asp?ID=970415113709AB5782

National Institute of Standards and Technology (2005). *Malcolm Baldrige National Quality Award.* Retrieved December 29, 2005, from http://www.quality.nist.gov/

Nilsson, F., & Waidringer, J. (2002). Logistics management from a complexity perspective. *Managing the Complex IV, Conference on Complex Systems and the Management of Organizations, 7-10 December 2002,* Naples, Florida.

Piller, F. T. (2003). *Mass customization. Ein wettbewerbsstrategisches Konzept im Informationszeitalter.* Wiesbaden, Germany: Deutscher Universitätsverlag.

Pine II, B. J. (1993). *Mass customization: The new frontier in business competition.* Boston: Harvard Business School Press.

Pine II, B. J., & Gilmore, J. H. (1999). *The experience economy.* Boston: Harvard Business School Press.

Popper, K. (1944). *The poverty of historicism, Routledge Classics, 2002.* Routledge & Kegan Paul, 1957, originally published in Economia, 1944/5.

Project Management Institute (2005). *PMBOK® Guide.* Retrieved December 29, 2005, from http://www.pmi.org/prod/groups/public/documents/info/pp_pmbok2000welcome.asp

Schlott, S. (2005). *Wahnsinnn mit Methode.* Automobil-Produktion, (January, 2005), 38-42.

Sheard, S. A. (1997). The frameworks quagmire, A brief look. *Software Productivity Consortium,* Herndon, VA. Retrieved December 23, 2005, from http://www.software.org/quagmire/frampapr/frampapr.html

Sheffi, Y. (2005). *The resilient enterprise: Overcoming vulnerability for competitive advantage.* Cambridge, MA: The MIT Press.

SIEMENS (2003). *Erster Prozessmanagement-Summit in Wien. Plenarvortrag von PSE zeigt "State of the art" bei Siemens.* 2003-11-10. Retrieved March 11, 2005, from http://www. pse.siemens.at/apps/pseauftritt/ge/pseinternet. nsf/CD_Index?OpenFrameset&Bookmark&/0/ PK18C3295572D27C4AC1256DD4002DFF2B

Software Process Improvement and Capability. *Determination.* Retrieved December 5, 2005, from http://www.sqi.gu.edu.au/spice/

Software Quality Institute (2005). *Software Process Improvement and Capability determination.* Retrieved December 29, 2005, from http://www.sqi.gu.edu.au/spice/

Supply Chain Council (2005). *Supply-Chain Operations Reference Model: SCOR Version 7.0 Overview.* Retrieved December 23, 2005, from http://www.supply-chain.org/galleries/default-file/SCOR%207.0%20Overview.pdf

Thomas, C. (1996). *Ein objektorientiertes Konzept zur Modellierung und Simulation komplexer Systeme.* Düsseldorf, Germany: VDI.

Thomsen, E. (1997). *OLAP solutions building: Multidimensional information systems.* Chichester, England: John Wiley & Sons.

Ulrich, H. (1968). *Die Unternehmung als produktives soziales System.* Bern/Stuttgart, Germany: Paul Haupt Verlag.

Ulrich, H., & Probst, G. J. B. (1995). *Anleitung zum ganzheitlichen Denken und Handeln: ein Brevier für Führungskräfte* (4th ed). Bern, Germany: Paul Haupt Verlag.

Ulrich, K. T., & Eppinger, S. D. (1995). *Product design and development.* New York: McGraw-Hill.

Westphal, J. R. (2000). *Komplexitätsmanagement in der Produktionslogistik.* Institut für Wirtschaft und Verkehr, Lehrstuhl für Verkehrsbetriebslehre und Logistik, Technische Universität Dresden. Retrieved December 15, 2005, from http://www.tu-dresden.de/vkiwv/VWL/diskussion/diskp/dskp0004.pdf

Wildemann, H. (1998). Komplexitätsmanagement durch Prozess- und Produktgestaltung. In D. Adam, et al., *Komplexitätsmanagement,* Schriften zur Unternehmensführung (pp. 29-45). Wiesbaden, Germany: Gabler.

Winkler, R. (2005). *Modulare Auftragsbewirtschaftung. Methode der virtuellen Modularisierung in der automobilen kundenindividuellen Serienfertigung aus logistischer Perspektive.* Unpublished doctoral dissertation, constituent of a current doctoral project, publication in preparation, Graz University of Technology, Industrial Management and Innovations Research.

Winter, R. (2001). Mass customization and beyond - Evolution of customer centricity in financial services. In M. F. Sebaaly (Ed.), *Proceedings of the International NAISO Congress on Information Science Innovations (ISI'2001).* ICSC Academic Press. 8 pages (CDROM) Re-published in C. Rautenstrauch, R. Seelmann-Eggebert, & K. Turowski (Eds.), *Moving into mass customization - Information systems and management principles* (pp. 197-213). Berlin: Springer.

Zhang, X. Y., & Huan, G. Q. (2005). Integrated platform product development and supply chain configuration for manufacturing firm in mass customization. In T. Blecker & G. Friedrich (Eds.), *Mass customization, concepts - Tools - Realization. Proceeding of the International Mass Customization Meeting 2005 (IMCM'05). Gito, Berlin* (pp. 457-470).

Section II
Frameworks in
Mass Customization

Chapter V
An Associative Classification–Based Recommendation System for Personalization in B2C E–Commerce Applications

Yiyang Zhang
Nanyang Technological University, Singapore

Jianxin (Roger) Jiao
Nanyang Technological University, Singapore

ABSTRACT

This chapter presents an associative classification-based recommendation system to support online customer decision-making when facing a huge amount of choices. Recommendation systems have been recently introduced to e-commerce sites in order to solve the information overload and mass confusion problem. This chapter applies knowledge discovery techniques to overcome the drawback of conventional approaches to recommendation systems. The framework of the associative classification-based recommendation system has been addressed in this chapter. The system analysis, design, and implementation issues in an Internet programming environment are also presented. Taking the advantage of accumulative knowledge from historical data, the efficiency and effectiveness of B2C e-commerce applications are improved.

INTRODUCTION

With the advent of customer-driven marketing, it has been envisioned that e-commerce will emerge as a primary style of manufacturing in the coming decade and beyond. The capabilities of e-commerce enable the customer's involvement in design, manufacturing, and service, thus to make it possible for product/service providers to interact directly with their customers and capture the customer requirements. A number of online product customization systems have been launched recently (for example, Dell.com, Idtown.com, and Cannondale.com). These systems support providers to respond to a high variety of requirements and orders by customizing the offerings and anticipating the customer requirements.

However, the online customization systems encounter the difficulties when dealing with the support for customers' finding the valuable products that match their heterogeneous needs, namely, the personalization problem. It is not uncommon that searching for information or buying complex products (e.g., digital products) via the Internet are always frustrated (Francisco, Rafael, & Rodrigo, 2005). As in the World Wide Web, the available products and the corresponding electronic information lead to the problem of information overload. Online customers have to access all the information contents in order to find what they mostly prefer. Without the face-to-face advice, customers always have difficulties in making trade-offs among numerous competing products on the Internet. For example, as in real purchase decisions, buyers cannot get all the best features at the lowest prices. In some cases, for specific products, especially for digital products, professional knowledge is always required for evaluation. It is difficult for non-experts to compare products' performances. For example, online customers may be frustrated by the information of digital camera products because they do not know how each feature or its parameters can influence the picture quality.

Recommendation systems are traditionally used in e-commence sites to solve the personalization problem by guiding customers to find the products they would like to purchase (Yong, Yum, Song, & Su, 2005). A number of recommendation systems have been proposed for different businesses (for example, Group-Lens recommendation system and Ringo). Most of them are either homogeneous (i.e., content-based filtering) or heterogeneous (i.e., collaborative filtering) product recommendation systems (Yuan & Cheng, 2004). However, both of the two paradigms yielded few promising results. The content-based filtering (CBF) approach recommends products to target customers according to the preferences of their neighbors (Hill, Stead, Rosenstein, & Furnas, 1995). However, it is often inhibitive to estimate the preference similarities between various customers. For example, similar preferences may be defined as the preferences of customers who have similar ratings of items (Yoon & Jae, 2004). It is difficult to obtain the accurate customer ratings of products, especially when special knowledge is needed for rating. The collaborative filtering (CF) approach, on the other hand, recommends products to target customers based on their past preferences (Basu, Hirsh, & Cohen, 1998). When facing new customers, this type of recommendation system cannot recommend any product as no historical preference records are available (Avery & Zeckhauser, 1997). Nevertheless, both approaches require the customers to express their requirements according to system predefined formats (e.g., product ratings or customer profiles), and thus real customer requirement information may be distorted.

Due to the drawbacks of traditional approaches, new paradigm is preferred to advise proper products by capturing accurate individual requirement information (Cheung, Lee, Wang, Chu, & To, 2003). As individual customer requirements are heterogeneous, an open environment is required to allow customers to express their diverse requirements completely to their manner. On the other hand, to avoid the difficulties involved in preference estimation, it is preferred to establish such models that allow the prediction of product labels according to customer requirements directly. As a result, the main difficulties involved in establishing recommendation systems for personalization in B2C e-commerce applications can be summarized as two categories. First, customers always use their natural languages to express what they need. Their requirements are normally qualitative and tend to be imprecise and ambiguous due to their linguistic origins. Synonymous words are expected to express the same requirements. Further, numerous words that contribute nothing to information retrieval are always found. Second, classification methods have been proven to be effective means to predict future data objects for which the class label is unknown. Many efficient methods, such as decision tree, regression model, and so forth, are developed to identify the relationships between the objects and class labels. However, these methods only excel in classifying the structured data; the object data are organized into a fixed set of attributes or dimensions. Therefore, commonly-used relational data-oriented classification methods cannot be adopted to classify customer requirements which are organized into a set of text-based documents.

In this regard, this chapter proposes an associative classification-based recommendation system for personalization in B2C e-commerce applications. Due to the difficulties inherent in designing efficient recommendation systems, customer requirements are processed by semantic analysis and represented as text documents. A set of significant phrases are identified to describe diverse requirements. As the *association rule learning* method excels in dealing with semi-structured data, the associative classification approach is employed to establish the customer requirement classification model. By reusing the knowledge from historical data, a set of associated, frequently-occurring text patterns (classifiers) are built by applying an association rule learning method to a training set of requirement text documents. These classifiers are used to predict the product labels for new customer requirements and distinguish one label from others.

BACKGROUND REVIEW

Diverse *recommendation systems* have been developed. Tapestry (Goldberg, Nichols, Oki, & Terry, 1992) is one of the earliest recommendation systems. It is a mail-filtering system that allows its members to annotate each document in detail to represent how interesting the reader found the document. This system selects neighbored people to measure their preference similarities. Based on this work, several automated recommendation systems have been developed. Hill et al. (1995) proposed Video Recommender for movie suggestions. Konstan, Miller, Maltz, Herlocker, Gordon, and Riedl (1997) developed a recommendation system for news and movie recommendations. Shardanand and Maes (1995) developed Ringo to make personalized recommendations on music and artists. Schafer, Konstan, and Riedl (1999) proposed a taxonomy recommendation system to help e-commerce sites increase sales. Mooney and Roy (2000) proposed a content-based system for book recommendations. McNee, Albert, Cosley, Gopalkrishnan, Lam, Rashid, Konstan, and Riedl (2002) proposed a recommendation system to help research paper citation.

With the increasing applications of recommendation systems in a variety of fields, various approaches to *recommendation systems* have been developed. There are two paradigms for recommendation systems, namely, content-based filtering (CBF) and collaborative filtering (CF) approaches (Chen & Chen, 2001; Ghani & Fano, 2002). The CF method has thus far been the most successful recommendation techniques. It is firstly used to process huge volumes of e-mails (Goldberg et al., 1992). To enhance the quality of the recommendation system, some researchers improved the methodology for CF (CBF)-based recommendation systems. Chalmers, Rodden, and Brodbeck (1998) proposed a path-based CF methodology to utilize online information. Kohrs and Merialdo (2001) improved the quality of CF method using multimedia indexing techniques. Han, Xie, Yang, and Shen (2004) suggested a distributed CF algorithm to construct a scalable distributed recommendation system. Yong et al. (2005) proposed a novel CF-based recommendation system for e-commerce sites by analyzing customer behaviors based on their navigational patterns. Yu, Liu, and Li (2005) explored a hybrid CF method in which CF-I (collaborative filtering based on item) and CF-U (collaborative filtering based on user) are combined together to address multiple-interests recommendation problems. Yeong, Yoon, and Soung (2005) proposed a new methodology in which customer purchase sequences are used to improve the quality of CF-based recommendations.

As data mining techniques become more and more mature, researchers have begun to explore their applications to recommendation systems. Fu, Budzik, and Hammond (2000) tried to incorporate CF method and association rule learning technology to recommend Web pages on the Internet. Lee and Yang (2003) presented a multi-agent framework in which a decision tree-based approach is proposed to learn users' preferences. Films and news are recommended to a user based on the identified preferences. Wang and Shaob (2004) proposed a personalized recommendation system integrating clustering and association rule mining techniques to establish a recommendation model for e-learning Web sites.

PROBLEM DESCRIPTION

By semantic analysis, customer requirements can be described as a set of phrases; let $P \equiv \{p_1, p_2, \cdots, p_I\}$. Let $C \equiv \{c_1, c_2, \cdots, c_J\}$ be a set of class labels, each representing a specific product. Suppose there are sales records for S customers and all the sales records comprise a transaction database, T. Every transaction record, $t_s \mid \forall s = 1, 2, ..., S$, comprises the customer requirement record and

the record of the product he/she purchased. For each customer $s \mid \forall s = 1, 2, ..., S$ in the transaction database, the corresponding requirement record is described as a set of phrases, P^{t_s}, where $P^{t_s} \subseteq P$. The corresponding product record indicates a class label, $C(t_s)$, where $C(t_s) = c_j \mid \exists j \in [1, ..., J]$, showing which product he/she purchased. Thus, transaction records can be summarized as $\langle P, C \rangle$ pairs with the form of $t_s = \{P^{t_s}, C(t_s)\} \mid \forall s = 1, 2, ..., S$. Suppose there are K new object customers for whom the class labels are unknown. The object customers comprise an object database, O, where $O = \{o_k\}_K$. For each customer $k \mid \forall k = 1, 2, ..., K$ in the object database, the requirement record is described as a set of phrases, P^{o_k}, where $P^{o_k} \subseteq P$ and $P^{o_k} \neq P^{t_s} \mid \forall s = 1, 2, ..., S$. Thus, the recommendation problem based on customer requirements is noted as $P^{o_k} \Rightarrow c_j \mid \exists j \in [1, ..., J]$ where an association rule, $\Rightarrow$, indicates an inference from the customer requirements (P^{o_k}) to the class label ($c_j \mid \exists j \in [1, ..., J]$).

FRAMEWORK AND METHODOLOGY

Based on an associative classification method, an inference system can be constructed for recommendation problems. The system comprises four consecutive stages, namely the requirement preprocessing module, associative classifier generation module, classification module, and system performance validation module. First, historical requirement data are selected and transformed into proper phrase data sets. The data mining procedure then starts to search for a set of associated, frequently-occurring phrase patterns (classifiers). The generated classifiers are pruned by which only those classifiers with good quality are kept for recommendations. When new requirement information comes, the system identifies the corresponding class labels using multiple classifiers. Finally, the performance of the whole system is validated to evaluate how accurately the system will give recommendations.

Requirement Preprocessing Module

Customer requirements are usually expressed by natural languages where many common words occur which contribute nothing to information retrieval. For example, the words "a", "the", "of", "for", and so forth, are irrelevant for information even though they may appear frequently. These common words should be filtered out. On the other hand, a group of different words may share the same word stem. To reduce variations in words and increase the scope of searches, these words should be transformed into their canonical forms. In this regard, stemming algorithm (Porter, 1980) and a common stopword list in English (Fox, 1992) are adopted to reduce the dimensions of the text documents and to improve the efficiency of the classifier extraction.

Customer requirements may bear the same semantic meaning even though they are represented by different expressions (Carbonell, 1992). To generalize the requirement information, semantic analysis is adopted. In this research, four thesaurus collections are used to match the requirements. Each collection is composed of several sub-collections, each containing a set of synonyms. The four thesaurus collections are represented as $N = \{N_1, N_2, ...\}$, $V = \{V_1, V_2, ...\}$, $ADJ = \{ADJ_1, ADJ_2, ...\}$, $ADV = \{ADV_1, ADV_2, ...\}$, for noun, verb, adjective, and adverb, respectively. A lot of semantic rules are represented as IF-THEN rule formats and stored in the semantic rule database to indicate the inference relationship between requirements and a set of predefined phrases, $P \equiv \{p_1, p_2, \cdots, p_I\}$. Suppose after stopwords removal and stemming, a particular customer requirement is transformed into a word set, $Y \equiv \{y_1, y_2, y_3\}$, and the semantic meaning of such a requirement is represented as IF-THEN rule formats in the following:

IF $y_1 \in V_2$, $y_2 \in ADJ_1$, and $y_3 \in N_3$
THEN the semantic meaning of Y is associated with p_2.

After preprocessing, customer requirements are represented as a set of phrases which are used in the following procedures to generate the classifiers.

Associative Classifier Generation Module

Association rule learning is a data mining technique aiming at discovering the relationships among a large set of data items. Let $\eta = \{i_1, i_2, ...i_x, ...i_y, ...i_m\}$ be a set of items, and T a set of database transactions, where $T \equiv \{t_1, t_2, \cdots, t_Q\}$. Each transaction, $t_q \mid \forall q = 1, 2, ..., Q$, comprises a set of items and a given unique identifier. A transaction $t_q \mid \exists q \in [1, ..., Q]$ is said to contain i_x if and only if $i_x \subseteq t_q$. An association rule is an implication of the form $i_x \Rightarrow i_y$, where $i_x \subseteq \eta$, $i_y \subseteq \eta$, and $i_x \cap i_y = \Phi$. The rule $i_x \Rightarrow i_y$ in the transaction set T holds the support $s\%$, where $s\%$ is the probability that i_x and i_y hold together among all the transactions. This is taken as a probability, that is, $P(i_x \cap i_y)$. The rule $i_x \Rightarrow i_y$ in the transaction set T holds the confidence $c\%$, where $c\%$ is the conditional probability that i_y is true under the condition of i_x, that is, $P(i_y / i_x)$.

As the association rule learning method excels in finding the complex relationships among a huge number of semi- or non-structured items, it is adopted here to generate the classifiers. Traditional association rule mining ($i_x \Rightarrow i_y$) assumes that all items belong to one itemset of transaction data ($i_x \subseteq \eta$, and $i_y \subseteq \eta$). For recommendation problems, only those rules that indicate class labels are needed. In this regard, association rule learning for building classifiers involves two different itemsets, that is, $i_x \subseteq P$ and $i_y \subseteq C$, corresponding to requirement phrases and class labels, respectively.

As a result, the general form of associative classifiers is given as the following:

$$\alpha_1 \wedge \alpha_2 \cdots \wedge \alpha_i \cdots \wedge \alpha_Z \Rightarrow \beta$$
$$[Support = s\%; Confidence = c\%] \qquad (1)$$

where $\forall z = 1, 2, ..., Z$, $\alpha_z = p_i \mid \exists i \in [1,...,I]$, $\beta = c_j \mid \exists j \in [1,...,J]$; and for any two elements in the precedence, α_x and α_y, where x, $y \in [1,...,Z]$ and $x \neq y$, $\alpha_x \cap \alpha_y = \Phi$; $s\%$ and $c\%$ refer to the support and confidence levels for this rule, respectively. They are calculated based on the following:

$$s\% = \frac{count(\alpha_1 \wedge \alpha_2 \cdots \wedge \alpha_z \wedge \beta)}{count(T)} \times 100\%, \quad (2)$$

$$c\% = \frac{count(\alpha_1 \wedge \alpha_2 \cdots \wedge \alpha_z \wedge \beta)}{count(\alpha_1 \wedge \alpha_2 \cdots \wedge \alpha_z)} \times 100\%, \quad (3)$$

where $count(\alpha_1 \wedge \alpha_2 \cdots \wedge \alpha_z \wedge \beta)$ is the number of transaction records in database T containing all items α_1, α_2, ..., and α_z, as well as β; $count(T)$ is the total number of data records contained in T; and $count(\alpha_1 \wedge \alpha_2 \cdots \wedge \alpha_z)$ is the number of transaction records in T containing all items α_1, α_2, ..., and α_z. In addition, the set $\{\alpha_1, \alpha_2, \cdots, \alpha_z, \cdots, \alpha_Z\}$ embodies a non-empty subset of P, whereas the set $\{\beta\}$ exhibits a non-empty subset of C. The association rule in equation (1) means that the data occurrence of α_1, α_2, ..., and α_z associates with the data occurrence of β at a $s\%$-support and a $c\%$-confidence levels.

A priori algorithm is adopted in this research to generate the classifiers. The idea driving a priori algorithm is to use an iterative approach known as a level-wise search, where k-itemsets (the itemsets that containing k items) are used to explore $(k+1)$-itemsets. A priori property, where all nonempty subsets of a frequent itemset must also be frequent, helps reduce the search space and improve the efficiency of the level-wise generation of frequent itemsets. After all the frequent itemsets are discovered, association rules can be generated with the corresponding support and confidence levels.

Classification Module:

1. **Classifier pruning:** For the classifiers generated by association rule learning, one

important problem is that the number of the classifiers could be very huge. Excessive classifiers extend the time to identify the class labels for given requirement information. Besides, noisy and redundant information impairs the classification quality. To enable the timely and accurate responses, this research applies CBA-CB algorithm (Liu, Hsu, & Ma, 1998) to produce the best classifiers out of the whole set of rules. The driving idea of CBA-CB algorithm is that only those rules which are more general and hold high confidence levels are necessary for the classification task. The unnecessary rules should be pruned by database coverage. Thus, a small number of rules are kept for efficient recommendations. The principles of CBA-CB algorithm are as follows:

1. Given two rules, $r_x \Rightarrow c_j \mid \exists j \in [1, ..., J]$ and $r_y \Rightarrow c_j \mid \exists j \in [1, ..., J]$, the first rule is more general than the second one if $r_x \subseteq r_y$; and

2. Given two rules, r_x and r_y, r_x has a higher precedence than r_y, namely $r_x \succ r_y$, if (a) the confidence of r_x ($con(r_x)$) is greater than that of r_y; or (b) $con(r_x) = con(r_y)$, but the support of r_x ($sup(r_x)$) is greater than that of r_y; or (c) $con(r_x) = con(r_y)$ and $sup(r_x) = sup(r_y)$, but r_x is generated earlier than r_y.

Suppose M rules are generated by the classifier generation module and comprise a rule set, R, where $R \equiv \{r_1, r_2, ..., r_M\}$. Each rule, $r_m \mid \forall m = 1, 2, ..., M$, is pruned according to the first principle. After pruning, general rules are selected and stored in a pruned rule set, R_P. Rank all the rules in R_P in a descendent order according to the second principle and then record the ranked rules in a rule set, R_D. For each rule in R_D, $r_m \mid \forall r_m \in R_D$, the phrases involving in its precedent part comprise a set, PR^{r_m}, where $PR^{r_m} \subseteq P$. Let $C(r_m)$ present the class label associated with r_m, where

$C(r_m) = c_j \mid \exists\, j \in [1,...,J]$. Set a cover-count zero for each transaction record, $t_s \mid \forall\, s = 1, 2, ..., S$, namely $CC(t_s) = 0$. With respect to each rule, $r_m \mid \forall\, r_m \in R_D$, search all the records in the transaction database. For any record, $t_s \mid \exists\, s \in [1, ..., S]$, if it satisfies the condition, $PR^{r_m} \subseteq P^{t_s}$, it is selected. All the selected transaction records comprise a new set, T', where $T' \subseteq T$. Increase the cover-count by one for all the transaction records in set T'. For any rule, $r_m \mid \forall\, r_m \in R_D$, if it satisfies the condition, $C(r_m) = C(t_s) \mid \exists\, s \in [1,...,S]$, where $t_s \in T'$, it is put into the filtered rule set, R_F. Then delete the corresponding rule in set R_D and empty set T'. Finally, delete record $t_s \mid \exists\, s \in [1,...,S]$ in the transaction database that satisfies the condition, $CC(t_s) \geq \delta \mid \exists\, s \in [1,...,S]$, where δ is a threshold for cover-count.

2. **Classification based on multiple classifiers:** By CBA-CB algorithm, the pruned rules in set R_F are the most significant and finally selected as classifiers to predict the class labels for new requirement information. Suppose the object customers comprise an object database, O, where $O = \{o_k\}_K$. For customer $k \mid \exists\, k \in [1, ..., K]$ in the object database, the requirement record is described as a set of phrases, P^{o_k}, where $P^{o_k} \subseteq P$ and $P^{o_k} \neq P^{t_s} \mid \forall\, s = 1, 2, ..., S$. Select rules from set R_F which satisfy the condition, $PR^{r_m} \subseteq P^{o_k} \mid \forall\, r_m, r_m \in R_F$, and put the selected rules in the classifier rule set, R_C. Group all the rules in set R_C based on their associated class labels. Suppose N groups are generated, where $G \equiv \{g_1, g_2, ..., g_N\}$. Each group, $g_n \mid \forall\, n = 1, 2, ..., N$, associates with a class label, namely $C(g_n) = c_j \mid \exists\, j \in [1,...,J]$. Thus, the classification based on multiple classifiers can be formulated as the follows:

$$P^{o_k} \Rightarrow C(g_n) \mid \forall n = 1, 2, ..., N, \qquad (4)$$

$$\text{s.t. } \sum_m con(r_m) \geq \psi \mid \forall r_m,\ r_m \in g_n, \qquad (5)$$

where P^{o_k} represents the requirement information of customer $k \mid \exists\, k \in [1, ..., K]$ in the object database; $C(g_n)$ means the class label associated with n-th group $\mid \exists\, n \in [1, ..., N]$; $con(r_m)$ is the confidence of rule $r_m \mid \forall\, r_m, r_m \in R_F$; and ψ is the threshold. Equations (4) and (5) indicate that for the rules selected as classifiers, their associated class labels are selected as recommended ones only if their accumulative confidence satisfies the particular threshold. This enables multiple class labels to be identified based on strong patterns, thus adapting to the recommendation problems where multiple recommendations are preferred by allowing customers to make comparisons among a small set of similar products.

System Performance Validation Module

To evaluate how accurately the proposed recommendation system assigns class labels based on future customer requirements, this research applies the accuracy measurement (Han & Kamber, 2001) to validate the system performance. A test set is used to measure the recommendation accuracy. Suppose the test set $\overline{T}$ comprises S records, where $\overline{T} = \{\overline{t}_s\}_S$. For each record in set,

$$\overline{T}, \overline{t}_s = \{P^{\overline{t}_s}, C(\overline{t}_s)\} \mid \forall s = 1, 2, ..., S,$$

the associated class labels assigned by the classification module comprise a set $C^{\overline{t}_s}$.

Then the recommendation accuracy is computed as the following:

$$a = \sum_{s=1}^{S} v_s / S, \qquad (6)$$

$$\text{s.t } v_s = \begin{cases} 1 & \text{if } C(\overline{t}_s) \in C^{\overline{t}_s} \mid \forall\ \overline{t}_s \in \overline{T} \\ 0 & \text{otherwise} \end{cases}$$

$$\forall s = 1, 2, ..., S, \qquad (7)$$

where a means the recommendation accuracy, namely the percentage of the transactions in the test set that are correctly classified; $v_s \mid \forall s = 1, 2, ..., S$ is a binary variable where it is set to one if transaction $\bar{t_s} \mid \forall s = 1, 2, ..., S$ is correctly classified, and zero otherwise.

SYSTEM ANALYSIS AND DESIGN

To enable the application of the associative classification-based recommendation system to personalization in B2C e-commerce, this research implements the proposed recommendation system in an Internet programming environment. Figure 1 illustrates the function model of the associative classification-based recommendation system. The model comprises five functions. First, customer requirements in the transaction database are extracted and transformed into a set of predefined phrases. The requirement transformation is implemented by the requirement preprocessing function where stemming algorithm, stopwords removal methodology, and semantic analysis are integrated to process the natural requirements. Allowing the transformed transaction records, the second function, classifier generation function, creates a set of classifiers using a priori algorithm. The classifier pruning function then implements

the pruning work to remove the noisy and redundant information, and the refined rules are stored in the classifier rule database. To validate the system performance, the testing function uses the generated classifiers to assign the class labels for a test set where the class labels are already known. If the performance is validated, the classifiers stored in the classifier rule database are used for future classification task. Finally, when new customer requirements occur, they are firstly processed by the requirement preprocessing function and transformed into the corresponding phrases. Then the classification function searches all the classifiers that satisfy the transformed requirements and thus assigns the corresponding class labels.

WEB-BASED ARCHITECTURE AND IMPLEMENTATION

The design, development, and database access for the associative classification-based recommendation system in an Internet environment can be illustrated by the three-tier architecture (Huang & Mak, 2000) as shown in Figure 2.

The first tier includes the application clients, namely the customers shopping online. The application clients are involved in the

Figure 1. Function model of the associative classification-based recommendation system

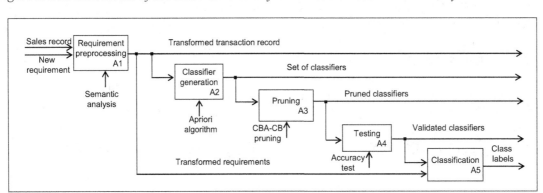

recommendation system only when they are connected with the Web server. There are two types of middle tier: the Web server and the application server. The Web sites are created by the Web server for applications. The application server is a piece of software to execute the computation activities. In this research, as the pruned classifiers have been generated and stored in the classifier rule database via complex off-line work, the Web server and the application server are deployed on the same computer to handle the simplified online tasks. The third tier is the database server to manage the relevant data and rules. In this research, the database is deployed on a computer separate from the Web server.

1. **Client:** The clients can be HTML pages, attached components to HTML pages, and programs that can be downloaded from a Web site and then installed, configured, and executed on the client machine. Clients and servers communicate with each other through HTTP by exchanging HTML files.

Figure 2. Three-tier architecture of the associative classification-based recommendation system in an Internet environment

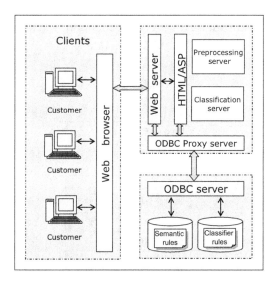

For the proposed recommendation system, in the client side, customers who search and buy products via the Internet, are allowed to log in the Web page and submit their requirement information expressed by their languages to the server and ask for recommendations for the most valuable product alternatives via HTML file format.

2. **Application server:** The application server deals with the computation tasks. It receives the client-side request and information and then processes the data. For the proposed system, the application server comprises two individual servers: the requirement preprocessing server, and the classification server. The requirement preprocessing server deals with the requirement information preprocessing task. When new customer requirement information comes, the requirement preprocessing server searches the semantic rule database where a set of semantic rules are stored as "IF-THEN" rule formats to indicate the relationships between phrases and natural requirement information. All the rules that satisfy the condition of the requirements are triggered, and the corresponding action clauses (phrases) are identified to match the original requirement information. The classification server handles the issues to assign the class labels for specific requirement information. Via a lot of off-line work, such as classifier generation, pruning, and testing, a set of classifiers are built and stored in the classifier rule database for future classification tasks. Allowing the new transformed customer requirements, the server finds all the classifiers that satisfy the conditions of such requirements by searching the classifier rule database. The proper class labels are then recommended to match the new requirements based on the identified multiple classifiers.

3. **Database server:** For the conventional way, if there are changes, the Web designers have to manually adjust all the related categories to reflect the changes. With the database, the Web designers are only required to update those tables containing the related categories without altering the interface. The database server is deployed to manage the data and rules. There are two rule databases in the proposed system, namely, the semantic rule database and the classifier rule database. All the rules in both of the two databases are described as "IF-THEN" rule formats to represent the relationships between original requirement information and phrases, as well as transformed requirement information and class labels, respectively. To enable the Web application work with rule databases, ODBC, which is a system level interface communicating with the database, is necessary. ODBC provides a common set of application interfaces (API) to communicate with the database using SQL and Access. For each application server, ODBC is adopted to work with other databases, thus integrating diverse applications.

To implement the associative classification-based recommendation system in an Internet environment, this research applies Active Server Pages (ASP) to create the dynamic and interactive personalized pages for the Web site. ASP is a language-independent server-side scripting technology. The most two common scripting languages, VBScript and Jscript, are supported by ASP. ASP provides an open, compile-free application environment in which HTML, scripts, and reusable ActiveX server components can be combined to create dynamic and powerful Web-based solutions. In addition, ASP runs on the server; thus, most browsers will be supported to gain the entire contents of the Web pages to ensure the accessibility to the clients. Further, ASP allows the connection to a database using active data objects (ADO). Data can be simply displayed from an ODBC-compliant database and formatted. To allow the rules to be queried and managed efficiently, this research deploys the Web database query run on Internet Information Server (IIS). All the rules in the two databases, the semantic rule database and the classifier rule database, are represented as "IF-THEN" (condition-action) formats. Given the query request, query processor searches for a set of rules whose conditions (IF) satisfy the request. The actions (THEN) of the fired rules are then triggered.

PROTOTYPE DEMONSTRATION

The prototype of the proposed associative classification-based recommendation system has

Table 1. Transaction database records

Record t_s	Requirement Phrases $P \equiv \{p_1, p_2, \cdots, p_I\}$	Product Class Label $C \equiv \{c_1, c_2, \cdots, c_J\}$
t_1	More functions, smallest, lightest, camera, large buttons	Samsung SGH-D730
t_2	Larger screen, office function, USB connectivity, picture transfer	Panasonic X800
t_3	Scheduler, e-mail, news, voice communication	Nokia 9300
...	...	...
t_{2162}	Stylish, elegant, black, video, friendly keypad, small, camera	Nokia 7610
t_{2163}	Stylish, elegant, black, light, colorful screen	Nokia 8910

been constructed for personalization in mobile phone B2C e-commerce application. Based on the historical sales records, transaction database is established comprising 2,163 transaction records, as shown in Table 1, where customer requirements are described as a set of phrases, and the corresponding class labels indicate the mobile phone that has been purchased. Allowing the transaction database, the classifiers are identified. After pruning, the pruned classifiers are used to assign the class labels for future customer requirements. Figure 3 shows part of the classifiers where the second column indicates the customer requirements represented as phrases, the third column shows the confidence levels, and the fourth column represents diverse mobile phone products.

Figure 3. Classifier rule database

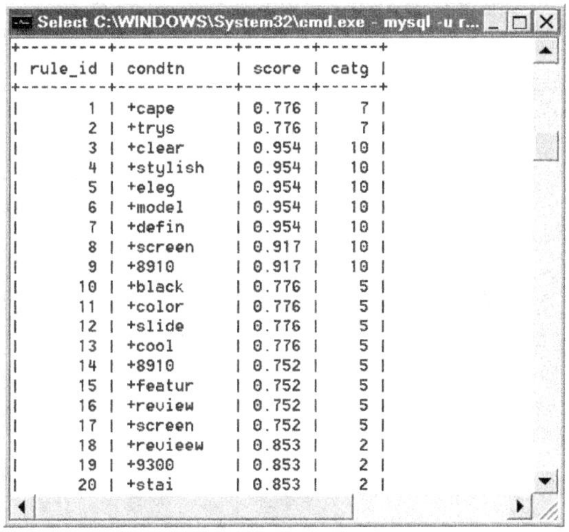

Select C:\WINDOWS\System32\cmd.exe - mysql -u r...

rule_id	condtn	score	catg
1	+cape	0.776	7
2	+trys	0.776	7
3	+clear	0.954	10
4	+stylish	0.954	10
5	+eleg	0.954	10
6	+model	0.954	10
7	+defin	0.954	10
8	+screen	0.917	10
9	+8910	0.917	10
10	+black	0.776	5
11	+color	0.776	5
12	+slide	0.776	5
13	+cool	0.776	5
14	+8910	0.752	5
15	+featur	0.752	5
16	+review	0.752	5
17	+screen	0.752	5
18	+revieew	0.853	2
19	+9300	0.853	2
20	+stai	0.853	2

The system performance has been validated using 1,000 test records. As shown in Table 2, the second column indicates the mobile phone product that has been purchased in each test record, and the third column lists the mobile phone products that are recommended by the associative classification-based recommendation system using classifiers. The value of v_s shown in the fourth column is either one or zero to indicate whether the recommendation system advises the correct products. In this case, 932 test records are correctly recommended resulting in the recommendation accuracy of 93.2%. After validation, the generated classifiers are stored in the classifier rule database for further retrieval, update, and query.

Online customers are allowed to search and buy mobile phone products via the Internet. The dynamic Web pages produced by ASP are not affected by the type of browser the online customer is using. Thus, online customers can access the recommendation system through the Internet more conveniently. To enable the right

Table 2. System performance results

Record $\bar{t}_s$	**Original Class Label** $C(\bar{t}_s)$	**Recommended Class Labels** $\bar{C}^{t_s}$	v_s
$\bar{t}_1$	Motorola E680i	Motorola E680i, Nokia N70	1
$\bar{t}_2$	Siemens SX1	Nokia E70, Samsung SGH-D720	0
…	…	…	…
$\bar{t}_{999}$	Nokia 7610	Nokia 7610, Nokia 8910	1
$\bar{t}_{1000}$	Samsung E628	Samsung E628, Nokia 9300	1
$\sum_{s=1}^{S} v_s$	932		
a	93.2%		

recommendation for a specific online customer, online customers are assigned credentials to log in the Web page and submit their requirements. By connecting with the database through ODBC proxy server, data and rules can be easily retrieved to support the application server to process the classification tasks. The most valuable product alternatives are then identified and represented to the online customers via HTML file format. Figure 4 shows the recommendation results for two different customer requirements. For example, Figure 4(a) indicates that the customer asks for a mobile phone that has a scheduler and can send e-mail. The recommendation result is Nokia 9300 shown in Figure 4(b), which is deemed as the most valuable mobile phone for the corresponding requirements supported by the associative classification-based recommendation system. Figure 4(c) and 4(d) show another customer requirement and the corresponding result, where the customer asks for the mobile phone that is stylish, elegant, and in black color,

Figure 4. Customer requirements and the recommendation result

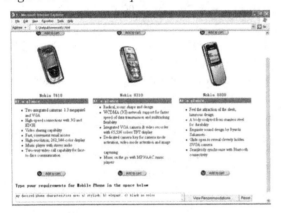

Figure 4(a). The first customer requirement for mobile phone product

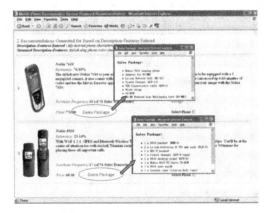

Figure 4(b). Recommendation result for the first customer requirement

Figure 4(c). The second customer requirement for mobile phone product

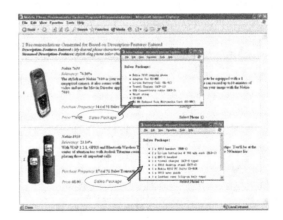

Figure 4(d). Recommendation result for the second customer requirement

and Nokia 7610 and 8910 are recommended for the customer's further comparison.

Supported by the associative classification-based recommendation system, online customers are able to find the mobile phone products that accord the most with their requirements among numerous available mobile phones. The multiple recommendations also allow online customers to make further comparisons among a reduced product set. This solves the information overload problem, thus improving the efficiency and effectiveness of B2C e-commerce.

CONCLUSION

To solve the information overload problem in B2C e-commerce, recommendation systems are always used by e-commerce sites to suggest the most valuable products to online customers. This chapter proposes an associative classification-based recommendation system for B2C e-commerce application. The associative classification-based recommendation system supports online customer decision-making by helping them find the products that they would like to purchase among overwhelming information. By applying knowledge discovery techniques, the associative classification-based recommendation system overcomes the drawback of the popular methods for recommendation systems, namely content-based and collaborative-based method. Thus, it is particularly useful in e-commerce sites that offer millions of products. To implement the proposed recommendation system in an Internet programming environment, three-tier architecture is adopted which enables the communication between the client server, the application server, and the database server. Thus, every customer requirement is processed in the server side which is powerful enough to handle complex computation tasks. An SQL server and an ODBC package are adopted to allow the data

and rules to be queried and managed by involved application servers.

REFERENCES

Avery, C., & Zeckhauser, R. (1997). Recommender systems for evaluating computer messages. *Communications of the ACM, 40*(3), 88-89.

Basu, C., Hirsh, H., & Cohen, W. (1998). Recommendation as classification: Using social and content-based information in recommendation. *CD-ROM Proceedings of the 1998 Workshop on Recommender Systems*, Menlo Park, CA (pp. 11-15).

Carbonell, J. G. (1992). *Natural language understanding.* In S. C. Shapiro (Ed.), *Encyclopedia of artificial intelligence* (pp. 997-1015). New York: John Wiley & Sons.

Chalmers, M., Rodden, K., & Brodbeck, D. (1998). The order of things: Activity-centered information access. *Computer Networks and ISDN Systems, 30*, 359-367.

Chen, H. C., & Chen, A. L. P. (2001). A music recommendation system based on music data grouping and user interests. CD-ROM *Proceedings of the 2001 ACM CIKM International Conference on Information and Knowledge Management,* Atlanta, GA (pp. 231-238).

Cheung, C. F., Lee, W. B., Wang, W. M., Chu, K. F., & To, S. (2003). A multi-perspective knowledge-based system for customer service management. *Expert Systems with Applications, 24*, 457-470.

Fox, C. (Ed.). (1992). *Information retrieval: Data structures and algorithms.* Englewood Cliffs, NJ: Prentice-Hall.

Francisco, G. -S., Rafael, V. -G., & Rodrigo, M. -B. (2005). An integrated approach for developing e-commerce applications. *Expert Systems with Applications, 28*, 223-235.

Fu, X., Budzik, J., & Hammond, K. J. (2000). Mining navigation history for recommendation. CD-ROM *Proceedings of the 5ᵗʰ International Conference on Intelligent User Interfaces,* New Orleans, LA (pp. 106-112).

Ghani, R., & Fano, A. (2002). Building recommender systems using a knowledge base of product semantics. CD-ROM *Proceedings of the International Conference on Workshop on Recommendation and Personalization in E-Commerce,* Malaga, Spain.

Goldberg, D., Nichols, D., Oki, B. M., & Terry, D. (1992). Using collaborative filtering to weave an information tapestry. *Communications of the ACM, 35,* 12.

Han, J., & Kamber, M. (Ed.). (2001). *Data mining: Concepts and techniques.* San Francisco: Morgan Kaufmann Publishers.

Han, P., Xie, B., Yang, F., & Shen, R. (2004). *A scalable P2P recommender system based on distributed collaborative filtering. Expert Systems with Applications, 27,* 203-210.

Hill, W., Stead, L., Rosenstein, M., & Furnas, G. (1995). Recommending and evaluating choices in a virtual community of use. CD-ROM *Proceedings of the 1995 ACM Conference on Factors in Computing Systems,* New York (pp. 194-201).

Huang, G. Q., & Mak, K. L. (2000). Webid: A Web-based framework to support early supplier involvement in new product development. *Robotics and Computer Integrated Manufacturing, 16*(2-3), 169-179.

Kohrs, A., & Merialdo, B. (2001). Creating user-adapted Websites by the use of collaborative filtering. *Interacting with Computers, 13,* 695-716.

Konstan, J., Miller, B., Maltz, D., Herlocker, J., Gordon, L., & Riedl, J. (1997). GroupLens:

Applying collaborative filtering to usenet news. *Communications of the ACM, 40*(3), 77-87.

Lee, W. -P., & Yang, T. -H. (2003). Personalizing information appliances: A multi-agent framework for TV programme recommendations. *Expert Systems with Applications, 25,* 331-341.

Liu, B., Hsu, W., & Ma, Y. (1998). Integrating classification and association rule mining. CD-ROM *Proceedings of the 4ᵗʰ International Conference on Knowledge Discovery and Data Mining,* New York (pp. 27-31).

McNee, S. M., Albert, I., Cosley, D., Gopalkrishnan, P., Lam, S. K., Rashid, A. M., Konstan, J. A., & Riedl, J. (2002). On the recommending of citations for research papers. CD-ROM *Proceedings of the 2004 Conference on Computer-Supported Cooperative Work,* New Orleans (pp. 116-125).

Mooney, R. J., & Roy, L. (2000). Content-based book recommending using learning for text categorization. CD-ROM *Proceedings of the ACM International Conference on Digital Libraries,* San Antonio, Texas (pp. 195-204).

Porter, M. F. (1980). An algorithm for suffix stripping. *Program, 14*(3), 130-137.

Schafer, J. B., Konstan, J.. & Riedl, J. (1999). Recommender systems in E-Commerce. CD-ROM *Proceedings of the 1ˢᵗ ACM Conference on Electronic Commerce,* Denver, Colorado (pp. 158-166).

Shardanand, U., & Maes, P. (1995). Social information filtering: Algorithms for automating word of mouth. CD-ROM *Proceedings of the 1995 Conference on Human Factors in Computing Systems,* Denver, Colorado (pp. 210-217).

Wang, F. -H., & Shaob, H. -M. (2004). Effective personalized recommendation based on time-framed navigation clustering and association mining. *Expert Systems with Applications, 27,* 365-377.

Yeong, B. C., Yoon, H. C., & Soung, H. K. (2005). Mining changes in customer buying behavior for collaborative recommendations. *Expert Systems with Applications, 28*, 359-369.

Yong, S. K., Yum, B. -J., Song, J., & Su, M. K. (2005). Development of a recommender system based on navigational and behavioral patterns of customers in e-commerce sites. *Expert Systems with Applications, 28*, 381-393.

Yoon, H. C., & Jae, K. K. (2004). Application of Web usage mining and product taxonomy to collaborative recommendations in e-commerce. *Expert Systems with Applications, 26*, 233-246.

Yu, L., Liu, L., & Li, X. (2005). A hybrid collaborative filtering method for multiple-interests and multiple-content recommendation in e-commerce. *Expert Systems with Applications, 28*, 67-77.

Yuan, S. -T., & Cheng, C. (2004). Ontology-based personalized couple clustering for heterogeneous product recommendation in mobile marketing. *Expert Systems with Applications, 26*, 461.

Chapter VI
Knowledge–Based Recommender Technologies Supporting the Interactive Selling of Financial Services

Alexander Felfernig
University Klagenfurt, Austria

ABSTRACT

Selling financial services requires deep knowledge about the product domain as well as about potential wishes and needs of customers. In this context, sales representatives can differ significantly in their expertise and level of sales knowledge. Therefore, financial service providers ask for tools supporting sales representatives in the dialog with the customer. In this chapter we present the knowledge-based recommender environment KOBA4MS (Knowledge-based Advisors for Marketing and Sales) which allows a flexible mapping of product, marketing, and sales knowledge to the representation of a recommender knowledge base. In KOBA4MS, we integrate diagnosis, personalization, and knowledge acquisition techniques, thus providing an infrastructure for the interactive selling of financial services.

INTRODUCTION

Due to a restricted knowledge about product assortments and sales processes, sales representatives in the financial services domain are often overwhelmed and prefer a product-oriented advisory approach leading to low quality results for the customer (Eckert-Niemeyer, 2000; Felfernig & Kiener, 2005a; Keltner & Finegold, 1996). In this context, financial service providers ask for tools supporting sales representatives in the dialog with the customer. Such tools should provide adaptive interfaces (Ardissono, Felfernig, Friedrich, Jannach, Petrone, Schaefer, & Zanker, 2003), personalized product recommendations fitting to the customer's goals, needs, and wishes, with explanations increasing the customer's confidence in a recommended product (Jiang, Wang, & Benbasat, 2005; Wind, 2001). KOBA4MS[1] is designed for the development of such knowledge-based recommender applications (advisors) (Burke, 2000; Felfernig, 2005b). KOBA4MS technologies have been successfully applied within the scope of industrial projects. A couple of applications has been implemented for financial service providers supporting the interactive selling of financial services which cover areas of interest such as financing, investment, pension, or insurances. In this context, KOBA4MS technologies are used for the following purposes:

- Formalization of product, marketing, and sales knowledge, that is, implementing a recommender knowledge base (product properties, customer properties, and constraints) and a corresponding recommender process (which questions should be posed to a customer in which situation);
- Test and debugging of recommender knowledge bases, that is, validating the results/ solutions calculated by the recommender

knowledge base and (if needed) automatically identifying faulty constraints in the knowledge base;

- Consistency check of customer requirements and (if needed) supporting the calculation of repair actions (minimal changes to a given set of customer requirements); for example, high return rates are incompatible with a low willingness to take risks; therefore, these requirements have to be changed (repaired) in order to enable the recommender application to find a solution; and
- Explanation of the calculated results in order to increase a customer's confidence in a presented solution; in order to be helpful for customers, recommender applications must provide explanations why a certain product fits to the wishes and needs of a customer (Jiang et al., 2005).

This chapter is organized as follows: In Section 2 (KOBA4MS Overview), we present the KOBA4MS architecture. In Section 3 (KOBA4MS Technologies), we discuss KOBA4MS recommender technologies and give examples for their usage in the financial services domain. In Section 4 (Experiences from Projects), we report experi-

Figure 1. KOBA4MS architecture

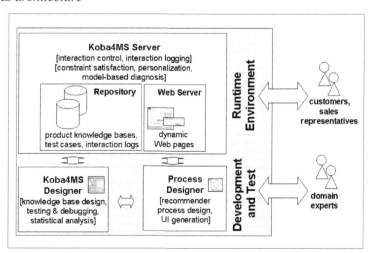

ences from applying KOBA4MS technologies in commercial settings.

KOBA4MS OVERVIEW

The Koba4MS architecture is shown in Figure 1. The development and test environment supports the design of the knowledge base and the corresponding process definition which represents a generic model of the behavior of the recommender user interface. The runtime environment (represented by KOBA4MS Server) is responsible for controlling the user interface and for calculating personalized solutions fitting to the wishes and needs of the customer.

KOBA4MS Designer is a recommender knowledge base (Felfernig, Friedrich, Jannach, Stumptner, & Zanker, 2003; Mittal & Frayman, 1989; Soininen, Tiihonen, Maenistoe, & Sulonen, 1998) development environment. The supported concepts are based on long-term research in the area of knowledge-based configuration and personalization (Ardissono et al., 2003; Felfernig, 2005b; Felfernig, Friedrich, & Jannach, 2000; Felfernig, Friedrich, Jannach, & Stumptner, 2004a; Felfernig et al., 2003; Friedrich, Mehlau, Wimmer, Zanker, & Russ, 2004b). KOBA4MS Designer supports the

development of multi-lingual applications, that is, recommender knowledge bases can be maintained for different languages.

A recommender knowledge base consists of the following parts (see Figure 2):

- Product properties describe the provided set of products, for example, name of the product, recommended investment period for the product;

- Customer properties (represented as questions posed to customers) describe the possible set of customer requirements, for example, willingness to take risks or expected return rates; and

- A set of constraints restricting the combinations of customer requirements and product properties, for example, return rates above 9% per annum require a high willingness to take risks.

Recommender processes (designed by **Process Designer**) are models of the intended behavior of the recommender user interface (see, e.g., Figure 3). Such process definitions define the way the system adapts its dialog style to the knowledge level and interest areas of a customer. Recommender applications typically have a finite num-

Figure 2. Knowledge base construction using KOBA4MS designer

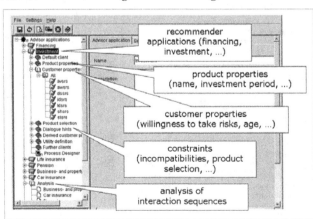

ber of states, where transitions are triggered by actions of the user (navigation to the next page, selection of the preferred answer to a given question, etc.). Formally, process definitions are based on predicate-augmented finite state recognizers (PFSR) (Felfernig, & Shchekotykhin, 2006; van Noord & Gerdemann, 2001) where constraints describe transitions between states of a recommender process. The execution of recommender processes is based on the evaluation of transition conditions. After each user input, post-conditions of the actual state are evaluated in order to determine the next state. The recommender knowledge base and the corresponding process

Figure 3. Recommender process definition using process designer

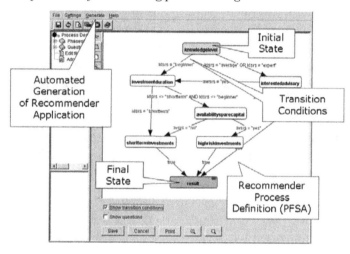

Figure 4. Types of advisors in typical application scenarios

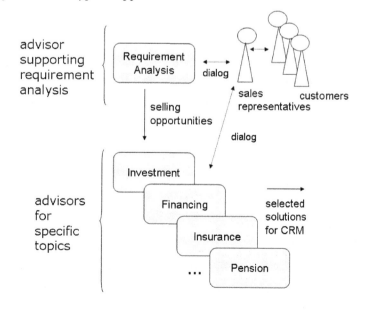

definition are represented as graphical models which are automatically translated into a corresponding recommender application (see, e.g., Figure 5). Java Server pages are generated, which are based on a custom JSP tag library (Goodwill, 2002) for recommender applications.[2] For each state in the process definition, a corresponding JSP file is generated which includes, for example, questions and possible answers (see, e.g., Figure 5). Templates contain placeholders which are replaced by concrete values when generating a JSP file. Having completed this generation task, the resulting advisor application can be executed on a standard Web server.

Typically, sales representatives analyse customer goals which depend on, for example, the life phase of the customer. In this situation, KOBA4MS supports the matching of customer life phases and personal goals (e.g., starting to build a house in three years, to provide for one's old age,

or to provide for one's children) to a set of **selling opportunities** (e.g., medium-term investments for building a house, long-term investments for closing the pension gap) (see Figure 4).

After such an initial analysis phase (the result is a set of topics/selling opportunities to be discussed with the customer), one or more detailed advisory sessions can be started; for example, an investment advisor is used to identify an investment solution which fits to the customer's preferences related to the dimensions profit, availability, and risk. Having completed such an advisory session, the customer decides which solutions she/he wants to buy. Selected solutions (orders) are returned to the CRM system which manages customer orders. If no solution can be found for a given set of customer requirements, a repair process is started which calculates a set of possible (minimal) changes to the given requirements, thus allowing the derivation of a solution for the customer.

Figure 5. Example recommender user interface

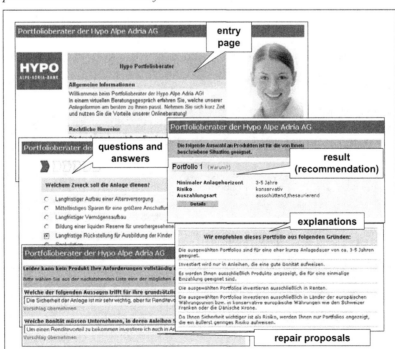

KOBA4MS TECHNOLOGIES

In contrast to Collaborative Filtering (Herlocker, Konstan, Terveen, & Riedl, 2004; Sarwar, Karypis, Konstan, & Riedl, 2001) and Content-based Filtering (Burke, 2002; Pazzani, 1999) approaches, Knowledge-based Recommenders (Ardissono et al., 2003; Burke, 2000; Felfernig, 2005b) exploit deep knowledge about the product domain. Using such an approach, the relationship between customer requirements and financial services can be explicitly modelled in a product knowledge base (Felfernig et al., 2003). Such model-based representations are an excellent basis for applying model-based diagnosis techniques which are discussed in the following sections.

Calculating Solutions

Basically, KOBA4MS uses constraint-based knowledge representations (Tsang, 1993). A Constraint Satisfaction Problem (CSP) (C,V,D) (Tsang, 1993) is defined by a set V of variables x_i, a set C of constraints c_j and a set D of domains d_i which defines for each variable the set of possible values. A CSP is solved if there exists a set of instantiations of the variables $x_1, x_2, ..., x_n$ s.t. all constraints contained in C are satisfied. A *recommendation task* can be defined as a CSP $(C,V_{SRS}, V_{PROD}, D_{SRS}, D_{PROD})$, where V is additionally divided into V_{SRS} (set of variables describing customer requirements) and V_{PROD} (set of variables describing product properties). The constraint solver tries to find a solution for a given recommendation task. If no solution can be found, constraints with a priority > 0 (0 is the highest priority) are relaxed, starting with constraints with the lowest priority. If nothing but non-relaxable constraints (priority = 0) remain, a corresponding repair mechanism is activated.

If no results could be found, typical recommender applications tell the user that no solution was found. KOBA4MS supports the calculation of **repair actions for customer requirements** (a minimal set of changes allowing the calculation of a solution). If $\Sigma = \{x_1=a_1, x_2=a_2, ..., x_n=a_n\}$ is a set of customer requirements (instantiations of customer properties) and C is a set of constraints ($\Sigma \cup C$ has no solution), a repair is a minimal set of changes to Σ (resulting in Σ') s.t. $\Sigma' \cup C$ has a solution. The computation of repair actions (Felfernig et al., 2004a) is based on concepts of model-based diagnosis (Reiter, 1987) (see Figure 5 for the representation of repair alternatives/proposals).

Figure 6. Repairing customer requirements

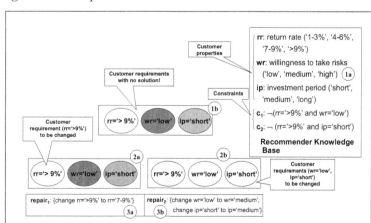

Model-based diagnosis starts with the description of a system (SD – System Description) which is, in our case, the recommender knowledge base. If the actual behavior of the system (set of customer requirements imposed to the knowledge base) conflicts with the intended system behavior (no solution can be found), the diagnosis task is to determine a minimal set of customer requirements which, when assumed to be functioning abnormally, will explain the discrepancy between the actual and the intended system behavior. An example for determining repairs using model-based diagnosis is depicted in Figure 6.

In this example Σ = {rr='>9%', wr='low', ip='short'} (Figure 6-1b), C={c_1, c_2} (Figure 6-1a) and $\Sigma \cup C$ has no solution since $c_1 \cup \Sigma$ is inconsistent and $c_2 \cup \Sigma$ is inconsistent as well. One possible repair of Σ is to change the requirement related to the return rate rr='>9%' (to, e.g., rr='7-9%') (Figure 6-2a, Figure 6-3a) which makes $\Sigma \cup C$ consistent. *Another repair alternative is to change the requirements related to the investment period (e.g., ip='long') and the willingness to take risks (e.g., wr='medium')* (Figure 6-2b, Figure 6-3b). *A detailed discussion on the calculation of repair actions can be found in Reiter (1987) and Felfernig et al. (2004a).*

Validating Knowledge Bases

The complexity of recommender knowledge bases makes **quality assurance** a critical task (Kirani, Zualkernan, & Tsai, 1994; Preece, Talbot, & Vignollet, 1997). Within KOBA4MS, process definitions are the basis for automatically generating test cases (**Automated Test Case Generation**). Solutions (results calculated by the knowledge base) for generated test cases are presented to the domain expert who decides on their validity (**Result Validation**). Test cases deemed as correct by the domain expert are used for future **Regression Testing** (Fleischanderl, 2002). Automated test case generation in KOBA4MS is based on the definition of a constraint satisfaction problem.

For this purpose, a complete set of possible paths through a recommender process is determined. For each path in the set, a CSP is generated and executed; identified results correspond to test cases. Test case generation follows a path-oriented approach which allows a high degree of coverage (Edvardson, 1999; Ferguson & Korel, 1996). Our experiences from developing recommender applications show that domain experts agree with accepting additional efforts related to the inspection of test sets, since the quality of the recommendations is of serious concern. The disposable time of domain experts for testing is restricted; therefore, mechanisms are provided which reduce the amount of tests. Details on approaches to reduce the number of test cases can be found in Felfernig (2005b).

Personalization

KOBA4MS includes mechanisms allowing the adaptation of the dialog style to the user's skills and needs (**management of customer profiles**). The user interface relies on the management of a user model that describes capabilities and preferences of individual customers. Some of these properties are directly provided by the user (e.g., age, nationality, personal goals, or self-estimates such as knowledge about financial services); other properties are derived using personalization rules and scoring mechanisms which relate user answers to abstract dimensions (Ardissono et al., 2003) such as preparedness to take risks or interest in high profits (dimensions describing the users' interests), and knowledge about funds (dimensions describing the users' knowledge about the domain). Initial values for the customer profile are collected in a requirements analysis phase where best-matching stereotypes are applied to complete profiles.

Customers have different approaches to specify their requirements which range from the direct specification of product parameters (e.g., a certain savings account, running for three years)

Table 1. Customer-individual utility values for requirements

	utility(rr)	utility(ip)	utility(wr)
customer₁	2	3	4
customer₂	5	2	1

Table 2. Personalized determination of repair actions

		utility customer₁	utility customer₂
repair₁	{rr='7-9%'}	2	5
repair₂	{ip='medium', wr='medium'}	7	3

to a very general specification of their personal goals (e.g., financing their children's education). An adaptation of the interaction style contributes to an improved approximation to the behavior of a human sales expert. Depending on a set of answers already provided by the customer, the following concepts support the **personalization of the dialog style**:

- Alternative formulation of questions, for example, questions posed to experts can be differentiated from those posed to customers with less knowledge about financial services;
- Rule-based formulation of default-answers, for example, in an investment advisory session where the goal of the customer is to put money by for a rainy day, the default answer to a question related to the maximum accepted decrease in value is no decrease in value accepted; and
- Alternative explanations for constraint violations, for example, if the customer is a novice, a very general explanation about changes in the pension law is given, while more detailed information can be included for experts.

If no solution can be found for a given set of customer requirements, KOBA4MS calculates a set of possible **repair actions** which allow the calculation of a solution. Different customer properties (variables) have an assigned priority (represented by a utility value) which indicates the utility of the variable for the customer. The lower the utility of the variable, the higher the probability is that the variable is considered as the focus of repair actions, for example, if the return rate is less important for a customer; this property is primarily considered as a potential candidate for repair actions, that is, repair actions are adapted to the customer's preferences. Table 1 and Table 2 depict a simple example for personalizing repair actions depending on defined utilities for variables (customer requirements). Table 1 shows the utility of the variables *rr* (return rate), *ip* (investment period), and *wr* (willingness to take risks) for customer₁ and customer₂, for example, the utility of the variable *rr* is higher for customer₂. Table 2 depicts the application of the different utility values to proposed repair actions (repair₁, repair₂). The sum of the utility values of repair₂ for customer₁ is seven (utility(*ip*) + utility(*wr*)), of repair₁ for customer₁ it is two. Consequently, repair₁ is proposed to customer₁, since it has the lowest utility for the customer. Vice versa, repair₂ is proposed to customer₂.

Figure 7. Faulty recommender knowledge base

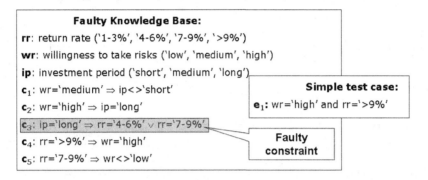

Knowledge Acquisition

One major requirement imposed by financial service providers is the availability of a **graphical design environment** for recommender knowledge bases. KOBA4MS Designer and Process Designer allow the design of recommender knowledge bases and process definitions by non-programmers. In this context, constraint schemes, that is, graphical interfaces for defining constraints are an important means to alleviate the management of recommender knowledge bases.

Debugging support for recommender knowledge base development is a critical issue for a successful development and maintenance of recommender applications. In KOBA4MS we have implemented model-based diagnosis algorithms (Felfernig et al., 2004a; Reiter, 1987) supporting the identification of minimal sources of inconsistencies in recommender knowledge bases. Similar to the diagnosis and repair of customer requirements, we apply model-based diagnosis techniques in order to identify a minimal set of constraints which, when deleted from the recommender knowledge base, allow consistency restoration. Test cases automatically generated by the test environment are applied to identify faulty regions in a given recommender knowledge base. Validated test cases and the corresponding

results are applied as positive examples for results to be calculated by the recommender knowledge base. If such a positive example is not accepted by the knowledge base, a corresponding diagnosis process is activated. KOBA4MS supports the calculation of diagnoses for recommender knowledge bases (a minimal set of constraints responsible for the nonacceptance of a set of positive examples). Let $\Pi = \{c_1, c_2, ..., c_m\}$ be a set of constraints in the recommender knowledge base and $\Omega = \{e_1, e_2, ..., e_n\}$ be a set of test cases (positive examples) and *not* ($\Pi \cup e_i$ consistent $\forall\ e_i \in \Omega$), then a corresponding diagnosis is a minimal set of changes to Π (deletions of constraints from Π) resulting in Π', s.t. $\Pi' \cup e_i$ consistent $\forall\ e_i \in \Omega$. Similar to the computation of repair actions for inconsistent customer requirements, the computation of diagnoses (Felfernig et al., 2004a) is based on the Hitting Set algorithm (Reiter, 1987). An example for the calculation of diagnoses is shown in Figure 7.

In this example, $\Pi = \{c_1, c_2, c_3, c_4, c_5\}$ and $\Omega = \{e_1:$ wr='high' and rr='>9%'$\}$. $\Pi \cup \Omega$ is inconsistent, that is, e_1 is not accepted by the recommender knowledge base. One possible diagnosis (constraints to be changed) for our simple scenario is c_3, since $\Pi - \{c_3\} \cup \Omega$ is consistent.

EXPERIENCES FROM PROJECTS

One example for the application of Koba4MS technologies is the Wüstenrot Building and Loan Association[3], where financial service recommenders have been deployed for about 1,400 sales representatives (Felfernig & Kiener, 2005a). In this case, the motivation for the application of knowledge-based recommender technologies was to improve the efficiency and effectiveness of sales processes in terms of solution quality (substituting a product-oriented advisory approach with a customer-oriented one), error reduction (checking the feasibility of calculated solutions at the customer side), and intelligent documentation of advisory sessions due to regulations of the European Union (EU, 2002). The sales volume of Wüstenrot in 2004 was about 345,000 products. On the average, a sales representative sells about 60-70 products per year (high performers, that is, sales experts sell up to 500 products per year). Further details on the deployment of financial service recommenders for Wüstenrot can be found in Felfernig (2005a).

Koba4MS technologies have been applied for implementing online investment advisors for the Hypo Alpe-Adria-Bank[4] for about 60 financial services. We have evaluated those applications on the basis of an online questionnaire (n=152 participants, 23% denoted themselves as experts, 40% as beginners, the rest as having average knowledge in the financial services domain), where about 51% of the participants actively applied the recommender applications. Of those who applied the recommender applications, 98.5% were judging the provided recommender functionality as very useful when searching for financial service solutions. Within the scope of the questionnaire, the participants had the task to identify a specific type of product on the bank's homepage. In this context, we have compared search times of those participants using a recommender application and those simply browsing Web pages of the bank (product fact sheets, etc.). Comparing the search efforts of the two groups indicated a clear potential for reducing search costs. The average search time was 10.5 min.; a one-sample z-Test ($z=2.75$, $p < 0.01$) indicates that participants invested less time for product search if they used a corresponding recommender application. In addition to search efforts, we also analyzed the subjective satisfaction with the provided advisory functionality of the homepage. The result of this analysis indicates an increased satisfaction with the overall advisory quality when having applied a recommender ($z=3.04$, $p < 0.01$). A number of additional applications have been implemented on the basis of KOBA4MS technologies, for example, recommenders for www.quelle.at, one of the leading online selling environments in Austria and the digicam advisor for www.geizhals.at, the largest product platform in Austria.

RELATED WORK

An overview of different types of recommender applications can be found, for example, in Schafer, Konstan, and Riedl (2000) and Montaner, Lopez, and De la Rose (2003). Overviews of different recommender technologies can be found in Burke, 2000, 2002; Sarwar et al., 2001; and Terveen and Hill (2001). Basically, there exist three technological recommender approaches. Collaborative Filtering (Herlocker et al., 2004; Sarwar et al., 2001) and Content-based Filtering (Burke, 2002; Pazzani, 1999) do not exploit deep knowledge about the product assortment. Collaborative Filtering is based on the assumption that customer preferences are correlated, that is, recommendations given to a customer are derived from preferences of customers who have similar interests, for example, if two customers have bought similar books in the past and have rated those books in a similar way, books (with a positive rating) read by only one of the two can be recommended to the other one. Similarly, Content-based Filtering does not exploit deep knowledge about the product domain but uses customer preferences to infer future recommendations. In this context, products are described by a set of keywords/categories which are stored in a customer profile if a customer buys a certain product. The next time the customer interacts with the recommender application, already-stored preferences from previous sessions are used for offering additional products which are assigned to similar categories. Both techniques suffer from problems when calculating recommendations for new users or new items (where no user ratings exist).

The reason for choosing a knowledge-based recommendation approach stems from requirements of the financial services domain where the user typically needs deep domain knowledge about the products in order to find a solution that corresponds to his/her demands. Knowledge-based Recommenders (advisors) (Ardissono et al., 2003; Burke, 2000; Felfernig, 2005b) exploit deep knowledge about the product domain in order to determine solutions for the customer. When selling financial services, a customer's taste is not of primary concern; primarily, solutions must be correct. This requirement can be met by explicitly representing product-, marketing-, and sales knowledge (Felfernig et al., 2003; Mittal & Frayman, 1989), that is, Knowledge-based Recommenders are the natural choice in this context. Compared to other knowledge-based approaches (Burke, 2002), KOBA4MS additionally includes model-based diagnosis (Felfernig et al., 2004a; Reiter, 1987) concepts allowing the calculation of repair actions in the case of inconsistent customer requirements (no solution can be found) and the determination of constraints responsible for an unintended behavior of a recommender knowledge base. Furthermore, repair actions related to customer requirements can be personalized using multi-attribute object rating (Ardissono et al., 2003).

Stolze, Field, and Kleijer (2000) present applications of knowledge-based technologies for the selection of insurance products. An interactive product configuration is shown by giving an impression of the overall system architecture and additional application examples. Compared to the work presented in this chapter, Stolze et al. (2000) do not discuss experiences related to the effectiveness of development and maintenance processes. Using retirement planning as application scenario, Dziarsteck, Farnschläder, Gilleßen, Süßmilch-Walther, and Winkler (2004) present their financial services recommender application. The system is based on a process-oriented approach, where the user is guided through the whole financial planning process. Although Dziarsteck et al. (2004) provide a good impression of the underlying recommender process, no details are provided about the underlying reasoning mechanisms of the system. Based on the scenario of composing insurance and investment services with the goal to provide an integrated (configured) solution for young families with children, the concept of customer- and needs-oriented product configuration is presented in Felfernig et al. (2004b). In the context of this scenario, different types of constraint representations are discussed (e.g., constraints between customer requirements or constraints establishing the relationship between customer requirements and product properties); these types of constraint representation are included in the KOBA4MS system.

CONCLUSION

KOBA4MS has been successfully applied for supporting customers and sales representatives of financial service providers in Austria. Model-Based Diagnosis technologies allow the retrieval of repair alternatives in situations where no solution can be found and provide support for knowledge engineers searching for faults in the recommender knowledge base. These technologies allow the construction of more intuitive online sales dialogs and can contribute to a significant reduction of development and maintenance efforts for knowledge-based recommender applications.

REFERENCES

Ardissono, L., Felfernig, A., Friedrich, G., Jannach, D., Petrone, G., Schaefer, R., & Zanker M. (2003). A framework for the development of personalized, distributed Web-based configuration systems. *AI Magazine, 24*(3), 93–108.

Burke, R. (2000). Knowledge-based recommender systems. *Encyclopedia of Library & Information Systems, 69*(32).

Burke, R. (2002). Hybrid recommender systems: Survey and experiments. *User Modeling and User-Adapted Interaction, 4*, 331-370.

Dziarstek, C., Farnschläder, F., Gilleßen, S., Süßmilch-Walther, I., & Winkler, V. (2004). A user-aware financial advisory system. *Multikonferenz Wirtschaftsinformatik (MKWI) 2004, Universität Duisburg-Essen,* Berlin (pp. 217-229).

Eckert-Niemeyer, V. (2000). Innovative tools zur Realisierung der virtuellen Beratung. *Banking and Information Technology, 1*(1), 23-31.

Edvardson, J. (1999). A survery on automatic test data generation. In *Proceedings of the 2nd Conference on Computer Science and Engineering CCSSe'99.*

EU (2002). *Richtline 2002/92/EG des Europäischen Parlaments und des Rates vom 9. Dezember 2002 über Versicherungsvermittlung,* Amtsblatt der Europäischen Gemeinschaften.

Felfernig, A. (2005b). Koba4MS: Selling complex products and services using knowledge-based recommender technologies. In *Proceedings of the*

7th *IEEE Conference on e-Commerce Technology,* München, Germany (pp. 92-100).

Felfernig, A., Friedrich, G., & Jannach, D. (2000). UML as domain specific language for the construction of knowledge-based configuration systems. *IJSEKE, 10*(4), 449-469.

Felfernig, A., Friedrich, G., Jannach, D., & Stumptner, M. (2004a). Consistency-based diagnosis of configuration knowledge bases. *AI Journal, 2*(152), 213-234.

Felfernig, A., Friedrich, G., Jannach, D., Stumptner, M., & Zanker, M. (2003). Configuration knowledge representations for Semantic Web applications. *AI Engineering Design, Analysis, and Manufacturing Journal, 17*, 31-50.

Felfernig, A., & Kiener, A. (2005a). Knowledge-based interactive selling of financial services using FSAdvisor. In *Proceedings of the 17th Innovative Applications of Artificial Intelligence Conference (IAAI'05),* Pittsburgh, PA (pp. 1475-1482). AAAI Press.

Felfernig, A., Mehlau, J., Wimmer, A., Zanker, M., & Russ, C. (2004b). Konzepte zur flexiblen Konfiguration von Finanzdienstleistungen. *Banking and Information Technology, Sonderheft zur Multi-Konferenz Wirtschaftsinformatik 2004, 5*(1), 5-17.

Felfernig, A., & Shchekotykhin, K. (2006). Debugging user interface descriptions of knowledge-based recommender applications. *ACM Conference on Intelligent User Interfaces (IUI'06),* Sydney, Australia (pp. 234-241).

Ferguson, R., & Korel, B. (1996). The chaining approach for software test data generation. *IEEE Transactions on Software Engineering, 5*(1), 63-86.

Fleischanderl, G. (2002). Suggestions from the software engineering practice for applying consistency-based diagnosis to configuration knowledge bases. In *Proceedings of the 13th International Workshop on Principles of Diagnosis (DX-02).*

Friedrich, G. (2004). Elimination of spurious explanations. In *Proceedings of the 16th European Conference on Artificial Intelligence (ECAI'04),* Valencia, Spain (pp. 813-817).

Goodwill, G. (2002). *Mastering JSP custom tags and tag libraries.* Wiley.

Herlocker, J. L., Konstan, J. A., Terveen, L. G., & Riedl, J. T. (2004). Evaluating collaborative filtering recommender systems. *ACM Transactions on Information Systems, 22*(1), 5-53.

Jiang, Z., Wang, W., & Benbasat, I. (2005). Multimedia-based interactive advising technology for online consumer decision support. *Communications of the ACM, 48*(9), 92-98.

Keltner, B., & Finegold, D. (1996). Adding value in banking: Human resource innovations for service firms. *Sloan Management Review, 38*(1), 57-68.

Kirani, S. H., Zualkernan, I. A., & Tsai, W. T. (1994). Evaluation of expert system testing methods. *Communications of the ACM, 37*(11).

Mittal, S., & Frayman, F. (1989). Towards a generic model of configuration tasks. In *Proceedings of the 11th International Joint Conference on AI,* Detroit, MI (pp. 1395-1401).

Montaner, M., Lopez, B., & De la Rose, J. (2003). A taxonomy of recommender agents on the Internet. *Artificial Intelligence Review, 19*, 285-330.

Pazzani, M. (1999). A framework for collaborative, content-based, and demographic filtering. *Artificial Intelligence Review, 13*(5-6), 393-408.

Preece, A., Talbot, S., & Vignollet, L. (1997). Evaluation of verification tools for knowledge-based systems. *International Journal of Human-Computer Studies, 47*, 629-658.

Reiter, R. (1987). A theory of diagnosis from first principles. *Artificial Intelligence, 23*(1), 57-95.

Sarwar, B., Karypis, G., Konstan, J. A., & Riedl, J. T. (2001). Item-based collaborative filtering recommendation algorithms. In *Proceedings of the 10th International World Wide Web Conference* (pp. 285-295).

Schafer, J., Konstan, J., & Riedl, J. T. (2000). Electronic commerce recommender applications. *Journal of Data Mining and Knowledge Discovery, 5*(1/2), 115-152.

Soininen, T., Tiihonen, J., Maenistoe, T., & Sulonen, R. (1998). Towards a general ontology of configuration. *AI Engineering Design Analysis and Manufacturing Journal, 12*(4), 357-372.

Stolze, M., Field, S., & Kleijer, P. (2000). Combining configuration and evaluation mechanisms to support to selection of modular insurance products. In *Proceedings of the 8th European Conference on Information Systems* (pp. 858-865).

Terveen, L., & Hill, W. (2001). Beyond recommender systems: Helping people help each other. In J. Carroll (Ed.), *HCI in the new millennium.* Addison Wesley.

Tsang, E. (1993). *Foundations of constraint satisfaction.* London: Academic Press.

vanNoord, G., & Gerdemann, D. (2001). Finite state transducers with predicates and identities. *Grammars, 4*(3), 263-286.

Wind, Y. (2001). The challenge of "customerization" in financial services. *Communications of the ACM, 44*(5), 39-44.

ENDNOTES

[1]   *Knowledge-based Advisors for Marketing and Sales* is funded by the Austrian Research Fund (No. 808479). Koba4MS is the research version of the commercial toolsuite CWAdvisor (www.configworks.com).

[2]   See e.g. sun.java.com.

[3]   www.wuestenrot.at.

[4]   www.hypo-alpe-adria.at.

Chapter VII
Developing Interoperability in Mass Customization Information Systems

Ricardo Jardim-Goncalves
Universidade Nova de Lisboa, Portugal

António Grilo
Universidade Nova de Lisboa, Portugal

Adolfo Steiger-Garcao
Universidade Nova de Lisboa, Portugal

ABSTRACT

This chapter proposes a standard-based framework to assist industrial organizations to develop interoperability in mass customization Information Systems. After identifying the major challenges for business and information systems in mass customization, the authors propose an innovative standard-based conceptual architecture for a combined model-driven and services-oriented platform. The chapter concludes by describing a global methodology for integration of models and applications, to enhance an enterprise's interoperability in the support of mass customization practices, keeping the same organization's technical and operational environment, but improving its methods of work and the usability of the installed technology through harmonization and integration of the enterprise models in use by customers, manufacturers, and suppliers. Its platform aims to stimulate the adoption of mass customization concepts and improve those practices through proper integration and harmonization of information system models, knowledge, and data.

INTRODUCTION

The advance of mass customization principles can only be sustainable if supported with changes in how value is created, namely in the way goods and services are defined, and how logistics, operations, and customer interaction are designed. These changes must occur both internally, within organizations value chain, and also in the network wherein companies are embedded, further exploiting relationships with suppliers, distributors, and consumers. Nevertheless, all these changes in business can only occur if enabled by adequate interoperable information systems.

Nowadays, many enterprises already have information technology that can fulfill their mass customization requirements in each activity and with external organizations, like, for example, suppliers and customers. Also, in an industrial environment, many applications are available to support operating the product life cycle (PLC) stages. However, organizations typically acquire their applications with an aim to solve focused needs, without an overall view of the global enterprise's system integration. This essentially results from the way companies are organized, with internal departments usually adopting different frameworks. Even when enterprise models are interoperable, when information has to be exchanged, very often difficulties arise with respect to data semantics, since common reference models are not in place.

Mass customization and interoperability can be identified as key factors for enterprise success on a constantly-changing global custom-driven environment, enabling companies to act in networked partnership to strengthen their position facing the market. However, due to the difficulty of maintaining and integrating existing heterogeneous information systems, languages, and applications, the interoperable platforms are urging to emerge.

Applications developed using standard-based architectures present a systematic approach to enterprise integration and promotion of interoperability among different enterprises. Several reference models designed and developed using standard methodologies and techniques have already been developed for covering many industrial areas and related application activities, from design to production and sales, for example, ISO 10303 STEP, ebXML, EDI. Also, proposals for standardized architectures have been evolving, and they are expected to be shown as the standard way of handling middleware and infrastructure development for enterprise systems groups, like the model-driven architecture (MDA) and service-oriented architecture (SOA).

However, implementing new technology in organizations is a complex task that must be developed according to a suitable methodology supported by a proper and easy-to-implement platform. The advent of continuous technological evolution and business challenges makes companies unable to be constantly updated, and such dynamics have a recognized impact in organizations' strategies and resources with costs that they cannot afford.

This chapter proposes a framework to enhance an enterprise's interoperability in the support of mass customization practices, keeping the same organization's technical and operational environment, but improving its methods of work and the usability of the installed technology through harmonization and integration of the enterprise models in use by customers, manufacturers, and suppliers. Its platform aims to stimulate the adoption of mass customization concepts and improve those practices through proper integration and harmonization of information system models, knowledge, and data.

CHALLENGES FOR BUSINESS IN MASS CUSTOMIZATION

Mass customization implementation in companies requires intervention at business processes, production network, and information systems. Integrating the value chain, together with a flexible supply chain management, and supported by an information-rich supply and distribution chains is crucial for the success of companies in the advent of mass customization practices.

Integrated Value Chain

Mass customization principles promote the individual possibilities and unique features for the customer, and this must be supported accordingly by design, production, and sales processes. To compete in a mass customization strategy, companies must have capacities, competencies, and resources to cope with evolving product configurations, variable output frequency, and dynamic customer profiles, providing thus product and services that will differentiate from commodity type of products (Gilmore & Pine, 1997; Pine, 1993).

Diverse solutions have been considered to sustain these business demands, like product platforms, modularity, commonality, or postponement (Anderson & Pine, 1997; Da Silveira, Borenstein, & Fogliaatto, 2001; O'Grady, 1999). These solutions imply greater efficiency of internal business processes, and effective coordination mechanisms between its different functions.

Competition in highly-dynamic and agile production environments require a significant reduction of setup time in the production cycle to deal with flexible order-taking from customers. As companies reverse their traditional market push systems to market pull systems, it is the consumer who drives product configuration requirements. Thus, organizations must have new methods of work, where more precise and evolving forecasting models have to be deployed, based on the late interaction and marketers' fine analysis of consumer patterns. This implies the use of advanced algorithms for aggregate planning based on a generic and intelligent bill of materials. Additionally, demands are posed in inbound and outbound logistics, and in the way stocks are managed; also, the manufacturing systems need to assemble the production basic blocks according to a set of evolving rules (Robertson & Ulrich, 1998; Simpson, 2005).

More than simple mass personalization of products and services that occurs in the late stages of the whole PLC, mass customization requires that the value chain's primary and secondary activities are linked together dynamically according to the product and customer profiles. These links need to be seamlessly established and error free. Since clients require highly-specific product or specific requirements, companies must be able to design products that both satisfy clients and are easily manufactured (Cusumano & Nobeoka, 1998; Liker, 2004). Thus, products must be designed to be manufactured.

These operations management challenges cannot be fulfilled if not supported by specialized computer applications, together with automation in the production line. To achieve agile and flexible response, these applications need to be integrated. Commercial ERP systems promise this integration, but real-world practice shows that too often companies choose fragmented, vertical, and functionally-oriented specialized applications rather than complete commercial ERP solutions (empírica GmbH, 2005). This poses challenges for information integration and therefore systems interoperability, as many applications run on disparate operating systems and use heterogeneous reference models and technologies.

Flexible Supply Chain Management

A mass customization paradigm requires enhanced flexible and efficiency in the supply chain, supported by seamless data exchange (Cusumano & Nobeoka, 1998; Hegge & Wortmann, 1991; Huang, Zhang, & Lo, 2005). Flexibility in the supply chain is necessary to respond to more complex products configuration and their fast-changing characteristics. However, this flexibility cannot compromise the efficiency of the businesses interaction, but rather increase it. Simultaneous flexibility and efficiency of the supply chain management can only be achieved through simplification. This requires standardization, automatic resupply mechanisms, and rationalization (Anderson, 2004).

Most products are designed without considering the benefits of using standardization. Thus, contrary to common practice, mass customization does not imply proliferation of elements to build products and services, if a focus on reuse of elements is considered since the design phase. Parts, components, and material diversity can be significantly reduced through standardization techniques. Automatic resupply is now well known and being used by many firms, as modern *kanban* or just-in-time techniques. Still, many firms are adverse to these techniques, as they do not recognize its benefits, and maintain the traditional issue of expensive time and resource-consuming purchase orders of parts, components, and materials. Also, it is fundamental that companies rationalize their product line to eliminate or make the outsourcing of the unfrequent, unusual, and low-volume products and services that marginally contribute to the profitability of the company.

Therefore, the supply chain simplification should be focused on reducing the variety of parts, components, and materials, in order to enable automatic and pull-based procurement of supplies. Also, it should reduce the number of qualified suppliers, developing partnerships to move away from price-based supplier competition, rather to flexibility and time- and quality-response selection (Anderson, 2004).

The enhanced flexibility and efficiency through supply chain simplification can only be achieved if electronic platforms are deployed, linking suppliers, producers, distributors, and customers. These e-platforms can have informational, collaborative, or transactional functions, enabling the definition of product characteristics, implementing joint product development, and sustaining distributed collaborative demand forecasting and stock management (Balakrishman, Kumara, & Sundaresan, 1999).

The success or failure of the adoption of these e-platforms is very much dependent on many business factors, like: (i) companies' individual business and IT strategies, processes, resources, and infrastructure; (ii) business relationships exchange episodes and atmosphere; and (iii) the characteristics of the production network governance structure and its input-output structure (Grilo & Jardim-Goncalves, 2005). However, to overcome hurdles posed by these business factors, it is important to develop interoperability between systems beyond the value chain, that is, at an inter-organizational dimension.

Information-Rich Supply and Distribution Chains

In traditional business approaches, the conventional value creation process implied that companies and consumers had distinct roles of production and consumption. Products and services contained value, and markets exchanged this value, from the producer to the consumer, that is, the value creation occurred outside the markets.

Mass customization allows a different process, a move towards cocreation of value, where consumers engage in the process of both defining and creating value. This approach is based on individual-centered cocreation of value between consumers and companies, grounded on the experience of the individual, whether as an individual consumer or as a "consumer" from an institutional client (Prahalad & Ramaswamy, 2004).

Thus, companies that wish to be competing in the market need to understand well the personalized experiences of consumers. Then, they need to extract the real attributes that are relevant for value creation, and modularize or define product platforms that can be mass-produced (Schooler, 2005). Definition of meta-data enables that a personalized user experience focused on certain attributes can go one step further in creating a customized user experience based on products and their attributes, and sharing that information across the production network. This requires that information systems are able to support not only the interaction between the parties but also have the capability to acquire and share knowledge on collaborative networks of people and companies (Balakrishman et al., 1999, Prahalad & Ramaswamy, 2004).

Hence, mass customization requires the existence of an information-rich enterprise system, where data is stored and processed on product types, rates, features, promotions, distribution channels, or customer interaction arrangements. This implies that sales and servicing people must be supported by integrated information systems that are able to give adequate answers to customer interaction.

To implement systems that can support global seamless information flow across the value chain, its heterogeneous and fragmented applications must be integrated. In such an environment, the information systems must: (1) support client personalization, enabling them to interact with design, production, and delivery systems in order to do the planning of what, when, and where to deliver; (2) have rule-based functionality that bound clients' choices to companies' production capabilities and eventual regulatory and legal constraints; and (3) provide a customer interaction system that records each individual interaction and purchase, for fine-tuned sales forecasting, production, and supply planning. Personal details, tastes, and opinions should also be kept and then analyzed through data mining techniques.

CHALLENGES FOR INFORMATION SYSTEMS IN MASS CUSTOMIZATION

Mass customization implementation in companies requires integrated information systems. Today, a principal driver to reach this aim is enterprises interoperability, through the use of reference models and ontology in open platforms.

Interoperability Driver

According to the IEEE Standard Computer Dictionary, interoperability is "the ability of two or more systems or components to exchange information and to use the information that has been exchanged". In 2002, the European Group for Research on Interoperability informed the European Commission's Information Society Directorate General of the fact that "enterprise systems and applications need to be interoperable to achieve seamless operational and business interaction, and create networked organizations".

Recent observations state: "30-40% of companies' IT budget is spent on integration [Gartner and AMR], 30% of entire IT budget is spent on building, maintaining, and supporting application integration [Forrester], 61% of CIOs consider integration of systems and processes a key priority [CIOMagazine], $29 billion by 2006 for application integration by IT professional services [Gartner Group]".

While some companies have been able to master a mass customization approach with the support of an adequate information system infrastructure, large-scale improvements in the use of IT will come only when the networked production systems engendered by technology allows for the realization of positive network externalities to their fullest extent.

Part of the reason why organizations looking for mass customization practices have not yet been able to exploit the positive network externalities comes from their lack of full interoperability. As SMEs are often the largest part of the manufactures' supplier base in disparate industries, this issue becomes more severe due to the inexistence of internal know-how and resources to solve it (Fenves, Sriram, Choi, Elm, & Robert, 2004; Fenves, Sriram, Choi, & Robert, 2003).

Recent studies have uncovered the cost of interoperability barriers of the IT systems used in engineering and manufacturing in the U.S. auto industry, estimated to be of the order of

$1 billion per year (Gregory, 1999). Similarly, for the construction industry, a study prepared for NIST by RTI International and the Logistic Management Institute, to identify and estimate the efficiency losses in the U.S. capital facilities industry resulting from inadequate interoperability among computer-aided design, engineering, and software systems estimates the cost of inadequate interoperability in the U.S. capital facilities industry to be $15.8 billion per year (Gallaher, 2004). These studies are an indication of the industry's inability to exploit IT to realize its full benefits. It is in this context that standards for information exchange are also critical in the mass customization paradigm.

Reference Model Driver

Many standard-based application protocols (APs) and business objects (BOs) are available today. They cover most of the major manufacturing and business activities, and come from ISO, UN, CEN, or OMG. However, most of these standards are not widely adopted, either by lack of awareness or due to private commercial interests of the software developers. Moreover, when they are selected, they are frequently used inadequately in most of the situations, due to an imprecise interpretation of the scope. This results in difficulties in achieving interoperability with others and introduces limitations in potential future reuse and model extensibility when creating new components (Jardim-Goncalves & Steiger-Garcao, 2002a).

However, a standard for data representation cannot usually cover all the range of activities one application needs to handle. As it is often the case that several of the enterprise's applications must operate side by side (horizontally), it is necessary to pay strong attention to the integration and cooperation of multiple standard application protocols and business objects.

The adoption of a strategy to help develop and implement architectures to support horizontally-oriented applications and to reuse vertically-de-

veloped APs and BOs, stimulates the intensive use and extensive reuse of existent standards. It also stimulates development of methodologies to specify and design flexible supportive architectures (Motta, 1999).

Hopefully, this will result in a framework to support extensive interoperability between standard models, based on the development of meta-protocols aimed to represent the overall organization structure and business activities in open platforms. This framework can also be a basis for the development of components.

Recently, XMI, one of the most promising tools for metamodel representation, revealed very able to assist on integration based on the concept of extending and reusing existent objects, and also on the development of compilers and code generators to assist in the development of new components (Jardim-Goncalves & Steiger-Garcao 2002b).

Complementing this, ISO13584 PLib is the standard suggested for representation of catalogues of objects and components (e.g., units of functionality, application objects and assertions, integrated resources, data access interfaces, object business data types, etc.), with direct link with a multi-level, multi-language ontology system. This multi-level characteristic also assists with the development of hierarchical components, while the multi-language mechanism will provide the adequate description of the objects and components in many native languages, for an easier understanding and better usage.

The architecture of standards for data exchange is typically complex. Due to its extent, it is a long and arduous task to fully understand a standard. This fact has been observed as one of the main obstacles for the adoption of standard models by the software developers. For this reason, even when software developers are aware of a standard which fits the scope for which they are looking, often they prefer to not adopt it, but rather to create a new specific framework.

However, most of the standards for data exchange contain a framework that includes a language for data model description, a set of application reference models, libraries of resources, mechanisms for the data access, and representation in neutral format. Examples are the DOM for XML, or the Part 21 of standard STEP (DOM, 2006; ISO10303-1, 1994).

Open Platform Driver

Generally, a standard data access interface (SDAI) is defined for each standard. Although it is of major importance to motivate implementers to adopt one standard, very low level interfaces were made available, with all the complexity of the standard's architecture to be managed and controlled by the user. Such interfaces require a significant effort from the implementers to use, and it has been a source of systematic errors. When functionalities for data access are very similar with slight differences in attribute names or data types, errors often occur.

Automatic code generators are state-of-the-art and can stimulate implementers to adopt the standards and implement them with more ease, minimizing the already-mentioned problems. These generators automatically produce code ready to be linked to the applications. The generated methods for data access act as a high-level interface on the top of the standard data access interface, offering a simpler interface that hides the detailed complexity of the standard architecture.

The code generated represents an abstract data type (ADT) as an implementation of the conceptual standard description of the standard model. The interface offered by the ADT virtualizes the complexities of the standard architecture, which will instantiate the ADT structure through the set of methods for putting and getting data in its attributes, and import and export data to the neutral format.

Using these generators, the applications become less exposed for coding errors once the code generator has itself been validated. Having them available for several platforms further enables

applications to adopt the standards with relative ease. Should the generated interfaces be universally harmonized and adopted as a reference for data access, independently of the standard and platform in use, this will enable the construction of very powerful configurable architectures, offering the flexibility that systems nowadays desire in order to face the rapid changes in the business requirements.

With this methodology, changing one of the adopted standards for data exchange will not imply updating the interfaces. Only the low level library, which interfaces with the data in neutral format and is linked with the generated code, needs to be substituted.

If the platform stores a repository with several implementations of standard data access interfaces, the implementer can multiplex the one he would like to use for the specific case, and keep using the higher level because the SDAI is not changed. In this case, the adoption of the new interface will be automatic, and the access to the new standard will be immediate.

To avoid the explosion on the number of required translators to cover all the existing standard data models, this methodology proposes the use of standard metamodel descriptions, that is, the Metamodel, using a standard Meta language, for example, XMI, to link the generators with this Metamodel information.

ONTOLOGY DRIVER

Ontology is the study of the categories of things within a domain and reflects a view of a segment of the reality. Its definition comes from philosophy and provides a logical framework for research on knowledge representation, embracing definition, classification, and relationships of concepts (IDEAS Project, 2003).

In this context, two or more communities (e.g., organizations, teams), operating in the same domain, may use different terminologies and have different views on the same concept, leading to different underlying ontologies, and consequently conducting to problems of interoperability. At a first level, this problem comes out in the communication between humans, then between humans and computer systems, and finally between computer systems.

For example, when a client talks with suppliers searching for a specific customization, they all need to understand each other. If for any reason this is not the case, humans are able to use reasoning and combine their knowledge, attempting to converge to a common understanding and, hence, to communicate. In opposition to this interactive and intelligent human-to-human process, computer systems communicate under a well-established syntax, through rigid communication protocols. However, the inclusion of semantics in the communication protocol under a well-established classification mechanism, making use of knowledge modeling components described according established semantic representation paradigms, complements the information exchanged contributing for an enhanced understanding between the systems.

Therefore, an interoperable system that seamlessly communicates and understands each other requires the comprehensive understanding of the meaning of the data exchanged within the domains which are involved. This can be realized, if the communication process is supported by an ontology developed under global consensus (Jardim-Goncalves, 2004; JTC 1/SC 7/WG 17, 2006).

To obtain this consensual model, it is necessary to classify and merge the concepts from the different sources within the domain of applicability, describing them in a unique harmonized structure of classes, attributes, relationships, knowledge components, and definitions. Through a combining procedure, the harmonized classification is defined, structuring the various suppliers' information from different sources and for diverse product categories.

CONCEPTUAL IS ARCHITECTURES FOR INTEROPERABILITY

With the large diversity of today's software applications, models, data repositories, programming languages, and operating systems, developers face difficulties to produce applications enabled to interoperate with any other. Therefore, to design their applications, they need to search for a common reference architecture that can guarantee interoperability with the others.

The Model-Driven Architecture

The Object Management Group (OMG) has been proposing the model-driven architecture (MDA) as a reference to achieve wide interoperability of enterprise models and software applications (JTC 1/SC 7/WG 17, 2006). MDA provides specifications for an open architecture appropriate for the integration of systems at different levels of abstraction and through the entire information systems' life cycle (Mellor & Balcer, 2002; Miller & Mukerji, 2001). Thus, this architecture is designed to incite interoperability of the information models independently of the framework in use (i.e., operating system, modeling and programming language, data servers, and repositories).

The MDA comprises three main layers (AlMellor, 2004; MDA, 2006). The Computation-Independent Model (CIM) is the top layer and represents the most abstract model of the system, describing its domain.

A computation independent model (CIM) is a stakeholders-oriented representation of a system from the computation-independent viewpoint. A CIM focuses on the business and manufacturing environment in which a system will be used, abstracting from the technical details of the structure of the implementation system.

The middle layer is the platform-independent model (PIM), and defines the conceptual model based on visual diagrams, use-case diagrams, and meta-data. For that it uses the standards UML (unified modelling language), OCL (object constraint language), XMI (XML metadata interchange), MOF (metaobject facility) and CWM (common warehouse metamodel). Thus, the PIM defines an application protocol in its full scope of functionality, without platform dependencies and constraints. For an unambiguous and complete definition, the formal description of the PIM should concern using the correct business vocabulary, choosing the proper use-cases and interface specifications.

The platform-specific model (PSM) is the bottom layer of the MDA. It differs from the PIM as it targets a specific implementation platform. Therefore the implementation method of the MDA, also known as model-driven development (MDD), is achieved through a transformation that converts the PIM to the PSM. This procedure can be done through automatic code-generation for most of the system's backbone platforms, considering middleware-specific constraints, for example, CORBA, .NET, J2EE, Web Services. Figure 1 depicts the Model-Driven Architecture, compared with the traditional scenario.

Catalysis is one example of a method adopting MDA (D'Souze & Wills, 1998). Based on one

extension of the UML, it was initially conceived by Desmond D'Souza and Alan Wills to model businesses processes. It describes and documents business models and collaborative processes, developing patterns to be employed as a reference and assist the applications to achieve interoperability (Trireme International, 2006).

The research community is also developing and validating other proposals, like those known as *executable UML*. With it, the abstract models described in UML are implemented and tested at a conceptual level, that is, PIM, before transforming them to be implemented in the targeted platform (AlMellor, 2004).

Recently, the ISO TC184 SC4 community has been developing the parts 25 and 28 of the standard ISO10303, known as STEP, the STandard for the Exchange of Product model data (ISO TC184/SC4 2006). These two new parts are reinforcing the implementation of STEP Application Protocols according to MDA.

Indeed, part 25 of STEP provides the specification for the XMI binding of EXPRESS schemata. The part 28 specifies the implementation method of ISO10303 product data according to XML. With them, a STEP Application Protocol can be implemented using a MDA, with the PIM represented in EXPRESS and transformed to XMI

Figure 1. The model-driven architecture

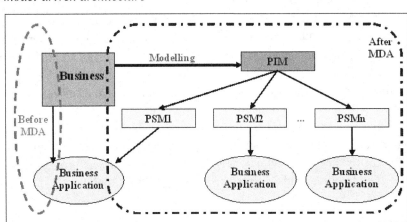

and UML according to Part 25 of this standard, and implemented in a specific platform in XML according to Part 28.

The Service-Oriented Architecture

The World Wide Web Consortium (W3C) refers to the service-oriented architecture (SOA) as "a set of components which can be invoked, and whose interface descriptions can be published and discovered" (W3C, 2006). Also, according to Microsoft, the goal for SOA is a world-wide mesh of collaborating services that are published and available for invocation on a service bus (SOA, 2006).

SOA does not consider the services architecture just from the technology perspective, but also proposing a normalized service-oriented environment (SOE) offering services' description, registration, publication, and search functionalities (Figure 2). Placing emphasis on interoperability, SOA combines the capacity to invoke remote objects and functions, that is, the services, with standardized mechanisms for dynamic and universal service discovery and execution.

The service-oriented architecture offers mechanisms of flexibility and interoperability that allow different technologies to be dynamically integrated, independently of the system's platform in use. This architecture promotes reusability,

and it has reduced the time to put available and get access to the new system's functionalities, allowing enterprises to dynamically publish, discover, and aggregate a range of Web services through the Internet.

Thus, SOA encourages enterprises to be focused on their business and services, not constrained by the specificities of the applications and platforms. This is an essential requirement for organizations to achieve information technology independence, business flexibility, agile partnership, and seamless integration in dynamic collaborative working environments and in digital ecosystems.

Some known service-oriented architectures are Microsoft's DCOM, IBM's DSOM protocol, or the OMG's Object Request Brokers (ORBs) based on the CORBA specification. Nowadays, the use of W3C's Web services is expanding rapidly as the need for application-to-application communication and interoperability grows. They can implement a business process integrating services developed internally and externally to the company, providing a standard means of communication among different software applications running on a variety of heterogeneous platforms through the Internet.

Web services are implemented in XML (extended markup language). The network services are described using the WSDL (Web services description language), and the SOAP (simple object access protocol) is the communication protocol which is adopted. The registration of the services is in the UDDI registry (universal description, discovery, and integration).

Although providing a significant contribution, the SOA alone is not yet the answer to achieve seamless interoperability between applications. For example, despite the efforts done to ensure compatibility between all the SOAP implementations, currently there is no unique standard. The Web Services Interoperability Organization (WS-I) is a good example of an organization supporting Web services interoperability across

Figure 2. Service oriented environment based on SOA

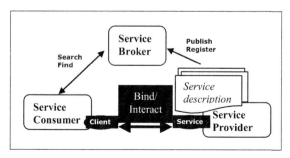

platforms, operating systems, and programming languages, and that has been developing efforts for the convergence and support of generic protocols for the interoperable exchange of messages between Web services (WS-I, 2006).

Combining MDA and SOA

Most of the standards contain a framework including a language for data model description, a set of application reference models, libraries of resources, mechanisms for the data access, and representation in neutral format. However, its architecture is typically complex. Especially due to its extent, to understand and dominate a standard completely is a long and arduous task (Bohms, 2001; Dataform EDIData, 1997; IAI/IFC, 1997; ISO10303-1, 1994).

This fact has been observed as one of the main obstacles for the adoption of standard models by the software developers. Even when they are aware of a standard which fits the scope of what they are looking for, quite often they prefer not to adopt it, and instead, create a new framework of their own (aecXML, 2006; Berre, 2002; CEN/ISSS, 2006; Clements, 1997).

Generally, the standard data access interfaces are described at a very low level. Moreover, they are made available with all the complexity of the standard's architecture to be managed and controlled by the user. This circumstance requires a significant effort from the implementers to use it, and is a source of systematic errors of implementation, for instance when there are functionalities for data access very similar with slight differences in attributes, names, or data types (ENV 13550, 2006; Pugh, 1997; Vlosky, 1998).

To avoid the explosion in the number of required translators to cover all the existent standard data models, an extension of this methodology proposes the use of standard metamodel descriptions, that is, the metamodel, using a standard meta-language, and putting the generators to work

with this metamodel information (Jardim-Goncalves & Steiger-Garcão, 2001; Umar, 1999)

With this methodology, changing one of the adopted standards for data exchange does not imply an update of the interface with the application using it, where only the low-level library linked with the generated code needs to be substituted. If the platform stores a repository with several implementations of standard data access interfaces, the implementer can choose the one that he would like to use for the specific case, for example, through a decision support multiplexing mechanism. In this case, the change for the new interface will be done automatically, and the access to the new standard will be immediate.

A proposal to contribute to face this situation considers the integration of SOA and MDA to provide a platform-independent model (PIM) describing the business requirements and representing the functionality of their services. These independent service models can then be used as the source for the generation of platform-specific models (PSM), dependent of the Web services executing platform.

Within this scenario, the specifications of the execution platform will be an input for the development of the transformation between the MDA's PIM and the targeted Web services platform. With tools providing the automatic transformation between the independent description of the Web services and the specific targeted platform, the solution for this problem could be made automatic and global.

PROPOSED CONCEPTUAL PLATFORM FOR INTEROPERABILITY

An integration platform (IP) is characterized by the set of methods and mechanisms capable of supporting and assisting in the tasks for integration of applications. When the data models and toolkits working for this IP are standard-based, they would be called Standard-based Integration Platforms (Boissier, 1995; Nagi, 1997).

The architecture of an IP can be described through several layers, and proposes using an *onion layer model* (Figure 3). Each layer is devoted for a specific task, and intends to bring the interface with the IP from a low to a high level of abstraction and functionality. The main aim of this architecture is to facilitate the integration task, providing different levels of access to the platform and consequently to the data, covering several of the identified requirements necessary for integration of the applications (Jardim-Goncalves & Steiger-Garcao, 2002b).

Layer 1 (L1) is the lowest of this architecture, and is the one dealing with the representation of data in neutral format (NF). L1 provides the possibility for applications to translate its own data to the NF using a Pre/Post Processor and use this format as the means for data exchange.

Figure 3. Layers of an integration platform

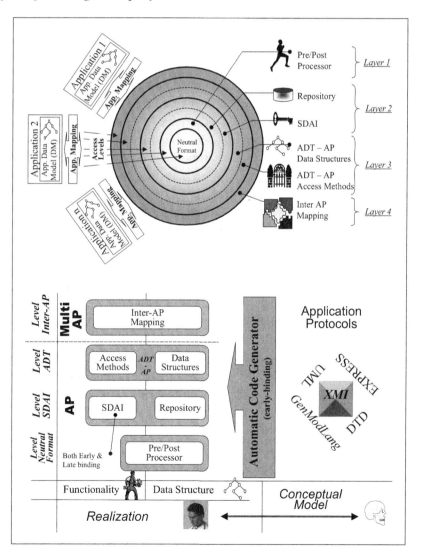

IPs must adopt for its set of available NFs those from the set of available standards, for example, ISO10303, Part 21 (STEP neutral format representation of data) or XML, and include in the IP the correspondent Pre/Post Processor.

The standard data access interface (SDAI) Layer comprehends the set of commands to handle and manage the data in NF. The SDAI acts as a low-level interface for Applications willing to handle Neutral Format data, using the repository as its support for handle and management of data and meta-data. Examples of components of a SDAI layer are the bindings for programming languages of ISO10303, Part 22, and the document object model (DOM). The repository could be any database or engine with persistence capabilities, although most SDAIs are released bundled with a proprietary database.

Nevertheless, to have SDAI with a standard interface to the repository (e.g., SQL) is a very important added value, though users become independent of any proprietary system (Loffredo, 1998). The low-level interface of SDAI has shown to be one of the main obstacles for the integration of Application in IPs. To provide higher-level interfaces using latest generation programming languages would make the development of translators easier and would stimulate users to plug in such platforms and consequently adopt the standards.

The Layer 3 (L3), abstract data type – application protocol, provides a higher-level interface on top of SDAI, developed in one of the popular programming languages. This layer offers to the applications' integrators Data Structures and Access Methods. They act as an early binding mapping from the application protocols used in the scope of the platform and described in a standard language for model representation (e.g., ISO10303, Part 11-EXPRESS, XMI) (ISO10303-11, 1998; XMI, 2006).

The need to plug into an IP is most often related with the usage of one application in an inter-cross industrial environment. Layer 4 (L4) deals with this issue. In this case, the use of a unique AP is often considered not enough, once APs are developed for a specific scope of industrial use. Thus, harmonization from more than one AP is necessary to cover all needs.

To develop interfaces for applications integrating such inter-cross platforms requires an additional effort to map, develop, and implement those APs required for the target integrated system. To facilitate this task, such mapping should be done in a descriptive high-level language (e.g., ISO10303, Part4 - EXPRESS-X), and generate automatically code in a program language ready to be linked with the Layer below, that is, L3.

However, to enable one application to be integrated in such an environment, not all layers are required to be implemented in its integrator interface. The interface can be developed at a lower or higher level, depending at what level the application intends to connect with the IP. For instance, if one application already adopts the same SDAI as the IP, the integration can be done at this level, avoiding the bi-directional translation down to the neutral format level, and up in the way back.

Levels of Integration of an Integration Platform

The described layered architecture of IPs renders to the integrator several levels of integration corresponding to the many ways to access to the standard-based data. When an application is integrated through a neutral format access level, it accesses to data in NF using the translator as a pre/post processor to generate/parse the neutral format data based on the AP from/to the application's internal data structure.

The use of the SDAI level for integration implies the direct use of a SDAI by the application using SDAI's set of commands to handle the data and communicate through it. Because the commands of SDAI allow the management of the SDAI's repository at data and meta-data level, and include direct connection to the generator and parser for neutral format data, the interface of the application dealing with SDAI should read/write the data from/to the repository using the SDAI commands, and commit/revoke such data in the repository to keep it updated with the exchanged information.

Integration at ADT level means that the applications use the high-level interface to establish communications and exchange data with third parties. Because the ADT data structures are a mapping resulting from the early-binding code generation from the AP in use, the integrator

should create and instantiate objects correspondent to the entities in the conceptual model. It should access to its attributes by putting and getting the required data using the ADT access methods, and thus call the import and export methods to access to the neutral format data.

Whenever inter-APs mapping is required for the integration of one application, this should be done at the mapping access level. This integration level releases the mapping interface generated through the inter-AP mapping description to applications, thus establishing the links between the several data structures corresponding to entities

Figure 4. Two views of the levels of integration in an IP

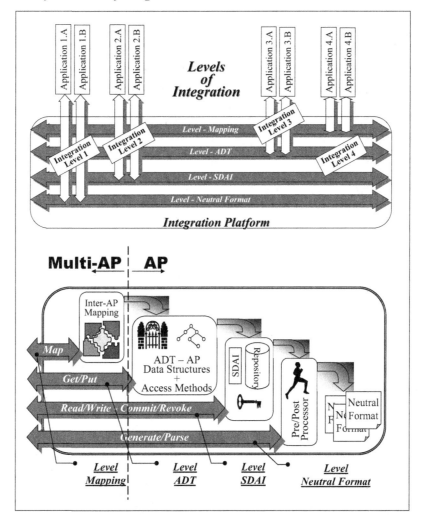

from the APs in use by the IP, and the application's internal data structure.

These present four levels of access conduct to the statement of four levels of integration (Figure 4) dependent on the selected access levels. These levels of integration let the integrator decide how deep he would like to go to enable the change of the standard-based data with the platform. For instance, an integration of one application in the IP at a Level 3 – ADT, means that the integrator does not need to understand all the details related with the commands and functionalities of the SDAI nor the syntax of the neutral format to enable his application to communicate via IP. To handle and manage all issues at ADT level should be enough.

Execution and Entry Point Level of IP

The realization of an application integration task in an IP is conducted by one of the presented integration levels, through one of its levels of access to data. The IP's levels of execution and entry point are the gates that provide entrance to the mechanism for the execution of commands and information exchange between the applications and the platform, and therefore among applications.

Each level of data access makes available different execution and entry point levels at which its functionality depends directly on the intended level of integration, with a specific level of abstraction. Figure 5 describes many execution and entry point levels that could be identified in an IP, in the extent of the levels of integration.

For the neutral format level, the entry point for execution is the sum of the mechanisms that allow writing and reading the information in NF. For instance, in the case of STEP Part 21, or XML, those are the commands that enable applications to read and write characters and strings in the syntax defined by the standard. In the case of Java or Corba objects, they are those that generate and handle directly the representation of the instances of these objects at its very low level (e.g., in binary format, under its data structure).

Figure 5. Execution and entry point levels of IP

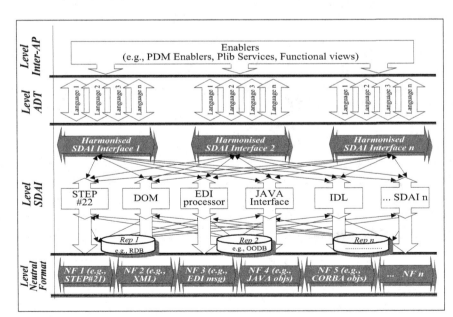

The entry point at SDAI level offers executable commands suitable to handle and manage repositories of data and meta-data compatible with the APs adopted by the IP, and to import and export such data in neutral format. The main aim of these commands is to virtualize the data represented in neutral format, providing to the integrators a unique interface independent of the standard adopted to represent the data. Since in the market there are several libraries that can be adopted with the role of a SDAI, there is a need to harmonize such interfaces, defining a new one on top of them which represents those commands that are universal to a set of SDAIs, and which applications can use universally.

Adopting this approach, one application can, for example, move immediately from one neutral format in STEP Part 21 to XML, by just changing the library of software, that is, by just changing SDAI. At this level, the kind of repository used is also very important to give persistence to the data in the IP. The ideal scenario would be the one where a unique repository is used and accessed using a standard data access mechanism, like SQL. In fact, what has been found is that each SDAI uses its property repository, not providing an easy connection to the others for sharing. This implies a propagation of repositories inside the IPs.

The ADT level makes available a set of methods that allows the new AP's objects to be created, instantiating them through its access methods, and importing and exporting such objects to the neutral format, using methods that communicate with one of the harmonized SDAIs adopted by the IP. For implementation, ADTs should be developed in some of the programming language in frequent use by the applications to facilitate immediate usage.

The high-level nature of the methods provided by the ADT's classes of objects, designed to be a steady mapping from their conceptual representation in the AP, provides a natural and easier way for integrators to handle the integrated data. Using the execution and entry points at the ADT level provide to the integrators an interface independent of the SDAI and consequently to the neutral format adopted by the IP.

When a mapping between ADTs is required, the mapping rules should be coded and made available to the integrator as a set of commands that allows it to easily instantiate the attributes of the required objects at once. This level of execution and entry points enables the integrator to see the global IP designed as a metaprotocol, in which its constituents are APs or parts of linked APs based on mapping and transformation rules between them. Working on the top of ADTs, this meta-AP could be accessed and handled independently of the SDAI or neutral format which has been adopted.

Using the inter-AP level raises the level of the IP to the one where access to it is done by mechanisms assigning data to the related APs. When reference between data from different standards is required, mechanisms to support this link should be supported. Examples are the STEP's PLib services and the Plib's view exchange protocols to join the standards STEP and PLib (Fowler, 2000; PLib, 2000).

Metadata and Model Morphisms

Nowadays UML is a main framework supported by toolkits in the market (Rumbaugh, 1998). However, major standard models are not represented using it, as are the cases of the ISO10303-STEP application protocols. To avail the existent models and reuse and put them in the market in popular formats like UML, a solution could be to develop model translators to UML. But the kernel of the problem still persists, since UML models are described in proprietary formats depending on the tools managing them. There is no established neutral way to represent them.

The Object Management Group (OMG) released a proposal entitled XML metadata interchange (XMI) with the intention of providing a common mechanism for interchange of models.

Today, XMI has been universally accepted as a standard for metamodel representation. Major groups involved with electronic data exchange, and most of the popular toolkits available in the market, have been adopting XMI as the standard for import/export of modeling information, supporting direct translation of major modeling technologies like UML and UMM (XMI, 2006).

Contradictory facts:

There is huge investment in developing models using standard-based methodologies, for example, STEP.

There is a technology that is very well accepted by the market, using methodologies like the unified modeling language (UML) that, besides the modeling features provided, also offers others like process design or system's deployment (Rational, 2006; Rumbaugh, 1998).

Question:

How can we take the large number of existing models described in languages like EXPRESS or XML and reuse them and put them in the market in a popular format like UML?

One immediate answer could be to develop model translators to UML, but the core of the problem still persists. Once UML models are represented in proprietary internal formats depending on the tools managing them, there is still not an established neutral way to represent them.

To translate from one modeling *Language 1* (e.g., EXPRESS) to XMI, first the model should be compiled, using the parser to populate a Meta-dictionary repository according to the processed information. For each language considered for the translation process, for example, EXPRESS and XMI, a library of commands to handle the metadata dictionary repository will be provided. This library acts as a meta-SDAI for each language, and it is the bridge between the model in one language and its representation in the meta-dictionary repository.

Hence, the access to the repository should be done using the meta-SDAI for the model language. Afterwards, the Mapping module is executed, translating the metadata from *Language 1*'s repository format, to XMI's repository language format. To have a mapping and translators from XMI to all languages in which models developed by the major standards exist, as are the cases of STEP APs or several of the registered DTDs, would be an important step to assure reusability and acceptance of these models.

The mapping between such languages is not direct, and therefore complete translations are sometimes difficult to achieve (Breton & Bézivin, 2001). To give a practical example identified during one of the real implementations of this framework, one of the difficulties found in translating an EXPRESS model to UML via XMI is related with the *classtoclass* relationship. While in EXPRESS this is represented using an attribute value, in UML it could be represented using aggregation or association mechanisms. There is no way to automatically infer from the EXPRESS model which is the correct semantic in order to translate it according to UML.

A mapping specification should document the correspondence between the information requirements defined by the reference model of an AP and how the requirements are satisfied by the objects in the integrated format. The mapping specification is established through analysis of the information requirements and the definition of a mapping for each application object, application object attribute, and application object assertion. It takes into account the scope and context of the AP, semantics of the application objects and resource constructs, together with the definition of constraints on the population of the resource constructs used in the integrated model. Therefore, the mapping specification should be understood as defining the complete correspondence between instances in the reference model and instances in the integrated model.

Figure 6. Translation between EXPRESS, UML, DTD, and XMI

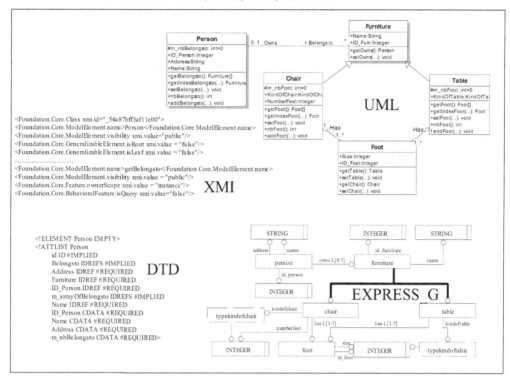

When the mapping module is executed, it translates the metadata from *Language 1*'s repository format to XMI's repository language format. One the other side, a generator will interpret the metadata in the XMI's repository, and generates the XMI model. Standards for data model exchange and inter-model mapping, like XMI or EXPRESS-X, together with code generators for mapping and high-level interfaces, have shown potential to be an ever increasing reference adopted by industry in general. Figure 6 gives an example of a translation between EXPRESS, UML, DTD, and XMI.

This platform is designed based on the concept of model morphisms (MoMo), which addresses the problem of mapping and transformation of models. The research community identifies two core classes of morphisms: nonaltering morphisms and model altering morphisms. In nonaltering, given two models, source and target model, a mapping is created relating each element of the source with a correspondent element in the target, leaving the two models intact. In model-altering morphism, the source model is transformed using some kind of transformation function which outputs the target model.

The proposed framework is according to the altering morphism class, as it gets the mapping rules already defined. As well, the framework is designed with extensibility in mind, so one can easily plug in other translators according to specific needs, as long as their implementations follow specific rules. Some of the proposed outputs to be available in the framework are XMI, XML, OWL, RDB, and visualization formats of EXPRESS schemas.

GLOBAL METHODOLOGY FOR INTEGRATION OF MODELS AND APPLICATIONS

After selecting the AP to be used as integrator of one application in an IP using an AP, the next stage is the development of its translator, and, as presented in a previous section, different levels of integration and levels of access to the platform become possible. In order to accelerate the development of these translators, and consequently the integration of the application in the IP, code can be generated based on the model adopted, thus providing faster development and better conformance of data and interoperability of applications with the IP.

For the implementation of inter-modeling mapping and generation of the ADT from a XMI model description, the architectures described in Figure 7 and Figure 8 are proposed. The modules to be considered are those directly related with the programming language selected for the code generation. Nevertheless, the mapping in this case is specialized in the generation of implementable

Figure 7. Architecture for inter-modeling mapping

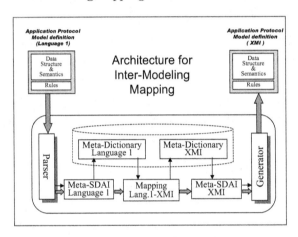

Figure 8. Architecture for ADT generation and early-binding SDAI

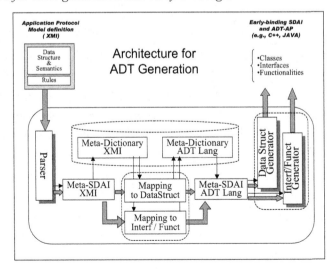

data structures and methods from the conceptual model. These methods will provide the functionalities to access to the class members, and virtualize the low-level layers of the IP architecture, as are the SDAI and the neutral format generators.

To have a complete system able to generate interfaces for several programming languages, and to have a general architecture supporting a flexible code generation, the requirement is that each programming language provides its meta-SDAI ADT, data structure, and interface/functionalities mapping, altogether with the respective generators.

The basis for the inter-AP mapping is the description of the mapping between the APs using a specialized language, like EXPRESS-X or

Figure 9. Architecture for inter-AP mapping

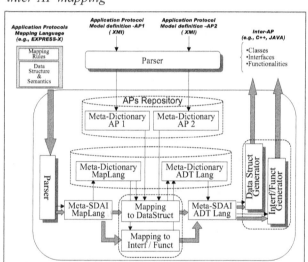

Figure 10. Methodology for integration of applications using general APs

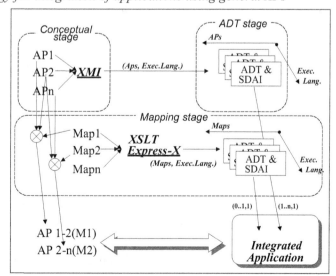

XSLT. The architecture to support the inter-AP mapping generation is an extension of the two architectures previously presented (Figure 9). The procedure to execute the inter-AP mapping should first compile the mapping description and store it in the repository. For that, a parser to this language, together with a meta-SDAI, should be plugged in the system.

In this architecture, the mapping is the core module. It runs by analyzing the mapping rules stored in the inter-AP mapping repository, together with the meta-dictionary information of the two APs and the one for the target ADT language. Therefore, this module will generate the data structure and functionalities to support the mapping between the models described in XMI.

To produce accurate mapping, the mapping tool needs to have knowledge about the mechanism for interoperability between the standards that originate the model in XMI, in order to implement in the translators the inter-reference mechanisms, accordingly with such standards. For instance, the reference from one model described in STEP to PLib should be done using the PLib services, as recommended by the ISO TC184/SC4 community (Staub, 1998).

The usage of the general architecture presented for inter-AP modeling, inter-AP mapping, and code generation must be driven by a methodology for the integration of applications in IPs (Jardim-Goncalves & Steiger-Garcao, 2002b).

The proposed methodology is described in four stages by Figure 10. They are:

Conceptual stage:
a.   Select the APs and models to be used as support for the integration of the application in the IP;
b.   Select the parser, meta-SDAI, and mapping module for each of the selected AP's language; and
c.   Translate those conceptual models to XMI.

ADT stage:
d.   Select the programming languages to be used for the implementation of the translators;
e.   Select the ADT generator, meta-SDAI, and mapping module for each of the selected programming language; and
f.   Generate for each AP the correspondent ADT in the set of selected programming languages.

Mapping stage:
g.   Select the set of APs that is required for the mapping;
h.   Define the mapping rules between them, using EXPRESS-X;
i.   Select the ADT generator, meta-SDAI, and Mapping module for each of the selected programming languages; and
j.   Generate for each mapping the correspondent inter-model mapping ADT, in the set of selected programming languages.

=» *Integrate the Application in the IP using the generated code.*

CONCLUSION

Companies need to fulfill a customer's expectations in terms of product and service specifications, price, and quality, in a dynamic environment, where products life cycle is dramatically reduced and competitors appear from everywhere, anytime. The globalization process of the last decade has exposed companies to wider markets, with an increasing number of potential clients. Competition on a global market means that clients are becoming more demanding, either through producing and selling products and services across the world, or by selling locally but competing with global players.

Mass customization is a rational way for firms to cope with this continuously-evolving business environment. To be able to produce based on the mass customization paradigm, companies must change the way they innovate and produce, requiring an increased productivity and enhanced flexibility, that must be sustained through the integration of their value chain, flexibility in the supply chain management, and exploitation of the information-rich supplier and distribution chain.

The required business changes must be enabled by adequate support of information systems and technology, along with an appropriate methodology. In the last decade, companies have made heavy investments in IT, both to support their internal business and manufacturing systems and to take advantage of new business opportunities in the emergence of the Internet.

Yet most of these implemented systems are unlikely to automatically exchange services and data, not only between internal applications but especially with trading partners' applications. This mainly results due to incompatibility of data formats, reference models, and semantics between the components to be exchanged between the systems. Indeed, the identified interoperability problems between applications are typically related with data model compatibility and mapping, different languages and methodologies for model representation, correctness in the semantics of the data being exchanged, and lack of accurate conformance and interoperability checking.

Companies are thus often facing a dilemma. They must respond to the demands posed by global competition and the need to mass-customize their production which needs to be supported by interoperable IT systems. But usually, even after large investments in IT applications, they are still not able to communicate and exchange data, information, and knowledge with other applications. Companies cannot afford to scrap everything and deploy new IT systems that are interoperable. Ideally they, require plug-and-play solutions that overcome existing technical barriers.

Despite this, there are an increasing number of specialized and complementary software applica-

tions working for each industry, together with a strong support for reuse, integration, and extension of already-existent application protocols, intending to cover the needs for inter-cross industrial scope, and trying to save most of the existent standardized work. Hence, mass customization can only be a viable manufacturing paradigm for companies having traditional operations management systems and IT systems, if they start investing in the development of interoperability for their business and information systems.

Conceptual IS architectures for interoperability are the foundation for the development of platforms for mass customization. The emerging model-driven architectures, combined with the promising service-oriented architectures, seem to be an adequate proposal to face seamless communication between systems and applications, integrating internal and external organizations. Also, reference models, like the standard ISO10303 STEP application protocols, and standard technologies for data representation, like XML, are today available to integrate the product life cycle.

However, even with such variety of available tools and methods, their adoption requires skilled expertise, usually not available in traditional organizations. Thus, to motivate the adoption of these available technologies, a proper methodology, supported by a set of tools that can facilitate the integration of these models using the proper technology, needs to be used. These should be part of the framework based on a conceptual platform to develop interoperability in mass customization information systems.

The presented work has been developed and applied in the scope of the intelligent manufacturing systems (IMS) SMART-fm programme (www.ims.org) and European ATHENA IP and INTEROP NoE projects (www.athena-ip.org, www.interop-noe.org), under real industrial environments.

ACKNOWLEDGMENT

The authors would like to thank all the national and international organizations that have been supporting and funding, during the last fifteen years, a significant number of international projects in the area of interoperable systems, which resulted in the framework presented in this chapter.

Major organizations are the European Commission, CEN/ISSS, Ministry of Industry of Portugal, Ministry of Economy of Portugal, Portuguese Foundation for Science and Technology, Portugal/USA Foundation for Development, IPQ, and the Portuguese Standardization Body.

Also, we express our recognition for the project partners that work and contribute substantially in the mentioned projects.

REFERENCES

aecXML (2006). Retrieved March 22, 2006, from http://www.iai-na.org/aecxml/mission.php

AlMellor (2004). *Introduction to model-driven architecture.* Addison-Wesley.

Anderson, D. (2004). *Build-to-order and mass customization: The ultimate supply chain and lean manufacturing strategy for low-cost on-demand production without forecasts or inventory.* CIM Press.

Anderson, D. M., & Pine II, B. J. (1997). *Agile product development for mass customization.* Chicago: Irvin Publishers.

Balakrishman, A. Kumara, S., & Sundaresan, S. (1999). Manufacturing in the digital age: Exploiting information technologies for product realization. *Information Systems Frontiers, 1,* 25-50.

Berre, A. (2002). Overview of international standards on enterprise architecture. *SINTEF.*

Böhms, M. (2001). Building construction extensible markup language (bcXML) description: E-construct bcXML. *A Contribution to the CEN/ISSS eBES Workshop, Annex A, ISSS/WS-eBES/01/001.*

Boissier, R. (1995). Architecture solutions for integrating CAD, CAM and machining in small companies. In *Proceedings of the IEEE/ECLA/IFIP International Conference on Architectures and Design Methods for Balanced Automation Systems* (pp. 407-416). London: Chapman & Hall.

Breton, E., & Bézivin, J. (2001). Using metamodel technologies to organize functionalities for active system schemes. In *Proceedings of the 5th International Conference on Autonomous Agents,* Canada.

CEN/ISSS (2006). *European Committee for Standardisation - Information Society Standardization System.* Retrieved March 22, 2006, from http://www.cenorm.be/isss

Clements, P. (1997). Standard support for the virtual enterprise. In *Proceedings of the International Conference on Enterprise Integration Modeling Technology – ICEIMT'97, Torino, Italy.* Retrieved March 22, 2006, from http://www.mel.nist.gov/workshop/iceimt97/pap-cle2/stdspt2.htm

Cusumano, M. A., & Nobeoka, K. (1998). *Thinking beyond lean.* New York: Free Press.

D'Souza, D., & Wills, A., (1998). *Objects, components, and frameworks with UML: The catalysis.* Addison-Wesley. Retrieved March 23, 2006, from http://www.catalysis.org

Da Silveira, G., Borenstein, D., & Fogliaatto, F. S. (2001). Mass customization: Literature review and research directions. *International Journal of Production Economics, 72*(1).

DATAFORM EDIData (1997). *UN/EDIFACT Release 93A.*

DOM (Document Object Model) (2006). Retrieved March 23, 2006, from http://www.w3.org/TR/REC-DOM-Level-1

empirica GmbH (2005). *The European e-Business Report: A portrait of e-business in 10 sectors of the EU economy, 2005 edition*. Retrieved March 23, 2006, from http://www.ebusiness-watch.org/resources/documents/Pocketbook-2005_001.pdf

ENV 13 550 (1995). *Enterprise Model Execution and Integration Services (EMEIS)*. Brussels, Belgium: CEN.

Fenves, S. J., Sriram, R. D., Choi, Y., & Robert, J. E. (2003). *Advanced Engineering Environments for Small Manufacturing Enterprises, 1*.

Fenves, S. J., Sriram, R. D., Choi, Y., Elm, J. P., & Robert, J. E. (2004). *Advanced Engineering Environments for Small Manufacturing Enterprises, 2*.

Fowler, J. (2000). *Co-operative use of STEP and PLib*. Retrieved March 22, 2006, from http://www.nist.gov/sc4

Gallaher, M. (2004). *Cost analysis of inadequate interoperability in the U.S. capital facilities industry* (NIST GCR 04-867). Washington, DC: National Institute of Standards and Technology, Department of Commerce.

Gilmore, J. H., & Pine II, B. J. (1997). The four faces of mass customization. *Harvard Business Review*, (January-February).

Gregory, T. (1999). *Interoperability cost analysis of the U.S. automotive supply chain* (99-1 Planning Rep.). Washington, DC: National Institute of Standards and Technology, Department of Commerce.

Grilo, A., & Jardim-Goncalves, R., (2005). Analysis on the development of e-platforms in the AEC sector. *International Journal of Internet and Enterprise Management, 3*(2).

Hegge, H. M., & Wortmann, J. C. (1991). Generic bill-of-material: A new product model. *International Journal of Production Economics, 23*.

Huang, G. Q., Zhang, X. Y., & Lo, V. H. (2005). Optimal supply chain configuration for platform products: Impacts of commonality, demand variability, and quantity discount. *International Journal of Mass Customization, 1*(1).

IAI/IFC (1997). *IFC End User Guide. International Foundation Classes Release 1.5. IAI*.

IDEAS Project (2003). Ontology state of the art - Final report.

ISO TC184/SC4 Standards (2006). Retrieved March 23, 2006, from http://www.tc184-sc4.org

ISO1030-1 (1994). ISO 10303 - Standard for the exchange of product data, Part 1, Overview and fundamentals principles. *International Organization for Standardization*.

ISO10303-11 (1998). ISO 10303 Standard for the exchange of product data (STEP), Part 11, Description methods, The EXPRESS language reference manual. *International Organization for Standardization*.

ISO10303-22 (2001). ISO 10303 Standard for the exchange of product data (STEP), Part 22. *International Organization for Standardization*.

Jardim-Goncalves, R. (2004). Ontology-based framework for enhanced interoperability in networked industrial environments. In *Proceedings of the 11ᵗʰ IFAC Symposium on Information Control Problems in Manufacturing, INCOM2004*. Salvador, Brazil.

Jardim-Goncalves, R., & Steiger, A. (2002). Integration and adoptabilidade of APs – The role of ISO TC184/SC4 standards. *Special issue: Applications in Industry of Product and Process Modelling Using Standards International Journal of Computer Applications in Technology*.

Jardim-Goncalves, R., & Steiger-Garção, A. (2001). Supporting interoperability in standard-based environments - Towards reliable integrated systems. Advances in Concurrent Engineering. In *Proceedings of the 8ᵗʰ ISPE International Conference on Concurrent Engineering (CE2001),* Anaheim, CA.

Jardim-Goncalves, R., & Steiger-Garção, A. (2002a). Implicit hierarchic metamodeling - In search of adaptable interoperability for manufacturing and business systems. In *Proceedings of the 5ᵗʰ IEEE/IFIP BASYS2002,* Mexico.

Jardim-Goncalves, R., & Steiger-Garção, A. (2002b). Implicit multi-level modeling to support integration and interoperability in flexible business environments. *Communications of ACM, Special Issue on Enterprise Components, Services, and Business Rules,* 53-57.

JTC 1/SC 7/WG 17 (2006). *ISO - International Organization for Standardization.*

Liker, J. (2004). *The Toyota way.* McGraw Hill.

Loffredo, D. (1998). *Efficient database implementation of EXPRESS information models.* PhD thesis, Rensselaer Polytechnic Institute, Troy, NY.

MDA (2003). *Model Driven Architecture, MDA Guide Version 1.0.1, June 2003.* Retrieved March 23, 2006, from http://www.omg.org/mda

Mellor, S., & Balcer, M. (2002). *Executable UML - A foundation for model-driven architecture.* Addison-Wesley.

Miller, J., & Mukerji, J. (2001). *Model driven architecture white paper.* Retrieved March 23, 2006, from http://www.omg.org/cgi-bin/doc?ormsc/2001-07-01

Motta, E. (1999). *Reusable components for knowledge modelling.* Amsterdam, The Netherlands: IOS Press.

Nagi, L. (1997). Design and implementation of a virtual information system for agile manufacturing. *IIE Transactions on Design and Manufacturing, Special issue on Agile Manufacturing, 29,* 839-857.

O'Grady, P. (1999). *The age of modularity.* Iowa City, IA: Adams and Steele Publishers.

Pine II, B. J. (1993). *Mass customization: The new frontier in business competition.* Boston: Harvard Business School Press.

PLib (2000). ISO 13584 Parts Library, ISO TC184/SC4, Part 102, View Exchange Protocol: View Exchange Protocol by ISO10303 conforming specification. *International Organization for Standardization.*

Prahalad, C. K., & Ramaswamy, V. (2004). *The future of competition: Co-creating unique value with customers.* Boston: Harvard Business School Press.

Pugh, S. (1997). *Total design: Integrated methods for successful product engineering.* Wokingham: Addison-Wesley.

Rational (2006). Retrieved March 22, 2006, from http://www.rational.com/uml

Robertson, D., & Ulrich, K. (1998). Planning product platforms. *Sloan Management Review, 39*(4).

Rumbaugh, J. (1998). *UML - The unified modeling language.* Addison-Wesley.

Schooler, S. B. (2005). Toward a multi-agent information management infrastucture for product family planning and mass customization. *International Journal of Mass Customization, 1*(1).

Simpson, T. W. (2005). Product platform design and customization: Status and promise. *Special Issue on Platform Product Development for Mass Customization, AIEDAM, 18*(1).

SOA (2006). *The Service-Oriented Architecture.* Retrieved March 23, 2006, from http://msdn. microsoft.com/architecture/soa/default.aspx

Staub, G. (1998). ISO TC184/SC4QC N068, *Interpretation of PLib Services-Guideline for the common interpretation of the "services" provided by PLib using the STEP IR.*

Trireme International (2006). Retrieved March 23, 2006, from http://www.trireme.u-net.com/catalysis

Umar (1999). A framework for analyzing virtual enterprise infrastructure. In *Proceedings of the 9th International Workshop on Research Issues in Data Engineering - IT for Virtual Enterprises, RIDE-VE'99* (pp. 4-11). IEEE Computer Society.

Vlosky, R. P. (1998). Partnerships versus typical relationships between wood products distributors and their manufacturer suppliers. *Forest Products Journal, 48*(3)*,* 27-35.

W3C (2006). *World Wide Web Consortium.* Retrieved March 23, 2006, from http://www. w3c.org

WS-I (2006). Web services interoperability organization. *WS-I.* Retrieved March 23, 2006, from http://www.ws-i.org

XMI, XML Meta-data Interchange (2006). Retrieved March 23, 2006, from http://www.omg. org/technology/xml/index.htm

Chapter VIII
An Agent–Based Information Technology Architecture for Mass Customized Markets

Manoochehr Ghiassi
Santa Clara University, USA

Cosimo Spera
Zipidy, Inc., USA

ABSTRACT

This chapter presents a Web-enabled, agent-based information system model to support mass-customized markets. We present a distributed, real-time, Java-based, mobile intelligent information system that interfaces with firms' existing IT infrastructures, follows a build-to-order production strategy, and integrates order-entry with supply chain, manufacturing, and product delivery systems. The model provides end-to-end visibility across the entire supply chain, allows for a collaborative and synchronized production system, and supports an event-based manufacturing environment. The system introduces four general-purpose intelligent agents to support the entire mass customization process. The adoption of this approach by a semiconductor manufacturing firm resulted in reductions in product lead time (by half), buffer inventory (from five to two weeks), and manual transactions (by 80%). Similarly, the adoption by a leading automotive manufacturer resulted in a 51% total inventory reduction while increasing plant utilization by 30%. These results verify that the successful adoption of this system can reduce inventory and logistic costs, improve delivery performance, increase manufacturing facilities utilization, and provide a higher overall profitability.

INTRODUCTION

The globalization of businesses and the infusion of information technology (IT) into every aspect of operations have introduced a strong demand for product variety and transformed business environments from a production-centric model to one that is information- and customer-centric (Arjmand & Roach, 1999). Although the Internet has strengthened business with its convenience and 24-7 global accessibility, it has also dramatically shifted the traditional business model to a new, competitive market space. People can now purchase anything, anywhere, at any time, and both product customization and customer requirements are increasing exponentially, making sales and inventory prediction a challenge. Meeting the wants and needs of such a heterogeneous customer population, in a global market, inevitably calls for product variety, while every efficiency-seeking supply chain prefers to process as few "flavors" as possible.

Mass customization seeks an economical resolution of this fundamental conflict. Taking mass production as a foil implies that a mass-customized product should not cost end customers much more than a mass produced near-equivalent, and that the customization process should not create too much of a delay. We believe that this can be realized with consistency and at scale only with a *customer-centric production system*. This is one that enables an end-customer to configure (partially design) the product online and provides real-time visibility of the resulting order directly to the manufacturing floor and throughout the supply chain. In such a production system, businesses focus on their core competencies and outsource activities that are not essential to this core. Improvements in information technology infrastructures and worldwide acceptance of the Internet have strengthened this transition. As a result, complex products in the market can be the result of collaborative efforts of many companies (Anderson & Lee, 1999). The auto industry is an excellent example of such a collaborative effort. A car can have over 10,000 parts, with multiple stages of production, many suppliers, a high degree of product complexity, and a high degree of customization. The manufacturing operation of such a business often requires a high production rate, time and space constraints, and often long cycle times. High technology is another example. Fabrication-less firms that design new components are common. These firms now concentrate on

their core business of designing a new component and outsource the manufacturing to specialized semiconductor and PC-board manufacturing contractors. Transportation and logistic systems are additional examples in which the Internet and online commerce have facilitated rapid movements of products and material in a time-sensitive production environment.

The participants in these markets include suppliers, retailers, and transportation services providers. The efficient operation of such markets requires extensive collaboration among its many members.

There are several common themes that characterize these markets. The first theme is the time-sensitive nature of the demand in such markets. The order stream for these markets can change in a short period of time. For example, for the semiconductor manufacturing system described later in this chapter, the order stream can arrive multiple times per day, creating a turbulent production environment requiring adjustments to production schedules. Similarly, transportation and delivery systems need to account for last-minute changes in orders, cancellation of existing orders, addition of new orders, breakdowns in the actual transportation facilities, and complications due to weather or traffic conditions, all within just a few hours (Dorer & Calisti, 2005). Most mass-customized production environments are time-sensitive and therefore exhibit such behavior. Traditional production systems cannot efficiently address these needs.

The second theme associated with such markets is the complexity of the supply chain system. The auto industry is an example of such a production environment. The supply chain is often multilayered with complex arrangements. Supporting mass customization of products in these markets can have a major impact on inventory levels for the suppliers that are located downstream from the final production vendor. If timely demand data reflecting the latest change in final product is not available to all suppliers, the inventory bullwhip effect may require downstream suppliers to stock up on the wrong components. The coordination requirements for an efficient operation of such a system are often lacking in traditional production systems.

These themes, associated with mass-customized markets, clearly introduce additional complexity into the production environment. For mass-customized markets, optimal production solutions tend to be order/demand-driven, are sensitive to each order quantity, and should account for more frequent changes in order streams. Obtaining optimality in such a production environment requires continuous analysis in very short time intervals. Effective analysis in this environment requires visibility of the changing demand data to all participants in the production system in real-time. The firms participating in such a system often follow a short-term optimization approach to production problems that require coordination and collaborations among local decision-makers. The decision-making for this environment is often: decentralized and distributed; more data-driven with less human intervention; benefits from a rule-based automated negotiation system; attempts to reach local optimal solutions for the participating firms; and performs final coordination and adjustment of these solutions in a short time interval. In contrast, the traditional production models rely on a centralized decision-making process that attempts to optimize a global, central production function representing the primary vendor, to address a longer-term production system.

For mass-customized production environments exhibiting these attributes, an agent-based information system solution can offer improved performance. We present two case studies that show how the implementation of such a system has improved the productivity and profitability for a semiconductor manufacturing company and an automotive firm. Actual and simulated results show that for the semiconductor firm, the implementation of our model improved product lead time by 50%, reduced buffer inventory from

five to two weeks, and reduced manual transaction processing by 80%. For the automotive case, our results show a total inventory reduction of 51%, and an increase in production facilities utilization rates by more than 30%. Other researchers report similar improvements in cost reduction (by 11.7%), reduced traveled kilometers (by 4.2%), and lower trucks employed (by 25.5%) in a transportation system utilizing an agent-based transportation optimization system (Dorer & Calisi, 2005), and a 15% increase in revenue with improved profit margin from 2% to 4% in a logistic provider after adoption of an agent-based adaptive transportation network (Capgemini, 2004).

MASS CUSTOMIZATION BUSINESS ENVIRONMENT

The business environment for successful implementation of a mass-customized market, thus, requires the establishment of business alliances and partnerships with selected suppliers. Mass-customized manufacturing systems need to support a *"demand-driven"* and *"make-to-order"* production system. Such a production system is often component-based and may involve many business partners, suppliers, and other companies that affect the delivery of products to customers (Gilmore & Pine, 2000). Outsourcing exacerbates the challenge of coordination and planning of any such production system. Supporting a mass-customized production system, therefore, requires a supply chain paradigm capable of a great degree of synchronization throughout the entire supply chain, including the entire inventory system. In particular, the order and reorder replenishment inventory cycle under this model will be more frequent, involve smaller lot sizes, and require shorter delivery schedules.

Such a synchronized production process will necessitate demand, manufacturing and production information transparency, and greater cooperation among the participating members, from the manufacturer to the primary and secondary suppliers (Ghiassi, 2001). Truly successful members of such a manufacturing environment must have stronger alliances and be willing to significantly improve their inter-firm communications. In addition, there is a need for an infrastructure that can:

- Reduce time-to-market for product development, enhancement, and customization;
- Provide end-to-end visibility along the entire supply chain;
- Directly tie order-entry and manufacturing planning systems to speed the availability of demand requirements and to react in real-time;
- Intelligently and selectively communicate with a manufacturer's strategic trading partners;
- Respond expediently to orders, changes in order configuration, and level of demand; and
- Support an event-based supply chain management system in a collaborative environment.

Supporting such a production system requires a collaborative, adaptive, and synchronized supply chain management system that spans multiple firms, is event-driven, distributed, and can operate in real-time and across many computer platforms (Ghiassi & Spera, 2003a). Such a synchronized supply chain operation no longer follows a linear model. This system must be a network-based operation that requires timely availability of information throughout the system in order to allow cooperative and synchronized flow of material, products, and information among all participants. The manufacturing environment for this system requires an operational structure and organization that can focus on building and maintaining the capacity to adapt quickly to a changing order stream while minimizing response time. Clearly, the decision-making process in this environment

needs to shift from a centralized to a distributed mode. In this model, operational and strategic decisions may still be driven centrally; however, the responsibility to adapt to a volatile condition needs to be resolved locally. The effects of a response to such events, then, must be communicated to all relevant layers of the organization, including participating suppliers. Obviously, the relationship among the supply chain members of such a production system also must be altered to support this new business paradigm. Transitioning from mass production to mass customization is a complex, enterprise-wide process which affects external supply chain members, which are not typically controlled by the core company, and thus necessitating alliances and collaborations among the entire supply chain members.

MASS CUSTOMIZATION IT INFRASTRUCTURE

Implementing such a system would require reliance on an interoperable open system IT structure, a high degree of automation in the decision process, and integration of customers, products, and production information across many participants with possibly heterogeneous IT infrastructures.

The technology infrastructure for a mass-customized production system requires a collaborative and adaptive supply chain management system that can account for the entire system: the customer, manufacturers, entire supply chain, and the supporting market structure (Ghiassi & Spera, 2003b). An effective infrastructure for such a vast domain requires an interoperable open system capable of operating in a multi-firm, heterogeneous IT infrastructure.

In this chapter, we present an IT framework and architecture to support a mass-customized production system. We report on prototype solutions that have helped firms achieve their mass-customized production strategies. We present an architecture that can manage production resources, perform negotiations, achieve supply chain information transparency, and monitor and manage processes. We use an intelligent agent technology that can tie together resources, parts, and process knowledge, in single or multiple locations, to create an agile production system. The system defines *"brokers and info-mediaries"* and uses an intelligent, mobile, agent-based trading system that can be utilized in an interactive mode that can react to job streams with customized orders, while bringing together buyers and suppliers in an efficient production environment. We have developed scheduling algorithms to balance the "time" versus "price" trade-off by examining the relations between manufacturers and their suppliers and subcontractors. A multi-agent technology is used to schedule, control, and monitor manufacturing activities, and facilitates real-time collaboration among design teams. Agents in this environment can provide information about the product development process, availability of resources, commitments to deliver tasks, and knowledge of expected product completion in a distributed platform. These mobile agents are used to reach across organizational boundaries to extract knowledge from resources in order to reconfigure, coordinate, and collaborate with other agents in solving enterprise problems. The agents can interface with a customer, a manufacturing resource, a database, or other agents anywhere in the network in seconds, enabling the supply chain system to continuously adapt to demand fluctuations and changing events. Agents in such an environment can facilitate a decentralized and bottom-up planning and decision-making process.

Our IT architecture supports an easily-accessible (Web-based) order and production management system where customers can:

- Configure a product according to their preferences;
- Monitor progress and obtain status reports; and

- Manage changes and gain overall visibility into production.

In this system, the firms can:

- Execute and support a demand-driven synchronized supply chain system;
- Select suppliers for non-strategic commodity components using mobile intelligent agents; and
- Employ intelligent agent technology to support the human stakeholders for strategic sourcing in an expedient manner.

We describe a distributed, Java-based, event-driven system that uses mobile agent technologies over the Internet to monitor multiple production systems, sense exceptions as they occur, and dispatch intelligent agents to analyze broken links and offer alternative solutions. The system is designed to improve the coordination and control of the total supply chain network, through the real-time optimization of material movement. This network encompasses all entities of the supply chain, and builds a demand recognition capability that is as close to the demand source as possible, and then uses this information to drive and synchronize the replenishment of all interim raw materials, components, and products.

The availability of this system enables all participants to monitor, detect, predict, and intelligently resolve supply chain problems in real-time. Participants can obtain up-to-date, customized visibility into other members of the marketplace and can measure historical supply chain performance activities. This information can lead to a manufacturing operation that supports a *"make-to-order"* strategy and avoids inventory bloat. In a mature implementation, the supply chain operation can be transformed into a *"demand chain"* operation, in which inventory is reduced to its minimal level throughout the entire system.

OVERVIEW OF THE MODEL

By providing a common communication infrastructure along with intelligent agents and optimization algorithms, we offer a system for transforming static supply chains into dynamic, Web-centric trading markets that are closely integrated with the manufacturer's systems. This system formulates the production problem as a set of distributed, decentralized, event-driven optimization sub-problems that can efficiently support a mass-customized production environment, which are often characterized by high-demand variability, fixed capacity, time-to-market sensitivity, and/or complex supply chain network.

This approach models the supply chain problem as a hierarchical framework and extends it to support a synchronized production system. The framework presented in this chapter partitions the mass customization production environment into hierarchical levels of process, plan, and execution. The framework offers facilities for process monitoring and analysis, short- and long-term planning capabilities, and efficient, optimized execution of production opportunities. It also provides visibility throughout the system by allowing changes in orders to be communicated to all impacted participants. Each participant in turn reacts to these changes and broadcasts its locally optimized solutions. In the next level of the hierarchy, the local optimum solutions are coordinated and synchronized, and discrepancies are broadcasted again to all affected parties. In the final decision-making level of the hierarchy, automated and human-assisted negotiating agents resolve all production conflicts in support of the final committed production. The responsiveness required for such a highly-synchronized production system is significantly higher than those of non-synchronized systems. This requirement necessitates real-time collaboration among all supply chain members. The supporting IT infrastructure and applications presented in this model are able to cope with high-demand variability, short product life cycles, and tight collaboration and interactions with suppliers.

In this model, information about the entire supply chain system is visible to all authorized members, especially through any device that is Internet-enabled. Our system allows the up-to-date demand data to drive the production system following a "*make-to-order*" production policy. In solving the production allocation sub-problems, the up-to-date demand data is used to monitor production allocation at various plants. The fluidity of the demand undoubtedly can create many exceptions to the centrally-designed production plan. Decentralized decision-making can allow local players to alter execution plans that satisfy their constraints. To manage such scenarios, a system must be able to detect an exception or unplanned event, identify the players impacted by the exception and its resolution, and develop the models necessary to solve the local sub-problem and to resolve the exception. To be fully effective, such a decentralized decision-making environment requires real-time data running across an intelligent peer-to-peer infrastructure and integrated with contextual understanding of the local production sub-problems.

In the past years, many researchers have examined using "agent technology" to find solutions to problems arising in supporting mass-customized production. Sundermeyer (2001) and Wilke (2002) present an agent-based, collaborative supply chain system for the automotive industry (DaimlerChrysler). These authors identify rapidly-changing consumer demands, planning uncertainties, information flow delays, and sequential, batch-oriented policies as elements of traditional production systems that contribute to an inefficient production environment. The authors offer an agent-based, Web-centric, collaborative solution that integrates the entire supply chain and provides a more efficient production system. They report results from a simulation study which show that using a collaborative, distributed, agent-based supply network management system can reduce production and inventory oscillations, safety stock levels, and working capital. Similarly, Dorer and Calisti (2005) report on the integration of an agent-based system into a real-world IT architecture in order to solve and optimize transportation problems facing a major logistics provider. They note that "conventional systems for transportation optimization are limited in their ability to cope with the complexity, and especially with the dynamics, of global transportation business where plans have to be adjusted to new, changing conditions within shortest time frames."

In the following, we describe a Java-based software system that uses intelligent agents to constitute a theoretical and practical basis for addressing mass customization markets.

Agent Taxonomy

We define a mobile intelligent agent to be an autonomous software program, capable of driving goals defined by a set of rules, with learning and adaptive capabilities that are loosely or tightly coupled with other peers. Software agents are often designed to perform a task or activity on behalf of the user and without constant human intervention (Adam, Dogramaci, Gangopadhyay, & Yesha, 1999; Ma, 1999).

Existing literature lists applications for intelligent agents in a wide array of electronic businesses, including retailing, purchasing, and automated negotiation (Jain, Aparicio IV, & Singh, 1999; Ma, 1999; Maes, Guttman, & Moukas, 1999; Sandholm, 1999). These software tools are used as *mediators* that act on behalf of their users. Specifically, these agents perform repetitive and predictable actions, can run continuously without human intervention, and are often stationary.

The authors in Singh, Salam, and Iyer (2005) present an agent-based model that uses e-marketplaces and info-mediaries to register suppliers and consumers of an e-supply chain. This system facilitates purchasing of material by collecting demands from the participants, then locating and matching this demand with suppliers. The proposed system develops supplier profiles based on a satisfaction survey of past performances. When extended to multiple e-marketplaces, a global balancing of supply and demand becomes viable. This system, however, does not include the actual manufacturing operations and relies heavily on the existence of e-marketplaces, info-mediaries, and the willingness of all participants to register their demands, their capacities, and their services.

Researchers have also applied intelligent agent technology to manufacturing and production systems (Kalakota, Stallaert, & Whinston, 1998), and mass-customized production environments (Baker, Van Dyke Parunak, & Kutluhan, 1999). Others have used agent technology to support what they have termed as "*adaptive virtual enterprises*" (Pancerella & Berry, 1999). They have used mobile agents to extend across organizational boundaries. In their model, these agents extract knowledge from resources in order to reconfigure, coordinate, and collaborate with other agents in solving enterprise problems.

There are many mobile agent systems that provide a platform for agent applications; most of these systems are Java-based. Some examples include "Aglets" from IBM, "Concordia" from Mitsubishi, and "Voyager" from ObjectSpace (Lang & Oshima, 1998).

We have applied agent technology to mass-customized production problems. We use mobile software agents to support a distributed decision-making process. A mobile agent, unlike a stationary agent, is not bound to one execution environment. A mobile agent can transport itself and its supporting data to other execution environments. It can then begin execution or use data from both sites to perform its tasks. The mobility also allows the agent to interact with other agents or traditional software systems on the new site. Mobile agents introduce a new paradigm to distributed computing. In this paradigm, any host computer in the network can benefit from the *"know-how"*, resources, and processors throughout the network.

We introduce an architecture that deploys mobile agents in the value chain to streamline the efficiency and performance of the entire network under various constraints of materials and time. The agents perform the following primary functions:

1. Distribute and collect data at the right time to process and analyze;
2. Coordinate inter-enterprise business processes and propose the best response to avoid disruptions throughout the supply chain;
3. Tactically and strategically adjust the supply network in an optimal and timely manner to changes in market conditions; and
4. Assist the decision-makers in their learning processes.

The four functionalities (monitoring, analyzing, acting, and coordinating) characterize the first dimension of our agent taxonomy, the second being given by the role that each agent assumes in the value chain. We have identified three types of roles:

1. Consumer assistant,
2. Demand management, and
3. Supply and resource management.

The agents performing these roles are mobile and ubiquitous. These agents address the needs of end users, manage product demands, and coordinate supply and resource management continuously. The time-sensitive nature of a mass-customized production environment requires the decisions to be made expediently. The mobility of the agents allows the communication between them to occur in real-time. For instance, consider the auto industry case discussed in this chapter. The consumer assistant agent is used by the end user to define product features, place an order, check order processing, and monitor production

status of the product all the way through actual delivery. Similarly, in a transportation/package delivery system, the consumer assistant agent can be used to even alter the actual delivery location of a package as the recipient relocates before the final routing of the scheduled delivery of the product.

The demand and supply management agents can also perform their roles in real-time and assist decision-makers in resolving conflicts and coordinating operations. In particular, conflict resolutions caused by supply or capacity shortages can be handled more expediently. The mobility of the agents and their real-time connectivity within the production system and with the actual end user is utilized to alter the production schedule and inventory levels. These agents can be preprogrammed to handle some decisions automatically to conduct some negotiations on behalf of their clients. For example, when a product feature is in short supply, the demand management agent can notify the consumer assistant agent of possible delays in delivery and to offer alternative resolutions. At the same time, this agent can negotiate with supply management agents to locate new sourcing of components that are hindering timely production of the final product. Additionally, the mobility of the agents allows managers and consumers to participate in decision-making in real-time, using the Internet or even hand-held devices. The technology used to implement these agents and their communication protocols are presented in the next section.

The complete functionality vs. role determining our agent taxonomy is reported next. Agent goals are reported in the corresponding cell (Table 1).

The entire system uses an event-based architecture (Figure 1). An event in this system is defined as actionable information (an object) that appears as a message in the system. The monitoring agents are registered to listen to certain messages. These messages are interpreted and processed synchronously (without explicitly waiting for a response)

Table 1. Agent taxonomy and functionality

Functionality versus Role	Consumer Assistant	Demand Management	Supply and Resource Management
Monitoring	Detect variations of any relevant (for the consumer) product features	Detect key demand variable changes at product model and location level	Detect key supply variable changes or resource constraints at product model and location level
Coordinating	Bring order and semantic structure to the collection of demand and supply events gathered from multiple sources by the mobile assistant	Bring order and semantic structure to the responses for the mix of demand events that are firing synchronously from multiple sources	Bring order and semantic structure to the responses for the mix of supply events that are firing synchronously from multiple sources
Analyzing	Rationalize the follow-on actions for comparative analysis based on features and customers preferences	Rationalize the follow-on actions from excess inventory projections, suboptimal minimum inventory levels, networked replenishment requirements, and multiple shipping alternatives and constraints	Rationalize the follow-on actions from excess/shortage inventory projections, suboptimal minimum inventory levels, networked replenishment requirements, and multiple assembling/shipping alternatives and production constraints
Acting	Adjust customers' decisions as their preference changes	Adjust projected demand through mix of techniques: Optimize base parameters, modify elasticity, adjust for cannibalization, and influence demand through dynamic pricing	Adjust projected supply and production rates through mix of techniques: Optimize base parameters, modify elasticity, adjust price, and optimize supply through tight collaboration.

or asynchronously (the message is blocked until a predefined state is reached). An event bus is introduced as a building block that receives, sends, and processes messages as objects. The event bus offers an interface that is visible to any component of the system that wishes to send and/or receive events (Figure 1).

The agents presented in this architecture behave dynamically, are rule-based, mobile, and respond to events. The behavior of the agents can be in reaction to both internal and external events. For instance, consider an inventory management scenario; the "analyze" and "act" agents can use parameters defined by other agents (monitoring and/or coordinating agents) to determine inventory replenishment policies that reflect up-to-date information about market conditions or even macroeconomic indicators,

in addition to specific product parameters such as available sources, lead time information, the supplier's recent behavior profile, and the latest speed of inventory deliveries. The supporting agents (monitoring and coordinating agents) can monitor internal and external events and processes to acquire and coordinate the necessary data that allows the analyzing and acting agents to manage inventory levels dynamically rather than the traditional static models that use predetermined inventory replenishment parameters.

Finally, in production environments for which e-marketplaces exist, this architecture allows the agents to seamlessly interface with these markets to execute procurement activities. When e-marketplaces do not exist, the agents can additionally perform market-making activities, such as identifying candidate suppliers, communicating requirements, and soliciting quotations.

AGENT SERVICE ARCHITECTURE FOR MASS CUSTOMIZATION

We present an architectural design which is agent-based, supports mass customization, and uses a "cluster model" representation as depicted in Figure 1. This architecture supports the firm's IT infrastructure, and interfaces with existing DBMS, ERP, and other manufacturing support database systems. The architecture uses existing IT networking systems to establish connectivity across participating firms in the marketplace. Clusters of agents can support multiple product lines and/or even different features of a product.

The main features of the above design are:

- **Agents technology and architecture:**
  - Agents are developed using a framework based on the ABLE (agent building and learning environment, from IBM) (Bigus, Schlosnagle, Pilgrim, Mills III, & Diago, 2002) and JADE-LEAP (Java agent development framework and its extension light extensible agent platform) (Bellifemine, Caire, Poggi,

& Rimassa, 2003, Bergenti & Poggi, 2001) platforms. The multiagent system introduced in this architecture uses the ACL language (agent communication language) (ACL, 2006) which complies with FIPA (Foundation for Intelligent Physical Agents) specifications. The architecture employed is distributed, and supports multiple hosts and processes, including mobile systems. Each running instance of the JADE runtime environment is called a "container." A container can include multiple agents (Figure 2). A set of active containers is called a JADE platform which can be distributed across several hosts. The distribution can be from one platform to many hosts and/or many platforms to many hosts. The inter-agent and intra-agent communications occur via ACL messaging. Each agent is represented by one Java thread;

- Agents are registered in JNDI (Java naming and directory interface) for clustering support;

Figure 1. An agent-based architecture for mass customization

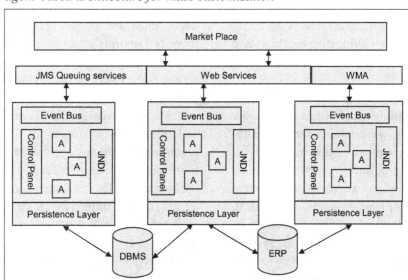

- Agents communicate asynchronously through the event bus among themselves, and can interface with external services (Web services, application services, and external agents) synchronously; and
- Agents learn and acquire intelligence through optimized algorithms per agent functionality.

- **Control panel:**
  - The control panel allows users to create a new agent on demand and register it with the event bus and the JNDI; and
  - The control panel allows users to modify agent parameters and thus modify the behavior of existing agents.

- **Communication interface:**
  - The event bus structure is introduced and developed to facilitate fast internal communications among agents; and
  - The JMS (Java message services) services are introduced to facilitate communications among agents and external applications, including Web services interface, WMA (Windows media audio) services, agents from other applications, external users, and the Web environment at large.

- **Persistent layer:**
  - The persistent layer assists agents in interfacing with existing databases and data retrieval systems.

These features offer the necessary elements for supporting visibility across the entire supply chain and allowing the establishment of collaborative efforts in support of a demand-driven, mass-customized production system. To illustrate these concepts, consider an agent-based system implementation for a manufacturing environment. Figure 2 presents the implementation of this technology to a hypothetical manufacturing system. In this system, agents are implemented as Java container classes that perform the monitoring, coordinating, analyzing, and acting functionalities. The server side of Figure 2 lists five agent containers. The client side shows how users can use mobile phones, PDAs, and similar devices to gain access to the system. In Figure 2, the "I/O container" offers monitoring agents that communicate with data entry systems and provide interface capabilities with existing DBMS, ERPs, and manufacturing databases. Agents from this container communicate and exchange information with the central coordinating agents. Similarly, the "inference container," an analyzing agent, stores information about the manufacturing operation for all possible product configurations. It continuously analyzes production schedules, capabilities, and equipment capacities. It also analyzes manufacturing requirements based on production status and the order stream information for new orders to form a batch and to hold them until notified by another agent (the optimizing agent) to release its information. The communications among these agents is in a synchronized mode. The "optimizing container" is an acting agent that is invoked upon receiving a new batch of orders from the agents of the "inference container." These agents optimize the processing of the orders. The optimization process includes: (a) scheduling optimization using tabu search and genetic algorithms; (b) resource planning using linear and integer programming; and (c) inventory optimization using stochastic optimization methods. The "back-end splits container" serves as the interface channel to the client side. The agents in this container receive and record orders from external agents. The orders are filtered and organized according to their manufacturing requirements and are aggregated and presented to the main container for further processing and optimization. The customers and/or external agents can use this interface to check the status of their orders. Finally, the "main container" serves as the coordinating agent. It interfaces with all other agents, provides supervisory functions to all agents, performs synchronization among processes, and serves as the conflict resolution authority among agents. In this architecture, a persistence layer is provided for interfacing with the external database and data retrieval systems. The entire system is Java-based and uses the agent technology framework developed by IBM (the "ABLE" technology) (Bigus et al., 2002) and JADE-LEAP framework from the open source software (Bellifemine et al., 2003; Bergenti & Poggi, 2001) and the ACL messaging language. These frameworks are extended and modified to support the mobile technologies that will allow users access to the system via mobile phones, PDAs, and any Web-enabled device or interface (Moreno, Valls, & Viejo, 2005).

The system presented supports the decentralized, distributed decision-making model discussed earlier. It is based on a distributed, Web-centric, client server architecture in which the server resides at the manufacturing (primary) vendor, and the client operates at each supplier site. The clients' implementations are lightly integrated into the suppliers' existing IT architectures. The Web-centric nature of the system ensures accessibility across the participating members

as depicted in Figure 2. The consistency of the system is ensured by the choice of the communications and the agent frameworks used in this implementation. The use of standard protocols such as XML and the collaborative nature of the environment require each participant to either directly comply with these protocols, or provide converters and translators in support of the communication systems. An implementation of such a system may include many geographical servers at various locations. Client installations can also be located at geographically- and/or organizationally-dispersed sites. Real-time production and consumption data is gathered from the entire supply chain system and distributed throughout the system for decision-making (Figure 2).

CASE STUDIES

In this section we will discuss case studies that report on adoption and implementation of our approach by two companies that produce mass-customized products. The first case study reports on adoption of this system in a semiconductor

Figure 2. An agent-based architecture for a manufacturing system

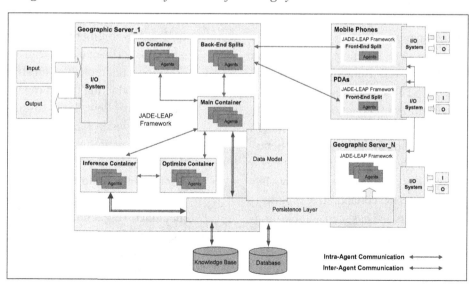

manufacturing environment, and the second case study presents our experience with implementation of the system in the automotive industry.

The ST Microelectronics System

The first case presents a semiconductor manufacturing firm (STM) that has adopted and implemented our software system. STM is the fourth largest semiconductor company in the world with revenue in excess of eight billion dollars. A large part of this revenue comes from integrated circuits that are heavily customized to STM's customer specifics.

STM is the primary supplier of assembled chip sets to a number of mobile telephone providers. The mobile telephone companies offer a mass-customized product line with multiple features (GPS, camera, and phone capabilities). There are a number of valid product configurations for consumers to choose. Orders from the phone companies to STM for the various chip sets often arrive daily or even twice per day. STM's production system needs to respond to demands on a daily or even shift-by-shift basis. The order/reorder processing system, defined by the demand at STM centers, requires agile manufacturing facilities capable of supporting a demand-driven supply chain system in real-time. The architecture described here, and its implementation at STM, enables the company to operate and manage a manufacturing system far more efficient than older, batch-driven, build-to-forecast alternatives. In July of 2000, STM adopted our software for their mass-customized production system. The server side of the software system was installed at STM manufacturing facilities and the clients' side at customers (the telephone manufacturers) and STM suppliers. This implementation has enabled STM to develop collaborative programs with its top customers and has seen notable progress in its delivery schedule, lead time, inventory management, and profit margins.

An important requirement of the project was the ability of STM to connect its IT infrastructure to its customers' existing installed IT systems using mobile intelligent agents. Our software system, sitting on top of STM's existing planning platform, detects the RosettaNet (1998) and XML messages, and provides visibility into different inventory scenarios, such as what parts to build and where to hold inventory to meet the highly-customized demand. The system offers a set of agent-based coordination tools for extracting and transmitting data across the entire IT infrastructures. This strategy has offered STM a proactive approach for supporting its mass customization strategy. It has allowed STM to connect its long-range plans with short-term execution and to optimize the inventory levels and production schedules in order to quickly build the integrated circuits that meet its customer's demands.

STM supplies IC boards (assembled chip sets) to several mobile phone providers. The boards need to be customized according to each customer's specification. The challenges facing STM in supporting their customers are to:

- Develop a long-term planning framework for process and systems improvements;
- Implement new demand planning, e-commerce communications, capacity planning, and efficient supply chain execution;
- Roll out e-commerce with supply chain partners, perform end-to-end supply chain planning, and implement an effective available-to-production (ATP) capability;
- Continue to follow a build-to-forecast (BTF) policy in wafer fabrication and probe to maintain a predefined level of inventory in the die bank;
- Implement a build-to-order (BTO) policy in the assembly and test phase of the IC manufacturing; and
- Develop a financial model to trade-off inventory, manufacturing, and supply chain costs with revenue potentials.

STM adopted the agent-based adaptive supply chain software system described earlier to achieve these objectives. The system is presented in Figure 3 and offers a collaborative supply chain network, supports adaptive demand synchronization and adjustment, provides an adaptive inventory opti-

Figure 3. STM adaptive supply chain system

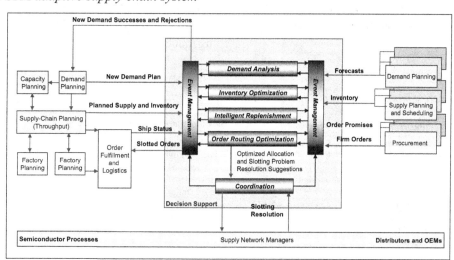

Table 2. Demand management activities for STM

Traditional Approach	Agent-Based Demand Management Approach

Forecast sharing is not traditional, but if it occurs, it follows a passive process like the following:
1. Semiconductor supplier receives forecasts and firm orders from Distributor and OEM on a weekly/daily basis by ship-to location and SKU;
2. Preprocess data to adjust for standard customer request dates, and account for uncertainty;
3. New forecast and firm order data are updated in demand planning system; and
4. Supply chain planners use new demand data to reevaluate and adjust production plans.
	Agent-based adaptive solution is driven by demand changes that impact as far downstream of the supply network as possible.
	1. Semiconductor supplier receives forecast or actual sales data from Distributors and OEMs on a daily/weekly basis; this will depend on cycle for forecast updates; if actual sales are given, then forecast from Distributor and OEM is also provided as it changes;
	2. Semiconductor supplier receives changes to firm orders from OEMs and Distributors on a daily basis;
	3. Event management system triggers a "New Demand" event whenever a new forecast or firm order is received into the system;
	4. MONITOR agents are listening for any demand event and will apply the appropriate business rules to adjust the input streams and trigger the required ANALYZE agents to check for any trending anomalies;
	5. ANALYZE agents perform the following actions:
	  a. ANALYZE "Order Synchronize" is designed to detect inconsistencies with transition from forecasted to firm orders;
	  b. ANALYZE "Volatility" is designed to check for excessive volatility between successive forecasts;
	  c. ANALYZE "Forecast Error" is designed to check for significant error between forecast and semiconductor shipments;
	  d. ANALYZE "POS Sales" is designed to check for significant error between customer forecast and daily/weekly sales from source location in supply network; in this case that is the OEM's and Distributor's; and
	6. ANALYZE agents will coordinate with ACT agents to engage demand synchronization actions:
	  a. ACT "Rationalize Error" agents deduce root cause actions from analysis results;
	  b. ACT "Optimize Parameters" agents adjust forecasting model parameters to minimize forecast error; and
	  c. ACT "Forecast" agents create and recommend new forecasts.

mization and replenishment policy, and optimizes order, material, and flow management systems. In Figure 3, the event management system models supply networks, monitors network input, and triggers events. The agents in the system provide demand synchronization, network inventory optimization, multi-echelon inventory replenishment, delivery and routing planning, and coordination

of the final decision resolution. Each of these components include multiple intelligent agents that perform the monitoring, coordinating, analyzing, and acting functions described earlier. The embedded decision support tools of the system offer performance visibility of suppliers through collection of rankings and metrics, and provides a library of optimization algorithms and learning models.

Table 3. Inventory management activities for STM

Traditional Approach	Agent-Based Inventory Management Approach

1. Inventory performance is reviewed on a periodic basis;
 2. Viewed from a single enterprise perspective; and
 3. Review of safety stock levels based on expected demand and variability, general service level targets, lead-times, and lead-time variability.
	1. Inventory management is driven from a network perspective;
	 2. Event management monitors demand trending, demand error trends, lead time trending, supply error trending, inventory level trends, and service level performance; if there is a threshold violation, an event is created;
	 3. MONITOR agents deduce the semantic value of the mix of events and will trigger the appropriate ANALYZE agents;
	 4. The ANALYZE agents will focus on the following:
	     a. ANALYZE "Stock Up" agents deduce where and why average inventory is increasing;
	     b. ANALYZE "Stock Out" agents deduce where and why stock-outs are excessive;
	     c. ANALYZE "Min Buffer" agents compute the minimum for all key buffers in the network; and
	 5. ANALYZE agents will coordinate with ACT agents to engage inventory optimization actions:
	     a. ACT "Balance Network" agents will be used to adjust inventory positions and levels via ACT "Replenishment" agents to adjust for both inventory shortage and excess scenarios; and
	     b. ACT "Set Level" agents make the appropriate safety stock parameter adjustments at all buffers.

Table 4. Replenishment management activities for STM

Traditional Approach	Agent-Based Replenishment Approach

1. Long-term forecasts are created by customers for up to three months lead-time;
 2. Forecast is frozen and used to negotiate for capacity from Semiconductor company;
 3. Semiconductor company realizes significant manual process costs to continually match capacity to expected customer demand;
 4. Semiconductor company is required to keep high levels of inventory to protect against high variability of demand; and
 5. Customers replenish inventory by continually placing orders with Semiconductor company.
	1. Updated demand plan is provided for target replenishment customers on a daily basis;
	 2. Event management system monitors the demand plan changes and inventory buffer changes; if a threshold limit is violated, an event is created;
	 3. MONITOR agents capture such events and engage the appropriate ANALYZE agent;
	 4. The ANALYZE agents are of the following two types:
	     a. ANALYZE "Buffer" agents compute the threshold values for all of the demand buffers for a new demand plan;
	     b. ANALYZE "Shortage" agents evaluate the shortage situation when inventory is low; and
	 5. ACT agents optimize replenishment over a targeted horizon in order to minimize costs and realize targeted service levels established by Semiconductor supplier and all OEM/Distributor customers:
	     a. ACT "Replenishment" agents create an optimized (min cost flow) replenishment plan for all items over supply/demand map and within targeted plan horizon; and
	     b. ACT "Shipment" agents coordinate with "Replenishment" agents to create and trigger shipments, with the goal of minimizing shipment costs over target shipping horizon.

In Table 2, we provide a comparison of the demand management activities of STM under both the traditional approach and the new agent-based adaptive approach.

Similarly, Table 3 presents the traditional and the new approach for inventory optimization module.

The adaptive replenishment collaboration process, its traditional implementation, and its new implementation are presented in Table 4.

Finally, the routing processes used to manage orders and the reordering of the IC boards, material flow, WIP, and movement of supplies throughout the supply chain and manufacturing plants are optimized to ensure timely availability of supplies and the fulfillment and delivery of customer orders. Table 5 presents the new routing processes employed and compares it with the traditional approach used by STM.

Table 5. Order routing process management activities for STM

Traditional "Commit" Approach	Agent-Based Routing Optimization

Whereas replenishment is used to support the indirect sales process, the "Order Commit" process supports direct sales:
1. Orders are entered and booked with a temporary Scheduled Ship Date and are localized in multiple offices;
2. Within 24 hours, the centralized Sales Planning team determines the initial commit date;
3. Sales orders are continuously revisited to bring the Schedule Date closer to the Customer Request Date; and
4. Management of sales order rescheduling is usually very manual, with limited ability for managing changes and exceptions.
	Adaptive Order Routing dynamically adjusts the slotting of orders to fulfillment routes that best meet the sales, service level, and supply chain cost goals across a network:
	1. Event management system is designed to monitor new orders, inventory, customer request date changes, and goods in transit; significant changes trigger events;
	2. MONITOR agents recognize such events and trigger the appropriate ANALYZE agents;
	3. ANALYZE agents interpret changes and recommend the best actions:
	  a. ANALYZE "Order" agents use order prioritization and current supply/demand state to correct order slotting;
	  b. ANALYZE "Supply" agents use change prioritization and current supply/demand state to correct order slotting response; and
	4. ACT agents are engaged by ANALYZE agents to continuously drive order schedule dates to the customer request date:
	  a. ACT "Simple Slotting" uses heuristics to slot or change an order to respond to a critical supply event; and
	  b. ACT "Allocation Optimization" optimizes order slotting, giving the user selectable weightings for sales, service levels, and cost or profit goals, subject to available material and capacity constraints.

Table 6. Overall improvements for STM manufacturing processes

Process	Results
Supply Chain Simplification	1. Non-value-added movement of wafers or packaged part is reduced; 2. Redefined the testing process to increase offshore testing; and 3. Reduced end-to-end cycle time by eight to ten days.
Logistic Improvements	1. Identified root cause of long transit between Asia and the U.S.; 2. Changed sourcing activities from multiple freight forwards to single 3PL (third-party logistic providers); 3. Reduced inter-company door-to-door cycle times from seven days to two days; and 4. Reduced total logistic costs by $2M/year.
Delivery Performance	1. Identified the root causes of the poor delivery performance; 2. Used inventory monitoring and optimization for allocating supply in capacity-constrained environments; and 3. Improved delivery performance to first commit by more than 35% within five months on pilot product line.

Implementation of the agent-based adaptive supply chain management system by STM has resulted in supply chain simplification, logistic process and provider improvements, and better delivery performance. Table 6 summarizes these improvements.

The agent-based system which has been presented offers an effective infrastructure that enables and encourages updated demand data to

be distributed among members of the production environment on daily or even shift-by-shift bases. In the traditional system, demand data was often only updated weekly. Clearly, accurate information offered by our solution allows decision-makers to optimize their operations throughout the system. The distributed nature of this system allows STM to validate orders for consistency by further monitoring and analysis of demand and

Figure 4. Supply chain model from plant B to plant A

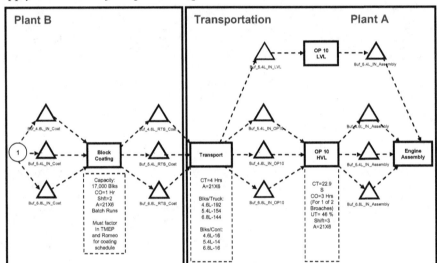

Figure 5. Supply chain model from plant C to plant B

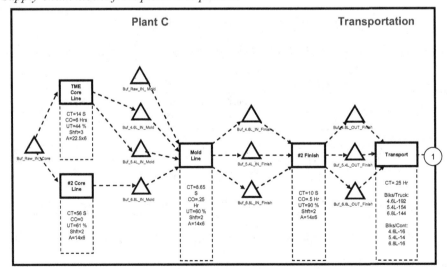

manufacturing data down the stream, up to the OEMs and distributors of its customers' (phone companies) products.

Since adoption and implementation of this strategy, STM has cut its product lead time in half, reduced buffer inventory from five to two weeks, and eliminated 80% of its manual transactions (Shah, 2002).

The Automotive Example: The XYZ Pickup Truck

Today, American, European, Japanese, and other automakers are fiercely competing among each other by giving consumers a unique level of choices in configuring their model. This extreme level of mass customization, for a market that until a few years ago was producing vehicles with very few choices, has introduced numerous challenges on how automakers have aligned and adjusted their supply chain. In the following, we report on the strategy and the solution adopted by one of the leading car manufacturers in addressing the challenges related to customization of one of the components of the pickup truck: the engine block.

This customization introduces a high degree of variability in the cylinder machining opera-

tion at Engine Plant A, the coating process at the Coating Plant B, and the block-casting process at the Casting Plant C. The mass customization process can often result in excessive inventory, which is not tolerable financially.

The objectives of the automaker were:

1. To increase the responsiveness to high customized demand;
2. To reduce the inventory level in the supply chain; and
3. To improve control of managing the overall material flow to the target performance levels.

We first summarize the inventory objectives and production features of each plant and report the "as is" supply chain from B to A and C to B in Table 7, and depict them in Figures 4 and 5 respectively.

To show the effect of mass customization to the supply chain, we consider the customization of the engine. There are two sets of choices for customers: engine size in liters (4.6, 5.4, and 6.8) and the number of cylinders (8 and 10). The only engine with 10 cylinders is the 6.8L V10. Even this simple set of choices can have a great impact on the production lead time. In particular, each time

Table 7. Plant inventory objectives and production features

Location	Inventory Objectives		Production Features	
Plant A	1.	Supply material needs for engine assembly, which is driven by end demand needs; and	1.	Unstable machine capability, and
	2.	Buffer against short supply from Plant B for the very near-term JIT windows.	2.	Low schedule stability.
Plant B	1.	Supply scheduled material needs (JIT schedule) at Plant A;	1.	Batch production,
	2.	Supply unexpected material needs at Plant A, which may be caused by end demand shift, high scrap rate or material consumption, overtime production, and so forth; and	2.	High demand uncertainty from Plant A, and
	3.	Buffer against short supply from Plant C, which may be caused by high changeover rate, unexpected machine downtime at Plant C, and so forth.	3.	High supply uncertainty from Plant C.
Plant C	1.	Supply scheduled material needs (JIT schedule) at Plant A; and	1.	Long changeover time,
	2.	Buffer against short material supply from internal or external suppliers.	2.	Batch production, and
			3.	Inflexible product switch.

that production shifts from V8 to V10, the line becomes idle for some period of time in order to set up the new configuration. Similarly, each time there is a change of configuration from 4.6L to 5.4L or 6.8L, the setup needs to be reconfigured and the line becomes idle.

The inability to proactively forecast and shape customers' demand results in:

- Unscheduled downtime at the block production line;
- Inability of block line to consistently support engine assembly at Plant A;
- Excessive inventory carrying costs;
- Transportation inefficiencies;
- Unplanned overtime at all the plants; and
- Scheduling instability.

To support this degree of mass customization, we have applied the "agent-based adaptive supply chain model" presented in this chapter to the manufacturing processes at the three plants. Since the auto industry's supply chain is complex and often includes many tiers, the agent-based solution provided in this model can make changes

in the demand data to be simultaneously visible throughout the system. The propagation of this up-to-date information will allow production and inventory level adjustments for all participants, including even downstream suppliers. This model minimizes downtime, reduces inventory throughout the production system, and offers a more efficient transportation system while achieving a more stable scheduling and delivering option. This model is presented in Figure 6.

There are seven components of this adaptive model:

1. **The event management:** The event management framework is a foundational capability of the adaptive supply chain solution. Its primary purpose is to monitor events and orchestrate the adaptive response to the significant event changes that occur in the supply chain. An event is any supply chain variable that represents some key dynamic in the operation of the supply chain process, for example, demand or inventory level. Throughout the supply chain, a change in an event can trigger one of two possible paths.

Figure 6. The adaptive supply chain model for engine assembly

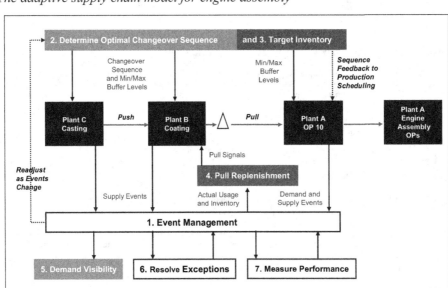

If the change is considered within the normal variability, it will trigger the changeover optimization engine, the pull replenishment engine, or both. If the change is outside a preset tolerance limit, it will trigger an exception and notify the appropriate user.

2 – 3. **Optimal changeover sequence and target inventory:** The optimal changeover and target inventory (OCTI) is an intelligent engine that will calculate both the optimal sequence of product runs and target inventory buffer levels for any series of product changeover constrained operations in the supply chain. The engine uses a mixed integer programming model to minimize the total supply chain costs subject to demand, inventory, and transportation and production constraints. The OCTI engine is used to calculate both the optimal block sequence for each of the supply chain operations and to adjust the associated min/max buffer levels. The supply chain system uses a push/pull control strategy for coordinating the material flow, with a pull replenishment buffer established at the ready to ship buffer in coating. The OCTI results are used as input to both casting and coating stages to drive the build schedules that are used to push the engine blocks through coating to the pull buffer. The min and max levels of the interim buffers are adjusted as needed. On the Plant A OP 10 side, the OCTI results are used as input to the OP 10 pull scheduling process to develop production runs that best support the actual engine assembly usage and the calculated optimal block sequence. When the event of the OP 10 input buffers reaches the reorder levels, it will trigger the pull replenishment engine to pull in blocks from the coating replenishment buffer

4. **Pull replenishment:** The pull replenishment is an intelligent replenishment engine designed to trigger and control the "pull" replenishment from any two entities in the supply chain. It also has a look-ahead capability, driven by forecasted demand that will assess the synchronization viability of the source supply. Plant A supply chain uses the pull replenishment engine to coordinate the pull signals between the OP 10 input buffer and the coating ready-to-ship buffer.

5. **Demand visibility:** The demand forecasting module offers intelligent agents that are invoked by the event management component. These agents use the longer-term demand values and parameters as guidelines and receive up-to-date demand information from the actual customer base. The agents revise and smooth the order stream using the longer-term demand values and parameters. They use the current production status, buffer values, and other production data to determine final manufacturing orders for both the casting and coating processes.

6. **Resolve exceptions:** Exceptions are defined to be violations of production values from manufacturing thresholds. In this system, thresholds have dynamic values and are determined by the demand levels. Once an exception is reached, that is, a threshold is violated, the conditions need to be restored to normality and full or near optimality. Reaching a restoration level is attempted while keeping the noise level in the entire manufacturing environment to a minimum and without causing major interruption to the system. For example, a generated exception might be allowed to proceed, and thus miss fulfilling a portion of the demand portfolio in the short term, in order to honor longer-term production goals and constraints.

7. **Measure performance:** This module uses intelligent agents to monitor key performances of the system through the event management component. It can measure performance of any event, both internal and external, by collecting statistics dynamically. Examples of internal events include

Table 8. Simulation results for the engine manufacturing plant

Models	Total Inventory	Utilization (Plant A)	Utilization (Plants B & C)
Existing System	27,000	60%	41%
Proposed System	13,283	90%	61%

inventory buffer levels, number of change-overs, production line throughput, and total inventory in the pipeline. Similarly, customer satisfaction and supplier performance, which are external events, can also be monitored and measured by this module.

Implementation of this system has used several features of the model, described in this chapter, in the engine manufacturing process. The data requirement of the system necessitated an information technology infrastructure based on the agent technology for decision-making, JDBC for data storage, and XML for interfacing and data access. The concept of synchronization was used to ensure sequencing of the steps. The system allowed for interaction with auto dealers, partners, and suppliers. This visibility brought demand information and fluctuation to the manufacturing floor and broadcasted manufacturing status, alerts, and exceptions to the affected targets. Finally, a graphical user interface was produced to allow authorized users to view, input, or edit the entire system information.

Prior to the implementation of the system, a simulation model was developed to assess the effectiveness of the proposed system and compare its performance to the existing one. The objectives of the simulation were to measure inventory levels, changeover time, and utilization of the manufacturing facilities for given demand values. The demand information represented a dynamic stream of customized orders and reorders recorded daily over a 90-day period. The objective function which was used represented total production costs while allowing for switching among the different configurations. The constraint set included the

various buffer limitations for inventory, change-over capacity and its opportunity cost, maximum throughput capacity, and equipment availability and maintenance constraints. The results of the simulation showed improved performance as measured by the two key indices (inventory levels and utilization rates) for the three plants. Table 8 shows that total inventory level for the system was reduced from 27,000 units to 13,283 units (a 51% reduction). The utilization rate for plant A increased from 60% to 90%, and the combined utilization rate for plants B and C was improved from 41% to 61%. These improvements have increased the automaker's responsiveness and its competitive edge in meeting customers' demands.

CONCLUSION

The goal of a mass customization strategy is to deliver customized products at costs that are near-equivalent to their mass-produced versions without significant delays. To achieve this goal, we presented a Web-enabled information system model that uses mobile intelligent agent technology and can be interfaced with the firms' existing IT infrastructures. Successful implementation of any mass-customized strategy requires a collaborative environment that follows a build-to-order production strategy. In such an environment, customers can configure their orders online and monitor any order's status at any time, suppliers can view demand stream dynamically in real-time, and the manufacturers can react to changing orders efficiently and expediently. We presented a distributed, Java-based, mobile intelligent information system model that is demand-driven, supports a build-to-order policy, provides end-to-end visibility along the entire supply chain, allows for a collaborative and synchronized production system, and supports an event-based manufacturing environment. The system introduces an agent-based architecture with four general-purpose intelligent agents to support the entire mass customization process. Experiences with implementations of this approach at a semiconductor and an automotive company show the effectiveness of the proposed architecture in enhancing the "*velocity of execution*" of supply chain management activities, including order management, planning, manufacturing, operations, and distributions. Results verified that successful adoption of this system can reduce inventory and logistic costs, improve delivery performance, increase manufacturing facilities utilizations, and provide a higher overall profitability.

REFERENCES

ACL: Agent Communications Language (2006). Retrieved May, 2006, from http://www.fipa.org/repository/aclspec.html

Adam, N. R., Dogramaci, O., Gangopadhyay, A., & Yesha, Y. (1999). *Electronic commerce.* NJ: Prentice Hall.

Anderson, D. L., & Lee, H. (1999). Synchronized supply chains: The new frontier. In *Achieving supply chain excellence through technology* (pp. 12-21). Montgomery Research.

Arjmand, M., & Roach, S. (1999). Creating greater customer value by synchronizing the supply chain. In *Achieving supply chain excellence through technology* (pp. 154-159). Montgomery Research. Also at http://arjmand.ascet.com

Baker, A. D., Van Dyke Parunak, H., & Kutluhan, E. (1999). Agents and the Internet: Infrastructure for mass customization. *IEEE Internet Computing,* (Sept.-Oct.), 62-69.

Bellifemine, F., Caire, G., Poggi, A., & Rimassa, G. (2003). *JADE: A white paper. Exp, 3*(3), 6-19.

Bergenti, F., & Poggi, A. (2001). LEAP: A FIPA platform for handheld and mobile devices. In *Proceedings of the Eighth International Workshop on Agent Theories, Architectures, and Languages (ATAL-2001),* Seattle, WA (pp. 303-313).

Bigus, J. P., Schlosnagle, D. A., Pilgrim, J. R., Mills III, W. N., & Diago, Y. (2002). ABLE: A toolkit for building multi-agent autonomic systems – Agent building and learning environment. *IBM Systems Journal,* (September), 1-19.

Capgemini (2004). *A collection of agent technology pilots and projects.* Retrieved May, 2006, from http://www.capgemini.com/resources/thought_leadership/putting_agents_towork/

Dorer, K., & Calisti, M. (2005). An adaptive solution to dynamic transport optimization. In *Proceedings of the Fourth International Joint Conference on Autonomous Agents and Multi-Agent Systems, AAMAS '05,* Utrecht, The Netherlands. Also at http://www.whitestein.com/pages/downloads/publications

Ghiassi, M. (2001). An e-commerce production model for mass-customized market. *Issues in Information Systems, 2,* 106-112.

Ghiassi, M., & Spera, C. (2003a). Defining the Internet-based supply chain system for mass-customized markets. *Computers & Industrial Engineering Journal, 45*(1), 17-41.

Ghiassi, M., & Spera, C. (2003b). A collaborative and adaptive supply chain management system. In *Proceedings of the 31st International Conference on Computers and Industrial Engineering,* San Francisco, CA (pp. 473-479).

Gilmore, J. H., & Pine II, B. J. (2000). *Markets of one: Creating customer-unique value through mass customization.* Harvard Business Review.

GPRS: General Packet Radio System. Retrieved May, 2006, from http://www.gsmworld.com/technology/gprs/index.html

JADE. Retrieved May, 2006, from http://jade.cselt.it & http://jade.tilab.com

Jain, A. K., Aparicio IV, M., & Singh, M. P. (1999). Agents for process coherence in virtual enterprises. *Communications of the ACM, 42*(3), 62-69.

Kalakota, R., Stallaert, J., & Whinston, A. B. (1998). Implementing real-time supply chain optimization systems. *Global Supply Chain and Technology Management, POMS,* 60-75.

Lange, D. B., & Oshima, M. (1998). *Programming and developing Java mobile agents with aglets.* Reading, MA: Addison-Wesley.

Ma, M. (1999). Agents in e-commerce. *Communications of the ACM, 42*(3), 79-80.

Maes, P., Guttman, R. H., & Moukas, A. G. (1999). Agents that buy and sell. *Communications of the ACM, 42*(3), 81-91.

MIDP: Mobile Information Device Profile. Retrieved May, 2006, from http://java.sun.com/products/midp/index.jsp

Moreno, A., Valls, A., & Viejo, A. (2005). *Using JADE-LEAP to implement agents in mobile devices (*Research Rep. 03-008, DEIM, URV*).* Retrieved May, 2006, from http://www.etse.urv.es/recerca/banzai/toni/MAS/papers.html

Pancerella, A., & Berry, N. (1999). Adding intelligent agents to existing EI frameworks. *IEEE Internet Computing,* (Sept.-Oct.), 60-61.

RosettaNet (1998). Retrieved May, 2006, from http://www.rosettanet.org

Sandholm, T. (1999). Automated negotiation. *Communications of the ACM, 42*(3), 84-85.

Shah, J. B. (2002). ST, HP VMI program hitting its stride. *Electronics Business News (EBN), 42.* Retrieved May, 2006, from http://www.ebnonline.com

Singh, R., Salam, A. F., & Iyer, L. (2005). Agents in e-supply chains. *Communications of the ACM, 48*(6), 109-115.

Sundermeyer, K. (2001). Collaborative supply net management. In F. Baader, G. Brewka, & T. Eiter (Eds.), *KI:2001, Advances in artificial intelligence* (pp. 467-470).

Wilke, J. (2002). Using agent-based simulation to analyze supply chain value and performance. In *Proceedings of the Supply Chain World Conference and Exhibition,* New Orleans, LA.

Chapter IX
Critical Role of Supply Chain Decoupling Point in Mass Customisation from Its Upstream and Downstream Information Systems Point of View

Soroosh Saghiri
The University of Greenwich Business School, UK

ABSTRACT

Concentrating on the role of supply chain decoupling point, this chapter introduces different levels of customisation and mass operations and three types of mass customisation. It argues that in each mass customisation type, information systems which are upstream and downstream of the decoupling point can be varied. Consequently, information flows in different types of mass customisation have been examined. This analysis is an endeavour to organise mass customisation information systems across the supply chain, while it can be a useful structure for future researches in this area as well.

INTRODUCTION

This chapter introduces mass customisation (MC) from the global perspective of supply chain. With this outlook, its focus point will lie on decoupling point (DP) and MC-associated information systems in DP upstream and downstream.

Mass customisation (MC) is known as a strategy in supply chain, which aims to meet market changing and ever-increasing requirements, while it tries to utilise mass production benefits (Hart, 1995; Kay, 1993). Towards exploring mass customisation strategy, the decoupling point (DP) analysis is viewed as an imperative section of supply chain management (SCM). DP can be implied as any stage of material/information flow in the supply chain where the customer order penetrates (Hoekstra & Romme, 1992). In effect, the position and the role of DP in supply chain have a direct influence on mass customisation strategy across the supply chain (Olhager & Wikner, 2000; van Donk, 2001; Yang & Burns, 2003).

Analysing various positions of DP across the supply chain, this chapter introduces different forms of mass customisation. Based upon this, it investigates the role of information systems in mass customisation supply chain strategy through particular concentration on DP. Finally, the role of information systems in production planning and order replenishment in upstream and downstream parts of DP is explored.

ROLE OF "DP" IN SUPPLY CHAIN STRATEGY POSITIONING

The organisation and structure of material flow, information flow, and customer-supplier relation-ships, and how they are managed across a supply chain has crucial correlation with the location of DP and supply chain strategy positioning. The DP is recognised as a business level concept with strategic, tactical, as well as operational implications, while its positioning affects the whole supply chain system (Wikner & Rudberg, 2005). Typically, DP upstream activities are performed to forecast, where in downstream they are performed in relation to the customer order. Accordingly, the general idea is using mass/lean production methods in upstream, up to the decoupling point, and customer-driven methods beyond it (Luna & Aguilar-Savén, 2004; Naylor, Naim, & Berry, 1999).

The DP position depends on a balance among several factors such as the product type, market atmosphere, production processes, and inventory characteristics. For example, in decisions for the location of the DP, firms usually consider the lead times imposed by the market and the inventories. If the lead time from the DP to the customer is longer than the market delivery time, companies will tend to react by moving the DP closer to the

Table 1. Attributes of supply chain upstream/downstream of DP (Adapted from Olhager, 2003)

Attribute	DP upstream	DP downstream
Product type	Standard, common	Special
Product range	Predetermined, narrow	Wide
Demand	High volume, predictable	Low volume, volatile
Order winner	Price	Flexibility, speed
Market qualifier	Quality, on-time delivery	Price, quality
Process	Flow shop	Job shop
Capacity	Lag/track	Lead/track
Facilities	Product focus	Process focus
Vertical integration	Supplier relationship	Customer relationship
Quality	Process focus	Product focus
Organisation	Centralised	Decentralised
Performance measurement	Cost, productivity	Flexibility, delivery lead times
Production planning and control	Order promising based on stock availability, rate-based material planning	Order promising based on lead time agreement, time-phased material planning

customer. An optimal DP changes as supply and demand conditions alter.

Based upon the above analysis of DP, Table 1 summarises various features of supply chain in "pre" and "post" DP. This will help in identifying the differences between the two sides of DP and its impact on information and material flow.

By moving DP from supply chain upstream (design) to supply chain downstream (retail), the supply strategy varies (see Figure 1). Each strategy could be described as follows:

• In engineer-to-order (ETO) supply chain, DP is positioned in design stage, where the customer can contribute to the design

and features of the product. The level of customer involvement is reduced when DP moves toward manufacturing and assembly stages;

• In make-to-order (MTO) and assemble-to-order (ATO) supply chains, although the design is firm, the product can be built or assembled based upon customer order;

• In ship-to-order (STO) supply chain strategy, DP is located in final product warehouses or distribution centres. In this case, although the product is not customised, its shipment follows the exact customer order (which can be interpreted as some sorts of customisation); and

Figure 1. Analysis of different positions of decoupling point in supply chain (Adapted from Olhager, 2003, and Naylor et al., 1999)

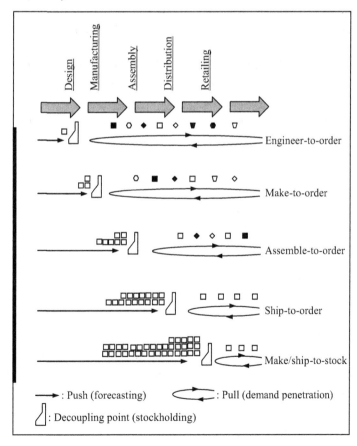

- When DP is positioned in point of sale (re-tailer), order penetration to the supply chain is in its lowest level, and the supply chain strategy will be make-to-stock (MTS).

As is clear from the above explanation, DP positioning and supply chain strategies are highly correlated. The position of DP impacts the supply chain strategy, and in any supply chain strategy, the recognition of the real position of the DP is crucial.

MASS-CUSTOMISATION AND DP

As reviewed before, mass customisation has been recognised as an operations strategy associated to the ability of providing customised products through flexible processes of high volumes (DaSilveira, Borenstein, & Fogliatto, 2001). Looking at this definition from the DP positioning viewpoint, it can be found that not every position of DP across the supply chain facilitates the implementation of mass customisation. In ETO supply chain, for example, although there is a high level of customisation, due to the position of DP, mass production is not possible. On the other hand, in the MTS supply chain, mass production works, where customisation has no opportunity to arise.

To find details of the relationship between the decoupling point and mass customisation, we investigate different types of mass customisation from the two perspectives of "mass operations" and "customisation".

Mass Operations Perspective

"Mass operations" has generally been recognised as a high-volume production system with a low variety of products (Slack, Chambers, & Johnston, 2004). However, in an extensive view of supply chain management, diverse aspects of

mass operations are recognised. The most typical understanding of mass operations is producing high volumes of the final product and shipping it in large lot sizes to mass markets. When the variety of the final product increases, and production volume of each product type decreases, supply of their parts and components can still follow the mass operations system. This particularly happens when those diverse final products use common parts and components. In such a situation, required raw material can be mass purchased, common parts can be mass produced, or even some parts of final assembly can follow the mass operations approach. These policies still tries to benefit from mass operations causes lower cost of procurement or production. Thus, from supply chain downstream to upstream there are different levels of mass operations to be applied. In supply chain view, any of them can be implied as an application of the mass operations concept, each to some extent. Levels of mass operations across the supply chain can be listed as follows:

- Mass shipment of final product to the demand point,
- Mass production of final product,
- Mass production of components, and
- Mass purchase.

Customisation Perspective

Customisation can also be interpreted in different ways and to different extents in supply chain. In fully-customised cases, the customer contributes in the design stage. Tailoring is a typical example of the highest level of customisation. Distancing from that level of customisation, the product may be built according to a firm design but varying in the material or manufacturing processes. In a less-customised case, diverse final products can be assembled based upon limited variety of components or modules. And sometimes, customisation can be realised in its lowest level of shipment of single model, final product to the demand point where customer expects it. Therefore, different levels of customisation can be listed as follows:

- Customised design,
- Customised manufacturing,
- Customised assembly, and
- Shipment to the right demand point.

Figure 2 compares different levels of mass operations and customisation, and illustrates where DP positioning and supply chain strategy let mass customisation be realised. As shown in Figure 2, except those areas which refuse customisation or mass operation totally, other areas can be potential conditions for mass customisation, each to a certain extent.

MASS CUSTOMISATION AND SUPPLY CHAIN INFORMATION SYSTEMS

Supply chain (SC) system can be seen as a business enterprise with a high level of data transaction. A well-organised information system is a foundation for high performance of SC, where the cost of different types of customisation is largely associated to information systems costs (Piller, 2002). Harmonised information flow enables the rapid sharing of demand and supply data at increasing levels of sophistication. The aim of integration is to achieve demand and supply data accuracy for business processes, markets, and customers. Such integration provides increasing competitive advantage accordingly (Post & Anderson, 2006).

Figure 2. Mass customisation opportunities in different supply chain strategies and different positions of DP

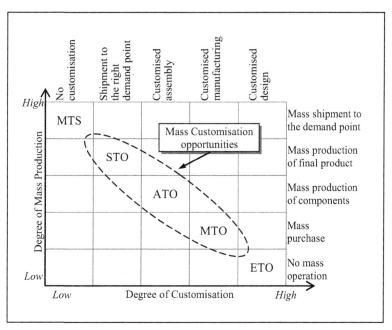

Supply chain management should emphasise the overall and long-term benefit of all parties on the chain through information sharing and coordination. This underlies the importance of the management of information flow. Information synchronisation between members of a supply chain using different levels of information technology should enhance shipment performance of supplier and reduce uncertainties in customer demands. Integration between employed information technology (IT) and business model, IT strategic planning, infrastructures for information systems, and effective application of IT based upon SC requirements are some key considerations in information flow management in SC.

With that respect, developments in IT have increased the probability of mass customisation being adopted as an acceptable supply chain strategy (Istook, 2002). Strategy of mass customisation needs the supply chain to be supported in the three levels of "infrastructure", "strategy", and "operations" (Post & Anderson, 2006).

On the other hand, considering the key role of DP in supply chain necessitates the analysis of those levels prior to and beyond it. Regarding the different types of mass customisation strategies, MTO, ETO, ATO, STO, and MTS, which have been recognised in the previous section, information systems in each are investigated in the following subsections.

STO-Type Mass Customisation Information Systems

Ship-to-order (STO) is a mass customisation strategy with a high level of mass operations and low customisation. While production activities prior to the decoupling point in STO follow mass operations system, shipment of the final product to the demand point is finalised after receiving the accurate quantity of demand. To increase customisation aspect of this strategy, transportation system and/or packaging of the final product can be customised as well. Hence, STO needs high-level communication between market and shipment point (final product warehouse or distribution centres). As the product in this strategy follows push system and is produced based upon total demand forecast, the supply chain could enjoy a stable condition for planning and control. Material requirement planning (MRP), enterprise resource management (ERP), and computer-aided quality control (CAQ) are some of the crucial information systems for the STO supply chain upstream. In

Figure 3. STO-type mass customisation and the associated information systems

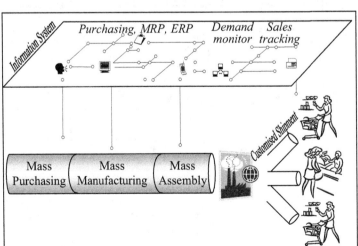

the downstream part, data communication systems between retail sector, distribution centres, and transportation system are the main required systems. Figure 3 illustrates the structure of the STO supply chain and some required information systems.

ATO-Type Mass Customisation Information Systems

With development based on a limited number of modules/subassemblies and numerous final products, assemble-to-order (ATO) is a mass customisation strategy with a moderate level of mass operations and customisation. In ATO, production of components and modules follows the mass operations rules, in which assembly of the final product for the exact demand point is customised. This type of mass customisation needs well-established procurement and manufacturing information systems before decoupling point, which can support mass production of components and modules. Due to the production of a variety of final products based on limited diversification in modules, production planning and control systems are advised to change their

traditional bill-of-material (BOM) systems with supper BOM and Modular BOM systems (Browne, Harhen, & Shivnan, 1996). If components and modules are planned to be subcontracted, then integrated information systems will be required to facilitate the transaction of engineering, financial, and planning information. Figure 4 shows the structure of the ATO supply chain and some associated information systems.

MTO-Type Mass Customisation Information Systems

Make-to-order (MTO) is a mass customisation strategy with a high level of customisation and moderated-to-low level of mass operations. Using almost similar raw material, MTO produces final products and their components based on customer orders. So, different processes, equipment, and facilities are to be employed. On the other hand, utilising similar raw material lets the firm purchase them in high quantity. This mass purchasing makes the cost manageable, where it also facilitates the mass production in suppliers.

Although MTO products are not designed according to the customer order, it still needs

Figure 4. ATO-type mass customisation and the associated information systems

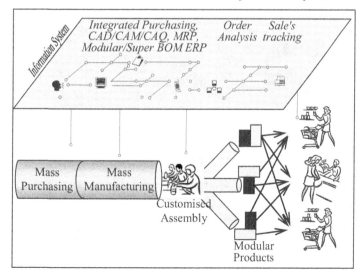

integrated information systems. These information systems are to cover product and process engineering information, financial and accounting databases, and customer order processing. Receiving the customer order, analysing features, and translating them to technical and engineering information create a demand for strong information systems, which are supported by decision support systems (DSS) and expert systems (ES). The architecture of the MTO supply chain and its supporting information systems are shown in Figure 5.

MASS CUSTOMISATION AND SUPPLY CHAIN PLANNING

Planning in mass customisation-oriented supply chains is critically dependent on the location of DP. Furthermore, the structure and relationships between DP's upstream and downstream information systems are vital for planning in a supply chain that follows the mass customisation strategy. Supply chain planning can be analysed in terms of time frames in the three levels of business planning, aggregate planning, and master production scheduling.

Business planning refers to long-term plans of the supply chain. In this level, the overall business in which the firm aims to work is planned. Based on this business plan, the decision has been made whether mass customisation is a supply chain strategy to be pursued or not. If mass customisation is chosen as the main supply chain strategy in the business plan, its type (STO, ATO, or MTO) will also be identified accordingly.

In a medium-range planning, aggregation helps us to identify the overall demand within the next 6-18 months, whereas in short-range planning, master production scheduling tries to plan the production of each type of product. Aggregate planning and master production scheduling have quite different outputs in different types of mass customisation. In STO, aggregation is implemented on overall demand of the final product. Since the variety of the products in STO is very limited, the disaggregating step on master production scheduling is done on different demand points. In other words, while aggregate planning estimates the total demand, master production

Figure 5. MTO-type mass customisation and the associated information systems

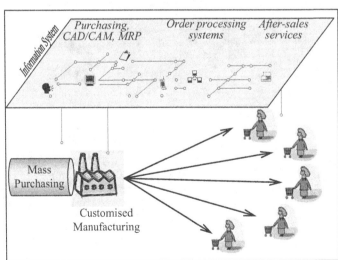

scheduling tries to identify the exact demand of each market in the short term. Figure 6 demonstrates information interchanges of supply chain planning in STO-type mass customisation.

In ATO-type mass customisation, due to the higher variety of final products, aggregate planning can estimate the total demand of all of the final products, where the demand for each product will be planned later in the master production schedule for the short term. Based upon the information of the aggregate plan, the demand for modules and components is approximately clear, so production plan and purchasing plan can be

developed in advance with less complexity, where the assembly plan should be postponed by the time the customer's order arrives. Since the time for planning assembly is very limited, there is a critical need for rapid data interchange which transfers the customer order to the sales department and the assembly plant. Information systems which support this quick data transaction should mainly work based upon online ordering and processing, and real-time updating capabilities. The information system design in ATO-type mass customisation should focus on quick reception of the order, quick transformation of the market information

Figure 6. Information flow in STO-type mass customisation

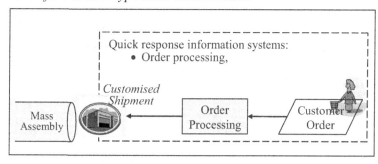

Figure 7. Information flow in ATO-type mass customisation

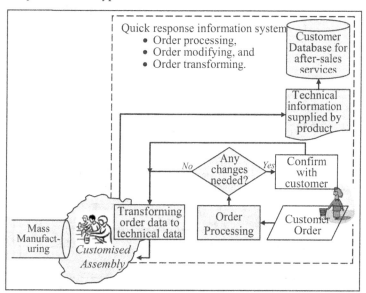

to assembly technical information, quick communication with the customer regarding changes in the order, and quick transferring of the order to the assembly point. Figure 7 points up the flow of information across the DP downstream, where the customer's order is to be met by a variety of ATO-type mass-customised products.

In MTO-type mass customisation, due to quite diverse products, aggregate planning can estimate the overall demand of all possible product very roughly. This can be helpful only for procuring raw material and purchasing planning. Since products are to be made based upon different orders of different customers, even master production scheduling cannot give an exact idea about the demand. In that respect, when the customer order arrives at the sales point, an initial review is done on the feasibility of accepting the order. This review is mainly about the customer's expected price, availability of manufacturing resources, and the delivery time. Based on this review, a preliminary agreement is made with the customer.

Then the order is submitted to the plant where more technical reviews are done on the order. Any changes on the order which is related to product features, manufacturing process, and so forth, are to be confirmed by the customer in this stage as well. The agreed order is built and shipped to the customer, where technical information is supplied with it. Due to the high-level customisation of the product, complete after-sales services should be provided to the customer, usually by the end of the product life cycle. All these data transactions are to be done with the highest accuracy and without delay. A customer is usually very tough about the deadline, and expects the order to be met on-time, with agreed specifications and price. These all demand a quick information system, with a high level of capability in communication with different parties in each order (i.e., customer, sales point, manufacturing plant, process engineers, etc.). Figure 8 shows the flow of information in a typical MTO mass customisation.

Figure 8. Information flow in MTO-type mass customisation

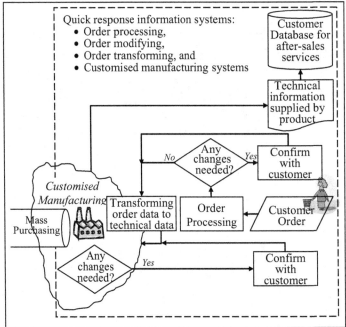

CONCLUSION

This chapter addressed mass customisation information systems, with particular focus on the decoupling point across supply chain. It investigated the concept of mass customisation from customisation and mass operations perspectives. Explaining different levels of mass operations and customisation, and considering the position of the decoupling point in each, the chapter brought in three types of mass customisation: ship-to-order, assemble-to-order, and make-to-order. Next, information systems in each type were dealt separately, where they were analysed in both decoupling point downstream and upstream. Completing that analysis, planning procedure was reviewed in different mass customisation types, and information flow in them was examined.

By investigating a total perspective for mass customisation information systems across the supply chain, this chapter can provide a well-established structure for future researches in this area. Examining compatible information systems strategies with mass customisation strategy, surveys on the applicability of different types of information systems which support mass customisation in supply chain, and case studies around how the decoupling point is recognised and how mass customisation information systems are established based upon that can be potential areas for future researches in this field.

REFERENCES

Browne, J., Harhen, J., & Shivnan, J. (1996). *Production management systems: An integrated perspective.* Harlow, UK: Addison-Wesley.

DaSilveira, G., Borenstein, D., & Fogliatto, F. S. (2001). Mass customization: Literature review and research directions. *International Journal of Production Economics, 72*(1), 1-13.

Hart, C. (1995). Mass customization: Conceptual underpinnings, opportunities, and limits. *International Journal of Service Industry Management,* 6(2), 36-45.

Hoekstra, S., & Romme, J. (1992). *Integrated logistics structures: Developing customer oriented goods flow.* London: McGraw-Hill.

Istook, C. L. (2002). Enabling mass customization: Computer-driven alteration methods, *International Journal of Clothing Science and Technology, 14*(1), 61-76.

Kay, M. (1993). Making mass customization happen: Lessons for implementation. *Planning Review, 21*(4), 14-18.

Luna, E. F. G., & Aguilar-Savén, R. S. (2004, April 30-May). Manufacturing strategy linked to product life cycle. In *Proceedings of the Second World Conference on POM and 15ᵗʰ Annual POM Conference,* Cancun, Mexico.

Naylor, J. B., Naim, M. M., & Berry, D. (1999). Leagility: Integrating the lean and agile manufacturing paradigms in the total supply chain. *International Journal of Production Economics, 62*(1-2), 107-118.

Olhager, J. (2003). Strategic positioning of the order penetration point. *International Journal of Production Economics, 85*(3), 319–329.

Olhager, J., & Wikner, J. (2000). Production planning and control tools. *Production Planning and Control, 11*(3), 210-222.

Piller, F. T. (2002). Customer interaction and digitalizability-A structural approach to mass customisation. In C. Rautenstrauch, R. S. Eggebert, & K. Turowski (Eds.), *Moving into mass customisation* (pp. 119-137). Berlin: Springer-Verlag.

Post, G. V., & Anderson, D. L. (2006). *Management information systems: Solving business problems with information technology.* New York: McGraw-Hill.

Slack, N., Chambers, S., & Johnston, R. (2004). *Operations management*. Essex, UK: FT/Prentice Hall.

Van Donk, D. P. (2001). Make to stock or make-to-order: The decoupling point in the food processing industries. *International Journal of Production Economics*, *69*(2), 297-306.

Wikner, J., & Rudberg, M. (2005). Integrating production and engineering perspectives on the customer order decoupling point. *International Journal of Operations & Production Management*, *25*(7), 623-641.

Yang, B., & Burns, N. (2003). Implications of postponement for the supply chain. *International Journal of Production Research*, *41*(9), 2075-2090.

Section III
Innovative Information Technology Approaches for Mass Customization

Chapter X
From Strategy Definition to Product Derivation Using a Scenario–Based Architecting Approach

Mugurel Ionita
University of Groningen, The Netherlands

Pierre America
Philips Research, The Netherlands

Dieter Hammer
University of Groningen, The Netherlands

ABSTRACT

Mass customization is a business strategy that aims at satisfying, in a timely and cost-effective manner, the various needs of different customers. For that purpose, a system architecture is needed that supports two different kinds of variability: Variability in space provides a range of different products where each addresses the specific needs of an individual customer; and variability in time allows the products to evolve and thus meet new requirements. In defining such an architecture, two issues should be considered. One is how to anticipate the most likely changes in the external business environment, and hence in the customers' future needs. The other is whether the architecture can address these changes effectively. This chapter presents a set of scenario-based methods and techniques to support the development of system architectures that are more future-proof, and also are advantageous for mass customization. These methods and techniques have originally been developed for highly-customized professional systems, in particular medical imaging equipment.

INTRODUCTION

In a competitive market, groups of customers have particular preferences for products that are more than just functional. Some are interested in a functional product which is also esthetic. Others set high store by the usability and ease of use of the product, or are interested in its cost of ownership or its interoperability. The ability to deal with the preferences expressed by an individual customer is now known as the process of product *customization* or *personalization*. The ability to identify and deal with the preferences of a group of individuals who share similar preferences with respect to a specific product is known as the process of *mass customization*. Mass customization is, therefore, the process of "producing goods and services to meet individual customer's needs with near mass production efficiency" (Tseng & Jiao, 2001).

The idea of mass customization also involves economic profitability. It has been observed that customers with a high level of product expertise consider a customized product as having a higher utility than a standard alternative (Dellaert & Stremersch, 2005). The equilibrium price and profit margin reached in the case of a customized product are therefore higher compared with the standard configuration. If this is the case, the question arises as to where to stop with customization. Reaching out to the individual customers and involving them in the codesign of the product proved to be complicated. Addressing communities proved to be a much more efficient way of collaborative customer codesign (Piller, Schubert, Koch, & Moeslein, 2004). Therefore, in highly competitive markets where customers set the rules and price, customization and personalization, that is, information about customers, their needs and wants, current markets, and future trends, is a key factor for success (Blattberg & Glaser, 1994; Hagel & Singer, 1999).

In this chapter, we look at the problems associated with designing customized systems in the context of professional products. In essence, this means being able to capture and manage change, in two of its forms. One is the modification of a product configuration to meet individual customer requirements, referred to as variability in space. The other is the evolution of one product into a new one to satisfy new requirements, referred to as variability in time. To deal successfully with these two issues, we look at techniques to discover and model variability at system architecture level, that is, ways to represent variability and to anticipate change in customers' future needs. The success of customization, therefore, depends on the degree to which we are able to manage change. Although the examples provided in this chapter refer to high-end professional products, the techniques and methods apply to a wider category of mass-customized systems such as information systems. These include customer relation management systems (CRM), enterprise content management systems (ECM), document management systems, and so forth. The variation modeling and the mass customization process for information systems can be performed following the same steps as for professional systems. These steps will be described in the next subsections.

The remainder of this chapter is organized as follows. Section 2 introduces scenario methods as powerful tools to capture change and innovation and to communicate ideas. Section 3 explains variation within the context of product customization. Here sources and types of variability are presented, as well as techniques to manage them. Section 4 presents the strategic option design and assessment (SODA) method, which is an approach for designing system architectures that support customization. The SODA method has been developed at Philips Research. In this section, the steps of the method are explained, and some examples are given based on a case study for professional medical systems. Section 5 presents some conclusions.

GUIDING THE EVOLUTION PROCESS USING SCENARIOS

When designing customized products, one can consider two approaches: A proactive approach, which involves designing for the current needs of the market while also trying to anticipate the most likely changes in the future business environment, or a reactive approach, which involves adapting the product offer after the change as we move along the timeline. There are many arguments in favor of a proactive approach: Organizations gain a competitive advantage if they detect change early; there will be an increase in market share due to early diversification of the product offering; minimized competition because few organizations are ready to compete for the same markets; discovery of new niche markets; and, probably most importantly of all, an improved company image as a leader and innovator. A proactive approach comes with higher costs, however, as few can invest in research and marketing of new products. A reactive approach involves lower marketing costs because the scouting and preparation has been done by the early entrants, but it also leads to a loss in market share and therefore profits because customers may already have chosen a different product or brand. A reactive approach is disregarded in this case.

To understand variation in terms of present and future changes, we need a good understanding of the environment of the organization. PEST (political, economical, societal, and technological) is an analysis framework used for scanning the relevant factors in the external macro-environment in which a company operates (Middleton, 2003). Political factors include, for example, legal issues under which the company should operate. Economic factors include, among others, the company's cost of capital. Societal factors describe demographic and cultural aspects of the business environment that might affect customer segmentation. Technological factors characterize the business environment in terms of expected technological progress and speed of innovation.

Once changes have been identified in various domains using the PEST framework, one can start to reason about their combined effect. A powerful way of organizing this kind of information is by using scenarios. Here a scenario is defined as a story written in natural language describing a plausible sequence of future events arranged in a timely manner. In our context, three types of scenarios are distinguished (see Table 1).

VARIABILITY MANAGEMENT ENABLING THE PRODUCT DERIVATION

Professional systems, for example in the medical domain, are typically used in different configurations by different users. One can observe that members of the same product family can be con-

Table 1. Scenario types and definitions

Scenario Type	Definition
Strategic	Based on the decisions made at the corporate level, strategists and marketeers scout different likely events, trends, or changes in the macroeconomic environment, organizing them in "plausible stories" about the future. The goal at this level is to stay in the business by exploring the future and the moves of the different competitors. Strategic scenarios can be defined at a business level, but applied at a system level as well.
Architecture	An architecture scenario is a set of choices made at an architectural level to describe a certain customization configuration. These choices are used to describe the variation in time and space of an architecture.
User	A user scenario is a story describing the user system interaction. It focuses on the specific functionality offered by the system, and the supported quality attributes. They are used to explain the customization that can be achieved by a system from a user perspective.

figured in many ways according to the purposes they are intended to serve. For example, an X-ray system can be used to acquire images of different parts of the human anatomy. Even within a product family for imaging blood vessels (known as angiography) (Philips Medical Systems, 2005), one can choose many different configurations. For blood vessels in the brain or in the heart, a compact X-ray detector can be chosen, whereas for blood vessels in the lower body a larger detector is required. The stand for the X-ray source and the detector can be positioned on the floor or attached to the ceiling. The same X-ray system can further be connected to various combinations of black-and-white or color display monitors. In addition, there are numerous configuration choices that are less easy to see, leading in total to thousands of configurations that are not only technically possible but also practically viable. Taking into account that only thousands (not millions) of such systems are sold, we can roughly say that no two systems are configured in the same way. Each hospital, clinic, or department will require a different configuration. We conclude that medical imaging systems are highly customized.

In addition to the variation in requirements from one customer to another, the requirements for these systems also change over time. For example, new medical procedures are developed that need a different kind of support from the system. It is also possible that the number of patients who need a particular procedure will rise, which will mean there is a need for greater optimization of the systems towards efficient usage.

In order to distinguish these two kinds of variation, we use the term "variation in space" to denote the variation among different systems at the same time. We refer to the evolution of systems, driven by new requirements, as "variation in time". The question that system developers are faced with is how to make customization possible. Customization should therefore be addressed at the system architecture level. In the remainder of this chapter,

we look at methods and techniques that support the design of customized systems.

Initially we defined customization as the process to address efficiently the specific needs of various customers. Customization can, therefore, be seen as the process of designing products that address these needs by considering multiple sources of variation. We identified at least three sources of variation:

- **External business environment:** This captures the future changes most likely to appear in the external macro business environment. This applies both to the customers' business and to the business of the developing organization. To identify these changes, one could look at the macro-changes that allow the development of new products (e.g., new technologies), which enable product variation in space, or at micro-changes in the use of existing products (e.g., features or quality requirements due to diversity in the current customers' needs), which enable customization in the form of product variants, or variation in time.

- **Customer needs and wants:** This describes the present and future needs of the different customers. To cover the possible variations within this domain, one could use techniques such as requirements elicitation, scenario-based customer segmentation and profiling, market share assessment, and so forth.

- **Technology:** This describes the possible variations in the technological solutions available for the design of the future system. Typically, technology evolves quickly over time, leading to new opportunities and fewer constraints. However, it is also possible that different technologies are needed at the same time to provide optimal solutions for systems with different requirements. For example, CRT monitors are ideal when the images have to look the same from different

Figure 1. From variation sources to customized products

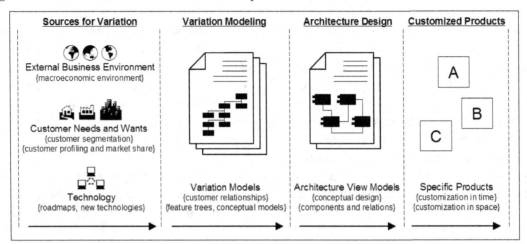

viewing angles, but LCD screens are better when there is limited space in a hospital room.

Customization in Time

Following the two dimensions of product variability (i.e., in time and in space), we can reason about the customization that is possible along these two lines. The difference between variation and customization is as follows. Variation accounts for any occurrence of differences, either in the systems under development or in their environment. Customization refers only to the explicitly-planned differences between systems.

Figure 2. Intra-architecture variation

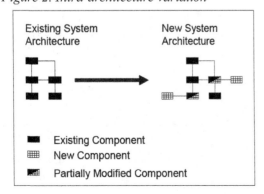

Given these differences, the customization in time refers to the timely incremental changes planned for the improvement of certain factors of an existing system. These changes affect a specific set of components of the existing system. An example here would be the architectural changes to improve the performance characteristics of an X-ray system. One solution would be to use a faster image processing algorithm. Another solution would be to add more processing power by means of dedicated hardware components. Therefore, the customization in time means managing the changes from one system version to another, referred to as intra-architecture variation.

The intra-architecture variation can be easily represented in terms of initial, modified, and new components, as shown in Figure 2. Here, the initial architecture consisting of five components (solid shading ■) is adapted to include two new components (texture shading ⊞). To make the adaptation possible, two other components have to be modified, as shown (solid and texture shading ◨). To make the adaptation possible, two other components have to be modified, as shown (solid and texture shading ⊞).

Customization in Space

Customization in space refers to the structural architectural changes to be made when new system features are added to enlarge the existing product portfolio. The inclusion of new features means that we have a new product that has evolved from the initial system. An example here would be a basic TV set, now equipped with Teletext and a VCR player, or a DVD player. Dealing with the variation to manage the architectural changes for the current product portfolio is also referred to as the inter-architecture variation. Inter-architecture variation is best represented by means of a feature tree. To do that, we first plot out the complete landscape of possible features

Figure 3. Inter-architecture variability

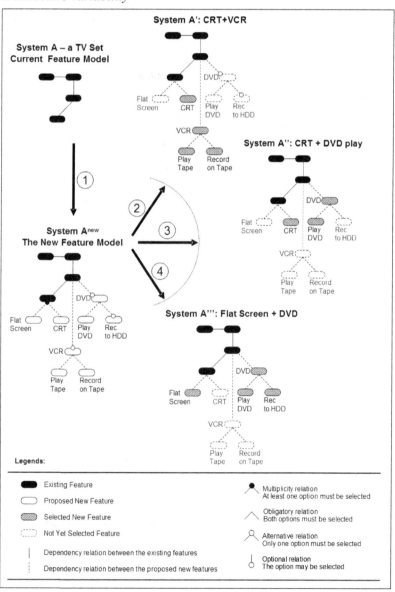

that could be included in new system versions. We then select those features that would define a new product. If more than one combination of new features exists, we could think of deriving two different systems from the initial one, as shown in Figure 3 (the top-left feature tree containing solid shadings ●).

In Figure 3, we represented the initial System A (i.e., a TV set) as a set of features (e.g., channel search, channel store, picture-in-picture, etc.). Based on this, in step ① we create a new landscape of features for System A NEW, such as CRT display vs. flat-screen, VCR (with two sub-features: play tape, record tape) and DVD (with two sub-features: play DVD and record to hard disk), as shown in Figure 3 (the middle-left feature tree containing solid ● and white shadings ○).

Next, in steps ②, ③, and ④, three possible system configurations are selected: configuration system A', consisting of the basic TV-set features for which we select the CRT display feature and the VCR feature; configuration System A'', consisting of the basic TV-set features for which we select CRT display and DVD Play features; and

configuration System A''', for which we select the flat screen display together with the DVD features, as shown in Figure 3 (the three middle-right feature trees containing solid ● and texture shading ●).

Customization in Strategy

Both customization in time and customization in space are often driven by the higher business goals of an organization. If such a business goal is, for example, to address the needs of a specialized segment of the market, one solution would be the product portfolio specialization, also known as a customization strategy. If the goal is to address the basic needs of the high-volume market, one solution would be the creation of standard products, also known as a standardization strategy. Targeting different groups of customers with different groups of products can be seen as a *customization in strategy*.

In our previous example, the TV set could be seen as the base configuration, addressing

Figure 4. Customization in strategy

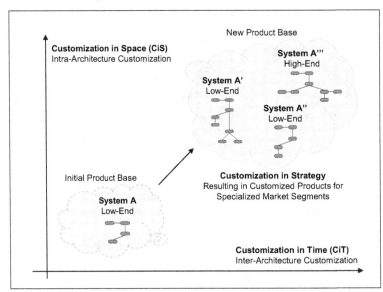

the low-end market. A customization in strategy thus refers to the improvement of the base product, addressing both the low-end and high-end market segments. In our previous example from Figure 3, the customization in strategy is the differentiation of System A into three new systems, Systems A' and A" to address the low-end market segments, and System A''' to address the high-end segments.

As one can observe, the customization in strategy actually has two components. One is the customization in space (new features appear), and the other is the customization in time (the evolution/adaptation of existing components).

THE STRATEGIC OPTION DESIGN AND ASSESSMENT (SODA) METHOD

This chapter presents the SODA method for developing highly-customized systems using a scenario-based architecting approach. The method supports the early design stages for system architectures, such as strategy definition, architectural options design, architectural options assessment, and product derivation. In the remainder of this chapter, we introduce the steps of the SODA method, showing how each of them contributes to the final design of customized products. The steps of the method are supported with examples from a case study conducted for the medical domain.

Introduction of the Case Study and Setting

The catheterization laboratory (cathlab) in a hospital or clinic is usually a special department where catheterization procedures are performed (see Figure 5). Such a catheterization uses a catheter, a thin, flexible pipe that can be inserted into a blood vessel and then moved to a position where the vessel has become narrowed or obstructed. In this example, we refer to heart interventions using specialized equipment such as X-ray-based systems.

The procedure is usually performed in the cathlab by the cardiologist, who is typically assisted by a technician and a nurse. First a catheter is inserted through one of the patient's main arteries and guided towards the heart using fluoroscopy, an X-ray imaging technique using a low dose of X-rays which provides just enough image qual-

Figure 5. Cathlab: The intervention room

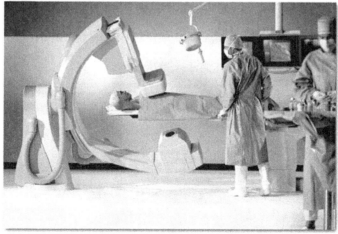

ity to navigate the catheter. Then angiography is performed, which is an X-ray-based technique that involves progressive diffusion of a low dose of contrast fluid into an artery to show the ramifications and the size of the vessels. The images are displayed on a set of monitors, as they are captured using X-rays. Based on this kind of information, a diagnosis is made of the obstructions or narrowing of the coronary vessels (i.e., the blood vessels around the heart).

Depending on the diagnosis, the narrowing or obstruction can be removed. For this purpose, a stent is delivered locally towards the tip of the catheter. The stent is a mesh of wire which can be expanded to enlarge the vessel section where it has been deployed.

The goal of this case study was twofold. On the one hand, the goal was to create the system architecture for a customized integrated cathlab for the various customers of such systems. On the other hand, the goal was to develop a systematic architecting method, based on the steps we took,

to show how to build customized systems. The SODA method is the result of this work, and it is presented below.

SODA Steps

SODA consists of four steps to guide the architecting process for customized system architectures (see Figure 6). It starts by looking at the possible changes in the future business environment, from which stories describing various plausible futures are then developed, hereafter called strategic scenarios. Based on the strategic scenarios, in step two of SODA, concrete business strategies are then developed. A business strategy defines the set of actions to be taken by an organization in order to achieve success (e.g., profit increase, market growth, product customization).

To implement the defined business strategies, concrete system architecture options that support the implementation of customized systems are created. This is done in step three of SODA.

Figure 6. SODA method: An overview

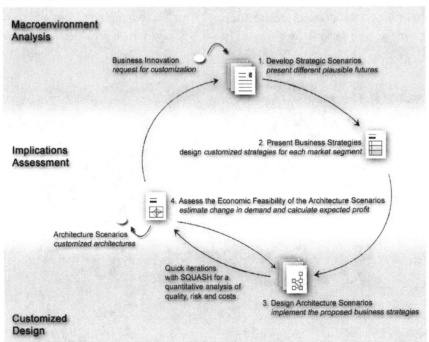

Each of the possible design options for the system architecture are described by means of scenarios, also called architecture scenarios.

As we show later, an architecture scenario is the technical representation of the system architecture, from different viewpoints. Finally, the proposed architecture scenarios are analyzed with respect to their overall economic feasibility. This is done in step four of SODA, as shown in Figure 6. In this step, issues such as quality and price elasticity of demand and estimated profit are analyzed. For this purpose, a quantification of the quality cost and the risks associated with the proposed architecture options is required. To support the feasibility assessment step (i.e., the

quick iteration performed between steps three and four of SODA), we developed the systematic quantitative assessment of scenarios heuristics (SQUASH) method, as introduced in Ionita, America, and Hammer (2005) and presented in more detail in Ionita (2005).

To introduce the SQUASH method briefly, we can say that it allows a systematic analysis of a quality attribute (e.g., usability, performance, or cost) as soon as the system architecture has been developed. Furthermore, when multiple architecture design options are available, SQUASH allows a comparison and visualization of the relative benefits for the proposed scenarios. This is realized by means of comparative representations as

Figure 7. A strategic scenario creation process

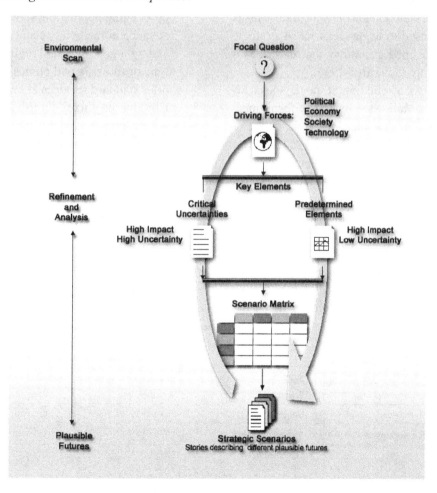

207

well as intuitive visualization for the data being analyzed.

SODA Step One:
Develop Strategic Scenarios

Changing a system architecture and implementing the changes is often expensive. In order to avoid these costs, architects should have a good understanding of the current and future customer needs, as well as of the future business environment of the system. Equipped with this knowledge, architects can create the basis for developing systems that have a higher customization palette.

The first step of SODA fills exactly this gap (see Figure 6). It provides the systematic means to explore the future business environment of the system and provide the architects with more insight into the most likely changes to occur in the near future in their domain of application. This is done by means of strategic scenarios. A strategic scenario is defined as a story that describes a plausible future (Schwartz, 1996).

The process of building strategic scenarios in SODA is as follows. Firstly, the focal question is posed. For example, what is the future of cardiology for the coming five years? To answer this question and subsequently to build different strategic scenarios, we look for those elements that can provide us with information about the most likely changes to appear in the future, the "driving forces" (see Figure 7). These driving forces are macroeconomic factors that cause changes in areas such as politics, economy, society, and technology. The identified forces can be further grouped into two categories: predetermined ele-

ments (i.e., changes that are observable or events that are in the pipeline, such as the aging of the population or a rise in the number of patients requiring cardiac treatment), and critical uncertainties (i.e., changes that are highly uncertain, such as adoption of new technologies, or economic boom or recession). These forces are the elements that shape the strategic scenarios to be developed. They are therefore combined in a balanced manner, so that the resulting scenarios are equally plausible (i.e., avoid having very likely vs. very unlikely scenarios). To achieve this result, a scenario matrix is used, which shows the main scenario lines (see Table 2).

For the cathlab case study, four strategic scenarios were developed. These were:

- McHealth, describing a future characterized by an aging population, slow technological advance in medicine, economic recession, and tight governmental regulations; in this type of future, small clinics appear, which offer standard services at low prices;
- Clinique de Luxe, describing a future in which the economic situation is one of stable growth, characterized by slow technological advance and population aging; this type of future enables clinics to offer diversified services at higher prices;
- See-Treat-Cure, describing a future in which technological advance gives rise to faster imaging modalities for large hospitals; in combination with a stable economic situation, patients too can afford more specialized types of treatment; and

Table 2. Scenario matrix

Trends in:		Strategic Scenarios		
		Scenario 1	Scenario 2	Scenario 3
Society	Lifestyle	Unhealthy	Preventive	Preventive
	Demographics	Aging Population		
	Patient Type	Governed by Strict Rules	Self Choosing	Consumer

- Brave New Pharma World, describing a booming economic situation, which fuels genomic research and technological advance; in this scenario, clinics can offer personalized treatments.

Strategic scenarios are the first step towards designing customized systems. Equipped with knowledge about the future context of a system, the architecting team can think in terms of possible changes and prepare alternative architectural designs.

SODA Step Two:
Present Business Strategies

In step two of SODA, business strategies are created as a response to the identified futures. A business strategy can be defined as the set of actions that need to be taken to achieve the specific business goals of an organization (Hill, 2002). In this step, a customization in strategy takes place. Different strategic futures require a different approach in the overall business strategy of an organization. In a booming economy, companies invest, insurance policies cover more of the costs, and patients require more specialized treatment. In such a situation, a diversification strategy is appropriate. Conversely, in times of recession, investment falls off, and we expect a dramatic reduction in costs. Insurance companies become more careful with expenditure to cover health care, and patients are therefore more likely to request only basic treatments. In such a situation a standardization strategy is recommended. Diversification and standardization are, therefore, two possible business strategies for coping with the envisaged futures.

As we deal with different scenarios that describe the future business environment of an organization, different business strategies can be developed.

In our case study, two possible strategies were considered for each future scenario. Firstly, a standardization strategy was proposed, which aimed to develop low-customized systems to offer basic functionality for the fast treatment hospitals. Secondly, a specialization strategy was proposed, which was aimed at developing highly-customized systems for the top-end market segments such as specialized clinics and academic hospitals.

SODA Step Three:
Design Architecture Scenarios

In step three of SODA, the goal is to develop concrete architectural solutions to implement the business strategies proposed in step two. These are called architecture scenarios because they describe different ways of representing the overall structure of the system (America, Hammer, Ionita, Obbink, & Rommes, 2005). Architectures are usually described from different viewpoints (e.g., a logical view that describes the main subsystems or packages of design, a use-case view that describes the interaction with the system from a user perspective) (Kruchten, 1995). In SODA, we use the CAFCR view model to represent the architecture, as it allows the representation of both technical- and business architecture-relevant details of the system (Muller, 2004; Obbink, Müller, America, van Ommering, Muller, van der Sterren, & Wijnstra, 2000). Other architecture view models are the 4+1 view model or the Soni model (Kruchten, 1995; Soni, Nord, & Hofmeister, 1995). However, these two models focus only on the technical aspects of the architecture.

CAFCR is an abbreviation of customer, application, functional, conceptual, and realization, which are five views to describe system architectures (see Figure 8). The first two views in CAFCR focus on the commercial aspects of the system, such as describing the stakeholders of the system (i.e., customer view) and showing how the system is used (i.e., application view). The last two views in CAFCR focus on the technical aspects, which involves the decomposition of the system into subsystems and components together with the relations between them (i.e., conceptual view), and the use of the available technology to implement the proposed architecture (i.e., realization view). The functional view is a combination of both commercial and technical aspects. It describes what the system offers in terms of functionality and quality.

The various system functions are referred to as external features. Qualities are also mentioned here, but specific knowledge for reasoning about them comes from other views as well.

When developing system architectures, we start by constructing variation models to plot the different ways of constructing the architecture. This usually begins with the customer view. Here we represent knowledge about the various customers and their concerns. Then we plot different ways of modifying or improving the current cathlab to address these concerns, by means of scenarios. A scenario here represents a set of choices in a certain architectural view. We also have to bear in mind that the resulting architectures should be in line with the business strategies defined in step two of SODA. A few examples are given for the various views to show how we represent the architecture by means of different views and variation models.

The Customer View

The customers of the cathlab are typically hospitals and clinics. To understand their needs and wants, in the customer view we look at variations across different dimensions, such as: customer size (with two options identified, large hospitals or small private clinics); customer profile (fast treatment hospitals focusing on intervention efficiency, and academic institutions also interested in research); capability coverage (here one could differentiate between customers interested in fast treatment procedures, diagnosis, personalized treatment, or a combination of all of these); the modalities of interest (various customers are interested in either a full X-ray-based cathlab or a combination of X-ray and MR capabilities); and procedure-type supported (customers may offer diverse cardiology services, such as angiography or electro-physiology).

Developing a customized system implies that choices have to be made with respect to which customer characteristics the new architecture is going to support. These choices can be communicated by means of scenarios. For the cathlab case, such customer scenarios are:

- Fast treatment hospitals focusing on angiography intervention procedures, requiring X-ray-based cathlabs with high throughput.
- Private clinics offering high-quality personalized angiography and electro-physiology type of interventions, for which X-ray-based cathlabs that support MR information are required.

Figure 8. CAFCR architecture view model: An overview

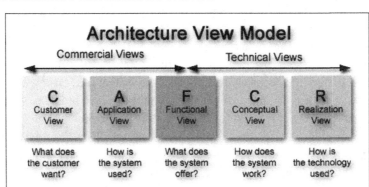

Next, we find that, consistent with the choices displayed in the customer view, other decisions are subsequently made in the rest of the CAFCR views in order to deliver the overall system architecture. The choices made in the customer view determine the level of intra-architecture variability for the future system. The more that customer attributes are considered, the higher the degree of customization for the final system will be.

The Application View

In this view, knowledge about the use of the cathlab is represented. Here we use both variation models for the technical representation of this information, and we use user scenarios as textual descriptions of the user interaction with the system, quality levels achieved, and so forth. The two representations complement each other.

From an application point of view, the cathlab can be used for diagnosis of the cardiac diseases and for cardiac interventions. The diagnosis can be performed using X-ray or MR technology. The intervention can follow a standard procedure type using X-ray technology and drug treatment, or it can be improved by using MR. The MR technology is able to provide the cardiologist with anatomical information about the heart, and it therefore provides the means to achieve higher treatment personalization levels.

The available choices are charted below in Figure 9. This figure presents the improvements that can be made to the existing cathlab in order to achieve a higher degree of customization. As in Figure 3, the shaded boxes denote existing activities performed in the cathlab. The white boxes denote new activities that enlarge the application domain of the current cathlab.

In line with the choices made in the customer view, two possible customization scenarios in this view would be: firstly, the integration of 3D information for stenosis measurement and localization to speed up the intervention procedure in hospital cathlabs and, secondly, the integration

Figure 9. Application view, using the same notation as in Figure 3

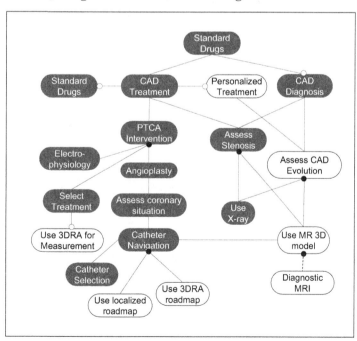

of MR studies to be used in parallel with X-ray-based information during the procedures, for private clinics offering some more personalized types of treatments. These two scenarios can be represented as follows.

The Functional View

This describes the functionality which the system provides, also referred to as external features. In our example, the cathlab should support the viewing of 3D images, generate these images, or do both. The part of functionality responsible for the generation of 3D images is called 3DRA support (where 3DRA = three-dimensional rotational angiography, which is a technique for reconstructing the 3D model of the heart vessels using individual 2D projections that are taken from different angles; the 3D model helps the cardiologist to diagnose or treat coronary artery diseases more effectively). This can be done us-

ing a remote (i.e., separate) workstation or a local 3D reconstructor (i.e., built into the current X-ray system). The viewing support is required for the manipulation of 3D images. This functionality can be achieved through graphical or non-graphical user interfaces (GUI or NGUI) as well as through multimodality support for viewing 3D images from other modalities, such as MR. Below we present two functional scenarios for the 3D feature of the cathlab. The purpose here is to give an example of how customization is applied for a feature model, rather than drawing the complete feature map for the cathlab (see Figure 11).

The two customization scenarios are in line with the choices made in the previous view. The first functional scenario (Figure 11– Left) is suitable for the standard cathlabs that focus on improving the intervention duration. The choices presented in the second functional scenario (Figure 11– Right) are made to support the personalized treatment idea presented in the application view,

Figure 10. Based on Figure 9, two possible application scenarios are proposed; Left – system customization focusing on presentation and control integration to reduce the intervention duration and improve accuracy; Right – system customization focuses on achieving higher accuracy by providing personalized types of treatment using MR.

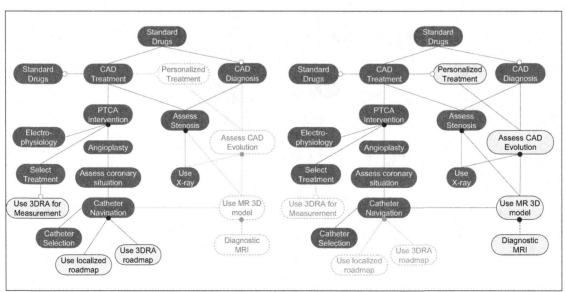

where the use of 3D MR is suggested to improve the quality of treatment.

The Conceptual View

This view presents the system in terms of internal features. These are properties of the system which cannot be observed from the way the system behaves, but they are a result of how the system is designed. Some of the features described in the functional view might be reused in this model to relate the concepts to the actual observable features. To continue the customization process from the functional view, an example of a conceptual model is given below (see Figure 12).

The local 3DRA feature can be designed internally in two different ways, namely by means of a real-time reconstructor which has been designed especially for this type of X-ray equipment, or by a slower but portable reconstructor.

The 3D viewing can be designed in two ways, namely using a native viewer or a hosted 3D PACS client (where PACS stands for Picture Archiving and Communication System, a system used for storing different types of medical images). The native viewer renders and displays the model without actually storing it. The hosted PACS client would allow extended storage and viewing of medical images from modalities other than X-ray as well. The 3D viewing feature could be implemented by hosting such a PACS client on the X-ray system.

Two possible scenarios, which describe the set of choices for the conceptual view, are shown below in Figure 12. The intra-architecture customization process is continued in this view. This process will be finalized in the last view, which is the realization view.

Figure 11. Functional variation model for the cathlab, showing two customization scenarios: Left – a scenario for 3D image visualization using a remote reconstructor; Right – a scenario for 3D image visualization using a local reconstructor enhanced with 3D viewing and multimodality support; here we use the same notation as in Figure 9.

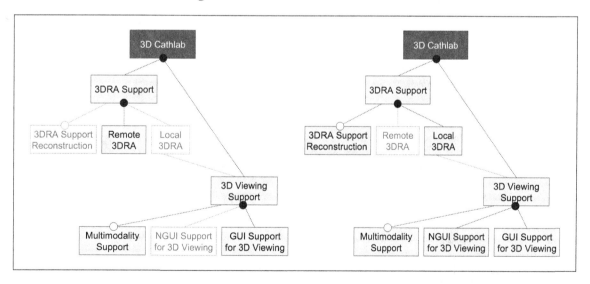

Figure 12. A piece of the variation model depicting the choices in the conceptual view for the cathlab architecture

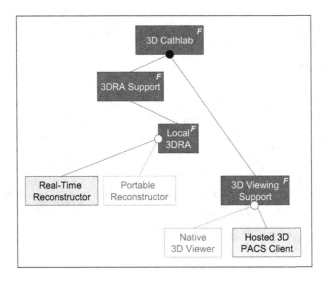

Figure 13. Two scenarios involving the conceptual view: Left – a scenario involving the internal design choices such as portable reconstructor using a native 3D viewer; Right – a scenario using a real-time reconstructor based on the concept of a hosted PACS client; the notation in this figure is similar to the one used in Figure 9.

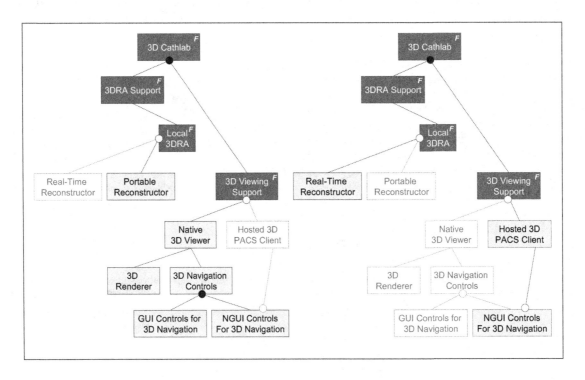

The Realization View

This last view of CAFCR shows exactly how the available technology can be used to implement the choices made in the previous views.

Below, we present two pieces of the variation model for the realization view (see Figure 13). The real-time reconstructor and the NGUI controls for 3D navigation are two design concepts introduced in Figure 13. These are realizable by means of either a dedicated processor or by using the default processor of the hosting workstation which, in this case, could be a multi-processor machine. The NGUI controls for 3D navigation can be realized using a trackball, a joystick, or proprietary hardware. The choices in this view depend again on the customization required by the customer. The architecture should, therefore, be ready to accommodate any of these possible options or a restricted set thereof.

After choices consistent with each other have been made across the CAFCR views, the result is a set of architecture scenarios. They describe ways in which the architecture can be customized to support the business strategies mentioned in SODA step two.

Table 3 shows the resulting set of architecture scenarios for the cathlab case study. These are based on the choices made in the variation models of the CAFCR views. For example, for

the fast treatment hospitals three application scenarios are proposed: *presentation and control*, *workflow*, and *full integration* scenarios. As explained below, these scenarios address different usability, performance, and cost objectives in the cathlab. With each of the application scenarios, a functional scenario was proposed, followed by a conceptual scenario and a concrete realization scenario, that is, cohost for the presentation and control and workflow scenarios, which describe the type of integration which is envisaged here, and flat screen for the luxurious integration as in the full scenario.

SODA Step Four:
Assess Economic Feasibility of Architecture Scenarios

In this last step of SODA, we are interested in assessing the economic feasibility of the proposed architecture scenarios. This is because, although technically realizable, for some scenarios the implementation costs will outweigh the few benefits they offer, and they are therefore unlikely to be considered further in the design. We choose profit, expressed in monetary units, as the overall measure to compare the economic feasibility of the different architecture scenarios. The feasibility assessment is performed in the macroeconomic context provided by the strategic scenarios from SODA step one.

Figure 14. A part of the variation model for the realization of two conceptual features

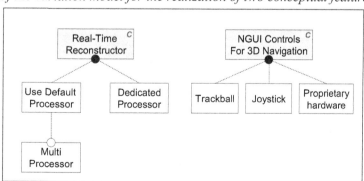

Table 3. Building architecture scenarios with CAFCR

Customer	Application	Functional	Conceptual	Realization
Academic	Minimal	Minimal	-	-
	Data	Data	DM Integration	Multi-host
	Presentation and Control	Presentation and Control	HW Switch	
Production			Alt-Tab	Cohost
	Workflow	Workflow	Coordinator	
	Full	Full	Luxury	Flat screen

For this purpose, the strategic scenarios are annotated with the market-related information, such as estimates of the current market share of the organization, customer segments and profiles, estimates of demand functions, estimates of competitor offer, and participation in similar market segments.

The resulting profit figures are plotted on a single graph, with the axes denoting the strategic future, and the values on these axes showing the estimated profit yielded by each of the proposed architecture scenarios, as shown in Figure 15.

This kind of representation allows us to compare the relative profits yielded by the various architecture scenarios for each strategic future. Next we show how such an analysis can be performed. In order to carry out such an analysis, we start from the simple assumption that profit (π) can be calculated as being the difference between sales price (p) and the cost (c) for one unit of output. The profit on total sales takes into account the revenues, which is price (p) times the product quantity demanded (Q), minus the total development cost (tc); see formula (1).

Figure 15. Architecture scenarios economic performance: Cumulative profit graph

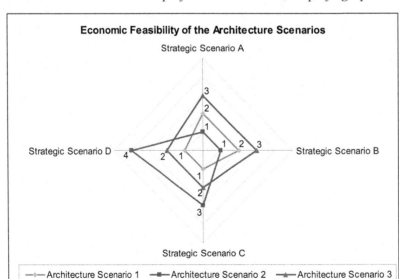

$$\pi = Q * p - tc \qquad (1)$$

The total cost (*tc*) has a few components, such as the development costs (*dc*) and production costs (*pc*) for each individual unit *j* produced, to which we add the marketing costs (*mc*) for the *Q* outputs. Therefore, for an output quantity *q* of products *i*, we calculate the total cost tc_i with the formula (2). The values for the individual $dc_{j,i}$ and $pc_{j,i}$ can be calculated on the basis of existing estimates for similar system configurations, corrected, of course, for the extra costs associated with the development of the new system.

$$tc_i = \sum_{j=1}^{q} (dc_{j,i} + pc_{j,i}) + mc_i \qquad (2)$$

The sales price (*p*) is given, as set by marketeers. The sales price is calculated on the basis of the demand and supply curve, competitor pricing strategies, and the position of the organization on the market. These values also differ from one market to another. The same product can be sold at different prices depending on the local business context of a specific market. Therefore, sales prices bear no relation to the actual production costs. It is important, however, that in the long run the revenues obtained from sales do cover the total costs incurred by production. For an accurate analysis, one should take into account all these issues when estimating the revenues ($Q*p$). In order to be brief, we use an operational definition for sales price *p* for a product *i,* which is the average sales price $\overline{p}_i$ calculated from the individual prices p_i over the whole sales *q*. In practice $\overline{p}_i$ would be calculated using formula (3).

$$p \Leftrightarrow \overline{p}_i = \frac{\sum_{m=1}^{q} p_{m,i}}{q} \qquad (3)$$

In an open healthcare market that offers professional services, the patient can choose the clinic or hospital from which he or she wants to receive treatment. The quality of care influences the patient choice for one or another healthcare provider. A low quality of care due to a healthcare system's low level of quality will result in patient and hence healthcare provider dissatisfaction (Wadhwa, 2002). As a result, healthcare providers will choose substitute products. This will lead to a decrease in demand for the low-quality healthcare systems.

When estimating profit, therefore, we must take into account the impact of the system-exhibited quality on demand. In literature, this effect is known as the elasticity of demand with respect to a variable, in our case the quality of the product (Pindyck & Rubinfield, 2001). Product quality elasticity of demand is the percentage change in the quantity demanded *Q* resulting from a 1% increase in the level of a quality attribute Ai.

It is usual to look at a set of quality attributes when we perform the impact estimation. To aggregate the effect of the individual quality attributes on the initial demand, we use a weighted sum function in which the individual positive or negative contributions ($c_{i,j}$) of a quality attribute of the demand are summed up, taking into account the relative importance ($w_{i,j}$) of all quality factors *k*.

With the formulae (2), (3), and (4), the expected profit for a product *i*, becomes Box 2.

The analysis is then repeated for each of the proposed cathlab architecture scenarios as these describe different system customizations for each of the strategic futures.

For a detailed example of how such an analysis was performed, we refer to Ionita (2005). The details of these calculations are not relevant for the purpose of this chapter as different organizations may use different models to estimate profit. The emphasis here is on the fact that the customized architecture scenarios are not just designed but also analyzed with respect to their economic feasibility in the different future contexts offered by the strategic scenarios.

Based on such results, as shown in Figure 15, one could observe the differences in the estimated

Equation 4.

$$Q \Leftrightarrow New\_demand_i = Initial\_demand_i + \sum_{j=1}^{k} w_{i,j} * c_{i,j}$$

Box 2.

$$\pi_i = \left(Initial\_demand_i + \sum_{j=1}^{k} w_{i,j} * c_{i,j} \right) * \overline{p}_i - \sum_{j=1}^{q} \left(dc_{j,i} + pc_{j,i} \right) - mc_i$$

economic performance associated with the proposed architecture scenarios. This would enable us to compare the various options proposed and to select one or more that are most likely to yield an economic profit in most of the futures which are envisaged.

SODA BENEFITS AND DISADVANTAGES

Our experience so far has shown that the SODA method contributes in several ways to the existing body of knowledge for system architecture design:

- It explicitly incorporates the use of strategic scenarios, which are useful tools for envisaging new future requirements from a macroeconomic perspective. Based on these strategic scenarios, major trends in the external business environment can be identified and therefore considered when architecture decisions are being made;
- It facilitates the design of highly-customized systems, based on an a priori exploration of the various design options performed in the early architecting phases; and
- It allows a quantitative assessment of the architecture scenarios proposed for customization. This is done by assessing the relative economic performance of the proposed customization options measured by the estimated profit figures calculated for each of the future business contexts which are envisaged.

The disadvantages of the SODA method are as follows:

- Considerable effort is devoted to preparing the grounds for customization: interviews with domain experts and business people for building the strategic scenarios, interviews with marketeers to understand the customer preferences, quality elasticity of demand for a certain product, future changes in customer markets, competition, and so forth. However, in large organizations this knowledge can be reused across related projects. Therefore, in such situations the effort invested in building the strategic scenarios is spread across the number of potential projects using this result;
- The kind of feasibility analysis performed in step four has to be repeated over time to keep up with the changes in the macroeconomic environment. To reduce this work, appropriate spreadsheet calculation tables can be used;
- The construction, maintenance, and consistency checking of the variation models across the five CAFCR views are also labor-intensive. As these models are built

by architects and involve a lot of domain knowledge, they cannot be automated yet; and

- Although the SODA method has not been specifically applied for the mass customization of information systems, we see no problem in applying it in this domain as well. This is because the SODA method deals with the early development stages of system architecture development, which is not much different when it comes to information or professional systems.

ACKNOWLEDGMENT

We are grateful to our colleagues: Eelco Rommes, Georgio Mosis, Hans Jonkers, Ron Koymans, André Postma, Marc Stroucken, Jan Gerben Wijnstra, Henk Obbink, and many people from Philips Medical Systems for their assistance and feedback. This research was funded by Stichting Technische Wetenschappen (STW) in the AIMES Project EWI.4877, and by the Eureka Σ! 2023 Program in the ITEA project ip02009 Families.

REFERENCES

America, P., Hammer, D. K., Ionita, T. M., Obbink, H. J., & Rommes, E. (2005). Scenario-based decision-making for architectural variability in product families. *Software Process - Improvement and Practice Journal, 10*(May), 171-187.

Blattberg, R., & Glaser, R. (1994). Marketing in the information revolution. In R. Blattberg, et al. (Eds.), *The marketing information revolution* (pp. 9-29). Boston:

Dellaert, B. G. C., & Stremersch, S. (2005). Marketing mass customized products: Striking the balance between utility and complexity. *Journal of Marketing Research*, (May), *219-227.*

Hagel, J., & Singer, M. (1999). *Net worth – Shaping markets when customers make the rules.* Harvard Business School Press.

Hill, C. W. L. (2002). *International business: Competing in the global marketplace.* New York: McGraw-Hill.

Ionita, T. M. (2005). *Scenario-based system architecting: A systematic approach to developing future-proof system architectures.* PhD thesis, University of Eindhoven, The Netherlands.

Ionita, T. M., America, P., & Hammer, D. K. (2005). A method for strategic scenario-based architecting. In *Proceedings of the 38th Hawaii International Conference on System Sciences (HICSS-38)* (p. 312).

Kruchten, P. B. (1995). The 4+1 view model of architecture. *IEEE Software, 12*(6), 42-50.

Middleton, J. (2003). *The ultimate strategy library: The 50 most influential strategic ideas of all time.* Capstone.

Muller, G. J. (2004). *CAFCR: A multi-view method for embedded systems architecting: Balancing genericity and specificity.* Ph.D. thesis. Retrieved February 23, 2006, from http://www.gaudisite.nl/

Obbink, H. J., Müller, J. K., America, P., van Ommering, R., Muller, G. J., van der Sterren, W., & Wijnstra, J. G. (2000). *COPA: A component-oriented platform architecting method for families of software intensive electronic products.* Tutorial for SPLC1, the First Software Product Line Conference, Denver, Colorado, August.

Philips Medical Systems (PMS) (2005). X-ray angiography. Retrieved February 23, 2006, from www.medical.philips.com/main/clinicalsegments/cardiology/angiography.html

Piller, F., Schubert, P., Koch, M., & Moeslein, K. (2004). From mass customization to collaborative customer co-design. In T. Leino, T. Saarinen, & S. Klein (Eds.), *Proceedings of the Twelfth European Conference on Information Systems, Turku School of Economics and Business Administration,* Turku, Finland.

Pindyck, R. S., & Rubinfield, D. L. (2001). *Microeconomics* (5th ed.). Prentice Hall International.

Schwartz, P. (1996). *The art of the long view.* Currency Doubleday.

Soni, D., Nord, R. L., & Hofmeister, C. (1995, April 23-30). Software architecture in industrial applications. In *Proceedings of the 17th International Conference on Software Engineering* Seattle, WA.

Tseng, M. M., & Jiao, J. (2001). Mass customization. In *Handbook of industrial engineering, technology, and operation management* (3rd ed.). (p. 685).

Wadhwa, S. S. (2002). Customer satisfaction and health care delivery systems: Commentary with Australian bias. *The Internet Journal of Nuclear Medicine.* Retrieved November 15, 2005, from www.ispub.com/ostia/index. php?xmlFilePath=journals/ijh/vol3n1/bias.xml

Chapter XI
Research Issues in Knowledge–Based Configuration

Dietmar Jannach
University Klagenfurt, Austria

Alexander Felfernig
University Klagenfurt, Austria

Gerold Kreutler
University Klagenfurt, Austria

Markus Zanker
University Klagenfurt, Austria

Gerhard Friedrich
University Klagenfurt, Austria

ABSTRACT

Knowledge-based configuration systems have made their way into industrial practice. Nowadays, all major vendors of configuration systems rely on some form of declarative knowledge representation and intelligent search techniques for solving the core configuration problem, due to the inherent advantages of that technology: On the one hand, changes in the business logic (configuration rules) can be accomplished more easily because of the declarative and modular nature of the knowledge bases, while on the other hand highly-optimized, domain-independent problem-solving algorithms are available for the task of constructing valid configurations.Still, the development has not come to an end as, in a world that becomes increasingly automated and wired together, constantly new challenges for the development of intelligent configuration systems come in: Web-based configurators are being made available for large heterogeneous user groups, the provision of mass-customized products requires the integration of companies along a supply chain, and configuration and reconfiguration of services become an increasingly important issue, just to name a few. This chapter gives an overview on these current and future research issues in the domain of knowledge-based configuration technology, and thus summarizes the state-of-the-art, recent achievements, novel approaches, and open challenges in the field.

INTRODUCTION

One of the earliest and most successful expert systems introduced in an industrial environment was a product configurator, when, in the early 1980s, Digital Corporation developed the R1/XCON (McDermott, 1982) system for automating the configuration process for their complex computer systems. Although R1/XCON was one of the first systems of that kind, two typical aspects in the context of configuration systems have not changed since then:

a. It has been proven that using an intelligent product configurator will lead to significant business benefits: Suitable configurations and accompanying offers can be calculated much faster, the quality of the configurations is comparable or better than the one of manually-engineered solutions, and the process itself is less error-prone, which in turn leads to considerable savings for a company (Barker, O'Connor, Bachant, & Soloway, 1989; McDermott, 1982).

b. There is also another side of the medal, which is, for instance, documented in Barker et al. (1989), also for the R1/XCON system: The configuration task itself can become very complex, and the corresponding knowledge bases soon have to contain information on thousands of components and configuration rules; that is, after 10 years of production, the R1/XCON system contained around 10,000 configuration rules. This in turn leads to different problems. So, for instance, maintenance of the knowledge base becomes an issue, in particular in domains where product life cycles are short and changes in the products are frequent. In addition,

when the knowledge bases grow, also the running times for checking or constructing a configuration can significantly increase, potentially resulting in performance problems. Finally, as also mentioned already in McDermott (1982), for all of the engineering tasks, highly-skilled and trained development staff is needed for maintaining the knowledge bases and/or improving the configurator software.

Due to the inherent complexity of the task, configuration problems have since then always been subjects of interest for researchers in different areas, in particular in the field of artificial intelligence (AI). In fact, significant advances have been made since these early, "rule-based" years: Powerful knowledge representation schemes for configuration problems have been developed (McGuiness & Wright, 1998b; Mittal & Frayman, 1989), a formalization of the problem has been done (Felfernig, Friedrich, Jannach, & Stumptner, 2004), the invention of new algorithms was driven by the challenges of the domain (Fleischanderl, Friedrich, Haselböck, Schreiner, & Stumptner, 1988; Mittal & Falkenhainer, 1990), industrial-strength software libraries are now available (Mailharro, 1998) and knowledge-based configurators are nowadays already incorporated in standard business software (see, for instance, Haag, 1998).

Nonetheless, the developments of today's networked economy constantly bring in new challenges and requirements for current and future product configuration systems. For instance, the life cycles of, for example, electronic products still continue to become shorter and shorter while, on the other hand, the products tend to be more complex, which in turn requires even better knowledge-representation and modeling schemes for alleviating the knowledge-engineering and maintenance tasks. In addition, with the growing complexity of the knowledge bases, we also need adequate means and tools to support the error detection and debugging phases, since standard debugging techniques are insufficient for such knowledge-based systems.

When looking at current developments from the business perspective, we can observe a trend that companies today aim at cooperating in supply-chain networks in the process of manufacturing and provisioning their configurable goods and services. So, in many cases, the customer requirements that determine the design of the final product have to be forwarded to the partners in the supply-chain while, on the other hand, overall consistency of the final configuration has to be ensured.

Another business-related aspect in some domains can be seen in the fact that sometimes a fully-configured product which has been already deployed at the customer's site for years, for example, a large telecommunication switch (Fleischanderl et al., 1988), has to be extended or adapted to reflect new customer requirements. In these cases, the existing configuration has to be reconfigured, and we have to consider different optimization goals, for instance, preserving most of the existing configuration.

An additional example where new requirements for product configuration systems can be seen is the fact that nowadays not only technical engineers or sales engineers are the users of configuration systems as it was in the early years. The mass customization paradigm is applied to various business branches, and in many domains the customers themselves use the configurator (over the Web) to tailor a product to their specific needs and demands. This in turn creates new challenging requirements on interactivity for configurators: End-users can be quite heterogeneous with respect to their background and capabilities, so things have to be simple for them. On the other hand, users may have different preferences and capabilities on how they want to or are able to express their requirements. As such, a personal-

ized and more intelligent user interface may be required to guarantee the success of an online configuration system.

This chapter gives an overview on such current and future research issues for intelligent product configuration systems and thus summarizes the state-of-the-art, recent achievements, novel approaches, and open challenges in the field. Quite naturally, of course, the selection of issues is determined by a somehow subjective viewpoint, but it is based both on long years of active research in the field as well as on the experiences and lessons learned from international workshops that have been held in the last decade on major artificial intelligence conferences.

KNOWLEDGE REPRESENTATION AND REASONING

Successful applications of configuration technologies can be found in various domains such as the automotive industry (Freuder, Likitvivatanavong, & Wallace, 2001), the telecommunication industry (Juengst & Heinrich, 1998), the computer industry (Barker et al., 1989), or power electric transformers (McGuiness & Wright, 1998a). *Rule-based* knowledge representations, such as used in R1/XCON (Barker et al., 1982), were the starting point for configuration knowledge representation. In later years, *model-based* knowledge representations have been developed, which strictly separate domain knowledge from problem-solving knowledge: Such a separation increases the effectiveness of configuration application development and maintenance (Forza & Salvador, 2002; Freuder et al., 2001; Juengst & Heinrich, 1998; Mailharro, 1998), since changes in the product knowledge do not affect the definition of the search process and vice versa. Overall, a comprehensive configuration environment (Mittal & Falkenhainer, 1990) has to support all major tasks of *core configuration,* that is, guiding the user and checking the consistency of user requirements with the knowledge base, solution presentation, and translation of configuration results into detailed bill-of-materials.

Typically, knowledge bases are built using proprietary languages (see, e.g., Forza & Salvador, 2002; Franke & Piller, 2002; Haag, 1998), where technical experts and knowledge engineers elicit product, marketing, and sales knowledge from domain experts. Knowledge bases thus consist of a description of the product structure and a set of constraints that restrict the combinations of components in a configuration result. Configuration problem-solving is, in many cases, based on a *constraint satisfaction problem* representation of a configuration task (Tsang, 1993). Depending on the size and complexity of the problem, different facets of constraint representations can be applied: In *generative constraint satisfaction* (Fleischanderl et al., 1998), components are dynamically generated on demand during the search process; when using a *dynamic constraint satisfaction* (Mittal & Falkenhainer, 1990) approach, depending on a specific state in the search process, only a relevant subset of the defined constraints and variables are active, that is, are taken into account for calculating a solution; in *distributed constraint satisfaction* (Yokoo, Durfee, Ishida, & Kuwabara, 1998), messages about changes in the problem space are exchanged between different local entities of constraint satisfaction problems. Such a distributed representation can primarily be applied in different variants of supply chain settings.

Although configuration systems have been successfully applied in various real-world applications, a number of challenges have to be tackled with respect to configuration knowledge representation: Knowledge-base development is a cooperative process between technical experts and domain experts, and the development of knowledge bases can be very expensive (Mittal & Frayman, 1989). In this context, the application of *standard representations* can help to reduce development and maintenance costs because

standards are known by technical experts and, in many cases, are also known by domain experts (generally non-programmers). Furthermore, information systems departments always aim at standardization and *interoperability* between various system components. Therefore, configuration systems are required to be equipped with standard representations which contribute to an improved flexibility of a company's software infrastructure: In the financial services domain, for instance, standardized interfaces are a major decision criterion for incorporating a configurator into their software environment. The amount of resources required to develop and maintain configuration knowledge bases can be substantial (see, e.g. Mittal & Frayman, 1998). In many cases, however, a configuration knowledge base is encoded in the proprietary language of the underlying configuration environment. This makes related investments particularly unsafe due to the fact that, for example, changing requirements on the configurator application could lead to a need of exchanging the whole configuration environment (Mittal & Frayman, 1998). In such cases, no support will be available for easily transforming an existing knowledge base into the representation of the new environment. Therefore, the following languages can play an important role in the context of standardized configuration knowledge and product data representation.

OIL and *DAML+OIL* (Fensel, van Harmelen, Horrocks, McGuinness, & Patel-Schneider, 2001) are ontology representation languages developed within the context of the *Semantic Web* (Berners-Lee, 2001). These languages support the design of ontologies on the formal basis of description logics. Felfernig, Friedrich, Jannach, Stumptner, and Zanker (2003) point out that Semantic Web representation languages are suitable for configuration knowledge representation. However, an additional language is needed for supporting an intuitive formulation of constraints on product structures; especially the definition of aggregation functions and complex structural properties is not supported by state-of-the-art Semantic Web knowledge representation languages. With respect to ongoing efforts to extend DAML+OIL or its successor *OWL* (van Harmelen, Patel-Schneider, & Horrocks, 2001), the work of Felfernig et al. (2003) contributes a set of criteria which must be fulfilled in order to apply those languages for full-fledged configuration knowledge representation.

Universal Standard Products and Services Classification Code (*UNSPSC*) is a coding system organized as product taxonomy. Levels of the taxonomy are *segments* denoting aggregations of families (e.g., computer equipment), *families* as groups of interrelated categories (e.g., software), *classes* as a group of elements sharing a common usage (e.g., text-editing), and *commodity* as a group of substitutable products (e.g., Linux text editors). *RosettaNet* classification schemes are restricted to the categorization of electronic equipment. RosettaNet has two taxonomy levels (product groups and products). Both standards focus on the categorization of products, but do not provide mechanisms for building models of generic product structures. Another standard related to product data representation is cXML (*commerce XML*—www.cxml.org) which also does not provide any mechanisms for configuration knowledge representation (Schmitz, Leukel, & Kelkar, 2004).

The *standard for product model interchange* (*STEP*—ISO, 1994) takes into account all aspects of a product, including geometry and even organizational data. The goal is to provide the means for defining application-specific concepts for modeling products in a particular product domain. Such application-specific concepts are denoted as *application protocols*, which are defined by using the *EXPRESS* DDL. EXPRESS includes a set of modeling concepts useful for representing configurable products; it can, however, not be used to define enterprise-specific configuration models without leaving the STEP standard: The reason is that STEP standards define a (although generic) fixed product structure, that is, they do not provide the freedom to design any type of configuration model. If a company models its products according to STEP, it should use an application protocol in order to conform to the STEP standard.

The *unified modeling language* (*UML*) and the *object constraint language* (*OCL*) (Warmer & Kleppe, 2003) include major language elements needed for the intuitive representation of configuration knowledge (Felfernig, Friedrich, Jannach, & Zanker, 2002). Such a standardized language is a crucial success factor for integrating configuration technologies into industrial software development processes. Object-oriented structure representation concepts of UML (Dennis, Wixom, & Tegarden, 2004; Rumbaugh, Jacobson, & Booch, 1989) and OCL constraint definitions allow the representation of configuration knowledge in a quite natural way: Product components are represented as classes and constraints between different components are represented by a set of corresponding OCL navigation expressions, that is, the basic concepts provided by UML/OCL should be integrated into existing configuration environments. From the viewpoint of knowledge acquisition support for configuration knowledge bases, the integration of industrial standard representations such as UML/OCL into configurator development environments is one of the major challenges for allowing effective knowledge acquisition processes, exchangeability of knowledge bases, and standardized interfaces to existing software components.

DEVELOPMENT AND DEBUGGING SUPPORT

Effective knowledge acquisition and maintenance support is one of the key issues in building configuration knowledge bases. The application of UML/OCL for configuration knowledge representation (Felfernig et al., 2002) can be seen as a quite intuitive and understandable representation of configuration knowledge. However, the application of such modeling languages for knowledge-base construction does not automatically guarantee the *validity* of the generated knowledge base: Validation is typically performed by testing the knowledge base using a set of *test cases* (examples) which are provided by domain experts or are taken from previously-calculated configurations. If a knowledge base is invalid, that is, some of the provided test cases are inconsistent with the actual version of the knowledge base, domain experts and knowledge engineers are faced with the challenge to identify a set of constraints in the knowledge base which are responsible for the faulty behavior of the knowledge base. Such a task becomes even harder when applying *rule-based* knowledge representations: In such a situation, domain experts and knowledge engineers need adequate tools that support automated identification of the faulty parts in a configuration knowledge base. *Automated debugging* concepts can improve the effectiveness of configuration knowledge-base development processes by significantly reducing development efforts: If a new version of a configuration knowledge base is created, regression tests can be automatically triggered in order to assure that the new version is still consistent with the defined test cases. Automated regression tests reduce development and maintenance costs since faults in the knowledge base can be detected early, that is, they are not propagated to the production environment.

In order to support an automated detection of faulty constraints in configuration knowledge bases, we can apply concepts from *model-based diagnosis* (Reiter, 1987): Model-based diagnosis is characterized as explanation of faulty behavior based on observations of the behavior of the concrete system (e.g., the behavior of a malfunctioning car engine) and the comparison with a corresponding system model representing the correct behavior of the system. The theory of Reiter (1987) includes the basic representational and computational assumptions which can be applied to a number of application domains. In Reiter (1987), a *system* is interpreted as a pair (SD, COMPS) where SD, the system description, is a set of first-order sentences and COMPS, the system components, is a finite set of constants. An observation, OBS, of a system is a finite set of first-order sentences. Thus (SD, COMPS, OBS) denotes a system (SD, COMPS) with observations OBS. A corresponding diagnosis for (SD, COMPS, OBS) is a minimal set $\Delta \subseteq$ COMPS such that SD $\cup$ OBS $\cup$ {ab(c)| c $\in \Delta$} $\cup$ {¬ab(c)| c $\in$ COMPS - Δ} is consistent. In other words, the assumption that the components of {ab(c)| c $\in \Delta$} behave abnormal, together with the assumption that the other components (i.e., {¬ab(c)| c $\in$ COMPS - Δ}) behave normal, is consistent with the given system description SD and the given observations OBS.

If we now interpret the logical sentences (constraints) of a configuration knowledge base as system components, we can introduce a *configuration knowledge base* (*CKB*) *diagnosis* problem and a corresponding *configuration knowledge base diagnosis*. A detailed discussion on the application of model-based diagnosis concepts to the automated debugging of configuration knowledge bases can be found in Felfernig et al. (2004): A CKB diagnosis problem is a triple (DD, E$^+$, E$^-$), where DD is a configuration knowledge base, E$^+$ is a set of *positive examples* (test cases), and E$^-$ is a set of *negative examples* (test cases). The examples are given as sets of logical sentences. Each example on its own is assumed to be consistent. Note that a positive test case is an example for the intended behavior of a knowledge base; a negative test case is an example for an unintended behavior of a knowledge base (i.e., an example for a result which should not be calculated by the knowledge base).

A CKB diagnosis for a CKB diagnosis problem is a set $\Delta \subseteq$ DD of sentences such that there exists an extension EX (EX is a set of logical sentences) such that DD-$\Delta \cup$ EX $\cup$ e$^+$ is consistent $\forall$ e$^+ \in$ E$^+$, and DD-$\Delta \cup$ EX $\cup$ e$^-$ is inconsistent $\forall$ e$^- \in$

E⁻. The result of a diagnosis task is a minimal set of constraints of the configuration knowledge base which should be taken into account in order to make all positive examples consistent with the knowledge base.

This process of a consistency-based diagnosis of a configuration knowledge base can be fully automated given a number of predefined test cases. The definition of test cases is an important precondition for the application of model-based diagnosis concepts: On the one hand, test cases can be derived from former valid configuration results. If such results are not available, test cases must be either manually specified by domain experts or can be semi-automatically generated from the specification of a configuration knowledge base. Although testing is considered the most pragmatic and successful technique in quality assurance, the research field is still insufficiently explored in the context of developing and maintaining knowledge-based systems (Preece, Talbot, & Vignollet, 1997; Pretschner, 2001). The development of intelligent concepts supporting the automated generation of test suites should, therefore, be one of the major focuses of current research. In that context, the major challenge with respect to validation of configuration knowledge bases is the development of intelligent concepts that support the *generation and administration of test cases*. Test cases can be automatically generated from a given definition of a configuration knowledge base by calculating possible user interactions (requirements specifications) for predefined interaction paths. The number of generated test cases has to be further reduced in order to make their validation feasible for domain experts within a reasonable time span (Felfernig, Isak, & Kruggel, 2005).

DISTRIBUTED CONFIGURATION

Most of the existing approaches in the area of knowledge-based product configuration rely on the assumption that the configurable product is provided by *one single supplier* who assembles the product according to the customers' needs. However, in today's networked economy, the provision of products and services in many domains requires the integration of different companies in a supply chain. Furthermore, in many cases the subassemblies are again designed to be configurable, and the detailed configuration of the subassembly partially depends on the configuration parameters of the product as a whole. The standard approach to solve such problems is to integrate the required configuration rules into a central knowledge base. While this seems intuitive and practicable at a first glance, such an approach may have the drawback that the resulting knowledge base will soon become complex, thus increasing the probability of errors and, consequently, maintenance costs. In addition, it may be undesirable for a supplier to expose all its configuration logic, which is in many cases connected to a company's pricing rules, for confidentiality or organizational reasons.

In the CAWICOMS project (Ardissono, Felfernig, Friedrich, Goy, Jannach, Petrone, Schäfer, & Zanker, 2000, 2003), a consortium strongly rooted in telecommunications industry was piloting a scenario of cooperating configuration systems in the domain of IP-based Virtual Private Networks (IP-VPN). In that business case, a reseller is contracting multi-national IP-VPN solutions to its clients: The reseller subcontracts parts of the network to different telecommunication service providers that might themselves introduce subsuppliers. In order to generate a full configuration of the overall solution including, for example, IP-settings, internal routings, and additional hardware requirements, the cooperation of the local problem solvers of the involved business entities is necessary. Thus, the value chain has a networked structure, where each node can be represented by a configuration agent; in addition, *mediating components* were introduced for the coordination of the different configuration systems.

The main findings of the project with regard to distributed configuration and issues for future work in the area can be summarized as follows:

a.   The interoperation of different configuration systems requires the establishment of a shared view on the interdependent fractions of the product model. Therefore, a common language and ontology has to be employed for describing the configurable product configuration problem in a tool-independent manner. A proposal for such a common knowledge representation mechanism and exchange format, based on a general configuration ontology in the sense of Felfernig et al. (2002), has been developed within the project. However, as already sketched in the section on knowledge representation, up to now a *lingua franca* does not yet exist for exchanging configuration knowledge, which is one of the major prerequisites needed in such distributed configuration scenarios.

b.   Standard algorithms for distributed solution search like Distributed Constraint Satisfaction (Yokoo, 2001) are not directly applicable for distributed configuration problems. Thus, domain-specific distributed algorithms (see e.g., Ardissono et al., 2003; Zanker, 2002), which address the particularities of the problem domain, have been designed and prototypically implemented in the CAWICOMS project. However, there is still room for improvement to ease the integration of distributed solving protocols with the different heterogeneous configuration systems on the market.

RECONFIGURATION

Nearly all of the existing product configuration frameworks, problem-solving algorithms, and configurator applications are designed for the use in business scenarios in which a customer-specific product variant is constructed "from scratch" (Männistö, Soininen, Tiihonen, & Sulonen, 1999).

Still, there are many domains in which the products or services have a longer lifetime and for which it is common that the original configuration has to be adapted or extended over time. A typical example can, for instance, be found in the domain of the configuration of large telecommunication switches (see, e.g., Fleischanderl et al., 1998): These large-scale complex electronic devices are configured once and set up at a location, and are then in productive use for several years or even decades. During this period of productive use, there might be several reasons why the original configuration has to be changed or extended: For instance, the requirements may change over time when new technologies become available or more switching-capacity has to be provided. On the other hand, it is also possible that individual broken components have to be replaced, and only newer versions of these components are available which have to be plugged into an existing configuration.

Quite obviously, the optimization goals for configuration from scratch and reconfiguration are not the same: While in an initial configuration the main focus will be, in general, on minimizing the number of components needed in the system, the reconfiguration goal in most cases is to preserve as many parts of the existing configuration as possible. When considering these two different goals of optimization, we see that a system which is designed to support *reconfiguration* has to be augmented with additional knowledge, configuration logic, or adequate heuristics beside the core business and configuration rules.

In principle, two different approaches for dealing with that challenge can be identified: First, the required reconfiguration knowledge can be modeled externally as an add-on to the existing knowledge base. Such an approach is, for instance, proposed in Männistö et al. (1999), where reconfiguration *operations* consisting of preconditions and actions are made explicit in a separate "reconfiguration model". Given an existing configuration and a set of new requirements, the reconfiguration problem then basically consists of finding a subset of these reconfiguration operations that change the system in a way that the new requirements are fulfilled. The main advantage of such an approach lies in the fact that the search space for possible modifications is limited by the number of existing reconfiguration operations: If we assume that none of the reconfiguration operations will lead to a violation of the original configuration constraints, the problem variables of the typically larger core configuration problem do not have to be taken into account during search. The main drawback of such an approach, however, can be seen in: (a) the problem of ensuring that particular consistency property for complex knowledge bases; and (b) the reconfiguration rules have to be maintained and updated every time the core configuration knowledge base is changed.

The other principle approach is to include all reconfiguration alternatives and knowledge in the knowledge base from the beginning and only change the optimization goal when it comes to reconfiguration when configurations which reuse more of the existing components are preferred over others. While such an approach in theory will lead to "optimal" reconfigurations and no additional modeling is required, the search problem is, in practice, intractable with today's search technology for realistic scenarios. In fact, in many cases, even the original configuration may already be suboptimal due to the complexity of the search space and the use of domain-specific heuristics (Fleischanderl et al., 1998), which are needed to find a *good* solution in an appropriate time frame. In addition, many problem solvers (e.g., based on Constraint Satisfaction) are based on *constructive search and backtracking*, that is, the configurations are incrementally constructed from scratch during the search process. Therefore, in our opinion, *local search techniques* or *evolutionary* algorithms are more promising for reconfigura-

tion problems and should be further investigated in future research: As a core characteristic, these algorithms start from an existing configuration (or variable assignment) and incrementally try to improve the current solution by exploring *neighboring* solutions which have a strong correlation to the reconfiguration problem.

A special form of reconfiguration support can be seen in what is called *parametric redesign*: Such approaches are basically suitable for configurable systems that are already "designed for reconfiguration". In such systems, the basic structure of the product remains static (e.g., there exists a given number of connected components), but the individual components can be parameterized such that they fulfill specific requirements. In Stumptner and Wotawa (1999), for instance, such an approach is described for the domain of telephone networks: Given an existing network configuration and a new functional requirement (in that case, a certain call type), the problem is to reconfigure the nodes in the telephone network such that this functionality becomes available. In their approach, Stumptner and Wotawa propose to employ model-based diagnosis techniques for determining these parameter sets and thus develop a general framework for parametric reconfiguration. The search space in their approach remains manageable due to the fact that they limit the reconfiguration options to alternative parameter settings. Model-based diagnosis techniques are also used for reconfiguration in the approach proposed by Crow and Rushby (1991): In contrast to the work of Stumptner and Wotawa, however, they base their approach on explicit reconfiguration knowledge. Their main goal was to extend existing diagnosis techniques toward automatic *repair*, where the goal not only is to identify faulty components of a system but also compute a set of actions to be taken in order to reestablish a functioning system.

From a business perspective, reconfiguration (adaptation/extension) of already-installed systems falls into the category of *after-sales* and *maintenance* activities, which we see as an increasingly important business area for many of today's companies (Männistö et al., 1999). As such, we argue that adequate tool support for such high-quality customer services can be extremely valuable for companies, in particular as a competition factor in markets where the products of different manufacturers are comparable, and differentiation from the market competitors has to be achieved by the provision of such *add-on* services.

In the context of reconfiguration and after-sales services, we also see *versioning* and *evolution* of configuration knowledge bases as additional, future challenges in the area of knowledge-based configuration, in particular, as almost no support exists in current configurator systems.

PERSONALIZED USER INTERACTION

In business-to-consumer environments, product configuration systems are one of the information systems that are directly located at the interface between customers and producers. They allow the automation of the order-taking process by capturing customer requirements without involving human intermediaries in an interactive process. This means that customers are enabled to self-configure their products to their individual requirements in Web-based applications, which has been proven to lead to a significant reduction of costs and errors. Thus, product configuration systems are one of the main enablers of the mass customization paradigm which aims at providing highly-tailored products and services to end users.

While technical experts have been the dominant user group of configuration systems in the early years, nowadays they are used by quite heterogeneous groups of online end users. Thus, these users have typically different backgrounds in terms of experience or skills, or are simply different in the way they prefer to or are able to express their needs and requirements.

Consequently, it is obvious that static "one-style-fits-all" approaches are not adequate for user interfaces of configuration systems in many current application environments. In Web-based applications, for instance, HTML forms, with which the user can specify technical product details in order to find a valid product configuration, are common. However, such static state-of-the-art technologies cannot ensure that the final configured product is tailored to the *real* customer preferences and expectations. Thus, the quality of the achieved results can be significantly improved when the system interacts with the user in a personalized way.

Up to now, there have been significant efforts for personalizing Web-based user interfaces of configuration systems. Besides "standard" personalization techniques for hypermedia applications (Kobsa, Koenemann, & Pohl, 2001), there are several approaches that are specific for personalization in the domain of configuration systems. In general, we can distinguish two basic strategies of how user requirements can be elicited: (a) The system poses explicit questions to the user; and (b) the system applies indirect reasoning techniques about, for instance, already-gathered information about the current user or some stereotype classification mechanisms.

In the CAWICOMS project (Ardissono et al., 2000, 2003), such a hybrid approach was chosen for the domain of configuration of complex telecommunication switches. The CAWICOMS system automatically adapts its user interaction to the user's skills by varying the complexity level of the configuration process based on information about the current user stored in a long-term user model (Thompson, Goeker, & Langley, 2004); on the other hand, a rule-based system is applied to determine a more "overall" personalization strategy. For instance, in the CAWICOMS system the user can delegate decisions about feature values to the system which infers the most suitable setting. Furthermore, the system hides or presents some details in the configuration process in order to focus the presentation on the most relevant information according to the current user's skills.

One of the major challenges of a hybrid approach, however, lies in the fine-tuning of the interoperation between the two techniques. The explicit personalization rules in such a system are, in many cases, driven by the estimates contained in user models based on Bayesian networks (cf. for instance, the POET tool, Royalty, Holland, Goldsmith, and Dekhtyar, 2002). As a side effect, small changes in such a user model can cause a threshold to be exceeded such that an expert rule fires, causing unexpected major effects.

Today, systems are wide-spread that base the personalization solely on long-term user models, reasoning on past behavior or stereotypes. These systems are producing promising results in particular in domains with revisiting users (see, for instance, Sung, 2002; Thompson et al., 2004). For first-time visitors, however, they typically face the *new user problem*, that is, in absence of suitable data for a new user they can base their personalization simply on a poor user model. In addition, user models that are maintained by such systems can often only capture high-level characteristics of the customer to be theoretically reusable across different applications.

Therefore, we claim that it is particularly important to consider extensive personalization of the interaction between the user and the configuration system to reach better results and higher customer satisfaction. Thus, it is not sufficient to adapt the content and the presentation of configuration application to the current user's skills, but also to tailor the interaction level (Jannach & Kreutler, 2005). For example, if we think of a system for configuring personal computers, there will be users who want to specify technical details of the desired model, whereas others will only be able to express for what purposes they intend to use the computer; yet others only want to compare

preconfigured models and decide by themselves. Up to now, such a personalization of the interaction with the user was primarily addressed in the context of recommender systems.

McGinty and Smyth (2002) propose an approach for recommender systems that is based on a more casual conversation. This means that there should be several degrees of feedback that an online user can provide during the dialog. For instance, leading users through deep dialogs that replicate customer buying models from the real world is not always appropriate in online settings. The authors argue that there should also be a low-cost form of feedback for users instead of complex dialogs. They propose a comparison-based approach for product recommendation, in which the user is asked to choose a recommended item as a preference (positive or negative). The further recommendation is based on the difference of the preferred products and the remaining alternatives.

In a further investigation, McGinty and Smith (2002a) give an overview on different techniques for user feedback which can be based, for example, on value elicitation, tweaking, ratings, and preferences. In their work, they focus on a low-cost preference-based feedback model which is evaluated in a recommendation framework. The proposed feedback techniques for recommender systems can also be applied in the context of configuration systems. For instance, comparison-based approaches could be applied when the final configurations are presented to the user.

In the domain of configuration systems, Pu, Faltings, and Torrens (2003) consider preference elicitation as a fundamental problem: Building on experiences in building decision support systems in various domains, they identify some principles for designing of the interactive procedure of finding a suitable configuration in the solution space. In a survey of ten commercial online flight reservation systems, they find out that a personalized user interaction significantly improves the preference elicitation process for the end-user.

They allow users to state values for those options that correspond to their main objectives, which lead more quickly to a more accurate preference model. Furthermore, example critiquing in a minimal context, that is, making critiques on a personalized (minimized) set of attributes, is also identified as adequate means. Finally, the authors also consider the visualization of the result set with the possibility of revising previously-stated preferences during the elicitation process as crucial because users can immediately see the consequences of their stated preferences and possible changes.

EXPLANATIONS AND PROBLEM RESOLUTION

Most of today's product configuration systems are highly-interactive software applications. Typically, users incrementally enter their requirements while the system continuously checks the constraints, eventually reports conflicts, or removes inconsistent options. Then, the user may be given the possibility to revise his/her requirements and finally, the system in many cases automatically completes the configuration by, for example, adding some mandatory components or by setting some variables with default values.

In particular for configuration applications where the end user is not a technical expert, for example, in a Web-based environment, it is important that the end user develops a good understanding of the behavior and logic of the configurator. Typical questions that arise in such interactive sessions are, for instance, *"why am I not allowed to select this option anymore?"*, *"what decision do I have to retract, if I want to have a particular functionality?"*, or *"why was an option automatically set by the configurator with a certain value?"* If the user is not provided with answers to these questions, there is a high chance that the user's confidence in the final configuration is low, or he/she is frustrated when using the system because no adequate help was available during the interactive configuration session. Overall, we therefore claim that the provision of explanations can significantly help to increase the acceptance and value of a configuration system.

In fact, the ability to provide explanations can be seen as one of the key features of knowledge-based systems in general, and there also exists long research history on how problem-solvers can be built that are capable of, for example, justifying conclusions, detecting inconsistencies, or keeping track of dependencies (see Forbus & deKleer, 1993) for an overview. Still, many of the proposed approaches, like so-called truth maintenance systems, are limited in their applicability, since the size of the dependency network which has to be maintained soon gets too large to manage problems of realistic size.

Today, constraint satisfaction (Tsang, 1993) is the most popular technique for representing configuration problems. Therefore, most of the current research efforts in the area of advanced user interaction and explanations are based on this technology. On the other hand, many researchers also use configuration problems as a test-bed for new algorithms because of the typically high complexity that is involved in solving such problems. A recent contribution in that area was introduced by Junker (2004), who developed QuickXPlain, a general algorithm for fast extraction of dependencies and detection of *minimal* conflicts for arbitrary constraint propagation and inference algorithms, which is in particular of importance because high-performance problem-solvers, in many cases, lack the ability to provide explanations. With the help of QuickXPlain, some of the answers mentioned above (e.g., why a certain value was chosen) can be answered without the need of costly bookkeeping of justifications and, in cases where a black-box propagation engine is used, that does not record the explanations.

Beside Junker's algorithm, other proposals for computing explanations for Constraint problems have been developed in recent years (see, e.g.,

Freuder et al., 2001; Jussien, 2001; Rochart, Jussien, & Laburthe, 2003). Still, many of them rely on the abduction principle which can lead to the problem of "spurious explanations" which were dealt with by Friedrich (2004). In this chapter, the notion of a "well-founded explanation" was introduced, which helps us to eliminate such inconsistent explanations.

Conflict detection and explanation of the situation is, however, only one part of the problem. In fact, for the end user, it may be desirable to get some advice on how to deal with the problematic situation, that is, how conflicts can be resolved and consistency can be restored. The work of Amilhastre, Fargier, and Marquis (2002) is one example of research in that direction. The main problem of consistency restoration in constraint-based configuration problems lies in the fact that most current approaches for performing the required tasks are computationally expensive, while at the same time the response times in an interactive configuration session are very restricted. The authors therefore propose a technique that relies on pre-compilation of the problem, which is, in our opinion, in general a technique which is also promising for other problem domains that require fast response times. In their work, the original constraint problem is preprocessed off-line, and an automaton is compiled that represents a set of possible solutions. At run-time, the generated data structures can then be exploited for consistency maintenance and restoration in an efficient way.

Despite these recent advantages, we still can identify additional challenges that have to be addressed in the context of explanations and consistency restoration in interactive configurator applications: Although there are already first commercial solutions that incorporate explanation facilities (like configurator software), support for *repair* in the case of inconsistent situations cannot be found in today's systems. We also think that still better algorithms are required in that

context that, for instance, take the particularities of configuration problems better into account – in contrast to only viewing the configuration problem as a binary constraint satisfaction problem.

From our subjective perspective, another challenge in that context lies in the automated construction of *understandable* explanations: If we look at what we can get from current configurator software solutions is in many cases not more than a *trace* of the inferences (e.g., propagations) that were made by the problem solver. In the best case, such traces are understandable for the knowledge engineer who designed the knowledge base, but not for the end user. Furthermore, we think that there is also an unexploited potential for personalization in explanations: Depending on the goal one wants to achieve with the explanations, for instance, increasing the user's confidence or helping the user to understand the logic behind, the style or technical depth of the explanations could be varied.

CONCLUSION

The technological and economical environment in which product configuration systems are embedded is rapidly evolving, which, as a consequence, constantly creates new challenges for today's and future software systems that shall efficiently support the process of configuring products and services according to the customers' needs. Although there exists a long history of applying knowledge-based technology for solving configuration problems, further research in various directions, from knowledge representation, over problem-solving, or personalization, will be required to cope with these new requirements. Within this chapter, an overview on these new challenges was given, and recent developments and novel approaches in knowledge-based configuration technology were summarized.

REFERENCES

Amilhastre, J., Fargier, H., & Marquis, P. (2002). Consistency restoration and explanation in dynamic CSPs - Application to configuration. *Artificial Intelligence, 135*, 199-234.

Ardissono, L., Felfernig, A., Friedrich, G., Goy, A., Jannach, D., Petrone, G., Schäfer, R., & Zanker, M. (2000). Personalizing online configuration of products and services. In *Proceedings of the 15th European Conference on Artificial Intelligence*, Lyon, France (pp. 225-229). IOS Press.

Ardissono, L., Felfernig, A., Friedrich, G., Goy, A., Jannach, D., Petrone, G., Schäfer, R., & Zanker, M. (2003). A framework for the development of personalized, distributed Web-based configuration systems. *AI Magazine, 24*(3/Fall, 2003), 93-110.

Barker, V. E., O'Connor, D. E., Bachant, J. D., & Soloway, E. (1989). Expert systems for configuration at Digital: XCON and beyond. *Communications of the ACM, 32*(3), 298-318.

Berners-Lee, T. (2001). *Weaving the Web*. Harper Business.

Crow, J., & Rushby, J. M. (1991). Model-based reconfiguration: Toward an integration with diagnosis. In *Proceedings of the National Conference on Artificial Intelligence – AAAI'91* (pp. 836-841). AAAI Press.

Dennis, A., Wixom, B., & Tegarden, D. (2004). *System analysis and design with UML version 2.0: An object-oriented approach* (2nd ed.). John Wiley & Sons.

Edwards, K., & Pedersen, J. (2004). Product configuration systems – Implications for product innovation and development. In *Proceedings of the International Conference on Economic, Technical and Organisational Aspects of Product Configuration Systems, Copenhagen*, Denmark (pp. 231-239).

Felfernig, A., Friedrich, G., Jannach, D., & Stumptner, M. (2004). Consistency-based diagnosis of configuration knowledge bases. *Artificial Intelligence, 152*(2), 213-234.

Felfernig, A., Friedrich, G., Jannach, D., Stumptner, M., & Zanker, M. (2003). Configuration knowledge representations for Semantic Web applications. *Artificial Intelligence in Engineering, Design, and Manufacturing, 17*(3), 31-49.

Felfernig, A., Friedrich, G., Jannach, D., & Zanker, M. (2002). Configuration knowledge representation using UML/OCL. In *Proceedings of 5th International Conference on the Unified Modeling Language (UML 2002)*, Dresden, Germany (pp. 49-62).

Felfernig, A., Isak, K., & Kruggel, T. (2005). Testing knowledge-based recommender applications. *OEGAI Journal, Special Issue on Recommender Systems, 24*(4), 12-18.

Fensel, D., van Harmelen, F., Horrocks, I., McGuinness, D., & Patel-Schneider, P. (2001). OIL: An ontology infrastructure for the semantic Web. *IEEE Intelligent Systems, 16*(2), 38-45.

Fleischanderl, G., Friedrich, G., Haselböck, A., Schreiner, H., & Stumptner, M. (1998). Configuring large systems using generative constraint satisfaction. IEEE Intelligent Systems, (July/August, 1998), 59-68.

Forbus, K., & deKleer, J. (1993). *Building problem solvers*. MIT Press.

Forza, C., & Salvador, F. (2002). Managing for variety in the order acquisition and fulfillment process: The contribution of product configuration systems. *International Journal of Production Economics, Elsevier, 76*, 87-98.

Franke, N., & Piller, F. T. (2002). *Configuration toolkits for mass customization: Setting a research agenda* (Working Paper No. 33 of the Department of General and Industrial Management). Technische Universität München.

Friedrich, G. (2004). Elimination of spurious explanations. In *Proceedings of the 16ᵗʰ European Conference on Artificial Intelligence (ECAI 2004)*, Valencia, Spain (pp. 813-817). IOS Press.

Freuder, E., Likitvivatanavong, C., & Wallace, R. J. (2001). Deriving explanations and implications for constraint satisfaction problems. In *Proceedings of Principles and Practice of Constraint Programming - CP 2001, LNCS 2239*, Paphos, Cyprus (pp. 585-589). Springer.

Haag, A. (1998). Sales configuration in business processes. *IEEE Intelligent Systems, 13*(4), 78-85.

ISO (1994). Standard 10303-1: Industrial automation systems and integration – Product data representation and exchange – Part 1: Overview and fundamental principles.

Jannach, D., & Kreutler, G. (2005). Personalized user preference elicitation for e-services. In *Proceedings of IEEE International conference on e-Technology, e-Commerce and e-Service*, Hong Kong (pp. 604-611).

Juengst, E. W., & Heinrich, M. (1998). Using resource balancing to configure modular systems. *IEEE Intelligent Systems, Special Issue on Configuration, 13*(4), 50-58.

Junker, U. (2001a). Preference programming for configuration. In *Proceedings of the Workshop on Configuration (IJCAI'01)*, Seattle, WA (pp. 50-56).

Junker, U. (2004). QuickXplain: Preferred explanations and relaxations for over-constrained problems. In *Proceedings of AAAI'2004*, San Jose (pp. 167-172).

Jussien, N. (2001). E-constraints: Explanation-based constraint programming. In *Proceedings of the CP'01 Workshop on User-Interaction in Constraint Satisfaction*.

Kobsa, A., Koenemann, J., & Pohl, W. (2001). Personalized hypermedia presentation techniques for improving online customer relationships. *The Knowledge Engineering Review, 16*(2), 11-155.

Mailharro, D. (1998). A classification and constraint-based framework for configuration. *Artificial Intelligence in Engineering, Design, and Manufacturing, 12*, 383-397.

Männistö, T., Soininen, T., Tiihonen, J., & Sulonen, R. (1999). Framework and conceptual model for reconfiguration. *Papers from the AAAI Configuration Workshop* (AAAI Tech. Rep. WS-99/05). AAAI Press.

McDermott, J. (1982). A rule-based configurer of computer systems. *Artificial Intelligence, 19*(1), 39-88.

McGinty, L., & Smyth, B. (2002). Deep dialogue vs. casual conversation in recommender systems. In *Proceedings of the Workshop on Personalization in eCommerce at the Second International Conference on Adaptive Hypermedia and Web-Based Systems (AH-02)*, Universidad de Malaga, Spain (pp. 80-89).

McGinty, L., & Smyth, B. (2002a). Comparison-based recommendation. *Lecture Notes of Computer Science 2416, Proceedings of the 6ᵗʰ European Advances in Case-Based Reasoning* (pp. 575-589). Springer.

McGuiness, D., & Wright, J. (1998a). An industrial strength description logics-based configurator platform. *IEEE Intelligent Systems, Special Issue on Configuration, 13*(4), 69-77.

McGuiness, D. L., & Wright, J. R. (1998b). Conceptual modelling for configuration: A description logic-based approach. *Artificial Intelligence in Engineering, Design and Manufacturing (AI EDAM), 12*(98), 33–344.

Mittal, S., & Falkenhainer, B. (1990). Dynamic constraint satisfaction problems. In *Proceedings of*

8th National Conference on Artificial Intelligence, AAAI-90 (pp. 25-32).

Mittal, S., & Frayman, F. (1989). Towards a generic model of configuration tasks. In *Proceedings of International Joint Conference on Artificial Intelligence, IJCAI-89* (pp. 1395-1401).

Preece, A., Talbot, S., & Vignollet, L. (1997). Evaluation of verification tools for knowledge-based systems. *International Journal of Human-Computer Studies, 47*, 629-658.

Pretschner, A. (2001). Classical search strategies for test case generation with constraint logical programming. In *Proceedings of Workshop on Formal Approaches to Testing of Software,* Aalborg, Denmark (pp. 47-60).

Pu, P., Faltings, B., & Torrens, M. (2003). User-involved preference elicitation. In *Proceedings of the 18th International Joint Conference on Artificial Intelligence (IJCAI'03), Workshop on Configuration,* Acapulco.

Reiter, R. (1987). A theory of diagnosis from first principles. *Artificial Intelligence, 23*(1), 57–95.

Rochart, G., Jussien, N., & Laburthe, F. (2003). Challenging explanations for global constraints. In *Proceedings of the CP'03 Workshop on User-Interaction in Constraint Satisfaction,* Ireland.

Royalty, J., Holland, R., Goldsmith, J., & Dekhtyar, A. (2002). POET: The online preference elicitation tool. In *Proceedings of AAAI'02 Workshop on Preferences in AI and CP: Symbolic Approaches,* Edmonton, CA.

Rumbaugh, J., Jacobson, I., & Booch, G. (1989). *The Unified Modeling Language Reference Manual.* Addison-Wesley.

Schmitz, V., Leukel, J., & Kelkar, O. (2004). XML-based data exchange of product model data in e-procurement and e-sales: The case of BMECAT 2.0. In *Proceedings of the International Conference on Economic, Technical, and Organisational Aspects of Product Configuration Systems,* Copenhagen, Denmark (pp. 97-108).

Stumptner, M., & Wotawa, F. (1999). Reconfiguration using model-based diagnosis. In *Proceedings of the International Workshop on Diagnosis (DX99),* Scotland.

Sung, H. H. (2002). Helping customers decide through Web personalization. *IEEE Intelligent Systems, 17*(6), 34-43.

Thompson, C. A., Goeker, M. H., & Langley, P. (2004). A personalized system for conversational recommendations. *Journal of Artificial Intelligence Research, 21*, 393-428.

Tsang, E. (1993). *Foundations of constraint satisfaction.* New York: Academic Press.

van Harmelen, F., Patel-Schneider, P. F., & Horrocks, I. (2001). *A Model-Theoretic Semantics for DAML+OIL.* Retrieved in December, 2005, from http://www.daml.org

Warmer, J., & Kleppe, A. (2003). *The Object Constraint Language 2.0.* Addison Wesley.

Yokoo, M. (2001). *Distributed constraint satisfaction.* Berlin/New York: Springer.

Yokoo, M., Durfee, E. H., Ishida, T., & Kuwabara, K. (1998). The distributed constraint satisfaction problem. *IEEE Transactions on Knowledge and Data Engineering, 10*(5), 673-685.

Zanker, M. (2002). *Distributed configuration.* PhD thesis, University Klagenfurt, Austria.

Chapter XII

Mass Customisation of Services and Processes Based on Fuzzy Cognitive Maps

Dimitris Kardaras
Athens University of Economics, Greece

Bill Karakostas
School of Informatics City University, UK

ABSTRACT

This chapter draws on the theory of fuzzy cognitive maps (FCM) to propose a modelling approach for mass customisation (MC) of services. The proposed model integrates concepts from service quality and customer preferences with business process and IT capabilities models. The model presented in this chapter is, to the best of our knowledge, the only fuzzy service model for MC that provides the means to consider the business objectives for service customisation, associate them with specific business areas, and suggest opportunities for MC. In contrast to other service designs and management approaches, the proposed model is dynamic, exhibits flexibility and responsiveness to environmental changes and customisability to specific organisational contexts, and allows the development of planning scenarios.

INTRODUCTION

In an era of increasing competition and demanding customers, businesses are investigating new ways of improving their performance and differentiating their products and services. Developed economies shift from manufacturing to service industries. As a result, service design and management has been a top concern for business management in the 1990s, and it continues to be so in the 21st century as well. Nowadays in order to be successful, services have to be more innovative, flexible, and customisable in order to achieve customer satisfaction. Mass production is not suitable anymore due to the current state of the global markets, which are characterised by the increasing variety of products and services, and the advent of electronic commerce.

It is argued that **mass customisation** (MC) is expected to be a critical strategic option for the survival and competitiveness of many organisations in the 21st century (Boynton, Victor, & Pine, 1993). MC focuses on delivering differentiated products and services at competitive prices. MC implies the development and distribution of products and services that are customised to specific customer needs and are made available at an acceptable cost and in accordance to customer's priorities with respect to quality factors. MC of markets means that organisations can reach the same large number of customers as in the mass markets, but additionally they have the ability to address their customers individually as in the customised markets. Business organisations already face intensive competitive pressure and can no longer capture market share and gain higher profits by supplying large volumes of standard products for mass markets. Firms that can understand, anticipate, and originate customer preferences, and then exhibit the necessary flexibility to respond with suitable products will become more competitive over their less-flexible competitors. It is argued that mass customisation is expected to be a critical strategic option for the survival and competitiveness of many organisations in the 21st century. A new market for mass customisation has already developed, and the growth of this concept is increasing. Thus organisations can address this new-segmented market, which is one of a series of niches, with each niche differentiated from the others by a number of factors.

Responding to the increasing interest in service design and the proliferation of Internet applications and e-services, researchers have developed a large number of methodologies and models for service management. However, none of the service management methodologies and models described in the relevant literature addresses the challenge of MC in services. This chapter draws on the theory of fuzzy cognitive maps (FCM) and proposes a modelling approach for services in MC. The proposed model integrates concepts related to service quality and customer preferences with business process and the capabilities of modern IT. The model presented in this chapter is, to the best of our knowledge, the only fuzzy service model for MC that provides the means to consider the business objectives and to associate them with specific business areas, which can represent opportunities for MC. In contrast to other service design and management approaches, the proposed model is dynamic, exhibits flexibility and responsiveness to environmental changes and customisability to specific organisational contexts, and allows for the development of planning scenarios.

The research objectives of the approach described in this chapter follow:

- Develop a new model based on the theory of cognitive maps to facilitate services of MC;
- Develop business process models that integrate services design priorities with process design options; and
- Develop a methodology and associated models that draw on the principles of MC, service quality, and customer satisfaction as well as on FCMs.

SERVICES AND E-SERVICES QUALITY

The concept of **service** and its quality is extensively discussed in the business literature. Ramaswamy (1996), for example, describes service as "the business transactions that take place between a donor (service provider) and receiver (customer) in order to produce an outcome that satisfies the customer". Gronroos (2000) defines service as "... an activity or series of activities of more or less intangible nature that normally, but not necessarily, take place in interactions between the customer and service employees and /or systems of the service provider, which are provided as solutions to customer problems". Services are often attributed as "experiences"; therefore, moods and emotions are critical factors that shape the perceived effectiveness of service encounters" (Pine & Gilmore, 1999).

In computer science, the term *service* has three different contexts: **Web services**, e-services, and services. **E-services** are "services that are delivered electronically, typically through the Internet" or "electronic services offered over the Internet are also referred to as electronic services, Web services, Internet services, Web-based services, or e-services" (Tut & Edmond, 2002).

With regards to **service quality,** it is argued that businesses need not only to correspond to their customers' needs but also to extend their customers' expectations (Gounaris, Stathakopoulos, & Athanassopoulos, 2003).

According to Wang (2003), the quality of e-services has seven dimensions, which are divided in two parts: The first part focuses on the quality of e-services, and the second focuses on the

resolution of the problems that appear during the provision of e-services (Table 1).

Services quality is strategically important, because it provides the companies with the ability to differentiate themselves from the competition and consequently to gain competitive advantage (Gounaris et al., 2003; Lassar, Manolis, & Winsor, 2000), through better customer service (Walker et al, 2002), as well as through better management of customer relationships (Gronroos, 1994).

Customer perceptions regarding quality have changed. Nowadays, customers require quality, and this is the reason why quality constitutes an entire and integral part of service, which means that quality and service are synonymous. Before taking any initiative regarding the quality of services, it is necessary to determine the needs and the preferences of the customers and the relative qualitative dimensions. The determination and the measurement of the expectations of the Internet service customers provide a framework for the evaluation of businesses in service industries regarding the provision of services quality (Jun & Cai, 2001). In their study, Jun and Cai (2001) determine extensively the fundamental qualita-

Table 1. Dimensions of e-service quality

The first part is divided into 4 dimensions:
1. **Efficiency:** It refers to the customer's ability to navigate easily in the website, to find the desired products, any relative information with a minimum of effort.
2. **Achievement:** It refers to the accuracy of realising what services promise to provide the customers with.
3. **Reliability:** It has to do with the technical reliability of the website.
4. **Privacy:** This dimension addresses the issue of data protection and it should include the reassurance that any personal data is treated with confidentiality and it will not be disclosed to a third party.

The second part includes the following personal services:
1. **Correspondence:** It measures the ability of a business to provide its customers with right and suitable information, when a problem appears.
2. **Compensation:** It refers to the money-back guarantee, when customers are not satisfied.
3. **Contact:** It refers to the customers' need to be able to talk to a "live" customer service agent online or through telephone.

Table 2. Service quality dimensions, the case of banking

a) Customer Service Quality	b) Online Systems Quality	c) Banking Service Product Quality
• Reliability • Responsiveness • Competence • Courtesy • Credibility • Access • Communication • Understanding customer • Collaboration • Continuous improvement	• Content • Accuracy • Ease of use • Timeliness • Aestetics • Security	• One dimension of product variety / diverse Features

tive attributes of Internet banking services and products, based on an analysis of the comments from e-banking customers.

According to this study, three quality categories of banking e-services were divided in 17 dimensions/attributes. These three categories and the corresponding 17 dimensions are shown in Table 2.

In order to maintain a high quality level of e-services, businesses have to pay attention to all the above 17 dimensions.

INTRODUCTION TO MASS CUSTOMISATION

Mass customisation implies the development and distribution of products and services that are customised to specific customer needs and are made available at acceptable cost and in accordance to customer's priorities with respect to factors that reflect quality in products and services (Fulkerson, 1997). The term MC was first coined by Davis (1987) who proposed the idea that a competitive advantage could be gained, through companies delivering customised goods on a mass basis. It is also suggested (Boynton et al., 1993) that MC is a "new" competitive strategy to challenge "old" strategies such as mass production.

Hart (1994) defines **mass customisation** as "... the use of flexible processes and organizational structures to produce varied and often individually customised products and services at the low cost of a standardized, mass-production system".

Mass customisation of markets means that organisations can reach the same large number of customers as in the mass markets, but additionally they have the ability to address their customers individually as in the customised markets (Hirschhorn, Noble, & Rnkin, 2001; Parker, 1996; Radder & Louw, 2000). Firms that can understand, anticipate, and originate customer preferences and then exhibit the necessary flexibility to respond with suitable products will become more competitive over their cumbersome competitors (Fulkerson, 1997). A new market for mass customisation is already developed and the growth of this concept is increasing (Parker, 1996). Thus organisations can address this new-segmented market, which is one of a series of niches, where each niche is differentiated from the others by a number of factors (Davis, 1987).

Five **approaches** are suggested through which enterprises can develop mass customisation (Parker, 1996):

- **Standardised products with customised services:** This approach suggests that companies enter mass customisation through their existing or new standard products with customised services;

- **Customise through standardisation:** This approach implies a standardised modular development of products. The standard modules can then be used to configure products for individual customers;
- **Create products that the customers can customise:** This approach assumes that an organisation develops a product architecture that allows a customer to choose several aspects of the products in order to customise it to his/her individual needs;
- **Move final manufacturing function close to the end customer:** The aim of this approach is to achieve point-of-sale customisation by the customer who can customise several aspects of the product; and
- **Flexible manufacturing technologies:** Flexible manufacturing technologies allow organisations to develop a large variety of products at relatively low cost.

However, a different classification of mass customisation **approaches** is suggested by Gilmore & Pine II (1997) as follows:

- The *collaborative customisers* approach suggests conducting a dialogue with individual customers to help them articulate their needs, to identify the precise offerings, and customise the products. This approach is most appropriate to use when customers cannot easily choose what they want or when they have to choose from a wide range of options;
- The *adaptive customisers* approach implies that an organisation offers a standard but customisable product that is designed so that customers can alter it themselves. This approach is best suited to businesses whose customers want the product to perform in different ways on different occasions;
- The *cosmetic customisers* approach sug-

gests that a standard product is presented differently to different customers. Rather than being customised, the product with this approach is displayed differently and its characteristics are advertised in different ways; and

- The *transparent customisers* approach implies that organisation should provide individual customers with unique products and services, without letting them know exactly how the products have been customised. This approach is suitable when the customers' specific needs are predictable or can be easily deduced.

THE NEED TO FOCUS ON SERVICES MASS CUSTOMISATION

Most of the research on MC focuses on tangible manufacturing products with little attention paid to services for MC; these have utterly been left in the shadow (Alford, Sackett, & Nelder, 2000; Brown & Bessant, 2003; Felfernig, Friedrich, & Jannach, 2001; Forza & Salvador, 2002). Related research is carried out in configuration tools and dynamic Web user modelling (Ardissono, Felfernig, Friedrich, Goy, Jannach, Petrone, Schafer, & Zanker, 2003; Ardissono, Goy, Petrone, & Segnan, 2002). Adrissono et al. developed a configuration platform that uses hypermedia and XML technologies, models domain-dependent knowledge of products and services, and delivers customised products and services through the Web to customers. MC in services is challenging because services are intangible; their existence depends on the time, and their quality reflects the customers' perceived quality. That means that service quality is highly related to customer individual needs, cognition, and personal characteristics. Research on mass-customised services is rather important if we consider the special **characteristics of the mass-customised service** operations. These are:

Figure 1. The diamond of competitive strategies

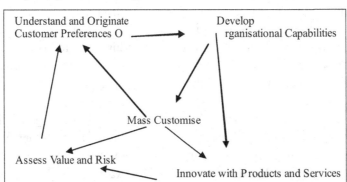

- They are more labour–intensive compared to manufacturing;
- They have greater customer involvement;
- They are more sensitive to quality errors;
- They have tighter delivery times;
- They are unable to rely on inventories to adjust to demand fluctuations; and
- They are more dependent on information reliability.

Both the insurance and the banking industries are showing strong signs of adopting a more customised approach towards their products. They are moving with the times, accepting the changes and new demands of the market. It is often attributed to the post industrial age or information age that customers set the rules and, as a consequence, an even greater extent of individualization must be realized in an efficient form. Customers are now seen as individuals rather than as objects to be standardized. Individuality is the new fashion, and the fashion has now spread from not only manufactured goods but also into the services we use. The financial sector has realized this shift in demand and is making preparations to meet it. It is claimed, "Through the application of technology and new management methods, they have found their way to a new paradigm by creating variety and customisation through flexibility and quick responsiveness". In order to achieve the MC of products and services, it is important to listen carefully to customers in order to design a set of product variants and individualization options that on the one hand has enough possibilities for customisation, and on the other is as easy as possible to reduce complexity, a main cost driver of MC. It is suggested that the goal is to ascertain, from the customer's perspective, the range within which a given product or service can be meaningfully customised (i.e., differentiated) for that customer, and then to facilitate the customer's choice of options from within that range. The key issue of any of the above approaches or combinations of customisation is to draw on whatever means of customisation prove necessary to create unique customer value within the limits of the organisations' capabilities and orientation. The organisational strategies for the 21st century should evolve around the "diamond" of Figure 1:

This is an inherently complex strategy for many companies, whose success depends on an organisation's abilities to find the "best" combination or sequence of service characteristics in order to form the processes that will address the specific needs of customers. The successful design and implementation of mass customisation requires organisational capabilities and services to be assessed in terms of their compatibility and suitability for specific processes and tasks, the associated risk and value, as well as in terms of customers' needs and priorities.

PROCESS MODELLING FOR MC

As MC literature suggests, organisations should refrain from keeping the same business processes, which are designed mainly with mass production in mind, when they embark on a MC initiative (Boynton et al., 1993; Pine, Victor, & Boynton, 1993). Mass customisation must be pursued through a stage of business process reengineering (BPR) (Boynton et al., 1993; Pine et al., 1993). Therefore, process modelling can be used to facilitate the analysis and design of business processes for mass customisation. Several process modelling approaches have been proposed, for example, data flow diagrams (DFDs), role activity diagrams (Wastell, White, & Kawalek, 1994), modelling of strategic actors relationships (Yu & Mylopoulos, 1995), communication-based and activity-based methodologies (Georgakopoulos, Hornick, & Sheth, 1995), and so forth. Object-oriented process models are also proposed in the use cases-based business reengineering approach (Jacobson et al, 1994).

Although none of the above approaches has been specifically designed or adopted for mass customisation processes, the suitability of intelligent agents and case-based design approaches for mass customisation have been suggested in Fulkerson (1997) and in Tseng and Jiao (1997).

Mass customisation requires the development of a flexible network of autonomous operating units or modules. These modules, which perform a specific task and communicate with each other with material or information flows, can be people, teams, or software components (Boynton et al., 1993) depending on the resources they use. These modules represent the business processes capabilities (Boynton et al., 1993; Fulkerson, 1997; Pine et al., 1993) and they are not pre-engineered or pre-aligned for some known end product. The flexible coordination and combination of the different modules gives an organisation the ability to produce virtually an infinite variety of products and services at costs which are competitive with the mass producer.

The **requirements for the specification and modelling of MC processes** should include the ability to cope with and provide the justification for the use of fuzzy logic technologies in MC process and services modelling (Kardaras, Karakostas, & Papathanassiou, 2000):

- Inexact information about customer needs, for example, how important is a particular aspect of a product or service, and so forth;
- Soft issues such as the specification of the "best" possible combination of modules to meet customer needs or the degree of the reusability potential of a particular resource;
- The assessment of customers' priorities of qualitative and rather intangible nature, for example, after-sales support issues;
- The need to resolve contradiction involved in mass customisation design such as between process efficiency and product variety, or between low-cost processes and product differentiation (Boynton et al., 1993);
- The development of a conceptual construction that is understandable to customers, since communication between the organisation and its customers is essential;
- The use of the Internet to facilitate communication and collaboration with the customers; and
- The development of flexible information systems architectures.

FUZZY COGNITIVE MAPS

Cognitive maps (CP) are signed digraphs designed to capture the causal assertions of a person with respect to a certain domain and then use them in order to analyse the effects of alternatives, for example, policies, business decisions, and so forth, upon certain goals (Axelrod, 1976). A signed digraph allows for a sign (+) or (-) to be assigned on each relationship, thus modelling just the direction of the change. A CP is a representation of the perceptions and beliefs of an individual or group about his own subjective world. A CP has only two basic types of elements: *concepts* and *causal beliefs*. The concepts are represented as variables and the causal beliefs as relationships among variables.

Weighted cognitive maps can be derived from the signed digraphs. The sign can be replaced with positive or negative numbers, which show not only the direction, but also the magnitude of the change. When the numbers on each relationship are replaced with a sign and a fuzzy weight, such as strong, weak, moderate, and so forth, the resulting map is called **fuzzy cognitive map** (Kosko, 1986). Figure 2 shows a FCM.

The terms "strong", "moderate", and so forth, are the fuzzy weights, which show the beliefs of the decision-makers with respect to the strength of the impact between two linked concepts.

Each weight (e.g., strong, weak, etc.) in the FCM is a fuzzy set. Fuzzy sets are characterised by a membership function, which is also called the *degree* or *grade* of *membership*. The definition of a fuzzy set is as follows (Tanaka, 1997; Zadeh, 1973):

"A **fuzzy set** A of a universe of discourse U is characterised by a membership function $\mu_A : U \rightarrow$ [0,1] which associates with each element y of U a number $\mu_A(x)$ in the interval [0,1] which represents the grade of membership of y in A."

Therefore, it can be defined in the interval [0, 1], or it can be defined with respect to a partially-ordered linguistic terms set such as {undefined, little, moderate, strongly}.

The following rules apply to the two-valued system; however, there are also rules proposed for the eight-valued system (Axelrod, 1976) as well.

- **Rule 1:** *The indirect effect of a path from a cause variable (X) to an effect variable (Y) I(x,y) is positive if the path has an even number of negative arrows, and it is negative if it has an odd number of negative arrows.* The indirect effect is defined as the multiplication of the signs of the causal relationships that form the path from the cause variable to the effect variable. The indirect effect of variable (X) to variable (Y) through path P(xwy) in Figure 1 is therefore positive (+).

- **Rule 2:** *The total effect of a cause variable (X) on an effect variable (Y) is denoted by T(x,y)* and is the sum of all the indirect effects from the cause variable X to the effect variable Y. In Figure 1, the total effect of variable (X) to variable (Y) is the sum of the indirect effect of (X) to (Y) through the paths P(xwy) and P(xfzy). Both indirect effects are positive, which means the total effect is positive (+) as well.

CMs and FCMs have been applied to ill-structured problems such as political science, in simulation, organisational strategies modelling, support for strategic problem formulation and decision analysis, knowledge bases construction, managerial problems diagnosis, failure modes effects analysis, modelling of social and psycho-

Figure 2. Example of fuzzy cognitive map

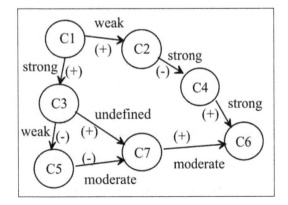

logical processes, modelling virtual worlds and analysis of their behaviour, requirements analysis, and systems requirements specification (Kardaras & Karakostas, 1999).

MODELLING SERVICES AND BUSINESS PROCESSES FOR MC WITH FCM

The proposed approach aims at modelling service quality and customer expectations of a service and then identifying opportunities for customising the required services so that customer satisfaction increases. The approach is realised with the development of models that use fuzzy logic and object-oriented technologies. This section presents the theoretical framework for services of MC and illustrates the proposed approach with a case study.

Overview of the Approach

A service consists of service components, with some of them being tangible and some being intangible in nature. The perceived quality of a service depends on each individual customer's overall expectations of a particular service and on each service component's quality in particular. The competitiveness of a business is often translated in terms of customer satisfaction and customer loyalty, as both reflect the customer's perceived quality of the services they acquire. As a first step to services of MC, the proposed approach models services and associates their characteristics with customer expectations. The comparison between the actual service quality as it is perceived by the customer and the customer expectations reveals areas of improvements. The required changes are translated in turn into components changes and subsequently into tasks and processes alignment. Further, the approach suggests that any changes in service components and corresponding process tasks should be considered as requirements for

changes in the resources portfolio and uses. The steps of the proposed approach follow:

Step 1: Modelling Services
Let $S(i)$ be a service, then $S(i)=[C_1, C_2, C_3, ..., C_n]$. Therefore, a service consists of a set of service components C_k. Service components can be specified with thorough analysis of the service management and service quality literature and, additionally, with knowledge extracted with interviews from domain experts. Each service component C_k, is modelled in terms of three characteristics, namely:

- The fuzzy set *importance* (i) of a particular component C_k to a corresponding service quality $S(i)$;
- The fuzzy set *degree of presence* (p) of a particular component $C_{(k)}$ in a service $S(i)$; and
- The fuzzy set *actual contribution* (c) of a particular component C_k to the $S(i)$ service quality, which is estimated using the formula $q(k)= p(k)* c(k)$.

Since all component characteristics are fuzzy sets, they take values in the interval $[0, 1]$. Different approaches have been proposed for the specification of the values for the fuzzy weights in a FCM (i.e., the values for the *importance* (i), *degree of presence* (p), and *actual contribution* (c), of the proposed approach). One suggestion is to ask the experts to assign a real number from the interval $[0,1]$ for each relationship and then calculate the average (Taber, 1991; Zhang, Chen, & Bezdek, 1989). For example, three experts estimate 0.3, 0.6, 0.6. The weight is the average, that is, 0.5. Other approaches suggest that data is collected with surveys, and this data is subsequently statistically analysed (Lee, Kim, & Lee, 2004), or they propose the use of heuristics and neural networks (Glorfeld, 1996), an approach that requires large data sets, larger than the statistical approach.

However, Kosko (1986) and Schneider, Scnaider, Kandel, and Chew (1998) suggest that experts' opinion is essential in determining the strength of each relationship.

Therefore services are modelled as:

$$S(i)=[C_1(i, p, q), C_2(i, p, q), C_3(i, p, q), ..., C_n(i, p, q)].$$

If a component is not part of a service, then its presence (p) degree=0, where if it is fully present in the service then (p) =1.

The set of components reflects not only the structural aspects of a service, but equally importantly the quality aspects of the services as discussed earlier in this chapter.

Step 2: Modelling Customer Expectations

Expectations of customer m, CE(m) are represented as a vector of service components. The service vector and the customer expectations vector consist of the same service components. Therefore, $CE(m)=[C_1(e1), C_2(e2), ..., C_n(en)]$, that means each customer expects a level of satisfaction (e) from each component. Each component's expectation is a fuzzy set, and it is associated with a value in [0, 1] that represents the degree of customer expectation for a particular component. The values that show the customer expectations for each service component, similarly as in step one, can be specified with surveys and statistical analysis of data, neural networks, and so forth. In this case, however, depending on the design of the system that may implement the proposed approach, a customer may be engaged in a dialogue and asked for a value that is an individual choice.

Step 3: Comparing Actual and Expected Level of Service Quality

The comparison between the perceived service quality and the customer expectations for the service is estimated by the distance of the two vectors S(i) and CE(m,i) for each customer m and service i. The distance is calculated according to the following rule (Schneider et al., 1998):

Consider the two vectors *(V1)* and *(V2)* that are monotonically increasing (direct relation), then the distance (di) between two elements (vi) of the vectors is defined as:

$$di = |\chi 1(vi) - \chi 2(vi)|,$$

where $\chi 1$ and $\chi 2$ is the degree of membership for the (i) element of the vectors *(V1)* and *(V2)* respectively.

In the case of monotonically decreasing vectors (reverse relation) the distance of the two elements (vi) is defined as: $di = |\chi 1(vi) - (1 - \chi 2(vi))|$.

For a company to be competitive, it needs to minimise the distance between perceived service quality and customer expectations.

The proposed approach does not aim at managing differences automatically; therefore, there is no need to specify a threshold for "accepted" or not differences. It rather encourages decision-makers to develop alternative scenarios based on their assumptions for the company, its services, and its customers. The differences indicate service designers, the service components and, subsequently, the tasks on which they should focus their attention. So, if there are components identified that do not perform as expected, the management can trace the business tasks (see step 4) that are responsible for delivering the components (e.g., with the biggest difference) and decide for the appropriate actions. Any changes or initiatives that may propose, that possibly alter the performance of tasks or change the service design, can be fed back to the service FCM and simulate the expected results.

Figure 3 shows a FCM that represents the components of the loan service in a bank. The numbers on the arrows represent the importance of each component. Note that some components may affect the importance of other components. The presence of each component is not shown in order to improve the readability of the Figure.

Figure 3. The FCM of perceived service quality

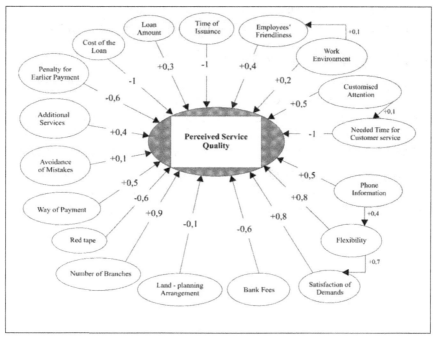

Figure 4. Loan management process

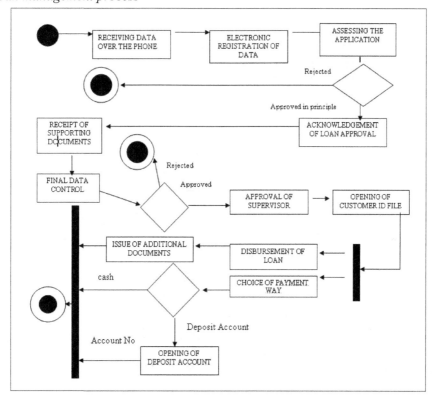

Both service vectors and customer expectation vectors are represented in terms of the concepts that appear in the FCM.

Step 4: Identifying the Business Task(s) That Delivers a Service Component

Each component is supported by one or more tasks in the "loan management" process. The business **process model** is shown in the following UML activity diagram.

Since process tasks are supporting service components, each task's performance is expressed and modelled in terms of service quality issues.

Therefore, the time that it takes to register the data electronically increases by "little" (+0.1) the time of issue of the loan, which in turn affects service quality.

Step 5: Identify MC Opportunities

Customer expectations are compared with the level of a service quality, by calculating the distance between the two vectors. If the service does not meet customer expectations, this is attributed to either a lower level of satisfaction of a component or the non-existence of a required component in the service. Therefore, the oppor-

Figure 5. The FCM of the task "electronic registration of data", of the process for issuing personal loans

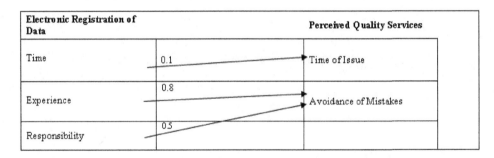

Figure 6. The FCM of the task "assessing the application", of the process of issuing personal loans

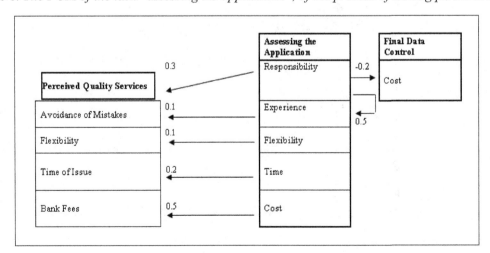

tunity for customising a service lies in the challenge to introduce components that are currently omitted from the service or improve components whose contribution is not at the required level. Given that the components importance (i) is not subject to changes, the actual contribution (q) of a component may be improved by changing its presence (p) in the service, that is, increasing or decreasing it, depending on the nature of the component and the required changes.

All vectors, that is, customer expectations, service quality, and distance between the two, are implemented as arrays. Therefore, if a service that consists of three components, for example, is $S(i)=[0.2, 0.8, 0.3]$ and expectations of customer (m) are $CE(m)=[0.8, 0.5, 0.6]$, then the Distance is $[0.6, -0.3, 0.3]$. The distance shows that component's C_1 actual contribution needs to increase by 0.6 that of component's C_2 to decrease by 0.3 and the contribution of component C_3 to increase by 0.3.

All service concepts and tasks performance issues (which are directly associated with service components) are interrelated. These interrelationships are implemented as a matrix (***service-task matrix***), which has columns and rows for all service concepts and tasks performance measures. The following table show what the matrix would look like.

The numbers in the first row of Table 3 show how each component affects or is affected by other components and task performance. The values are in the interval [-1, 1]. The multiplication of the *distance vector* and the above matrix indicates which tasks in which process(es) should change and in what direction (+ or –) in order to satisfy the requirements of the customers that are represented in the distance vector.

Therefore, the opportunities of service customisation are identified in terms of service components changes and processes tasks that are responsible for implementing the required changes.

The same approach works if the models are expanded to capture resources dependencies and characteristics such as cost, suitability, compatibility, availability, and so forth. In such a case, the proposed approach can be expanded in order to be able to suggest alternative service components. The development of a new component pertains into the area of new product development (NPD) and does not fall within the scope of this chapter. Such an attempt requires deeper knowledge that refers, among others, to the investigation and modelling of the resources which a new component needs, the business tasks' configuration in order to support its development, market trends, and the anticipated impact on the service quality from a customer's perspective.

However, at the current state of development, the models can suggest service variants to the customer. This can be achieved by offering the customer existing service components, which

Table 3. The service-task matrix that integrates service and tasks performance

	C_1	$C_2...C_n$	Task performance in terms of C_1	Task performance in terms of C_2	Task performance in terms of C_n
C_1	0	0.5	0.7	-0.4	0.8
$C_2, ..., C_n$					
Task performance in terms of C_1					
Task performance in terms of C_2					
Task performance in terms of C_n					

may have not been originally in the customer's priorities list, but according to the service FCM can possibly improve the perceived service quality. The multiplication of the *distance vector* and the *service-task matrix* shown in Table 3 produces such alternative service variants, for it shows how each component affects or is affected by other components, regardless to whether components are parts of the same service. Therefore, in order to improve the service quality, the service designers may consider adding to the service package existing components which were not on offer before.

Design Issues of an Intelligent Advisory System Based on the Proposed Approach

A system is designed as an intelligent *advisory* **system** which supports the decision-making process during service customisation and process modelling, rather than making the actual decision and recommending a solution through a prescribed computational approach. Therefore, it assists de-

cision-makers to gain a deeper understanding of their objectives and to consider the alternatives, but it refrains from choosing specific plans and strategies for customisation.

The components of the system are the following:

- **Fuzzy model designer (FMD):** This component assists in customising FCMs, that is, allows service designers to specify the weights on each relationship, and add or eliminate relationships according to the particular environment. FMD also allows planners to modify the structure of the model by, for example, adding or modifying variables. After changes in the FCMs, this component checks against the consistency of the model, for example, that variables should be connected to at least another one.

- **Scenarios developer (SDe):** This component allows service designers to specify their assumptions with regard to changes (positive or negative) of variables in FCMs. Scenarios

Figure 7. The architecture of an advisory system for customisation

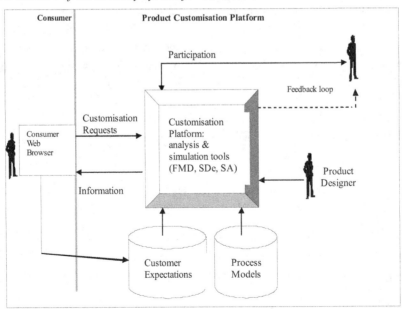

can, therefore, be developed in terms of increases or decreases of customer expectations or business processes performance issues. The results of the scenarios analysis can be used for designing or calibrating services.

- **Simulation and analysis (SA):** This component provides for the implementation of the reasoning and the analysis of the FCMs, that is, the propagation of the changes through the causal paths of the FCMs. Given the causal structure of a FCM and drawing on the scenarios which are developed during the service design and customisation, the functionality of this module provides the answers to the following queries:
  - What are the alternative ways to achieve a certain objective with regard to service quality improvement?
  - Which one of the alternatives enjoys the highest degree of belief among the designers or customers?
  - What will be the effect of the change (i.e., increase or decrease of certain variables) on business processes or service quality?

The following figure shows the major components of the advisory system.

FUTURE TRENDS

The proposed approach opens up new opportunities for research in services of MC. The intangible nature of services can be represented using fuzzy logic technologies. Lack of service models in contrast to manufacturing products where products models have long ago been developed. More research could focus in incorporating concepts from service management into fuzzy models. Moreover, the resources dependencies theory (Clemons & Row, 1991) is promising in investigat-

ing the resources necessary for the development of services.

Another direction for future research may be towards the investigation and modelling of MC principles and guidelines that would improve knowledge on service development. Finally, the development and use of MC metrics is an important research task, one that changes the way that MC is modelled and managed. Such a set of metrics could include the definition and measurement of concepts such as "compatibility", "reusability", "suitability", and so forth.

CONCLUSION

Despite the fact that service management is a top priority for researchers and practitioners, the MC of services has not been addressed yet. Service industries drive economies in the developed world, while an increasingly larger percentage of national wealth is attributed to services. MC principles can be applied to develop innovative strategies for businesses and produce new services. However, more research needs to be done in this area. This chapter discusses an approach that draws on fuzzy logic and service quality and management issues in order to develop models that can identify opportunities for service improvements and MC.

Benefits of the Approach

The proposed framework enables the service designers to consider the complex interactions between services, business processes, and customer-perceived quality. The innovation of the approach lies on its flexibility that it provides for the catering of different customer views and types of services. It can model individual perspectives of service quality and translate them into service design options. The flexibility which it exhibits, allows also for its models customisation in order to adequately represent the characteristics of a certain organisation, as well as to accommodate the most recent developments in its environment.

Moreover, it draws on fuzzy logic theory in order to manipulate qualitative concepts and measurement that are necessary in order to handle the subjectivity in service quality perceptions. The service designers and the customers may communicate in a commonly-understandable language with all technical terms hidden. This is expected to increase the applicability of the approach and its suitability to deal with complex problems such as that of service customisation.

In addition, the proposed approach allows for conflicting assumptions and biases to be realised, simulated, and resolved, through the development of scenarios during the service design process management. It introduces computational modelling to service customisation, which allows designers to cope with the complexity of the issue, to consider additional factors such as the belief among designers and customers with regard to the truth of a relationship, and so forth.

The proposed approach then takes a step further by translating the necessary service improvements into tasks and processes changes. Such changes may take the form of tasks or resources combinations in order to produce the required components in a service or to ensure the required level of presence of the particular component in a service. The authors believe that the proposed approach can be useful to both researchers and practitioners.

REFERENCES

Alford, D., Sackett, P., & Nelder, G. (2000). Mass customisation – An automotive perspective. *International Journal of Production Economics, 65*(1), 99-110.

Ardissono, L., Felfernig, A., Friedrich, G., Goy, A., Jannach, D., Petrone, G., Schafer, R., & Zanker, M. (2003). A framework for the development of personalized, distributed Web-based configuration systems. *AI Magazine, 24*(3), 93-110.

Ardissono, L., Goy, A., Petrone, G., & Segnan, M. (2002). The adaptive Web: Personalization in business-to-customer interaction. *Communications of the ACM, Special Issue "The Adaptive Web", 45*(5), 52-53.

Axelrod, R. (1976). *Structure of decision: The cognitive maps of political elites*. Princeton, NJ: Princeton University Press.

Boynton, A. C., Victor, B., & Pine II, B. J. (1993). New competitive strategies: Challenges to organisations and IT. *IBM Systems Journal, 32*(1), 40-64.

Brown, S., & Bessant, J. (2003). The manufacturing strategy-capabilities links in mass customisation and agile manufacturing - An exploratory study. *International Journal of Operations and Production Managament, 23*(7), 707-730.

Clemons, E. K., & Row, M. C. (1991). Sustaining IT advantage: The role of structural differences, *MIS Quarterly*, (September).

Davis, S. M. (1987). *Future perfect*. Reading, MA: Addison-Wesley.

Felfernig, A., Friedrich, G., & Jannach, D. (2001). Conceptual modelling for configuration of mass-customisable products. *Artificial Intelligence in Engineering, 15*(2), 165-176.

Forza, C., & Salvador, F. (2002). Product configuration and inter-firm co-ordination: An innovative solution from a small manufacturing enterprise. *Computers in Industry, 49*(1), 37-46.

Fulkerson, B. (1997). A response to dynamic change in the market place. *Decision Support Systems, 21*(3), 199-214.

Georgakopoulos, D., Hornick, M., & Sheth, A. (1995). An overview of workflow management: From process modelling to workflow automation infrastructure. *Distributed and Parallel Databases, 3*(2), 119-153.

Gilmore, J. H., & Pine II, B. J. (1997). The four faces of mass customisation. *Harvard Business Review, 75*(1), 91-101.

Glorfeld, L. W. (1996). A methodology for simplification and interpretation of back propagation-based neural network models. *Expert Systems with Applications, 10*(1), 37-54.

Gounaris, S. P., Stathakopoulos, V., & Athanassopoulos, A. D. (2003). Antecedents to perceived service quality: An exploratory study in the banking industry. *International Journal of Bank Marketing, 21*(4), 168-190.

Gronroos, C. (1994). From scientific management to service management. *International Journal of Service Industry Management, 5*(1), 5-20.

Gronroos, C. (2000). *Service management and marketing: A customer relationship management approach* (2nd ed.). Chichester, UK: John Wiley & Sons.

Hart, C. W. L. (1994). Mass customisation conceptual underpinnings, opportunities and limits. *International Journal of Service Industry Management, 6*(2), 36-45.

Hirschhorn, L., Noble, P., & Rnkin, T. (2001). Sociotechnical systems in the age of mass customisation. *Journal of Engineering and Technology Management, 18*(3-4), 241-252.

Jun, M., & Cai, S. (2001). The key determinants of Internet banking service quality: A content analysis. *International Journal of Bank Marketing, 19*(7), 276-291.

Kardaras, D., & Karakostas, V. (1999). The use of fuzzy cognitive maps to simulate the information systems strategic planning process. *Information and Software Technology, 41*(4), 197-210.

Kardaras, D., Karakostas, V., & Papathanassiou, E. (2000). Facilitating the mass customisation of services with a fuzzy object-oriented modelling approach. In *Proceedings of the 31st Annual Meeting: International Conference of the Decision Sciences Institute,* Florida (pp. 680-682).

Kosko, B. (1986). Fuzzy cognitive maps. *International Journal on Man-Machine Studies, 24,* 65-75.

Lassar, W. M., Manolis, C., & Winsor, R. D. (2000). Service quality perspectives and satisfaction in private banking. *International Journal of Bank Marketing, 18*(4), 244-271.

Lee, S., Kim, B. G., & Lee, K. (2004). Fuzzy cognitive map-based approach to evaluate EDI performance: A test of causal model. *Expert Systems with Applications, 27*(2), 287-299.

Parker, M (1996). *Strategic transformation and information technology: Paradigms for perfoming while transforming.* Prentice Hall.

Pine, B. J., & Gilmore, J. H. (1999). *The experience economy.* Boston: Harvard Business School Press.

Pine II, B. J., Victor, B., & Boynton, A. C. (1993). Making mass customisation work. *Harvard Business Review, 71*(5), 108-119.

Radder, L., & Louw, L. (2000). The readiness of selected South African organisations to mass customisation. *The TQM Magazine, 12*(4), 295-304.

Ramaswamy, R. (1996). *Design and management of service processes.* Addison-Wesley Publishing Company.

Schneider, M., Scnaider, E., Kandel, A., & Chew, G. (1998). Automatic construction of FCMs. *Fuzzy Sets and Systems, 93*(2), 161-172.

Taber, R. (1991). Knowledge processing with fuzzy cognitive maps. *Expert Systems with Applications, 12*(2), 83-87.

Tanaka, K. (1997). *An introduction to fuzzy logic for practical applications.* Springer Verlag.

Tseng, M., & Jiao, J. (1997). Case-based evolutionary design form mass customisation. In *Proceedings of the 21st International Conference on Computer and Industrial Engineering: Vol. 33*(1-2), 319-323.

Tut, M., & Edmond, D. (2002). The use of patterns in service composition. In *Proceedings of the Workshop on Web Services, e-Business, and the Semantic Web, held in conjunction with CAiSE02, Toronto, Canada, Lecture Notes in Computer Science, 2512* (pp. 27-28). Springer Verlag.

Walker, R.H., Craig-Lees,M., Hecker, R., & Francis, H. (2002). Technology-enabled service delivery: An investigation of the reasons affecting customer adoption and rejection. International *Journal of Service Industry Management, 13*(1), 91-106.

Wang, M. (2003). Assessment of e-service quality via e-satisfaction in e-commerce globalization. *The Electronic Journal on Information Systems in Developing Countries, 11*(10), 1-4.

Wastell, D. G., White, P., & Kawalek, P. (1994). A methodology for business process redesign: Experiences and issues. *Journal of Strategic Information Systems, 3*(1), 23-40.

Yu, E., & Mylopoulos, J. (1995). From E-R to A-R - Modelling strategic actor relationships for business process re-engineering. *International Journal of Cooperative Information Systems, 4*(2 & 3), 125-144.

Zadeh, L. A. (1973). Outline of a new approach to the analysis of complex systems and decision processes. *IEEE Transactions on Systems, Man, and Cybernetics, SMC-3*(1), 28-44.

Zhang, W. R., Chen, S. S., & Bezdek, J. C. (1989). Pool2: A generic system for cognitive map development and decision analysis. *IEEE Transactions on Systems, Man, and Cybernetics, 19*(1), 31-39.

Chapter XIII
Applying Service CAD System to Value Customization

Tomohiko Sakao
Darmstadt University of Technology, Germany and The University of Tokyo, Japan

Yoshiki Shimomura
Tokyo Metropolitan University and the University of Tokyo, Japan

Alberto Simboli
University "G.d'Annunzio", Italy

Andrea Raggi
University "G.d'Annunzio", Italy

Luigia Petti
University "G.d'Annunzio", Italy

Giuseppina Pagliuca
University "G.d'Annunzio", Italy

ABSTRACT

This chapter introduces a new concept, value customization, to increase the level of customer satisfaction. It presents methodologies and practice for designers to customize value in a service in industrial operation based on the discipline of service engineering (SE). SE aims at creating more value largely by knowledge and service contents rather than just materialistic contents. Especially, an information system named Service Explorer, an implementation of the methodologies, is applied to an Italian accommodation industry. After the application, five redesign options such as introducing a new service system with cash-back and a system of renting various goods were generated. Through this, the effectiveness of SE for value customization is suggested. This chapter addresses the importance of identifying value to be provided with specific customers based on their particular requirements, which has only briefly been discussed in researches of mass customization. In addition, both service activities and physical products can be crucial to realize value. Several further research issues such as general design methods for value customization were also identified.

INTRODUCTION

Mass customization (MC) is based on increasing differentiation levels of products and services depending on customers' needs, while reducing production costs and keeping levels of customer relationships (Pine, 1993; Tseng & Jiao, 2001; Tseng & Piller, 2003). To do so, MC incorporates partial variation on physical products and, in some cases, service activities employing the mass production technologies. On the contrary, a topic which is rarely discussed is what kind of value should be provided with specific customers based on their particular requirements. This should be regarded as an important question to be answered during design activities. It is the subject of this chapter. This subject has become more important according to the new circumstances which manufacturers have been facing recently (Sakao, Shimomura, Comstock, & Sundin, 2005c): One of these circumstances is the servicification of consumers' behaviors (Japanese Ministry—PMHAPT, 2002). This forces manufacturers to focus more on what services are really needed by customers rather than on what are provided physically. The other circumstance is the increasing seriousness of environmental problems (OECD, 2001) resulting from the mass production. This has raised for industry the necessity of dematerialization, which requires satisfying customers through limited resource consumption.

The authors define the problem as how an enterprise should design provided *service*. Service engineering (SE) (Arai & Shimomura, 2004, 2005; Sakao & Shimomura, 2004; Tomiyama, 2001), which aims at creating more value largely by knowledge and service contents rather than just materialistic value, will provide the basis. SE and MC have a common goal, customer-dependent satisfaction, while their approaches are different (Sakao et al., 2005c): Most of the MC technologies depend on designing properties of physical products, through an intermediate method lying somewhere between mass and customized produc-

tion, while SE pursues optimization of the value provided with customers. The technique of SE is innovative as most existing MC research has not tackled customization on the abstract level of value (Sakao et al., 2005c).

This chapter aims at presenting methodologies and practice for designers to customize value provided by a set of service activities and physical products based on the discipline of SE. Especially, an information system named Service Explorer, an implementation of the methodologies, will be applied to this purpose. Namely, how to increase the level of customer-dependent satisfaction with multiple stakeholders with support of the discipline of SE is presented through an application to an instance of service in industrial operation. Several further research issues are also identified.

The contents of this chapter begin with the background, including the methodologies of SE and the presented information system named Service Explorer. Then it describes the application of Service Explorer to value customization in an industry and some future research topics. These are followed by conclusions.

BACKGROUND

Importance of Service

It goes without saying that in the tertiary industry service activities are the source of core value and are regarded crucial. This paragraph describes a recent situation in the secondary industry. Manufacturers today encounter quietly but steadily growing trends. One is the servicification of consumers' behaviors, which means a shift from customers' consumption of physical products to their consumption of softer or solution-based services. Especially, this trend can be observed in statistics of the expenditure in a household with more than one person in Japan (Japanese Ministry—PMHAPT, 2002). If this is classified into the expenditure for "goods" and that for "services," the latter is steadily growing and accounts for 42% in the year 2002, while it accounted for just 36% in the year 1987. The other trend is environmental problems, which have been quite serious in some areas over a couple of decades. For instance, as for the global warming problem, which is one of the most seriously recognized ones, the annual average temperature on the earth has risen considerably (IPCC, 2001). As regards the waste generation problem, it is predicted that the volume of municipal wastes in OECD countries in the year 2020 will be more than double of that in 1980 (OECD, 2001). According to such trends, the current manufacturing paradigm, which produces mass products and mass wastes, seems unsustainable.

Motivated partially by the above-mentioned trends, industries have been increasingly focusing on services. As a result, new concepts such as product-service systems (PSS) (Goedkoop, van Halen, te Riele, & Rommens, 1999; McAloone & Andreason, 2004; Tischner, Verkuijl, & Tukker, 2002; Tukker, 2004), functional sales (Lindahl & Ölundh, 2001; Sundin, Lindahl, Shimomura, & Sakao, 2005), and functional products (Alonso-Rasgado, Thompson, & Elfstrom, 2004) have been developed so far. PSS can be defined as consisting of "tangible products and intangible services designed and combined so that they jointly are capable of fulfilling specific customer needs" (Tischner et al., 2002). The business concept of functional sales can be defined as "... to offer a functional solution that fulfils a defined customer need. The focus is, with reference to the customer value, to optimize the functional solution from a life-cycle perspective. The functional solution can consist of combinations of systems, physical products and services" (modified from Lindahl & Ölundh, 2001). Functional products, also known as "total care products" are products that comprise combinations of "hard" and "soft" elements (Alonso-Rasgado et al., 2004). In common to these three concepts, a service is trying to be incorporated into the design space, which has traditionally been dominated by physical products in manufacturing industries.

Need of Customization

In a competitive market, customization has been a promising strategy for enterprises to attract their customers (Bullinger, Wagner, Kürümlüoglu, & Bröcker, 2003; McLaughlin, 1996). Actually, the concept of mass customization (MC) (Pine, 1993; Tseng & Jiao, 2001; Tseng & Piller, 2003), which is defined, for instance, as "design and manufacture of customized products at mass production efficiency and speed" (Anderson, 1997), is already widespread.

Furthermore, Pine clarifies in what kind of cases an industry is moving towards higher levels of variety and customization by introducing a concept of *market turbulence* (Pine, 1993). He argues that an inner product of degrees of turbulence of the factors and their importance ratings yields an indicator for when to shift to MC.

Customization of Products and Services

There have been numerous theories and practices of MC presented throughout the years, but there has often been a focus on the customization of properties of physical products (Pine, 1993; Tseng & Jiao, 2001; Tseng & Piller, 2003). A relatively smaller number of researches have tackled so far the issue of customizing services. Jiao, Ma, and Tseng (2003) have proposed a strategy called design for MC (DFMC) which considers both product and service, namely a wider design space than normally targeted. In DFMC, they propose product family architecture (PFA) as a kernel as well as a process for developing service in a service delivery systems design. Cao, Wang, Law, Zhang, and Li (in press) have proposed a model and computer software for customizing services focusing on the interactiveness between customers and a company.

IT Systems for Customization

There are quite a few IT systems applicable for MC. A book by Blecker, Friedrich, Kaluza, Abdelkafi, and Kreutler (2005) discusses IT systems for MC focusing on a theory of product customization. They argue the importance of identifying customer requirements and so forth, and then explain development of IT systems, which deal with product configuration, an issue of complexity, and so forth. Frutos and Borenstein (2004) have proposed a framework of an IT system environment to support the interaction between customers and companies in customizing products or services. Kim and Gil (2004) have proposed a framework for composition of services applicable to Semantic Web services. A system called Service Explorer has been developed mainly for supporting service design (Arai & Shimomura, 2004, 2005; Hara, Shimomura, Uchida, & Sakao, 2004; Sakao & Shimomura, 2004) with a potential for the help of customization. This is explained in detail in the next section.

Service Explorer

Overview

A prototype system of a computer-aided design tool for service design, which is called Service Explorer, has been developed. Designers can describe services, and register them in a database, reload them, evaluate them, as well as design services from scratch using guidance functionality. This has a potential as a tool to support value customization. The aspect of information system, namely the theme of the whole book, is focused here, so that the model building is explained in relatively more detail.

Fundamentals of Service Engineering

A service is defined as an activity that a provider causes, usually with consideration, a receiver to change from an existing state to a new state that the receiver desires, where both contents and a channel are means to realize the service (Shimomura & Tomiyama, 2002; Tomiyama, 2001) (see Figure 1). Service contents are provided by a service provider and delivered through a service channel. Physical products are either the service contents or the service channel. Thus, selling physical products is also regarded here as a service. Hence, a service receiver is satisfied with just contents, which are any of material, energy, and information. A service channel is used to transfer, amplify, and control the service contents.

In this definition, artifacts can be either contents or channels. Artifacts have their own functions, behaviors, and states, and therefore they can be designed with conventional CAD (computer-aided design) systems. Hence, a methodology similar to conventional design will be introduced to the design of services.

The term "service" has been defined; however, what is service engineering (SE)? It is a discipline to increase the value of artifacts and to decrease the load on the environment by focusing on service. Note that SE has both analytical and synthetic aspects. SE aims at intensifying, improving, and automating this whole framework of service creation, service delivery, and service consumption. To increase the total satisfaction of receivers, we can improve the functions and/or the quality of both channels and contents. Traditionally, engineering design has aimed to improve only functions. A better function of a new product, we have believed, makes consumers satisfied. In SE, however, not only the functions of artifacts but also the meaning of contents must be matched to the specifications given by receivers. Then the satisfaction level of receivers increases.

Figure 1. The elements of service

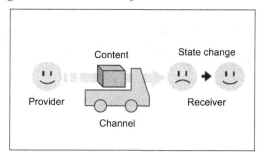

Figure 1. The elements of service

Modeling Methodology

The Outline of a Service Model

A service model consists of several sub-models: "flow model", "scope model", "view model", and "scenario model". The rest of this paragraph explains the four sub-models according to the literature (Arai & Shimomura, 2004; Shimomura & Tomiyama, 2002) with more focus on the latter two after describing an important concept in those sub-models called "receiver state parameter".

The reason for modeling "receiver state parameter" is as follows. Conventional design regards mainly the performance of physical products; it does not consider the state change of the receiver. Designing a service must be based on the degree of satisfaction with the state change of a receiver. Therefore, it is necessary to express receiver's state changes.

Receiver State Parameter

Receiver state parameters (RSPs) are classified into value and cost, depending on whether the customers like them or not. The term "value" here is different from that in Value Engineering (Miles, 1971), where it is defined as function over economic cost. In SE, value is defined as change of a receiver's state that he/she prefers, so that function is just a realization method to provide the value in SE.

Change of a receiver is represented by a set of receiver state parameters (RSPs). Since an RSP

consists of quantitative value, including Boolean logic and multi-value logic, we can compute any comparison between two RSPs. In addition, we introduced a new assumption that all RSPs are observable and controllable. This assumption has been unproven with human receivers because we have not had a reliable method to measure the consumer behavior.

RSPs change by received contents. Hence, we assume that contents consist of various functions, whose name is function name (FN), whose operating objects are function parameters (FPs), and whose effect is represented by function influences (FIs).

As the receiver's states may change with respect to supply of contents, RSPs can be written as functions of contents. Parameters expressing contents are called content parameters (CoPs). In the same way, the parameters of channel, which make the flow of CoPs change and thus influence RSPs indirectly, are called channel parameters (ChPs). Hence, we assume that both contents and channels consist of various functions, and both CoPs and ChPs belong to FPs.

These parameters create a network with one another. We studied several examples and chose different sets of parameters; some of the examples are from daily life such as restaurant operations, travel bureaus, and laundry services. Other studies are in manufacturing sectors with products such as disposable cameras, copiers, and elevators. The details are not discussed, but we need to point out that the selection of contents within various parameters is subjective; this seems the greatest reason that services have not been dealt with sufficiently as engineering issues have been.

Flow Model

One of the traditional and typical services is a travel bureau, which arranges and purchases various tickets on behalf of customers. Contents are different from one ticket to another, even if all the tickets are delivered to the customers. In this way, services can be delivered through complex multiple structures consisting of various go-betweens. The intermediate agents have double characteristics of a receiver and a provider, which is represented by a symbol of a smiling circle "intermediate agent".

When we focus on the relationship between a

receiver and a provider, many intermediate agents exist among them. We call the sequential chain of agents "a flow model" of a service (see the upper half of Figure 2, which takes an example from a cafe service). This model is needed because in SE, designers are supposed to consider how organizations participating in a concerned service can be successful in their business.

Scope Model

Practical services have complicated structures of intermediate agents, connected to one another on an almost infinite chain. Therefore, it is necessary to specify the effective range of the service from an initial provider to a final receiver. In comparison to the view model in which a single RSP is expressed, the scope model deals with all the RSPs within the provider and the receiver (see the lower half of Figure 2). In other words, a scope model handles multiple view models,

Figure 2. The relation among three sub-models: flow model, scope model, and view model

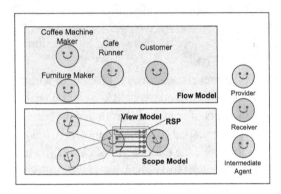

Figure 3. A simple example of a view model

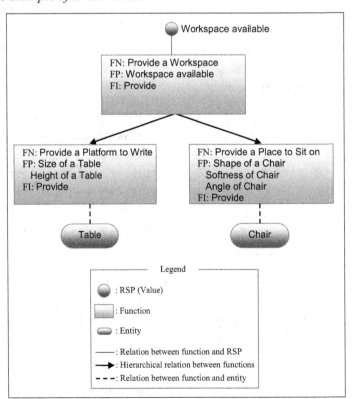

namely multiple RSPs. Thus, it helps designers to understand the activities between the provider and the receiver.

View Model

A view model expresses the relationships among the elements of the service; that is, the mutual relationships among the RSPs and FPs (CoPs and ChPs). It should be emphasized that not only products but also services are represented by CoPs and ChPs. Figure 3 depicts a simple example taken from a coffee shop service for the customers working there and drinking coffee. RSPs change according to how the receiver evaluates subjectively the received contents. An RSP is linked to several CoPs because the receiver evaluates the contents. The CoPs may be supported by several ChPs existing in the chain of several agents in the flow model.

The view model illustrates visually the relationships among the parameters (RSP, ChP, and CoP) in the graph of connected nodes. Thus, it helps designers with customizing value and costs in the form of RSPs by changing the corresponding realization structures represented in the form of FPs.

Physical structures are represented using function parameters. It should be emphasized that a view model works as a bridge between values represented in the form of RSP and physical structures.

Scenario Model

Last but not least, the scenario model is explained. This model represents receivers themselves and their behaviors in receiving the service. This is necessary because the grounds behind RSPs of service receivers should be understood. In other words, the scenario model serves as a direct source for producing a variety of RSP sets depending on customers' properties. Therefore, this will be a key element for understanding customers' needs and wants.

A scenario model represents two kinds of information: One is a behavior of a receiver, while the other is a property of the receiver. The former is described as a transition graph whose node represents a state of a receiver and whose arc refers to a transition between two states (either temporal or causal). A state is described as a set of parameters with their values. The parameters are classified into two types: internal ones for the states inside a receiver, and external ones for those outside. For instance, in a clothes-cleaning service, an amount of dirt on clothes to be cleaned off is a kind of external parameter, while coziness of the receiver is internal. Furthermore, those parameters have a hierarchical relation among themselves from end to means. By using this transition graph, the receiver's final goals and their activities can be described. RSPs are a partial set of parameters of a state selected by designers.

The latter is represented by an application of the concept called *persona* (Cooper, 1999). Persona is an imaginary target user and is frequently used in practical design of software interfaces. The information to identify persona is classified into two types: One is demographic data, such as age, gender, and professional carrier, while the other is psychological data, such as personality and lifestyle. The data for persona are given by objective information, for example, statistical data and results from marketing activities. It is important to determine the properties of persona concretely and accurately, rather than abstractly and correctly, since this can prevent the target customers from varying from one form to another during the whole design process. The psychological data are necessary because they let designers recognize the target customer like a real living person.

Design Methodology

The authors have already developed a generic method for service design that adopts the explained model of service, and have verified it through application to industrial cases (Lindahl et al., 2005; Sakao & Shimomura, 2004). Designers are able to design the target service efficiently by following this method.

Required Functionalities

This paragraph describes the required functionalities of Service Explorer.

a. **Model building:** It is necessary that Service Explorer has the following five types of functionality. Required specifications and implemented ones in detail are as follows:

1. **To input and edit a service model:** This is the most fundamental functionality of Service Explorer. In order to acquire the knowledge of service cases for service design in service CAD efficiently, it is necessary to provide the interface to describe a service model with ease. To do so, Service Explorer has a graphical user interface. In addition, a service model is described as a graph structure constituted by nodes and arcs.

2. **To display the component elements that designers focus on:** It is effective to be able to display (or not to display) the component elements selectively, depending on designers' demands, so that they can understand the structure of the service efficiently. To do so, Service Explorer provides the function to display (or not to display) the function topology and the parameter structure.

3. **To register service models in a service database:** On building a service database, it is desirable that the service database can store service models independently of the specific OS/application. For the sake of this, on Service Explorer, XML is adopted as a database description language. Herewith, input and edited service models are stored into a service database after being converted into XML data.

4. **To search the service database:** To support service design by using knowledge of existing service cases, it is necessary to be able to search the service database depending on designers' requests. On the current Service Explorer, designers can search the service database for service models with keywords contained in the composition elements (RSP, FN, FP, FI, and Entity).

5. **To reuse the service model data stored in the service database:** This is the function to reuse the elements or the structure of a service model stored in the service database, when designers input and edit a service model.

b. **Design guidance:** Service Explorer should be able to guide designers based on the design methodology mentioned previously.

c. **Reasoning:** Several types of reasoning engines shall be stored. This functionality is crucial from the viewpoint of information system, because designers can take good advantage of a computing power. One of the promising reasoning engines is abduction (Coyne, 1998; Roozenburg & Eekels, 1995). The authors' research group has already constructed a generic computer system employing abduction named Universal Abduction Studio (UAS) (Takeda, Sakai, Nomaguchi, Yoshioka, Shimomura, & Tomiyama, 2003). By having this reasoning module plugged in, Service Explorer will be able to help designers with creative design using knowledge in different business fields.

Prototype

Based on the above-mentioned functional specifications, the authors have been developing Service Explorer with Java SDK 1.4.1 and XML version 1.0. MVC (Model View Controller) model (Krasner & Stephen, 1988), which has been used widely in general GUI applications, was adopted as basic architecture of Service Explorer. By applying the MVC model, high flexibility and reusability of Service Explorer and robustness of the service model data are realized. Figure 4 depicts the system configuration of Service Explorer. The current version of Service Explorer was developed using Java (Java2 SDK, Standard Edition 1.4.1) and XML version 1.0 in the Microsoft Windows XP Home Edition environment.

Designers can build service models on Service Explorer following a guidance based on the methodology explained using some databases of Service Explorer. Namely, they construct flow models, scope models, view models, and sce-

nario models. This guiding functionality itself is implemented as a sub-module named "service design organizer" in Service Explorer (Figure 4). "Service Evaluator" is employed in the evaluation process (Sakao, Watanabe, & Shimomura, 2003). A reasoning engine for abduction will be stored in the near future as shown in the right-hand side of Figure 4.

Through this chapter, four screen shots of the prototype will be shown. One displays the widest coverage on the models. It shows a flow model with scope models, an action chain of a target receiver, and RSPs in an action. An example is shown later in Figure 7. Multiple scope models which represent provision/receipt relationships between them are shown there. The second one is for editing a persona for a target receiver. An instance of this is shown in Figure 8, which appears later, too. Figures 7 and 8 are taken from a case concerning the design of a hotel service. The third one is for extracting RSPs from an action chain. See an example of this in Figure 5. The upper half is for

Figure 4. Conceptual structure of Service Explorer

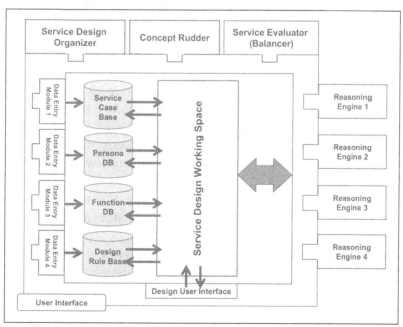

Figure 5. A screenshot of extracting RSPs for a persona

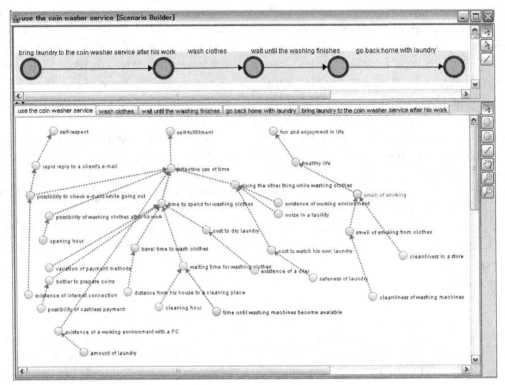

describing a chain of actions, corresponding to the lower middle part of Figure 7, while the lower one visualizes a hierarchy among the parameters. This is taken from a laundry service. The last one is for deploying RSPs further to obtain functions on a view model, as seen in Figure 10. Figure 10 is also an example from the hotel case.

APPLYING SERVICE EXPLORER TO VALUE CUSTOMIZATION IN INDUSTRY

Existing Problems

There are a number of theories and practices of MC and information systems for MC as reviewed previously. Nevertheless, the following three problems have not been solved well so far in the field of customization in industries.

1. What kind of value should be provided according to customer categories has only briefly been discussed.

   MC largely deals with partial variation on physical products employing the mass production technologies. Furthermore, in many cases of MC methods, physical products in some form are assumed to be adopted before design activities begin. However, this should be conducted only after the provided value is somehow defined. In most of the MC literature, the reason why customization is required for the design target is missing. What should be provided depending on customers has not been sufficiently discussed.

2. How to deal with both products and services in customization is poorly available.

   While products are discussed relatively more as a target of MC, fewer cases of service customization are found. In addition, in cases of service, they deal with services in a narrow sense (Cao et al., in press). In other words, their space of design is limited to service activities, although it is in principle more beneficial to include products and facilities associated with the services. In addition, Jiao et al. (2003) succeeded in targeting both products and services by DFMC; however, they do not discuss preparing a variety of different services depending on customer categories.

3. No existing information system has been applied to support design activities to answer the two questions above.

    Almost no information system in the field of customization in industries has so far succeeded in supporting design activities to determine what value is provided and how products and services are adopted to do so. It is taken for granted that an information management system is effective for achieving MC. However, supporting the activities of designing provided value is crucial for MC as well. Hence, a system to facilitate designers optimizing value as well as to manage the related information is necessary. Such information consists of required value specific to a customer category, the realization structures for the value, and the relations with other stakeholders. It should be noted that design support system, in this case, does not refer to a system for interactive design in which customers participate as well (Cao et al., in press; Kim & Gil, 2004).

On the contrary, Service Explorer has a potential as a tool to help designers with customizing value as implied in the previous section. The rest of this chapter describes application of Service Explorer to customizing value in service provided in an Italian hospitality industry.

Practice of Service Explorer for Value Customization

The Target of Service Design

As a target of service design with the methods and tool presented previously, redesigning a hotel service in the Abruzzo region of Italy was selected (Sakao, Shimomura, Petti, & Raggi, 2005d). This hotel has three-star certification, and is characterized by various efforts to reduce environmental impacts. The hotel management, indeed, regards the environmental consciousness as a sales point to its guests, and wants to reduce the environmental impact and develop a new attractive service for the guests (Watanabe, Shimomura, Sakao, Raggi, & Petti, 2004).

Investigation of the Current Service

For the sake of redesign of the hotel service, the authors carried out an on-site customer survey about guests' requirements, namely value and costs for the guests, through delivering questionnaires. Those questionnaires were collected in the spring of 2004, and the summer of 2005. During the time spans, 189 filled-in questionnaires were collected. The questionnaire, which was prepared by the authors, included a list of 38 requirements about the hotel accommodation and required hotel guests to rate them, on a scale from 1 to 10, on the basis of the importance level attributed to each requirement (1 meaning not important at all, 10 meaning very important). Such scores correspond to RSP weighting. At the end of the questionnaire, hotel guests were required to anonymously provide some additional information about their stay at the hotel (period and reason for the stay) and about their personal condition (gender, age, profession, and residence). In addition, the authors investigated the actual hotel service by interviewing the employees and the hotel owner (Watanabe et al., 2004).

The results include classification of customers into twelve (12) categories according to their trip purposes (business or others), ages (younger, middle, or elder), and genders (female or male). For each customer category, an average weighting for each RSP was calculated. Among them, Table 1 shows partially the average weightings for eleven (11) RSPs for five categories. Each RSP has its own ID from 1 to 11, and each weighting is denoted as L (low), M (middle), or H (high), depending on its numerical size. It should be noted that the L-M-H classification was in relative terms, not in absolute ones such as L for 1 to 3. It should be also mentioned that those range thresholds for age and RSP scores were subjectively selected. RSPs with italic characters refer to environmentally-related issues, though this information was not shown explicitly to the answerers.

For each RSP, frequencies of weighting were calculated. It is worth noticing that, even if the average values are more or less the same, some RSPs show completely different score distributions from others. For most RSPs, there appears to be a high concentration of scores in a higher

Table 1. Customer categories' weightings on RSPs in the hotel service

ID	RSP Content	ID Trip purpose Age Gender	a B L F	b B H F	c B L M	d B M M	e B H M
1	Adequate heating and/or air-conditioning		H	H	H	H	L
2	*Reduced release of pollutants into the environment*		H	M	M	M	L
3	*Reduced waste generation*		H	H	L	L	L
4	*Use of materials from renewable resources*		H	H	H	L	L
5	*Water saving*		M	H	M	H	L
6	*Energy saving*		H	H	M	H	L
7	Good lighting (both natural and artificial)		H	H	L	L	L
8	Freshness of towels and bed linen		H	H	H	H	H
9	Comfortable bathrooms provided with various amenities		H	H	H	L	H
10	Well-furnished and attractive rooms		L	H	H	L	L
11	Comfortable and spacious rooms		H	M	M	M	L

Trip purpose: B(business) / O(others)
Age: L(younger) / M(middle) / H(elder)
Gender: F(female) / M(male)
Weighting: L(low) / M(middle) / H(high)

Figure 6. Frequencies of each importance rating for Internet access in rooms

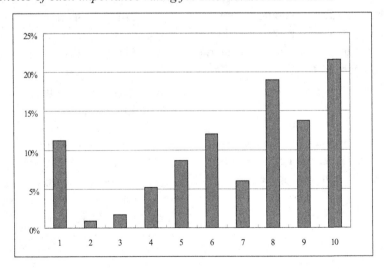

range. Other RSPs show a more homogeneous distribution of scores. Simultaneously, they have relatively higher peaks in a low-score range. Namely, lower importance is attached by a considerably higher share of respondents. An example is the availability of Internet access in rooms (see Figure 6).

It was investigated whether a property of a guest influences or does not influence his/her judgments of RSP weightings in order to obtain a clue to make effective personas. Among the properties possible to be input on persona, which were the gender, the age, and the profession, the age and the profession were found to be more highly influential. However, it should be noted that this can be partly explained by the higher number of classes (5 and 3 for the profession and the age, respectively, against 2 for the gender) and, consequently, by the lower number of instances in a class. Here, the options for the profession were based on the standardized ones in Italy (ISTAT,

2001): Those consisted of Group 1 (independent professionals, entrepreneurs, craftsmen), Group 2 (clerks, researchers, teachers), Group 3 (generic clerks, workers, etc.), Group 4 (tradespersons, etc.), and Group 5 (students, housewives, and pensioners). On environmentally-related RSPs as a whole, Group 4 put the highest scores.

Redesigning the Service

By applying the methods and tool of SE, especially Service Explorer, the designers generated five redesign options to improve the current service. First, they began with describing the flow model, activities of each agent, and associated value/cost in each activity as shown in Figure 7. "hotel," "customer," "linen company," "cleaning company," and "tenant" are arranged as agents which participate in the service. The generated solutions and the performed processes based on

Figure 7. The screen shot displaying some RSPs of a hotel guest in the category b on Service Explorer

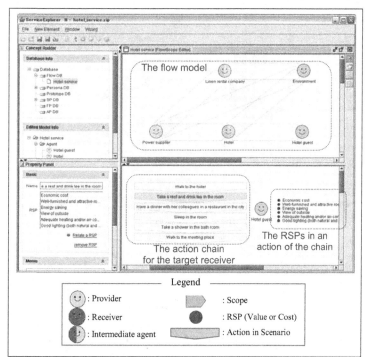

the above-mentioned design methodology are described below. Note that not all the options will be explained in detail due to the limited space. The first three options provide different solutions depending on guests' requirements, while the last two options present a unified solution for every type of hotel guests.

Option 1: "Cash-back per non-wash" system: From Table 1, two characteristic personas were generated. First, the customer category b of the hotel guest, namely elder women on a business trip, was selected as one of the target types of the customers. As Table 1 shows that their weightings on most of the RSPs from ID 2 to 6 are generally higher than the other categories, they are relatively environmentally conscious. The demographic and psychological data of this persona was described

on Service Explorer as shown in Figure 8. It should be mentioned that the persona is set to be a tradesperson from profession group 4 due to its highest weighting on environmentally-related RSPs among the profession groups. In addition, the persona was described to consider a great deal of some items of the LOV (List of Value) (Kahle, Beatty, & Homer, 1986) such as sense of security.

The other persona was prepared for elder males on a business trip, the category e, who put the lowest weightings on environmental RSPs. It was also confirmed that both of those two personas put a high weighting on the RSP, "freshness of towels and bed linen" (ID 8).

Currently, the hotel gives choices for the guests to decide whether the towels used in the bathrooms have to be washed or not. This system can give

Figure 8. The screen shot for editing the persona for the category b on Service Explorer

more satisfaction level to several RSPs. They include "reduced release of pollutants into the environment" (ID 2) in the scope models between the hotel and the guests, as well as between the hotel and the environment. Thus, the customer category with a higher environmental consciousness receives a higher level of satisfaction.

The newly-proposed system named "Cashback per non-wash" would not only allow guests to decide whether they have towels washed or not, but it would also give some form of discount to guests per a non-cleaned towel. This option would additionally decrease the economic cost of stay. Hence, this type of charging system would bring value to more categories of customers, which are, indeed, all the categories. Service Explorer supported designers to generate this option by providing them with a scheme for describing such value and costs of the current and new services.

It should be emphasized that the value provided in this option to several customer categories are different from each other; mere monetary cost reduction to the customers without a high environmental consciousness, and less environmental burdens, in addition, to highly environmentally-conscious customers. In addition, remarkably, service activities for giving back some cash were adopted to change the provided value.

Option 2: Various goods rental: According to the importance rating for the Internet access in rooms shown previously (Figure 6), it was found that some guests put no importance on some RSPs at all, while others appreciate them.

At present, the hotel provides guests with various goods and facilities such as bathroom amenities and telephone lines in a standardized

Figure 9. Illustration of option 2

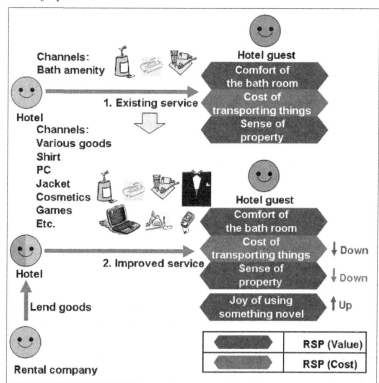

way. The goods or facilities provided by the hotel depending on the customer category could improve the quality of the hotel service. During their business trip stay hotel guests use various goods and facilities, including Internet access facilities, personal computers, bags, and jackets. The hotel can rent a variety of those useful goods or facilities to their guests. Thus, in this newly-proposed service, guests can be provided on demand with those various goods for rental. This option adds value to each guest with a specific request.

This improvement option would delete or reduce the degree of the negative RSP "cost of transporting things" of the guests, since they do not have to carry some of their own belongings with them and can just rent them on-site. In addition, this option can bring a totally new RSP "joy of using something new" even though it gives negative influence on the existing RSPs such as "comfort from one's own belongings" and "joy of owning". "Joy of using something new" in this case is meant as the joy of trying something they never or seldom own. The examples of that RSP may include enthusiasm to exchange one type of cosmetics for another, and excitement to wear a jacket with a remarkable brand name. It should be emphasized that this type of RSP used to be out of the scope of the hotel service. Figure 9 illustrates Option 2 by comparing the information described for the current and new services on Service Explorer.

If the hotel directly ran the rental service, it would probably cost too much. Thus, it is reasonable that the hotel receives the rental service by another agent, a rental company. It should be emphasized that in this option, several new RSPs for the hotel guests were added by setting a new provider so that the total satisfaction of the service might be increased. In addition, Service Explorer facilitates designers to investigate balance of value and costs of the related agents.

Option 3: A room customizing system: The hotel currently provides any type of guests with a standardized set of room furniture and equipment, such as a desk and an armchair in each room. This is a good solution from the viewpoint of mass production with a low cost (standardization). However, from the viewpoint of SE, service designers should pay more attention to a variety of customers' ways of satisfaction. An option to fill in the gap is a system to customize the furniture and equipment depending on a guest's needs. For instance, in this option, a business trip guest would be able to use a larger desk instead of a big sofa, contributing to the value of a good working environment. Service Explorer supported designers investigating balance of value and costs of multiple types of hotel guests.

Option 4: Window shielding films: For a target persona of hotel guest category b, the chain of actions was described as shown in the lower part of Figure 7, beginning with "walk to the hotel" and ending with "walk to the meeting place". A final goal of was set to be getting prepared for her forthcoming business meeting. A parameter to describe the goal was set to be relaxation, after the second action in the chain, "take a rest and drink tea in the room" was focused. The RSPs such as "adequate heating and/or air-conditioning" (ID 1), "good lighting" (ID 7), "energy-saving" (ID 6), "well-furnished and attractive room" (ID 10), and "economic cost" were extracted. The first three RSPs, in the summer, are rephrased as cool and light with less energy. Another target persona of hotel guest category e also has the same RSPs except for "energy-saving" (ID 6).

Here, the current realization structure of the service was referred. The existing hotel building has a roll shutter on the outside of a window to prevent the sunlight and heat from coming into the room. When it is in use, it gets cooler due to its performance to prevent the heat transfer. However, natural light does not come into the room, either. It was found in the function database that there exist special films attached on the window to shield a specific range of radiation frequency (Correa & Almanza, 2004). Installing these films is expected to decrease the energy usage by air conditioners for the rooms. This redesign option will achieve the change of all of the three RSPs mentioned above (cool and light with less energy).

The function structures for RSPs were developed in accordance with the processes in the previous paragraph, and then the entities for those functions were described on Service Explorer as well. Figure 10 shows just a small part of the developed view model of the service, corresponding to the RSP "adequate heating and/or air-conditioning" (a root element). In the view model, "Control the temperature and the humidity in the room" is described as a root function to change the RSP. The RSP is connected to CoPs of "comfortability of

the temperature in the room" and "comfortability of the humidity in the room". Then, the function is deployed into "Control the temperature in the room" and "Control the humidity in the room". By detailing gradually the functional structure which realizes the change of the RSP, the RSP is finally linked to the entity such as "Window", "Window film", or "Air-conditioner in the room". It should be noted that "Window film" is an additional part in this redesign option. Regarding function parameters, the first CoP is linked to a ChP of "capability to shield heat of the films". One can understand this by looking at functions and entities in the view model.

After reflection of such information on Service Explorer, an RSP named "view of outside" was newly recognized as value and was described.

Figure 10. The screen shot for a partial view model for the target RSP with its realization structures

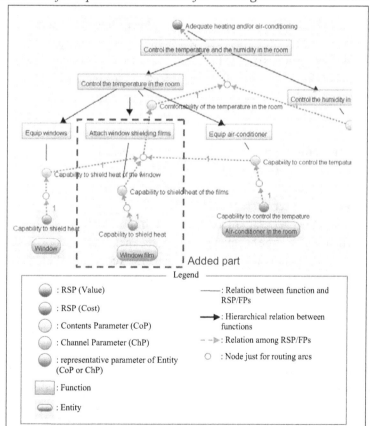

Option 5: A sunlighting system: The customer categories considered as targets are categories with high importance for "energy saving", which are categories a, b, and d. By considering that the RSPs for the persona for the category b include "good lighting" and "energy-saving", a lighting system was focused for the redesign target. During daytime, electric lighting is currently employed to provide illumination in some areas of the hotel building, such as corridors, underground parking places, and so forth. Substituting, at least partially, natural daylight for artificial lighting system was proposed. This has a potential to improve those two RSPs, "good lighting" and "energy-saving", though quantitative calculation of illumination level and needed electric power is necessary for evaluating the levels of those RSPs. A number of devices such as light pipes and fiber optics are commercially available to facilitate and optimize the effective use of natural daylight in a wide range of buildings. Such sunlighting systems (Jenkins & Muneer, 2003) are designed to gather the sunlight outside the building shelter and canalize it to the destination area(s) inside the building. It should be mentioned that a new RSP "comfort from natural lighting" was recognized after having proposed this option and described on Service Explorer.

This improvement is not only beneficial for the categories a, b, and d, but also has no big negative influences for the other categories. This is why a unified form of products and services in this case can be the solution. However, value from "comfort from natural lighting" may be beneficial especially for the category b, who is concerned about the environmental issues.

Feedbacks

Feedbacks on the options above were obtained from the hotel company as follows. The proposed improvement options were generally new to them. Actually, they started to investigate the feasibility of the light-shielding window films (Option 4) and "cash-back per non-wash" system (Option 1). They also began to collect the detailed product information of the sunlighting system (Option 5). However, they recognize that the various goods renting service (Option 2) would not necessarily be feasible. One reason is that clothes-renting is not familiar in the Italian culture at present. Another reason is that the target hotel is located in Abruzzo, where most guests travel for a short period and a short distance. On the other hand, in hotels located in international cities like Rome, this service might be more attractive to hotel guests. Furthermore, cosmetics renting service is quite interesting, because a cosmetics manufacturer can utilize a hotel as a channel, and a hotel could reduce the economic cost of preparing various types of goods at the same time. With regards to the room customizing system (Option 3), they consider it is necessary to better investigate the economic feasibility, given the likely increased labor costs related to that option.

According to the outputs from the application and the feedbacks to them, the methods and tool of SE are suggested to be effective for designing services for increasing the level of customer-dependent satisfaction. It should be further verified in the future how the satisfaction levels of the hotel guests are changed after those options are implemented.

Evaluations

It is important that redesign options generated out of the methods and tool of SE are evaluated from service receivers. Although evaluation results from hotel guests are not yet obtained, evaluation of Option 5 (a sunlighting system) from the viewpoint of environment, a receiver in the service, has been conducted as an example.

A preliminary approximate assessment of the main benefits in terms of reduced energy consumption and decreased environmental impact has been carried out on this option. Assumptions were made for the place of installation (an underground parking area) and some quantitative technical specifications with reference to some related literature (Canziani, Peron, & Rossi, 2004; Jenkins & Muneer, 2003; Shao & Callow, 2003).

The main results suggested that the installation of one commercial medium-sized light pipe might contribute quite marginally to decreasing the global electricity consumption required to meet the lighting needs of the hotel area under investigation. Only if these devices can be installed in such a number and configuration to thoroughly replace electric lighting during daytime would a more meaningful energy savings be achieved. A more comprehensive environmental assessment would require that all the life cycle stages of the options compared (conventional artificial lighting versus light pipes) are considered, to avoid that some environmental improvements in one life cycle stage are counterbalanced by worse environmental performance in other stages.

FUTURE TRENDS

Dealing with services in an engineering manner has just marked the beginning on its quite long history of engineering. It is only for the last decade that concepts like SE, PSS, functional sales, and functional products have been the focus of study. More researches, both on theories and practices, must be conducted in this domain. These are expected to expand the target area of the present MC research and technologies by taking advantage of SE's goals, which are the same as those of MC, such as customer satisfaction depending on customer categories (Sakao et al., 2005c). Apparently, it will be impossible to tackle this problem only within the framework of one single discipline, such as engineering, marketing, and management. Thus, researches to be achieved are expected to establish a new academic discipline (Sakao & Shimomura, 2005a).

More specifically, researches of design methods are needed. Design methods and IT systems

are complementary to each other. Promising topics for these researches include developing generic procedures to generate value-customizing solutions (Sakao, Shimomura, Comstock, & Sundin, in press). A way of balancing the value and cost provided by a service (Sakao & Shimomura, 2005b) is expected, too. This is critical because a service with more value and more cost might not be accepted. Another topic is solving conflicts in designing value and cost depending on customer categories. The conflicts here may be classified into two groups: the conflict among multiple categories of customers in one agent, and that among multiple agents.

CONCLUSION

The methodologies and tool presented in this chapter are verified here to check whether the problems pointed out were overcome, by reviewing the processes and the solutions explained in the application to the hotel case.

First, the presented methods and tool were proved to be able to deal with customization in an industry spanning from customer segmentation to product design. Actually, depending on customers' properties and requirements, different solutions were generated. Description of personas on Service Explorer to identify value effectively helped, as demonstrated in Option 1 ("Cash-back per non-wash" system). In Option 2 (various goods rental), identifying RSPs on Service Explorer especially supported designers. How a view model facilitates designers finding service structures, including employed physical products according to the identified RSPs, was demonstrated in Option 4 (window-shielding films).

Second, the processes and the solutions proved that the presented methods and tool allow designers to operate value and costs of a service as shown in all the options. For instance, new value, "view of outside", was added in Option 4 (window-shielding films). Another newly-added value was "comfort from natural lighting" in Option 5. This is a benefit mainly from the model representing value and cost.

Third, it was found that the supported customization utilizes both physical products and service activities. This is a benefit from the *soft* modeling scheme and design process which allow designers to handle products and services in a flexible way.

It should be explained why the Options 4 and 5 can be instances of customization in spite of unified services provided with every guest. These options are the results of finding solutions to satisfy multiple categories of the hotel guests and the environment. In these cases, a homogeneous solution for every type of guests is provided: These were *lucky* cases. In general, this is not always the case. As seen in Options 1, 2, and 3, heterogeneous services are, in many cases, the solutions to customize value. It should be noted that customization here means not merely generating various services depending on customer types. Rather, it means incorporating requests from multiple categories of service receivers to find a solution with the advantage of efficiency of mass production.

As explained above, using Service Explorer, value and costs associated with a service can be op-

timized on a view model whose value is produced from a scenario model depending on the target customer category. Designing products follows the outputs of a view model. It should be noted that Service Explorer deals with the upper stream of design activities rather than those handled by existing CAD tools (see Figure 11). Therefore, the design space given to a design discipline by SE is wider, resulting in more design options as well as differentiation solutions.

Remarkably, Service Explorer, namely the implementation of the presented methodologies, is innovative in such points that it supports design activities, and the target is services. It should be noted that none of the existing systems support designers as demonstrated in the chapter.

As suggested above, SE has a possibility to become a novel discipline. The methods and tool are constructed based on the engineering discipline, while taking advantage of other disciplines such as marketing and management. For instance, customer categorization, which is a typical marketing method, is employed. However, SE does not provide a new method within the marketing field. Thus, SE will be characterized as a novel discipline coupling marketing and engineering activities (Sakao & Shimomura, 2005a). They provide environment for design activities seam-

Figure 11. Various CAD tools applied to service design stages

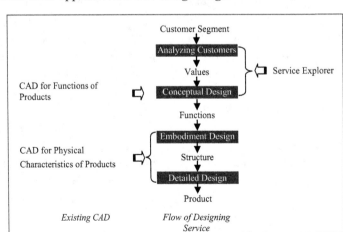

less from analyzing customers up to constructing physical structures.

Furthermore, the argument that the methods and the tool contribute to solving environmental problems is supported from the following two reasons. One is expected dematerialization through servicification, supported by the methods and the tool as seen in the presented five options. However, this is insufficient to raise such an argument. Thus, the second ground is provided: This is the power to help designers with adding appropriate value on services depending on customers' environmental consciousness as seen in Option 1 ("Cash-back per non-wash" system). As a result, even less-environmentally-conscious people have more chances to accept such services that prevent environmental damages.

In conclusion, this chapter has presented application of the methodologies and a tool based on SE to customizing value in industries. SE helps designers in utilizing both services and products, and can be a novel discipline in trying to integrate engineering and others like marketing and management. Especially, an innovative tool named Service Explorer was practiced in the field of customization. Actually, it was applied to a hotel accommodation service in Italy with the aim of increasing the level of customer-dependent satisfaction in multiple stakeholders. This is innovative, as most existing MC research has not tackled customization on the abstract level of value.

ACKNOWLEDGMENT

We would like to express our gratitude to Mr. Tatsunori Hara, Mr. Kentaro Watanabe, and Mr. Hiroki Doi from the University of Tokyo for their implementation of and execution of Service Explorer. This research was carried out within an official agreement between the University "G. d'Annunzio" and RACE, the University of Tokyo. This research was also partially supported by a Research Fellowship Program by Alexander von Humboldt Foundation in Germany. We express our appreciation for fruitful discussions with Prof. Birkhofer and other members of Institute for Product Development and Machine Elements, Darmstadt University of Technology, Germany. We give special thanks to Mr. Emilio Schirato, the owner of the hotel Duca d'Aosta, and his employees for their kind cooperation.

REFERENCES

Alonso-Rasgado, T., Thompson, G., & Elfstrom, B. (2004). The design of functional (total care) products. *Journal of Engineering Design*, *15*(6), 515-540.

Anderson, D. (Ed.). (1997). *Agile product development for mass customization*. Chicago: Irwin.

Arai, T., & Shimomura, Y. (2004). Proposal of service CAD system - A tool for service engineering. *Annals of the CIRP*, *53*(1), 397-400.

Arai, T., & Shimomura, Y. (2005). Service CAD system - Evaluation and quantification. *Annals of the CIRP*, *54*(1), 463-466.

Blecker, T., Friedrich, G., Kaluza, B., Abdelkafi, N., & Kreutler, G. (2005). *Information and management systems for product customization*. New York: Springer Publishing.

Bullinger, H., Wagner, F., Kürümlüoglu, M., & Bröcker, A. (2003). Towards the extended user-oriented shoe enterprise. In M. M. Tseng & F. T. Piller (Eds.), *The customer centric enterprise* (pp. 451-463). Heidelberg, Germany: Springer.

Canziani, R., Peron, F., & Rossi, G. (2004). Daylight and energy performances of a new type of light pipe. *Energy and Buildings*, *36*, 1163-1176.

Cao, J., Wang, J., Law, K., Zhang, S., & Li, M. (in press). An interactive service customization model. *Information and Software Technology*.

Cooper, A. (1999). *The inmates are running the asylum*. Sams.

Correa, G., & Almanza, R. (2004). Copper-based thin films to improve glazing for energy-savings in buildings. *Solar Energy, 76,* 111-115.

Coyne, R. (1998). *Logic models of design*. London: Pitman.

Frutos, J., & Borenstein, D. (2004). A framework to support customer-company interaction in mass customization environments. *Computers in Industry, 54,* 115-135.

Goedkoop, M. J., van Halen, C. J., te Riele, H. R., & Rommens, P. J. (1999). *Product service systems, ecological, and economic basics* (VROM 990570). Hague: Netherlands Ministry of Housing, Spatial Planning and the Environment.

Hara, T., Shimomura, Y., Uchida, M., & Sakao, T. (2004). Proposal of a computerized tool for service design. In *Proceeding of the 8th World Multi-Conference on Systemics, Cybernetics, and Informatics (SCI 2004)* (pp. 374-379). IEEE Computer Society.

IPCC (Intergovernmental Panel on Climate Change) (2001). *Climate change 2001: The scientific basis*. Cambridge University Press.

ISTAT (Italian National Institute of Statistics) (2001). *Classificazione delle professioni, Metodi e Norme - nuova serie. n. 12*. Rome: ISTAT (in Italian).

Japanese Ministry of Public Management, Home Affairs, Posts, and Telecommunications (PMHAPT). (2002). *Annual report on the family income and expenditure survey*. Tokyo: Japan Statistical Association (in Japanese).

Jenkins, D., & Muneer, T. (2003). Modelling light-pipe performances - A natural daylighting solution. *Building and Environment, 38,* 965-972.

Jiao, J., Ma, Q., & Tseng, M. (2003). Towards high value-added products and services: Mass customization and beyond. *The International Journal of Technological Innovation, Entrepreneurship, and Technology Management, 23,* 809-821.

Kahle, L., Beatty, S., & Homer, P. (1986). Alternative measurement approaches to consumer values, The list of values (LOV) and values and life style (VALS). *Journal of Consumer Research, 13,* 405-409.

Kim, J., & Gil, Y. (2004). Towards interactive composition of semantic Web services. *2004 AAAI Spring Symposium* (Tech. Rep. SS-04-06). Retrieved March 10, 2006, from http://www.isi.edu/ikcap/scec/papers/AAAI-Symp-04-Kim-Gil.pdf

Krasner, G. E., & Stephen, T. (1988). Pope for using the model-view-controller user interface paradigm in Smalltalk-80. *Journal of Object-Oriented Programing, 1*(August/September), 26-49.

Lindahl, M., & Ölundh, G. (2001). The meaning of functional sales. In A. J. de Ron (Ed.), *Proceedings of the 8th CIRP International Seminar on Life Cycle Engineering – Life Cycle Engineering: Challenges and Opportunities* (pp. 211-220).

Lindahl, M., Sundin, E., Shimomura, Y., & Sakao, T. (2005). Verification of a service design tool at a global warehouse provider. *CD-ROM Proceedings of the 15th International Conference on Engineering Design, ICED05*.

McAloone, T. C., & Andreason, M. M. (2004). Design for utility, sustainability, and social virtues: Developing product service systems. In *Proceedings of International Design Conference – Design 2004* (pp. 1545-1552).

McLaughlin, C. (1996). Why variation reduction is not everything: A new paradigm for service operations. *International Journal of Service Industry Management, 7,* 17-30.

Miles, L. (1971). *Techniques of value analysis and engineering.* McGraw-Hill.

OECD (2001). *OECD environmental outlook.* OECD.

Pine, J. (1993). *Mass customization: The new frontier in business competition.* Boston: Harvard Business School Press.

Roozenburg, M., & Eekels, J. (1995). *Product design: Fundamentals and methods.* Chichester, UK: John Wiley & Sons.

Sakao, T., & Shimomura, Y. (2004). A method and a computerized tool for service design. In *Proceedings of the International Design Conference (DESIGN 2004)* (pp. 497-502).

Sakao, T., & Shimomura, Y. (2005a). A novel design methodology for services to increase value combining service and product based on service engineering. *CD-ROM Proceeding of the 4th International Symposium on Environmentally Conscious Design and Inverse Manufacturing (Eco Design 2005).* IEEE Computer Society.

Sakao, T., & Shimomura, Y. (2005b). MVC (model for balancing value and costs): A fundamental model to design environmentally-conscious services. *CD-ROM Proceedings of the Fourth International Symposium on Environmentally Conscious Design and Inverse Manufacturing (EcoDesign 2005).* IEEE Computer Society.

Sakao, T., Shimomura, Y., Comstock, M., & Sundin, E. (2005c). Service engineering for value customization. *CD-ROM Proceedings of the 3rd Interdisciplinary World Congress on Mass Customization and Personalization (MCPC).*

Sakao, T., Shimomura, Y., Comstock, M., & Sundin, E. (in press). A method of value customization. *International Design Conference – (DESIGN 2006).*

Sakao, T., Shimomura, Y., Petti, L., & Raggi, A. (2005d). Applying service engineering methods and tools to improve various customers satisfaction in an accommodation service. *CD-ROM Proceedings of the 3rd Interdisciplinary World Congress on Mass Customization and Personalization (MCPC).*

Sakao, T., Watanabe, K., & Shimomura, Y. (2003). A Method to Support Environmentally Conscious Service Design Using Quality Function Deployment (QFD). In *The Third International Symposium of Environmentally Conscious Design and Inverse Manufacturing (Ecodesign 2003)* (pp. 567-574). IEEE Computer Society.

Shao, L., & Callow, J. M. (2003). Daylighting performance of optical rods. *Solar Energy, 75,* 439-445.

Shimomura, Y., Sakao, T., Hara, T., Arai, T., & Tomiyama, T. (in press). Service Explorer - A tool for service design. In E. Arai & T. Arai (Eds.), *Mechatronics for safety, security, and dependability in a new era.* Elsevier.

Shimomura, Y., & Tomiyama, T. (2002). Service modeling for service engineering. In *Proceedings of the 5th International Conference on Design of Information Infrastructure Systems for Manufacturing 2002 DIISM2002* (pp. 309-316).

Sundin, E., Lindahl, M., Shimomura, Y., & Sakao, T. (2005). New engineering design for functional sales business. *CD-ROM Proceedings of the 15th International Conference on Engineering Design ICED05.*

Takeda, H., Sakai, H., Nomaguchi, Y., Yoshioka, M., Shimomura, Y., & Tomiyama, T. (2003). Universal abduction studio - Proposal of a design support environment for creative thinking in design. *CD-ROM Proceedings of the 14th International Conference on Engineering Design, ICED03.*

Tischner, U., Verkuijl, M., & Tukker, A. (2002). *First draft PSS review.* Cologne, Germany: Econcept.

Tomiyama, T. (2001). Service engineering to intensify service contents in product life cycles. In *Proceedings of the Second International Symposium on Environmentally-Conscious Design and Inverse Manufacturing (EcoDesign 2001)* (pp. 613-618). IEEE Computer Society.

Tseng, M., & Jiao, J. (2001). Mass customization. In G. Salvendy (Ed.), *Handbook of industrial engineering,* (3rd ed.). (pp. 684-709). New York: Wiley.

Tseng, M., & Piller, F. (2003). The customer centric enterprise. In M. M. Tseng & F. T. Piller (Eds.), *The customer centric enterprise* (pp. 3–16). Heidelberg, Germany: Springer.

Tukker, A. (2004). Eight types of product-service systems: Eight ways to sustainability? Experiences from Suspronet. *Business Strategy and the Environment, 13,* 246-260.

Watanabe, K., Shimomura, Y., Sakao, T., Raggi, A., & Petti, L. (2004). Application of a service modeling tool to hotel industry. In *Proceedings of the Sixth International Conference on EcoBalance* (pp. 495-498).

Compilation of References

ACL: Agent Communications Language (2006). Retrieved May, 2006, from http://www.fipa.org/repository/aclspec.html

Adam, D., & Johannwille, U. (1998). Die Komplexitätsfalle. In D. Adam et al. (Eds.), *Komplexitätsmanagement* (pp. 5-28). Wiesbaden, Germany: Schriften zur Unternehmensführung, Gabler.

Adam, N. R., Dogramaci, O., Gangopadhyay, A., & Yesha, Y. (1999). *Electronic commerce*. NJ: Prentice Hall.

aecXML (2006). Retrieved March 22, 2006, from http://www.iai-na.org/aecxml/mission.php

Agrawal, M., Kumaresh, T. V., & Mercer, G. A. (2001). The false promise of mass customization. *The McKinsey Quarterly, 3,* 62-71.

Åhlström, P. & Westbrook, R. (1999). Implications of mass customization for operations management: An exploratory survey. *International Journal of Operations & Production Management, 19*(3), 262-274.

Aldanondo, M., Rougé, S., & Vérnon, M. (2000). Expert configurator for concurrent engineering: Caméléon software and model. *Journal of Intelligent Manufacturing, 11,* 127-134.

Aldanondo, M., Véron, M., & Fargier, H. (1999). Configuration in manufacturing industry, requirements, problems, and definitions. In *Proceedings of the IEEE International Conference on Systems, Man, and Cybernetics: Vol. 6* (pp. 1009-1014).

Alford, D., Sackett, P., & Nelder, G. (2000). Mass customisation – An automotive perspective. *International Journal of Production Economics, 65*(1), 99-110.

AlMellor (2004). *Introduction to model-driven architecture*. Addison-Wesley.

Alonso-Rasgado, T., Thompson, G., & Elfstrom, B. (2004). The design of functional (total care) products. *Journal of Engineering Design, 15*(6), 515-540.

America, P., Hammer, D. K., Ionita, T. M., Obbink, H. J., & Rommes, E. (2005). Scenario-based decision-making for architectural variability in product families. *Software Process - Improvement and Practice Journal, 10*(May), 171-187.

American Productivity and Quality Center (2005). Retrieved December 29, 2005, from http://www.apqc.org/portal/apqc/ksn/APQC_PCF_June_2005.pdf?paf_gear_id=contentgearhome&paf_dm=full&pageselect=contentitem&docid=121388

Amilhastre, J., Fargier, H., & Marquis, P. (2002). Consistency restoration and explanation in dynamic CSPs - Application to configuration. *Artificial Intelligence, 135,* 199-234.

Anderson, D. (2004). *Build-to-order and mass customization: The ultimate supply chain and lean manufacturing strategy for low-cost on-demand production without forecasts or inventory.* CIM Press.

Anderson, D. (Ed.). (1997). *Agile product development for mass customization.* Chicago: Irwin.

Anderson, D. L., & Lee, H. (1999). Synchronized supply chains: The new frontier. In *Achieving supply chain excellence through technology* (pp. 12-21). Montgomery Research.

Anderson, D. M., & Pine II, B. J. (1997). *Agile product development for mass customization.* Chicago: Irvin Publishers.

Andreasen, M. M. (1980). *Machine design methods based on a systematic approach – Contribution to a design theory.* Unpublished Ph.D. thesis, Lund Technical University, Sweden.

Andreasen, M. M. (1992). Designing on a designer's workbench (DWB). In *Proceedings of the 9th WDK Workshop,* Rigi, Switzerland.

Andreasen, M. M., Hansen, C. T., & Mortensen, N. H. (1997). *On the identification of product structure laws.* Paper presented at the 3rd WDK Workshop on Product Structuring, Delft, The Netherlands.

Arai, T., & Shimomura, Y. (2004). Proposal of service CAD system - A tool for service engineering. *Annals of the CIRP, 53*(1), 397-400.

Arai, T., & Shimomura, Y. (2005). Service CAD system - Evaluation and quantification. *Annals of the CIRP, 54*(1), 463-466.

Arana, J., Lakunza, J. A., & Astiazaran, J. C. (2005). *Product models and mass customization experiences in the Basque country.* Paper presented at the International Mass Customization Meeting, Klagenfurt, Austria.

Arana, J., Lakunza, J. A., Elejoste, M., & Mendizabal, B. (2005). *Configurators and product data management systems: Living together.* Paper presented at the Mass Customization and Personalization Congress, Hong-Kong, China.

Ardissono, L., Felfernig, A., Friedrich, G., Goy, A., Jannach, D., Petrone, G., Schäfer, R., & Zanker, M. (2000). Personalizing online configuration of products and services. In *Proceedings of the 15th European Conference on Artificial Intelligence,* Lyon, France (pp. 225-229). IOS Press.

Ardissono, L., Felfernig, A., Friedrich, G., Goy, A., Jannach, D., Petrone, G., Schäfer, R., & Zanker, M. (2003). A framework for the development of personalized, distributed Web-based configuration systems. *AI Magazine, 24*(3/Fall, 2003), 93-110.

Ardissono, L., Goy, A., Petrone, G., & Segnan, M. (2002). The adaptive Web: Personalization in business-to-customer interaction. *Communications of the ACM, Special Issue "The Adaptive Web", 45*(5), 52-53.

Ariano, M., & Dagnino, A. (1996). An intelligent order entry and dynamic bill of materials system for manufacturing customized furniture. *Computers in Electrical Engineering, 22*(1), 45-60.

Arjmand, M., & Roach, S. (1999). Creating greater customer value by synchronizing the supply chain. In *Achieving supply chain excellence through technology* (pp. 154-159). Montgomery Research. Also at http://arjmand.ascet.com

Ashby, W. R. (1960). *Design for a brain,* (2nd ed.). London.

Ashby, W. R. (1961). *An introduction to cybernetics,* (4th ed.). London: Chapman & Hall.

Avery, C., & Zeckhauser, R. (1997). Recommender systems for evaluating computer messages. *Communications of the ACM, 40*(3), 88-89.

Axelrod, R. (1976). *Structure of decision: The cognitive maps of political elites.* Princeton, NJ: Princeton University Press.

Axelrod, R., & Cohen, M. D. (2000). *Harnessing complexity – Organizational implications of a scientific frontier.* New York: Basic Books.

Baker, A. D., Van Dyke Parunak, H., & Kutluhan, E. (1999). Agents and the Internet: Infrastructure for mass customization. *IEEE Internet Computing*, (Sept.-Oct.), 62-69.

Balakrishman, A. Kumara, S., & Sundaresan, S. (1999). Manufacturing in the digital age: Exploiting information technologies for product realization. *Information Systems Frontiers, 1,* 25-50.

Bardacki, A., & Whitelock, J. (2003). Mass-customisation in marketing: The consumer perspective. *Journal of Consumer Marketing, 20*(5), 463-479.

Barker, V. E., O'Connor, D. E., Bachant, J. D., & Soloway, E. (1989). Expert systems for configuration at Digital: XCON and beyond. *Communications of the ACM, 32*(3), 298-318.

Basu, C., Hirsh, H., & Cohen, W. (1998). Recommendation as classification: Using social and content-based information in recommendation. *CD-ROM Proceedings of the 1998 Workshop on Recommender Systems*, Menlo Park, CA (pp. 11-15).

Beaty, R. T. (1996). Mass customisation. *IEE Manufacturing Engineer, 75*(5), 217-220.

Becker, J. (1999). *Branchen-Referenzmodelle, dargestellt am Beispiel des Handels-Referenzmodells.* In J. Becker et al. (Eds.), *Referenzmodellierung – State-of-the-Art und Entwicklungsperspektiven* (pp. 150-165). Heidelberg, Germany: Physica.

Beer, S. (1959). *Cybernetics and management.* London: The English Universities Press.

Beer, S. (1966). *Decision and control – The meaning of operational research and management cybernetics.* London: John Wiley & Sons.

Beer, S. (1972). *Brain of the firm – The managerial cybernetics of organization.* London: Penguin Press.

Beer, S. (1985). *Diagnosing the system for organizations.* Chichester, England: John Wiley & Sons.

Bellifemine, F., Caire, G., Poggi, A., & Rimassa, G. (2003). *JADE: A white paper. Exp, 3*(3), 6-19.

Bergenti, F., & Poggi, A. (2001). LEAP: A FIPA platform for handheld and mobile devices. In *Proceedings of the Eighth International Workshop on Agent Theories, Architectures, and Languages (ATAL-2001),* Seattle, WA (pp. 303-313).

Berman, B. (2002). Should your firm adopt a mass customization strategy? *Business Horizons, 45*(4), 51-60.

Berners-Lee, T. (2001). *Weaving the Web.* Harper Business.

Berre, A. (2002). Overview of international standards on enterprise architecture. *SINTEF.*

Bigus, J. P., Schlosnagle, D. A., Pilgrim, J. R., Mills III, W. N., & Diago, Y. (2002). ABLE: A toolkit for building multi-agent autonomic systems – Agent building and learning environment. *IBM Systems Journal,* (September), 1-19.

Blattberg, R., & Glaser, R. (1994). Marketing in the information revolution. In R. Blattberg, et al. (Eds.), *The marketing information revolution* (pp. 9-29). Boston:

Blecker, T., & Friedrich, G. (2005). Mass customization, concepts – Tools - Realization. In *Proceeding of the International Mass Customization Meeting 2005 (IMCM'05),* Gito, Berlin.

Blecker, T., Abdelkafi, N., Kreutler, G., & Friedrich, G. (2004). Product configuration systems: State of the art, conceptualization, and extensions, In A. B. Hamadou, F. Gargouri, & M. Jmaiel (Eds.), *Proceedings of the Eighth Maghrebian Conference on Software Engineering and Artificial Intelligence (MCSEAI 2004)* (pp. 25-36).

Blecker, T., Friedrich, G., Kaluza, B., Abdelkafi, N., & Kreutler, G. (2005). *Information and management systems for product customization.* New York: Springer.

Bliss, C. (2000). *Management von Komplexität. Ein integrierter systemtheoretischer Ansatz zur Komplexitätsreduktion.* Wiesbaden, Germany: Gabler.

Böhms, M. (2001). Building construction extensible markup language (bcXML) description: E-construct bcXML. *A Contribution to the CEN/ISSS eBES Workshop, Annex A, ISSS/WS-eBES/01/001.*

Boissier, R. (1995). Architecture solutions for integrating CAD, CAM and machining in small companies. In *Proceedings of the IEEE/ECLA/IFIP International Conference on Architectures and Design Methods for Balanced Automation Systems* (pp. 407-416). London: Chapman & Hall.

Bonehill, E., & Slee-Smith, P. (1998). Product configurator. *IEE Workshop on Responsiveness in Manufacturing (Digest No.1998/213)*, 9/1-9/4.

Boynton, A. C., Victor, B., & Pine II, B. J. (1993). New competitive strategies: Challenges to organisations and IT. *IBM Systems Journal, 32*(1), 40-64.

BPT (2005). *Supply-chain council partners with proforma to release object-oriented SCOR®-Model.* Retrieved March 11, 2006 from http://www.bptrends.com/news_items.cfm

Bramham, J., & MacCarthy, B. (2004). The demand-driven chain. *IEE Manufacturing Engineer, 83*(3), 30-33.

Breton, E., & Bézivin, J. (2001). Using metamodel technologies to organize functionalities for active system schemes. In *Proceedings of the 5th International Conference on Autonomous Agents*, Canada.

Broekhuizen, T. L. J., & Alsem, K. J. (2002). Success factors for mass customization: A conceptual model. *Journal of Market-Focused Management, 5*(4), 309-330.

Brown, A. O., Lee, H. L., & Petrakian, R. (2000). *Xilinx improves its semiconductor supply chain using product and process postponement.* Retrieved March 12, 2006, from http://markov.kaist.ac.kr/scm/refer/Semiconductor-postponement.pdf

Brown, S., & Bessant, J. (2003). The manufacturing strategy-capabilities links in mass customisation and agile manufacturing - An exploratory study. *International Journal of Operations and Production Managament, 23*(7), 707-730.

Browne, J., Harhen, J., & Shivnan, J. (1996). *Production management systems: An integrated perspective.* Harlow, UK: Addison-Wesley.

Bullinger, H., Wagner, F., Kürümlüoglu, M., & Bröcker, A. (2003). Towards the extended user-oriented shoe enterprise. In M. M. Tseng & F. T. Piller (Eds.), *The customer centric enterprise* (pp. 451-463). Heidelberg, Germany: Springer.

Burke, R. (2000). Knowledge-based recommender systems. *Encyclopedia of Library & Information Systems, 69*(32).

Burke, R. (2002). Hybrid recommender systems: Survey and experiments. *User Modeling and User-Adapted Interaction, 4*, 331-370.

Canziani, R., Peron, F., & Rossi, G. (2004). Daylight and energy performances of a new type of light pipe. *Energy and Buildings, 36*, 1163-1176.

Cao, J., Wang, J., Law, K., Zhang, S., & Li, M. (in press). An interactive service customization model. *Information and Software Technology.*

Capgemini (2004). *A collection of agent technology pilots and projects.* Retrieved May, 2006, from http://www.capgemini.com/resources/thought_leadership/putting_agents_towork/

Carbonell, J. G. (1992). *Natural language understanding.* In S. C. Shapiro (Ed.), *Encyclopedia of artificial intelligence* (pp. 997-1015). New York: John Wiley & Sons.

Carnegie-Mellon Software Engineering Institute (2005). *Capability Maturity Model for Software (SW-CMM).* Retrieved December 29, 2005, from http://www.sei.cmu.edu/cmm/

Caron, F., & Fiore, F. (1995). Engineer to order companies: How to integrate manufacturing and innovative processes. *International Journal of Project Management, 13*, 313-319.

CEN/ISSS (2006). *European Committee for Standardisation - Information Society Standardization System.* Retrieved March 22, 2006, from http://www.cenorm.be/isss

Chalmers, M., Rodden, K., & Brodbeck, D. (1998). The order of things: Activity-centered information access. *Computer Networks and ISDN Systems, 30*, 359-367.

Chen, F., Drezner, A., Ryan, J. K., & Simchi-Levi, D. (1999). The bullwhip effect: Managerial insights on the impact of forecasting and information on variability in a supply chain. In S. Tayur, et al. (Eds.), *Quantitative models for supply chain management* (pp. 417-440). New York: Springer.

Chen, H. C., & Chen, A. L. P. (2001). A music recommendation system based on music data grouping and user interests. CD-ROM *Proceedings of the 2001 ACM CIKM International Conference on Information and Knowledge Management,* Atlanta, GA (pp. 231-238).

Chen, I. J., & Paulraj, A. (2004). Understanding supply chain management: Critical research and a theoretical framework. *International Journal of Production Research, 42*(1), 131-163.

Cheung, C. F., Lee, W. B., Wang, W. M., Chu, K. F., & To, S. (2003). A multi-perspective knowledge-based system for customer service management. *Expert Systems with Applications, 24,* 457-470.

Christopher, M. (1998). *Logistics and supply chain management, strategies for reducing cost and improving service* (2nd ed). London: Financial Times Prentice Hall.

Clements, P. (1997). Standard support for the virtual enterprise. In *Proceedings of the International Conference on Enterprise Integration Modeling Technology – ICEIMT'97, Torino, Italy.* Retrieved March 22, 2006, from http://www.mel.nist.gov/workshop/iceimt97/papcle2/stdspt2.htm

Clemons, E. K., & Row, M. C. (1991). Sustaining IT advantage: The role of structural differences, *MIS Quarterly,* (September).

Commission de Surveillance du Secteur Financier (2005). *BASEL II Operational Risk Management Process Reference Model.* Retrieved December 29, 2005, from http://www.cssf.lu/docs/PRM_ORM_BALEII_V01_00.pdf

Comstock, M., Johansen, K., & Winroth, M. (2004). From mass production to mass customization: Enabling perspectives from the Swedish mobile telephone industry. *Production Planning & Control, 15*(4), 362-372.

Cooper, A. (1999). *The inmates are running the asylum.* Sams.

Correa, G., & Almanza, R. (2004). Copper-based thin films to improve glazing for energy-savings in buildings. *Solar Energy, 76,* 111-115.

Coyne, R. (1998). *Logic models of design.* London: Pitman.

Crow, J., & Rushby, J. M. (1991). Model-based reconfiguration: Toward an integration with diagnosis. In *Proceedings of the National Conference on Artificial Intelligence – AAAI'91* (pp. 836-841). AAAI Press.

Cusumano, M. A., & Nobeoka, K. (1998). *Thinking beyond lean.* New York: Free Press.

D'Souza, D., & Wills, A., (1998). *Objects, components, and frameworks with UML: The catalysis.* Addison-Wesley. Retrieved March 23, 2006, from http://www.catalysis.org

Da Silveira, G., Borenstein, D., & Fogliaatto, F. S. (2001). Mass customization: Literature review and research directions. *International Journal of Production Economics, 72*(1), 1-13.

DATAFORM EDIData (1997). *UN/EDIFACT Release 93A.*

Davis, S. (1989). From future perfect: Mass customizing. *Planning Review.*

Davis, S. M. (1987). *Future perfect.* Reading, MA: Addison-Wesley.

Dellaert, B. G. C., & Stremersch, S. (2005). Marketing mass-customized products: Striking a balance between utility and complexity. *Journal of Marketing Research, 42*(2), 219-227.

Dennis, A., Wixom, B., & Tegarden, D. (2004). *System analysis and design with UML version 2.0: An object-oriented approach* (2nd ed.). John Wiley & Sons.

DOM (Document Object Model) (2006). Retrieved March 23, 2006, from http://www.w3.org/TR/REC-DOM-Level-1

Dorer, K., & Calisti, M. (2005). An adaptive solution to dynamic transport optimization. In *Proceedings of the Fourth International Joint Conference on Autonomous Agents and Multi-Agent Systems, AAMAS '05*, Utrecht, The Netherlands. Also at http://www.whitestein.com/pages/downloads/publications

Du, X., Jiao, J. & Tseng, M. M. (2000). Architecture of product family for mass customization. In *Proceedings of the 2000 IEEE International Conference on Management of Innovation and Technology.*

Duray, R. (2002). Mass customization origins: Mass or custom manufacturing? *International Journal of Operations & Production Management, 22*(3), 314-328.

Dziarstek, C., Farnschläder, F., Gilleßen, S., Süßmilch-Walther, I., & Winkler, V. (2004). A user-aware financial advisory system. *Multikonferenz Wirtschaftsinformatik (MKWI) 2004, Universität Duisburg-Essen,* Berlin (pp. 217-229).

Eckert-Niemeyer, V. (2000). Innovative tools zur Realisierung der virtuellen Beratung. *Banking and Information Technology, 1*(1), 23-31.

ECR Europe (2005). *ECR Europe: Organisation and principles.* Retrieved December 29, 2005, from http://www.ecrnet.org/

Edvardson, J. (1999). A survey on automatic test data generation. In *Proceedings of the 2ⁿᵈ Conference on Computer Science and Engineering CCSSe'99.*

Edwards, K., & Pedersen, J. (2004). Product configuration systems – Implications for product innovation and development. In *Proceedings of the International Conference on Economic, Technical and Organisational Aspects of Product Configuration Systems, Copenhagen,* Denmark (pp. 231-239).

empirica GmbH (2005). *The European e-Business Report: A portrait of e-business in 10 sectors of the EU economy, 2005 edition.* Retrieved March 23, 2006, from http://www.ebusiness-watch.org/resources/documents/Pocketbook-2005_001.pdf

Engelhardt, C. (2000). *Betriebskennlinien. Produktivität steigern in der Fertigung.* München/Wien, Germany: Hanser.

ENV 13 550 (1995). *Enterprise Model Execution and Integration Services (EMEIS).* Brussels, Belgium: CEN.

Ericsson, A., & Erixon, G. (1999). *Controlling design variants: Modular product platforms.* ASME Press.

EU (2002). *Richtline 2002/92/EG des Europäischen Parlaments und des Rates vom 9. Dezember 2002 über Versicherungsvermittlung,* Amtsblatt der Europäischen Gemeinschaften.

European Foundation for Quality Management (2005). *The EFQM Excellence Model.* Retrieved December 29, 2005, from http://www.efqm.org/Default.aspx?tabid=35

European Logistics Association/A. T. Kearney Management Consultants (2004). *Differentiation for Performance – Excellence in Logistics 2004.* Hamburg, Germany: Deutscher Verkehrs-Verlag.

Eversheim, W., Schenke, F.-B., & Warnke, U. (1998). Komplexität im Unternehmen verringern und beherrschen – optimale Gestaltung von Produkten und Produktionssystemen. In D. Adam et al. (Eds.), *Komplexitätsmanagement* (pp. 29-45). Wiesbaden, Germany: Schriften zur Unternehmensführung, Gabler.

Feitzinger, E., & Lee, H. (1997). Mass customization at Hewlett-Packard: The power of postponement. *Harvard Business Review, 75*(1), 116-121.

Felfernig, A. (2005b). Koba4MS: Selling complex products and services using knowledge-based recommender technologies. In *Proceedings of the 7ᵗʰ IEEE Conference on e-Commerce Technology,* München, Germany (pp. 92-100).

Felfernig, A., & Kiener, A. (2005a). Knowledge-based interactive selling of financial services using FSAdvisor. In *Proceedings of the 17ᵗʰ Innovative Applications of Artificial Intelligence Conference (IAAI'05),* Pittsburgh, PA (pp. 1475-1482). AAAI Press.

Felfernig, A., & Shchekotykhin, K. (2006). Debugging user interface descriptions of knowledge-based recommender applications. *ACM Conference on Intelligent User Interfaces (IUI'06)*, Sydney, Australia (pp. 234-241).

Felfernig, A., Friedrich, G., & Jannach, D. (2000). UML as domain specific language for the construction of knowledge-based configuration systems. *IJSEKE, 10*(4), 449-469.

Felfernig, A., Friedrich, G., & Jannach, D. (2001). Conceptual modeling for configuration of mass-customizable products. *Artificial Intelligence in Engineering, 15*, 165-176.

Felfernig, A., Friedrich, G., Jannach, D., & Stumptner, M. (2004). Consistency-based diagnosis of configuration knowledge bases. *Artificial Intelligence, 152*(2), 213-234.

Felfernig, A., Friedrich, G., Jannach, D., & Zanker, M. (2002). Configuration knowledge representation using UML/OCL. In *Proceedings of 5th International Conference on the Unified Modeling Language (UML 2002)*, Dresden, Germany (pp. 49-62).

Felfernig, A., Friedrich, G., Jannach, D., Stumptner, M., & Zanker, M. (2003). Configuration knowledge representations for Semantic Web applications. *AI Engineering Design, Analysis, and Manufacturing Journal, 17*, 31-50.

Felfernig, A., Isak, K., & Kruggel, T. (2005). Testing knowledge-based recommender applications. *OEGAI Journal, Special Issue on Recommender Systems, 24*(4), 12-18.

Felfernig, A., Mehlau, J., Wimmer, A., Zanker, M., & Russ, C. (2004b). Konzepte zur flexiblen Konfiguration von Finanzdienstleistungen. *Banking and Information Technology, Sonderheft zur Multi-Konferenz Wirtschaftsinformatik 2004, 5*(1), 5-17.

Fensel, D., van Harmelen, F., Horrocks, I., McGuinness, D., & Patel-Schneider, P. (2001). OIL: An ontology infrastructure for the semantic Web. *IEEE Intelligent Systems, 16*(2), 38-45.

Fenves, S. J., Sriram, R. D., Choi, Y., & Robert, J. E. (2003). *Advanced Engineering Environments for Small Manufacturing Enterprises, 1.*

Fenves, S. J., Sriram, R. D., Choi, Y., Elm, J. P., & Robert, J. E. (2004). *Advanced Engineering Environments for Small Manufacturing Enterprises, 2.*

Ferguson, R., & Korel, B. (1996). The chaining approach for software test data generation. *IEEE Transactions on Software Engineering, 5*(1), 63-86.

Fetter, P., & Loos, P. (2004). Referenzmodelle für den Handel. In K. Hildebrand (Ed.), (Hrsg.), IT-Lösungen im Handel, dpunkt. Heidelberg, Germany: Verlag.

Fleischanderl, G. (2002). Suggestions from the software engineering practice for applying consistency-based diagnosis to configuration knowledge bases. In *Proceedings of the 13th International Workshop on Principles of Diagnosis (DX-02)*.

Fleischanderl, G., Friedrich, G., Haselböck, A., Schreiner, H., & Stumptner, M. (1998). Configuring large-scale systems with generative constraint satisfaction. *IEEE Intelligent System-Special issue on Configuration, 13*(7), 59-68.

Fohn, S. M., Liau, J. S., Greef, A. R., Young, R. E., & O'Grady, P. J. (1995). Configuring computer systems through constraint-based modeling and interactive constraint satisfaction. *Computers in Industry, 27*, 3-21.

Forbus, K., & deKleer, J. (1993). *Building problem solvers.* MIT Press.

Forrester, J. (1961). *Industrial dynamics.* Cambridge, MA: MIT-Press.

Forster, J., Fothergill, P., Lakunza, J. A., & Arana, I. (1995). *DEKLARE: Knowledge acquisition and support system for re-design.* Paper presented at the Expert Systems Annual Conference, Cambridge, UK.

Forza, C., & Salvador, F. (2002). Managing for variety in the order acquisition and fulfilment process: The contribution of product configuration systems. *International Journal of Production Economics, 76*, 87-98.

Forza, C., & Salvador, F. (2002b). Product configuration and inter-firm co-ordination: An innovative solution from a small manufacturing enterprise. *Computers in Industry, 49*, 37-56.

Fowler, J. (2000). *Co-operative use of STEP and PLib*. Retrieved March 22, 2006, from http://www.nist.gov/sc4

Fox, C. (Ed.). (1992). *Information retrieval: Data structures and algorithms*. Englewood Cliffs, NJ: Prentice-Hall.

Francisco, G.-S., Rafael, V.-G., & Rodrigo, M.-B. (2005). An integrated approach for developing e-commerce applications. *Expert Systems with Applications, 28*, 223-235.

Franke, N., & Piller, F. (2004). Value creation by toolkits for user innovation and design: The case of the watch market. *Journal of Product Innovation Management, 21*, 401-415.

Franke, N., & Piller, F. T. (2002). *Configuration toolkits for mass customization: Setting a research agenda* (Working Paper No. 33 of the Department of General and Industrial Management). Technische Universität München.

Franke, N., & Piller, F. T. (2003). Key research issues in user interaction with user toolkits in a mass customisation system. *International Journal of Technology Management, 26*(5/6), 578-599.

Freuder, E., Likitvivatanavong, C., & Wallace, R. J. (2001). Deriving explanations and implications for constraint satisfaction problems. In *Proceedings of Principles and Practice of Constraint Programming - CP 2001, LNCS 2239*, Paphos, Cyprus (pp. 585-589). Springer.

Friedrich, G. (2004). Elimination of spurious explanations. In *Proceedings of the 16th European Conference on Artificial Intelligence (ECAI 2004)*, Valencia, Spain (pp. 813-817). IOS Press.

Frutos, J. D., & Borenstein, D. (2004). A framework to support customer-company interaction in mass customization environments. *Computers in Industry, 54*, 115-135.

Fu, X., Budzik, J., & Hammond, K. J. (2000). Mining navigation history for recommendation. CD-ROM *Proceedings of the 5th International Conference on Intelligent User Interfaces*, New Orleans, LA (pp. 106-112).

Fulkerson, B. (1997). A response to dynamic change in the market place. *Decision Support Systems, 21*(3), 199-214.

Gallaher, M. (2004). *Cost analysis of inadequate interoperability in the U.S. capital facilities industry* (NIST GCR 04-867). Washington, DC: National Institute of Standards and Technology, Department of Commerce.

Geimer, H. (2005). Komplexitätsmanagement globaler Supply Chains. In K. Hildebrand (Ed.), *Supply chain management* (pp. 38-46). Heidelberg, Germany: HMD-Praxis der Wirtschaftsinformatik, HMD 243.

Gell-Mann, M. (1994). *Das Quark und der Jaguar: Vom Einfachen zum Komplexen*. München, Germany: Piper.

Georgakopoulos, D., Hornick, M., & Sheth, A. (1995). An overview of workflow management: From process modelling to workflow automation infrastructure. *Distributed and Parallel Databases, 3*(2), 119-153.

Ghani, R., & Fano, A. (2002). Building recommender systems using a knowledge base of product semantics. CD-ROM *Proceedings of the International Conference on Workshop on Recommendation and Personalization in E-Commerce*, Malaga, Spain.

Ghiassi, M. (2001). An e-commerce production model for mass-customized market. *Issues in Information Systems, 2*, 106-112.

Ghiassi, M., & Spera, C. (2003a). Defining the Internet-based supply chain system for mass-customized markets. *Computers & Industrial Engineering Journal, 45*(1), 17-41.

Ghiassi, M., & Spera, C. (2003b). A collaborative and adaptive supply chain management system. In *Proceedings of the 31st International Conference on Computers and Industrial Engineering*, San Francisco (pp. 473-479).

Gilmore, J. H., & Pine II, B. J. (1997). The four faces of customization. *Harvard Business Review, 75*(1), 91-101.

Gilmore, J. H., & Pine II, B. J. (2000). *Markets of one: Creating customer-unique value through mass customization.* Harvard Business Review.

Glorfeld, L. W. (1996). A methodology for simplification and interpretation of back propagation-based neural network models. *Expert Systems with Applications, 10*(1), 37-54.

Goedkoop, M. J., van Halen, C. J., te Riele, H. R., & Rommens, P. J. (1999). *Product service systems, ecological, and economic basics* (VROM 990570). Hague: Netherlands Ministry of Housing, Spatial Planning and the Environment.

Goldberg, D., Nichols, D., Oki, B. M., & Terry, D. (1992). Using collaborative filtering to weave an information tapestry. *Communications of the ACM, 35*, 12.

Goodwill, G. (2002). *Mastering JSP custom tags and tag libraries.* Wiley.

Gounaris, S. P., Stathakopoulos, V., & Athanassopoulos, A. D. (2003). Antecedents to perceived service quality: An exploratory study in the banking industry. *International Journal of Bank Marketing, 21*(4), 168-190.

GPRS: General Packet Radio System. Retrieved May, 2006, from http://www.gsmworld.com/technology/gprs/index.html

Gregory, T. (1999). *Interoperability cost analysis of the U.S. automotive supply chain* (99-1 Planning Rep.). Washington, DC: National Institute of Standards and Technology, Department of Commerce.

Grilo, A., & Jardim-Goncalves, R., (2005). Analysis on the development of e-platforms in the AEC sector. *International Journal of Internet and Enterprise Management, 3*(2).

Gronroos, C. (1994). From scientific management to service management. *International Journal of Service Industry Management, 5*(1), 5-20.

Gronroos, C. (2000). *Service management and marketing: A customer relationship management approach* (2nd ed.). Chichester, UK: John Wiley & Sons.

Gunasekarana, A., & Ngai, E. (2005). Build-toorder supply chain management: A literature review and framework for development. *Journal of Operations Management, 6*, 223-451.

Günter, A., & Kühn, C. (1999). *Knowledge-based configuration – Survey and future directions.* Paper presented at the XPS-99, Knowledge-Based Systems, Würzburg, Germany.

Haag, A. (1998). Sales configuration in business processes. *IEEE Intelligent Systems, 13*(4), 78-85.

Haag, A. (2005). "Dealing" with configurable products in the SAP business suite. *Workshop on Configuration, International Conference on Artificial Intelligence (IJCAI 2005), Edinburgh, Scotland* (pp. 68-71).

Haberfellner, R., & de Weck, O. (2005). Neuere Entwicklungen im systems engineering. In C. Engelhardt-Nowitzki & J. Wolfbauer, (Eds.), *Gelebtes Netzwerkmanagement* (pp. 129-149). Göttingen, Germany: Cuvillier Verlag.

Hagel, J., & Singer, M. (1999). *Net worth – Shaping markets when customers make the rules.* Harvard Business School Press.

Han, J., & Kamber, M. (Ed.). (2001). *Data mining: Concepts and techniques.* San Francisco: Morgan Kaufmann Publishers.

Han, P., Xie, B., Yang, F., & Shen, R. (2004). *A scalable P2P recommender system based on distributed collaborative filtering. Expert Systems with Applications, 27*, 203-210.

Hansen Harps, L. (2002). Super-charging your supply chain. Retrieved March 12, 2006, from http://www.inboundlogistics.com/articles

Hara, T., Shimomura, Y., Uchida, M., & Sakao, T. (2004). Proposal of a computerized tool for service design. In *Proceeding of the 8th World Multi-Conference on Systemics, Cybernetics, and Informatics (SCI 2004)* (pp. 374-379). IEEE Computer Society.

Hart, C. (1995). Mass customization: Conceptual under-pinnings, opportunities, and limits. *International Journal of Service Industry Management, 6*(2), 36-45.

Heatley, J., Agraval, R., & Tanniru, M. (1995). An evaluation of an innovative information technology - The case of carrier EXPERT. *Journal of Strategic Information Systems, 4*(3), 255-277.

Hegge, H. M., & Wortmann, J. C. (1991). Generic bill-of-material: A new product model. *International Journal of Production Economics, 23*.

Heiskala, M., Anderson, A., Huhtinen, V., Tiihonen, J., & Martio, A. (2003). A tool for comparing configurable products. *Workshop on Configuration, International Conference on Artificial Intelligence (IJCAI 2005), Acapulco, Mexico* (pp. 64-69).

Herlocker, J. L., Konstan, J. A., Terveen, L. G., & Riedl, J. T. (2004). Evaluating collaborative filtering recommender systems. *ACM Transactions on Information Systems, 22*(1), 5-53.

Heylighen, F. (1992). Building a science of complexity. Retrieved March 10, 2006, from http://pespmc1.vub.ac.be/papers/Buildingcomplexity.html

Heylighen, F. (1996). *The growth of structural and functional complexity during evolution.* Retrieved March 10, 2006, from http://pespmc1.vub.ac.be/papers/Complexitygrowth.html

Hicks, C., McGovern, T., & Earl, C. F. (2000). Supply chain management: A strategic issue in engineer to order manufacturing. *International Journal of Production Economics, 65*, 179-190.

Hill, C. W. L. (2002). *International business: Competing in the global marketplace.* New York: McGraw-Hill.

Hill, W., Stead, L., Rosenstein, M., & Furnas, G. (1995). Recommending and evaluating choices in a virtual community of use. CD-ROM *Proceedings of the 1995 ACM Conference on Factors in Computing Systems, New York* (pp. 194-201).

Hirschhorn, L., Noble, P., & Rnkin, T. (2001). Socio-technical systems in the age of mass customisation.

Journal of Engineering and Technology Management, 18(3-4), 241-252.

Hoekstra, S., & Romme, J. (1992). *Integrated logistics structures: Developing customer oriented goods flow.* London: McGraw-Hill.

Hopp, W. J., & Spearmann, M. L. (1996). *Factory physics. Foundations of manufacturing management.* Chicago: Irwin.

Hsu, H. -M., & Wang, W. -P. (2004). Dynamic programming for delayed product differentiation. *European Journal of Operational Research, 156*, 183-193.

Hsuan, J., & Skjoett-Larsen, T. (2003). *Mass customisation, postponement, and modularisation strategies in shaping supply chains.* Paper presented at the 12th International Conference on Management of Technology, Nancy, France.

Huang, G. Q., & Mak, K. L. (2000). Webid: A Web-based framework to support early supplier involvement in new product development. *Robotics and Computer Integrated Manufacturing, 16*(2-3), 169-179.

Huang, G. Q., Zhang, X. Y., & Lo, V. H. (2005). Optimal supply chain configuration for platform products: Impacts of commonality, demand variability, and quantity discount. *International Journal of Mass Customization, 1*(1).

Hubka, V., & Eder, W. E. (1988). *Theory of technical systems.* Berlin: Springer-Verlag.

Huffman, C., & Kahn, B. E. (1998). Variety for sale: Mass customization or mass confusion? *Journal of Retailing, 74*(4), 491-513.

Hvam, L. (1994). *Anvendelse af produktmodellering, -set ud fra en arbejdsforberedelsessynsvinkel.* PhD thesis, Driftteknisk Institut, DTU.

Hvam, L. (1999). A procedure for building product models. *Robotics and Computer-Integrated Manufacturing, 15*, 77-87.

Hvam, L., Malis, M., Hansen, B., & Riis, J. (2004). Reengineering of the quotation process: Application of knowledge-based systems. *Business Process Management Journal, 10*(2), 200-213.

IAI/IFC (1997). *IFC End User Guide. International Foundation Classes Release 1.5. IAI.*

IDEAS Project (2003). Ontology state of the art - Final report.

Ionita, T. M. (2005). *Scenario-based system architecting: A systematic approach to developing future-proof system architectures.* PhD thesis, University of Eindhoven, The Netherlands.

Ionita, T. M., America, P., & Hammer, D. K. (2005). A method for strategic scenario-based architecting. In *Proceedings of the 38th Hawaii International Conference on System Sciences (HICSS-38)* (p. 312).

IPCC (Intergovernmental Panel on Climate Change) (2001). *Climate change 2001: The scientific basis.* Cambridge University Press.

Ireland, R. (2005). *How to implement CPFR and other best collaborative practices.* Boca Raton, FL: J. Ross Publishing.

ISO (1994). Standard 10303-1: Industrial automation systems and integration – Product data representation and exchange – Part 1: Overview and fundamental principles.

ISO TC184/SC4 Standards (2006). Retrieved March 23, 2006, from http://www.tc184-sc4.org

ISO1030-1 (1994). ISO 10303 - Standard for the exchange of product data, Part 1, Overview and fundamentals principles. *International Organization for Standardization.*

ISO10303-22 (2001). ISO 10303 Standard for the exchange of product data (STEP), Part 22. *International Organization for Standardization.*

ISTAT (Italian National Institute of Statistics) (2001). *Classificazione delle professioni, Metodi e Norme - nuova serie. n. 12.* Rome: ISTAT (in Italian).

Istook, C. L. (2002). Enabling mass customization: Computer-driven alteration methods. *International Journal of Clothing Science and Technology, 14*(1), 61-76.

ITIL (2005). *What is ITIL.* Retrieved December 29, 2005, from http://www.itil.org/

JADE. Retrieved May, 2006, from http://jade.cselt.it & http://jade.tilab.com

Jahns, C., Gäde, C., & Langenhan, F. (2004). Der Management Navigator Logistics. Ein integrierter Managementansatz für die Waren- und Dokumentenlogistik,. In W. Dangelmaier, D. Kaschula, & J. Neumann (Eds.), *Supply chain management in der Automobil und Zulieferindustrie* (pp. 365-374). Paderborn, Germany: ALB-HNI..

Jain, A. K., Aparicio IV, M., & Singh, M. P. (1999). Agents for process coherence in virtual enterprises. *Communications of the ACM, 42*(3), 62-69.

Jannach, D., & Kreutler, G. (2005). Personalized user preference elicitation for e-services. In *Proceedings of IEEE International conference on e-Technology, e-Commerce and e-Service,* Hong Kong (pp. 604-611).

Japanese Ministry of Public Management, Home Affairs, Posts, and Telecommunications (PMHAPT). (2002). *Annual report on the family income and expenditure survey.* Tokyo: Japan Statistical Association (in Japanese).

Jardim-Goncalves, R. (2004). Ontology-based framework for enhanced interoperability in networked industrial environments. In *Proceedings of the 11th IFAC Symposium on Information Control Problems in Manufacturing, INCOM2004.* Salvador, Brazil.

Jardim-Goncalves, R., & Steiger, A. (2002). Integration and adoptabilidade of APs – The role of ISO TC184/SC4 standards. *Special issue: Applications in Industry of Product and Process Modelling Using Standards International Journal of Computer Applications in Technology.*

Jardim-Goncalves, R., & Steiger-Garção, A. (2001). Supporting interoperability in standard-based environments - Towards reliable integrated systems. Advances in Concurrent Engineering. In *Proceedings of the 8th ISPE International Conference on Concurrent Engineering (CE2001),* Anaheim, CA.

Jardim-Goncalves, R., & Steiger-Garção, A. (2002a). Implicit hierarchic metamodeling - In search of adaptable interoperability for manufacturing and business systems. In *Proceedings of the 5th IEEE/IFIP BASYS2002*, Mexico.

Jardim-Goncalves, R., & Steiger-Garção, A. (2002b). Implicit multi-level modeling to support integration and interoperability in flexible business environments. *Communications of ACM, Special Issue on Enterprise Components, Services, and Business Rules,* 53-57.

Jenkins, D., & Muneer, T. (2003). Modelling light-pipe performances - A natural daylighting solution. *Building and Environment, 38,* 965-972.

Jensen, T. (1999). *Functional modelling in a design support system.* Unpublished Ph.D. thesis, Technical University of Denmark, Denmark.

Jiang, Z., Wang, W., & Benbasat, I. (2005). Multimedia-based interactive advising technology for online consumer decision support. *Communications of the ACM, 48*(9), 92-98.

Jiao, J., Ma, Q., & Tseng, M. (2003). Towards high value-added products and services: Mass customization and beyond. *The International Journal of Technological Innovation, Entrepreneurship, and Technology Management, 23,* 809-821.

Jiao, J., Tseng, M. M., Duffy, V. G., & Lin, F. (1998). Product family modeling for mass customization. *Computers & Industrial Engineering, 35,* 495-498.

Jørgensen, K. A., & Petersen, T. D. (2005). *Product modelling on multiple abstraction levels.* Paper presented at the International Mass Customization Meeting, Klagenfurt, Austria.

Jørgensen, K. A. (2003). Information models representing product families. *Product Structuring Workshop, Technical University of Denmark,* January 23-24.

Jørgensen, K. A., & Petersen, T. D. (2005). Product modelling on multiple abstraction levels. In *Mass customization, concepts - Tools - Realization* (pp. 243-254).

JTC 1/SC 7/WG 17 (2006). *ISO - International Organization for Standardization.*

Juengst, E. W., & Heinrich, M. (1998). Using resource balancing to configure modular systems. *IEEE Intelligent Systems, Special Issue on Configuration, 13*(4), 50-58.

Jun, M., & Cai, S. (2001). The key determinants of Internet banking service quality: A content analysis. *International Journal of Bank Marketing, 19*(7), 276-291.

Junker, U. (2001a). Preference programming for configuration. In *Proceedings of the Workshop on Configuration (IJCAI'01)*, Seattle, WA (pp. 50-56).

Junker, U. (2004). QuickXplain: Preferred explanations and relaxations for over-constrained problems. In *Proceedings of AAAI'2004,* San Jose (pp. 167-172).

Jussien, N. (2001). E-constraints: Explanation-based constraint programming. In *Proceedings of the CP'01 Workshop on User-Interaction in Constraint Satisfaction.*

Kahle, L., Beatty, S., & Homer, P. (1986). Alternative measurement approaches to consumer values, The list of values (LOV) and values and life style (VALS). *Journal of Consumer Research, 13,* 405-409.

Kakati, M. (2002). Mass customization - Needs to go beyond technology. *Human Systems Management, 21,* 85-93.

Kalakota, R., Stallaert, J., & Whinston, A. B. (1998). Implementing real-time supply chain optimization systems. *Global Supply Chain and Technology Management, POMS,* 60-75.

Kardaras, D., & Karakostas, V. (1999). The use of fuzzy cognitive maps to simulate the information systems strategic planning process. *Information and Software Technology, 41*(4), 197-210.

Kardaras, D., Karakostas, V., & Papathanassiou, E. (2000). Facilitating the mass customisation of services with a fuzzy object-oriented modelling approach. In *Proceedings of the 31st Annual Meeting: International Conference of the Decision Sciences Institute,* Florida (pp. 680-682).

Kay, M. (1993). Making mass customization happen: Lessons for implementation. *Planning Review, 21*(4), 14-18.

Keltner, B., & Finegold, D. (1996). Adding value in banking: Human resource innovations for service firms. *Sloan Management Review, 38*(1), 57-68.

Kim, J., & Gil, Y. (2004). Towards interactive composition of semantic Web services. *2004 AAAI Spring Symposium* (Tech. Rep. SS-04-06). Retrieved March 10, 2006, from http://www.isi.edu/ikcap/scec/papers/AAAI-Symp-04-Kim-Gil.pdf

Kirani, S. H., Zualkernan, I. A., & Tsai, W. T. (1994). Evaluation of expert system testing methods. *Communications of the ACM, 37*(11).

Kirchhof, R. (2003). *Ganzheitliches komplexitätsmanagement.* Wiesbaden, Germany: Gabler.

Kitson, D. H., & Kitson, L. J. (1998). *ISO/IEC 15504 - Overview and Status.* Software Engineering Institute, Carnegie Mellon University, Pittsburgh, PA, September, 1998. Retrieved March 10, 2006, from http://www.sei.cmu.edu/iso-15504/resources/symp-se-98.pdf

Kobsa, A., Koenemann, J., & Pohl, W. (2001). Personalized hypermedia presentation techniques for improving online customer relationships. *The Knowledge Engineering Review, 16*(2), 11-155.

Kohrs, A., & Merialdo, B. (2001). Creating user-adapted Websites by the use of collaborative filtering. *Interacting with Computers, 13*, 695-716.

Konstan, J., Miller, B., Maltz, D., Herlocker, J., Gordon, L., & Riedl, J. (1997). GroupLens: Applying collaborative filtering to usenet news. *Communications of the ACM, 40*(3), 77-87.

Kosko, B. (1986). Fuzzy cognitive maps. *International Journal on Man-Machine Studies, 24*, 65-75.

Kotha, S. (1995). Mass customization: Implementing the emerging paradigm for competitive advantage. *Strategic Management Journal, 16,* 21-42.

Krasner, G. E., & Stephen, T. (1988). Pope for using the model-view-controller user interface paradigm in Smalltalk-80. *Journal of Object-Oriented Programing, 1*(August/September), 26-49.

Krause, F. L., Kimura, F., & Kjellberg, T. (1993). Product modelling. *Annals of the CIRP, 42*(2).

Kruchten, P. B. (1995). The 4+1 view model of architecture. *IEEE Software, 12*(6), 42-50.

Kühner, M. (2005). *Ein Verfahren zur Analyse prozessualer Logistikleistung auf Basis der Data Envelopment Analysis.* Dissertation thesis. Retrieved March 11, 2005, from http://elib.uni-stuttgart.de/opus/volltexte/2005/2321/pdf/Diss_Kuehner.pdf

Lampel, J. & Mintzberg, H. (1996). Customizing Customization. *Sloan Management Review, 38*(1), 21-30.

Lange, D. B., & Oshima, M. (1998). *Programming and developing Java mobile agents with aglets.* Reading, MA: Addison-Wesley.

Lassar, W. M., Manolis, C., & Winsor, R. D. (2000). Service quality perspectives and satisfaction in private banking. *International Journal of Bank Marketing, 18*(4), 244-271.

Lee, S., Kim, B. G., & Lee, K. (2004). Fuzzy cognitive map-based approach to evaluate EDI performance: A test of causal model. *Expert Systems with Applications, 27*(2), 287-299.

Lee, W. -P., & Yang, T. -H. (2003). Personalizing information appliances: A multi-agent framework for TV programme recommendations. *Expert Systems with Applications, 25,* 331-341.

Liening, A. (1999). *Komplexe Systeme zwischen Ordnung und Chaos. Neuere Entwicklungen in der Theorie nicht-linearer dynamischer Systeme und die Bedeutung für die Wirtschaftswissenschaft und Didaktik.* Lit. Münster etc.

Liker, J. (2004). *The Toyota way.* McGraw Hill.

Lindahl, M., & Ölundh, G. (2001). The meaning of functional sales. In A. J. de Ron (Ed.), *Proceedings of the 8th*

CIRP International Seminar on Life Cycle Engineering – Life Cycle Engineering: Challenges and Opportunities (pp. 211-220).

Lindahl, M., Sundin, E., Shimomura, Y., & Sakao, T. (2005). Verification of a service design tool at a global warehouse provider. *CD-ROM Proceedings of the 15th International Conference on Engineering Design, ICED05.*

Liu, B., Hsu, W., & Ma, Y. (1998). Integrating classification and association rule mining. CD-ROM *Proceedings of the 4th International Conference on Knowledge Discovery and Data Mining,* New York (pp. 27-31).

Loffredo, D. (1998). *Efficient database implementation of EXPRESS information models.* PhD thesis, Rensselaer Polytechnic Institute, Troy, NY.

Luczak, H., & Fricker, A. (1997). Komplexitätsmanagement – ein Mittel der strategischen Unternehmensgestaltung. In G. Schuh & H. P. Wiendahl (Eds.), *Komplexität und Agilität. Steckt die Produktion in der Sackgasse?* (pp. 309-323). Berlin: Springer.

Luna, E. F. G., & Aguilar-Savén, R. S. (2004, April 30-May). Manufacturing strategy linked to product life cycle. In *Proceedings of the Second World Conference on POM and 15th Annual POM Conference,* Cancun, Mexico.

Ma, M. (1999). Agents in e-commerce. *Communications of the ACM, 42*(3), 79-80.

MacCarthy, B., & Brabazon, P. (2003). In the business of mass customisation. *IEE Manufacturing Engineer, 82*(4), 30-33.

Maes, P., Guttman, R. H., & Moukas, A. G. (1999). Agents that buy and sell. *Communications of the ACM, 42*(3), 81-91.

Mailharro, D. (1998). A classification and constraint-based framework for configuration. *Artificial Intelligence in Engineering, Design, and Manufacturing, 12,* 383-397.

Mainzer, K. (1997). *Thinking in complexity* (3rd ed). Berlin: Springer.

Malik, F. (1996). *Strategie des Managements komplexer Systeme* (5th ed). Bern, Germany: Haupt.

Malik, F. (2000). *Systemisches Management, Evolution, Selbstorganisation – Grundprobleme, Funktionsmechanismen und Lösungsansätze für komplexe Systeme.* Bern, Germany: Haupt.

Manhart, P. (2005). Reconfiguration – A problem in search of solutions. In D. Jannach & A. Felfernig (Eds.), *Configuration – Papers from the Configuration Workshop at IJCAI'05* (pp. 68-71).

Männistö, T, Peltonen, H., Alho, K., & Sulonen, R. (1993). *A framework for long-term information management of product configurations* (Tech. Rep. TKO-B105). Helsinki University of Technology, Laboratory of Information Processing Science.

Männistö, T., Peltonen, H., Alho, K., & Sulonen, R. (1994). *Product configurations - An application for prototype object approach.* In M. Tokoro & R. Pareschi (Eds.), Object-Oriented Programming, 8th European Conference, ECOOP'94 (pp. 513-534). Springer-Verlag.

Männistö, T., Soininen, T., Tiihonen, J., & Sulonen, R. (1999). Framework and conceptual model for reconfiguration. *Configuration Papers from the AAAI Workshop* (AAAI Technical Report WS-99-05) (pp. 59-64). AAAI Press.

Martin, M. V., & Ishii, K. (2002). Design for variety: Developing standardized and modularised product platform architectures. *Research in Engineering Design, 13,* 213-235.

Massachussetts Institute of Technology (2005). *Lean Enterprise Model {LEM}.* Retrieved December 29, 2005, from http://process.mit.edu/Activity.asp?ID=970415113709AB5782

McAloone, T. C., & Andreason, M. M. (2004). Design for utility, sustainability, and social virtues: Developing product service systems. In *Proceedings of International Design Conference – Design 2004* (pp. 1545-1552).

McDermott, J. (1982). A rule-based configurer of computer systems. *Artificial Intelligence, 19*(1), 39-88.

McGinty, L., & Smyth, B. (2002). Deep dialogue vs. casual conversation in recommender systems. In *Proceedings of the Workshop on Personalization in eCommerce at the Second International Conference on Adaptive Hypermedia and Web-Based Systems (AH-02),* Universidad de Malaga, Spain (pp. 80-89).

McGinty, L., & Smyth, B. (2002a). Comparison-based recommendation. *Lecture Notes of Computer Science 2416, Proceedings of the 6th European Advances in Case-Based Reasoning* (pp. 575-589). Springer.

McGuiness, D., & Wright, J. (1998a). Conceptual modelling for configuration: A description logic-based approach. *Artificial Intelligence in Engineering, Design and Manufacturing (AI EDAM), 12*(98), 33–344.

McGuiness, D., & Wright, J. (1998b). An industrial strength description logics-based configurator platform. *IEEE Intelligent Systems, Special Issue on Configuration, 13*(4), 69-77.

McLaughlin, C. (1996). Why variation reduction is not everything: A new paradigm for service operations. *International Journal of Service Industry Management, 7,* 17-30.

McNee, S. M., Albert, I., Cosley, D., Gopalkrishnan, P., Lam, S. K., Rashid, A. M., Konstan, J. A., & Riedl, J. (2002). On the recommending of citations for research papers. CD-ROM *Proceedings of the 2004 Conference on Computer-Supported Cooperative Work,* New Orleans (pp. 116-125).

MDA (2003). *Model Driven Architecture, MDA Guide Version 1.0.1, June 2003.* Retrieved March 23, 2006, from http://www.omg.org/mda

Mellor, S., & Balcer, M. (2002). *Executable UML - A foundation for model-driven architecture.* Addison-Wesley.

Middleton, J. (2003). *The ultimate strategy library: The 50 most influential strategic ideas of all time.* Capstone.

MIDP: Mobile Information Device Profile. Retrieved May, 2006, from http://java.sun.com/products/midp/index.jsp

Mikkola, J. H., & Gassmann, O. (2003). Managing modularity of product architectures: Toward an integrated theory. *IEEE Transactions on Engineering Management, 50,* 204-218.

Miles, L. (1971). *Techniques of value analysis and engineering.* McGraw-Hill.

Miller, J., & Mukerji, J. (2001). *Model driven architecture white paper.* Retrieved March 23, 2006, from http://www.omg.org/cgi-bin/doc?ormsc/2001-07-01

Mittal, S., & Falkenhainer, B. (1990). Dynamic constraint satisfaction problems. In *Proceedings of 8th National Conference on Artificial Intelligence, AAAI-90* (pp. 25-32).

Mittal, S., & Frayman, F. (1989). Towards a generic model of configuration tasks. In *Proceedings of the 11th International Joint Conference on AI,* Detroit, MI (pp. 1395-1401).

Montaner, M., Lopez, B., & De la Rose, J. (2003). A taxonomy of recommender agents on the Internet. *Artificial Intelligence Review, 19,* 285-330.

Mooney, R. J., & Roy, L. (2000). Content-based book recommending using learning for text categorization. CD-ROM *Proceedings of the ACM International Conference on Digital Libraries,* San Antonio, Texas (pp. 195-204).

Moreno, A., Valls, A., & Viejo, A. (2005). *Using JADE-LEAP to implement agents in mobile devices (*Research Rep. 03-008, DEIM, URV*).* Retrieved May, 2006, from http://www.etse.urv.es/recerca/banzai/toni/MAS/papers.html

Mortensen, N. H. (1999). *Design modelling in a designers workbench.* Ph.D. project, Department of Control and Engineering Design, DTU.

Mortensen, N. H., & Hansen, C. T. (1999). Structuring as a basis for product modelling. In N. H. Mortensen & J. Sigurjonsson (Ed.), *Some implications in critical enthusiasm in contribution to design science* (pp. 111-128). Trondheim, Norway: P2005 Research Program - Norwegian Research Council.

Mortensen, N. H., Yu, B., Skovgaard, H. J., & Harlou, U. (2000). Conceptual modeling of product families in configuration projects. In *Proceedings of Product Models 2000-SIG PM,* Linköping, Sweden.

Motta, E. (1999). *Reusable components for knowledge modelling.* Amsterdam, The Netherlands: IOS Press.

Muller, G. J. (2004). *CAFCR: A multi-view method for embedded systems architecting: Balancing genericity and specificity.* Ph.D. thesis. Retrieved February 23, 2006, from http://www.gaudisite.nl/

Nagi, L. (1997). Design and implementation of a virtual information system for agile manufacturing. *IIE Transactions on Design and Manufacturing, Special issue on Agile Manufacturing, 29,* 839-857.

National Institute of Standards and Technology (2005). *Malcolm Baldrige National Quality Award.* Retrieved December 29, 2005, from http://www.quality.nist.gov/

Naylor, J. B., Naim, M. M., & Berry, D. (1999). Leagility: Integrating the lean and agile manufacturing paradigms in the total supply chain. *International Journal of Production Economics, 62*(1-2), 107-118.

Nilsson, F., & Waidringer, J. (2002). Logistics management from a complexity perspective. *Managing the Complex IV, Conference on Complex Systems and the Management of Organizations, 7-10 December 2002,* Naples, Florida.

O'Grady, P. (1999). *The age of modularity.* Iowa City, IA: Adams and Steele Publishers.

Obbink, H. J., Müller, J. K., America, P., van Ommering, R., Muller, G. J., van der Sterren, W., & Wijnstra, J. G. (2000). *COPA: A component-oriented platform architecting method for families of software intensive electronic products.* Tutorial for SPLC1, the First Software Product Line Conference, Denver, Colorado, August.

OECD (2001). *OECD environmental outlook.* OECD.

Olhager, J. (2003). Strategic positioning of the order penetration point. *International Journal of Production Economics, 85*(3), 319-329.

Olhager, J., & Wikner, J. (2000). Production planning and control tools. *Production Planning and Control, 11*(3), 210-222.

Orsvärn, K. (2005). Tacton configurator - Research directions. *Workshop on Configuration, International Conference on Artificial Intelligence (IJCAI 2005),* Edinburgh, Scotland.

Pahl, G., & Beitz, W. (1996). *Engineering design: A systematic approach, 2nd ed.* London: Springer-Verlag, Limited.

Paloheimo, K. -S., Miettinen, I., & Brax, S. (2004). *Customer-oriented industrial services.* Espoo, Finland: Report Series –Helsinki University of Technology BIT Research Centre.

Pancerella, A., & Berry, N. (1999). Adding intelligent agents to existing EI frameworks. *IEEE Internet Computing,* (Sept.-Oct.), 60-61.

Pargamin, B. (2002). Vehicle sales configuration: The cluster tree approach. *ECAI 2002 Workshop on Configuration* (pp. 35-40).

Parker, M (1996). *Strategic transformation and information technology: Paradigms for perfoming while transforming.* Prentice Hall.

Pazzani, M. (1999). A framework for collaborative, content-based, and demographic filtering. *Artificial Intelligence Review, 13*(5-6), 393-408.

Pedersen, J. L., & Edwards, K. (2004). Product configuration systems and productivity. In *Proceedings of International Conference on Economic, Technical and Organisational Aspects of Product Configuration Systems (PETO) 2004.*

Peltonen, H. (2000). *Concepts and an implementation for product data management.* Ph.D. thesis, Helsinki University of Technology, Department of Computer Science and Engineering. Published in Acta Polytechnica Scandinavica, Mathematics, and Computing Series. No. 105, Espoo.

Petersen, T. D., & Jørgensen, K. A. (2005). Product modelling for mass customisation in global ETO companies.

In *Mass customization, concepts - Tools - Realization* (pp. 333-344).

Philips Medical Systems (PMS) (2005). X-ray angiography. Retrieved February 23, 2006, from www.medical.philips.com/main/clinicalsegments/cardiology/angiography.html

Piller, F. T. (2002). Customer interaction and digitalizability-A structural approach to mass customisation. In C. Rautenstrauch, R. S. Eggebert, & K. Turowski (Eds.), *Moving into mass customisation* (pp. 119-137). Berlin: Springer-Verlag.

Piller, F. T. (2003). *Mass customization. Ein wettbewerbsstrategisches Konzept im Informationszeitalter.* Wiesbaden, Germany: Deutscher Universitätsverlag.

Piller, F. T., & Müller, M. (2004). A new marketing approach to mass customisation. *International Journal of Computer Integrated Manufacturing, 17*(7), 583-593.

Piller, F. T., Moeslein, K., & Stotko, C. M. (2004). Does mass customization pay? An economic approach to evaluate customer integration. *Production Planning & Control, 15*(4), 435-444.

Piller, F., Schubert, P., Koch, M., & Moeslein, K. (2004). From mass customization to collaborative customer co-design. In T. Leino, T. Saarinen, & S. Klein (Eds.), *Proceedings of the Twelfth European Conference on Information Systems, Turku School of Economics and Business Administration,* Turku, Finland.

Pindyck, R. S., & Rubinfield, D. L. (2001). *Microeconomics* (5th ed.). Prentice Hall International.

Pine II, B. J. (1993). *Mass customization: The new frontier in business competition.* Boston: Harvard Business School Press.

Pine II, B. J., & Gilmore, J. H. (1999). *The experience economy.* Boston: Harvard Business School Press.

Pine II, B. J., Victor, B., & Boynton, A. C. (1993). Making mass customisation work. *Harvard Business Review, 71*(5), 108-119.

Pine, B. J. II, Peppers, D., & Rogers, M. (1995). Do you want to keep your customers forever? *Harvard Business Review, 73*(2), 103-114.

PLib (2000). ISO 13584 Parts Library, ISO TC184/SC4, Part 102, View Exchange Protocol: View Exchange Protocol by ISO10303 conforming specification. *International Organization for Standardization.*

Popper, K. (1944). *The poverty of historicism, Routledge Classics, 2002.* Routledge & Kegan Paul, 1957, originally published in Economia, 1944/5.

Porter, M. F. (1980). An algorithm for suffix stripping. *Program, 14*(3), 130-137.

Post, G. V., & Anderson, D. L. (2006). *Management information systems: Solving business problems with information technology.* New York: McGraw-Hill.

Prahalad, C. K., & Ramaswamy, V. (2004). *The future of competition: Co-creating unique value with customers.* Boston: Harvard Business School Press.

Preece, A., Talbot, S., & Vignollet, L. (1997). Evaluation of verification tools for knowledge-based systems. *International Journal of Human-Computer Studies, 47,* 629-658.

Pretschner, A. (2001). Classical search strategies for test case generation with constraint logical programming. In *Proceedings of Workshop on Formal Approaches to Testing of Software,* Aalborg, Denmark (pp. 47-60).

Project Management Institute (2005). *PMBOK® Guide.* Retrieved December 29, 2005, from http://www.pmi.org/prod/groups/public/documents/info/pp_pmbok-2000welcome.asp

Pu, P., Faltings, B., & Torrens, M. (2003). User-involved preference elicitation. In *Proceedings of the 18th International Joint Conference on Artificial Intelligence (IJCAI'03), Workshop on Configuration,* Acapulco.

Pugh, S. (1997). *Total design: Integrated methods for successful product engineering.* Wokingham: Addison-Wesley.

Radder, L., & Louw, L. (1999). Research and concepts: Mass customization and mass production. *The TQM Magazine, 11*(1), 35-40.

Radder, L., & Louw, L. (2000). The readiness of selected South African organisations to mass customisation. *The TQM Magazine, 12*(4), 295-304.

Ramaswamy, R. (1996). *Design and management of service processes*. Addison-Wesley Publishing Company.

Rational (2006). Retrieved March 22, 2006, from http://www.rational.com/uml

Reichwald, R., Piller, F. T., & Möslein, K. (2000). Information as a critical success factor or: Why even a customized shoe not always fits. In *Proceedings Administrative Sciences Association of Canada, International Federation of Scholarly Associations of Management 2000 Conference.*

Reichwald, R., Piller, F., & Mueller, M. (2004). A multichannel interaction platform for mass customization – Concept and empirical investigation. *Workshop on Information Systems for Mass Customization (ISMC 2004), Fourth International ICSC Symposium on Engineering of Intelligent Systems (EIS 2004).*

Reiter, R. (1987). A theory of diagnosis from first principles. *Artificial Intelligence, 23*(1), 57-95.

Riis, J., Hansen, B. L., & Hvam, L. (2003). *Framework for product knowledge and product-related knowledge which supports modelling for mass customization.* Paper presented at the 2nd World Congress on Mass Customization and Personalization, Munich, Germany.

Robertson, D., & Ulrich, K. (1998). Planning for product platforms. *Innovation Driving Product, Process, and Market Change. MITSloan Management Review, 39*(4), 19-31.

Rochart, G., Jussien, N., & Laburthe, F. (2003). Challenging explanations for global constraints. In *Proceedings of the CP'03 Workshop on User-Interaction in Constraint Satisfaction,* Ireland.

Roozenburg, M., & Eekels, J. (1995). *Product design: Fundamentals and methods.* Chichester, UK: John Wiley & Sons.

RosettaNet (1998). Retrieved May, 2006, from http://www.rosettanet.org

Ross, A. (1996). Selling uniqueness. *IEE Manufacturing Engineer, 75*(6), 260-263.

Royalty, J., Holland, R., Goldsmith, J., & Dekhtyar, A. (2002). POET: The online preference elicitation tool. In *Proceedings of AAAI'02 Workshop on Preferences in AI and CP: Symbolic Approaches,* Edmonton, CA.

Rumbaugh, J. (1998). *UML - The unified modeling language.* Addison-Wesley.

Rumbaugh, J., Jacobson, I., & Booch, G. (1989). *The Unified Modeling Language Reference Manual.* Addison-Wesley.

Sabin, D., & Weigel, R. (1998). Product configuration frameworks – A survey. *IEEE Intelligent Systems & Their Applications, 13*(4), 42-49.

Sakao, T., & Shimomura, Y. (2004). A method and a computerized tool for service design. In *Proceedings of the International Design Conference (DESIGN 2004)* (pp. 497-502).

Sakao, T., & Shimomura, Y. (2005a). A novel design methodology for services to increase value combining service and product based on service engineering. *CD-ROM Proceeding of the 4th International Symposium on Environmentally Conscious Design and Inverse Manufacturing (Eco Design 2005).* IEEE Computer Society.

Sakao, T., & Shimomura, Y. (2005b). MVC (model for balancing value and costs): A fundamental model to design environmentally-conscious services. *CD-ROM Proceedings of the Fourth International Symposium on Environmentally Conscious Design and Inverse Manufacturing (EcoDesign 2005).* IEEE Computer Society.

Sakao, T., Shimomura, Y., Comstock, M., & Sundin, E. (2005c). Service engineering for value customization. *CD-ROM Proceedings of the 3rd Interdisciplinary World Congress on Mass Customization and Personalization (MCPC).*

Sakao, T., Shimomura, Y., Comstock, M., & Sundin, E. (in press). A method of value customization. *International Design Conference – (DESIGN 2006).*

Sakao, T., Shimomura, Y., Petti, L., & Raggi, A. (2005d). Applying service engineering methods and tools to improve various customers satisfaction in an accommodation service. *CD-ROM Proceedings of the 3rd Interdisciplinary World Congress on Mass Customization and Personalization (MCPC).*

Sakao, T., Watanabe, K., & Shimomura, Y. (2003). A Method to Support Environmentally Conscious Service Design Using Quality Function Deployment (QFD). In *The Third International Symposium of Environmentally Conscious Design and Inverse Manufacturing (Ecodesign 2003)* (pp. 567-574). IEEE Computer Society.

Salvador, F., & Forza, C. (2004). Configuring products to address the customization-responsiveness squeeze: A survey of management issues and opportunities. *International Journal of Production Economics, 91*(3), 273-291.

Sandholm, T. (1999). Automated negotiation. *Communications of the ACM, 42*(3), 84-85.

Sarwar, B., Karypis, G., Konstan, J. A., & Riedl, J. T. (2001). Item-based collaborative filtering recommendation algorithms. In *Proceedings of the 10th International World Wide Web Conference* (pp. 285-295).

Schafer, J. B., Konstan, J.. & Riedl, J. (1999). Recommender systems in E-Commerce. CD-ROM *Proceedings of the 1st ACM Conference on Electronic Commerce,* Denver, Colorado (pp. 158-166).

Schafer, J., Konstan, J., & Riedl, J. T. (2000). Electronic commerce recommender applications. *Journal of Data Mining and Knowledge Discovery, 5*(1/2), 115-152.

Schlott, S. (2005). *Wahnsinnn mit Methode.* Automobil-Produktion, (January, 2005), 38-42.

Schmitz, V., Leukel, J., & Kelkar, O. (2004). XML-based data exchange of product model data in e-procurement and e-sales: The case of BMECAT 2.0. In *Proceedings of the International Conference on Economic, Technical, and Organisational Aspects of Product Configuration Systems,* Copenhagen, Denmark (pp. 97-108).

Schneider, M., Scnaider, E., Kandel, A., & Chew, G. (1998). Automatic construction of FCMs. *Fuzzy Sets and Systems, 93*(2), 161-172.

Schooler, S. B. (2005). Toward a multi-agent information management infrastucture for product family planning and mass customization. *International Journal of Mass Customization, 1*(1).

Schwartz, P. (1996). *The art of the long view.* Currency Doubleday.

Shah, J. B. (2002). ST, HP VMI program hitting its stride. *Electronics Business News (EBN), 42.* Retrieved May, 2006, from http://www.ebnonline.com

Shao, L., & Callow, J. M. (2003). Daylighting performance of optical rods. *Solar Energy, 75,* 439-445.

Shardanand, U., & Maes, P. (1995). Social information filtering: Algorithms for automating word of mouth. CD-ROM *Proceedings of the 1995 Conference on Human Factors in Computing Systems,* Denver, Colorado (pp. 210-217).

Sheard, S. A. (1997). The frameworks quagmire, A brief look. *Software Productivity Consortium,* Herndon, VA. Retrieved December 23, 2005, from http://www.software.org/quagmire/frampapr/frampapr.html

Sheffi, Y. (2005). *The resilient enterprise: Overcoming vulnerability for competitive advantage.* Cambridge, MA: The MIT Press.

Shimomura, Y., & Tomiyama, T. (2002). Service modeling for service engineering. In *Proceedings of the 5th International Conference on Design of Information Infrastructure Systems for Manufacturing 2002 DIISM2002* (pp. 309-316).

Shimomura, Y., Sakao, T., Hara, T., Arai, T., & Tomiyama, T. (in press). Service Explorer - A tool for service design. In E. Arai & T. Arai (Eds.), *Mechatronics for safety, security, and dependability in a new era.* Elsevier.

SIEMENS (2003). *Erster Prozessmanagement-Summit in Wien. Plenarvortrag von PSE zeigt "State of the art" bei Siemens.* 2003-11-10. Retrieved March 11, 2005, from http://www.pse.siemens.at/apps/pseauftritt/ge/pseinter-net.nsf/CD_Index?OpenFrameset&Bookmark&/0/PK-18C3295572D27C4AC1256DD4002DFF2B

Silveira, G. D., Borenstein, D., & Fogliatto, F. S. (2001). Mass customization: Literature review and research directions. *International Journal of Production Economics, 72*, 1-13.

Simpson, T. W. (2005). Product platform design and customization: Status and promise. *Special Issue on Platform Product Development for Mass Customization, AIEDAM, 18*(1).

Singh, R., Salam, A. F., & Iyer, L. (2005). Agents in e-supply chains. *Communications of the ACM, 48*(6), 109-115.

Skjevdal, R., & Idsoe, E. A. (2005). *The competitive impact of product configurators in mass tailoring and mass customization companies.* Paper presented at the World Congress on Mass Customization and Personalization, Hong-Kong, China.

Slack, N., Chambers, S., & Johnston, R. (2004). *Operations management.* Essex, UK: FT/Prentice Hall.

Slywotzky, A. J. (2000). The age of the choiceboard. *Harvard Business Review, 78*(1), 40-41.

SOA (2006). *The Service-Oriented Architecture.* Retrieved March 23, 2006, from http://msdn.microsoft.com/architecture/soa/default.aspx

Software Process Improvement and Capability. *Determination.* Retrieved December 5, 2005, from http://www.sqi.gu.edu.au/spice/

Software Quality Institute (2005). *Software Process Improvement and Capability determination.* Retrieved December 29, 2005, from http://www.sqi.gu.edu.au/spice/

Soininen, T. (2002). *Configurable products and product configurators.* Helsinki University of Technology.

Soininen, T., Tiihonen, J., Maenistoe, T., & Sulonen, R. (1998). Towards a general ontology of configuration. *AI Engineering Design Analysis and Manufacturing Journal, 12*(4), 357-372.

Soni, D., Nord, R. L., & Hofmeister, C. (1995, April 23-30). Software architecture in industrial applications. In *Proceedings of the 17th International Conference on Software Engineering* Seattle, WA.

Spring, M., & Dalrymple, J. F. (2000) Product customisation and manufacturing strategy. *International Journal of Operations & Production Management, 20*(4), 441-467.

Staub, G. (1998). ISO TC184/SC4QC N068, *Interpretation of PLib Services-Guideline for the common interpretation of the "services" provided by PLib using the STEP IR.*

Steger-Jensen, K., & Svensson, C. (2003). Issues of mass customisation and supporting IT-solutions. *Computers in Industry, 54*, 83-103.

Stolze, M., Field, S., & Kleijer, P. (2000). Combining configuration and evaluation mechanisms to support to selection of modular insurance products. In *Proceedings of the 8th European Conference on Information Systems* (pp. 858-865).

Strom, U., & Axworthy, A. (2000). *Product configurators: The big picture.* Retrieved from http://www.midrangeERP.com

Stumptner, M., & Wotawa, F. (1999). Reconfiguration using model-based diagnosis. In *Proceedings of the International Workshop on Diagnosis (DX99)*, Scotland.

Suh, N. P. (1988). Basic concepts in design for producibility. *Annals of the CIRP, 37*(2), 559-567

Sundermeyer, K. (2001). Collaborative supply net management. In F. Baader, G. Brewka, & T. Eiter (Eds.), *KI:2001, Advances in artificial intelligence* (pp. 467-470).

Sundin, E., Lindahl, M., Shimomura, Y., & Sakao, T. (2005). New engineering design for functional sales business. *CD-ROM Proceedings of the 15th International Conference on Engineering Design ICED05.*

Sung, H. H. (2002). Helping customers decide through Web personalization. *IEEE Intelligent Systems, 17*(6), 34-43.

Supply Chain Council (2005). *Supply-Chain Operations Reference Model: SCOR Version 7.0 Overview.* Retrieved December 23, 2005, from http://www.supply-chain.org/galleries/default-file/SCOR%207.0%20Overview.pdf

Svensson, C., & Barfod, A. (2002). Limits and opportunities in mass customization for "build to order" SMEs. *Computers in Industry, 49,* 77-89.

Sviokla, J.J. (1990). An examination of the impact of expert systems on the firm: The case of XCON. *MIS Quarterly, 14*(2), 127-140.

Taber, R. (1991). Knowledge processing with fuzzy cognitive maps. *Expert Systems with Applications, 12*(2), 83-87.

Takeda, H., Sakai, H., Nomaguchi, Y., Yoshioka, M., Shimomura, Y., & Tomiyama, T. (2003). Universal abduction studio - Proposal of a design support environment for creative thinking in design. *CD-ROM Proceedings of the 14th International Conference on Engineering Design, ICED03.*

Tanaka, K. (1997). *An introduction to fuzzy logic for practical applications.* Springer Verlag.

Terveen, L., & Hill, W. (2001). Beyond recommender systems: Helping people help each other. In J. Carroll (Ed.), *HCI in the new millennium.* Addison Wesley.

Thomas, C. (1996). *Ein objektorientiertes Konzept zur Modellierung und Simulation komplexer Systeme.* Düsseldorf, Germany: VDI.

Thompson, C. A., Goeker, M. H., & Langley, P. (2004). A personalized system for conversational recommendations. *Journal of Artificial Intelligence Research, 21,* 393-428.

Thomsen, E. (1997). *OLAP solutions building: Multidimensional information systems.* Chichester, England: John Wiley & Sons.

Tiihonen, J., & Soininen, T. (1997). *Product configurators – Information system support for configurable products* (Tech. Rep. TKO-B137). Helsinki University of Technology, Laboratory of Information Processing Science. Also published in Richardson, T. (Ed.). (1997), *Using information technology during the sales visit.* Cambridge, UK: Hewson Group.

Tiihonen, J., Soininen, T., Männistö, T. & Sulonen, R. (1996). State-of-the-practice in product configuration—A survey of 10 cases in the Finnish industry. In T. Tomiyama, M. Mäntylä, & S. Finger (Eds.), *Knowledge Intensive CAD. Vol. 1* (pp. 95-114). Chapman & Hall.

Tiihonen, J., Soininen, T., Männistö, T. & Sulonen, R. (1998). Configurable products - Lessons learned from the Finnish industry. In *Proceedings of 2nd International Conference on Engineering Design and Automation (ED&A '98).* Integrated Technology Systems, Inc.

Tischner, U., Verkuijl, M., & Tukker, A. (2002). *First draft PSS review.* Cologne, Germany: Econcept.

Toffler, A. (1970). *Future shock.* New York: Bantam Books.

Tomiyama, T. (2001). Service engineering to intensify service contents in product life cycles. In *Proceedings of the Second International Symposium on Environmentally-Conscious Design and Inverse Manufacturing (EcoDesign 2001)* (pp. 613-618). IEEE Computer Society.

Trireme International (2006). Retrieved March 23, 2006, from http://www.trireme.u-net.com/catalysis

Tsang, E. (1993). *Foundations of constraint satisfaction.* London: Academic Press.

Tseng, M. M., & Jiao, J. (1998). Fundamental issues regarding developing product family architecture for mass customisation. In *Proceedings of the 5th International Conference on Industrial Engineering and Engineering Management,* Beijing, China.

Tseng, M. M., & Jiao, J. (2001). Mass customization. In *Handbook of industrial engineering, technology, and operation management* (3rd ed.). (p. 685).

Tseng, M. M., & Jiao, J. (1996). Design for mass customization. *Annals of the CIRP, 45*(1), 153-156.

Tseng, M., & Jiao, J. (1997). Case-based evolutionary design form mass customisation. In *Proceedings of the*

21st International Conference on Computer and Industrial Engineering: Vol. 33(1-2), 319-323.

Tseng, M., & Jiao, J. (2001). Mass customization. In G. Salvendy (Ed.), *Handbook of industrial engineering,* (3rd ed.). (pp. 684-709). New York: Wiley.

Tseng, M., & Piller, F. (2003). The customer centric enterprise. In M. M. Tseng & F. T. Piller (Eds.), *The customer centric enterprise* (pp. 3–16). Heidelberg, Germany: Springer.

Tukker, A. (2004). Eight types of product-service systems: Eight ways to sustainability? Experiences from Suspronet. *Business Strategy and the Environment, 13,* 246-260.

Tut, M., & Edmond, D. (2002). The use of patterns in service composition. In *Proceedings of the Workshop on Web Services, e-Business, and the Semantic Web, held in conjunction with CAiSE02, Toronto, Canada, Lecture Notes in Computer Science, 2512* (pp. 27-28). Springer Verlag.

Ulrich, H. (1968). *Die Unternehmung als produktives soziales System.* Bern/Stuttgart, Germany: Paul Haupt Verlag.

Ulrich, H., & Probst, G. J. B. (1995). *Anleitung zum ganzheitlichen Denken und Handeln: ein Brevier für Führungskräfte* (4th ed). Bern, Germany: Paul Haupt Verlag.

Ulrich, K. T., & Eppinger, S. D. (1995). *Product design and development.* New York: McGraw-Hill.

Ulrich, K. T., & Eppinger, S. D. (2000). *Product design and development.* McGraw Hill.

Umar (1999). A framework for analyzing virtual enterprise infrastructure. In *Proceedings of the 9th International Workshop on Research Issues in Data Engineering - IT for Virtual Enterprises, RIDE-VE'99* (pp. 4-11). IEEE Computer Society.

Van Donk, D. P. (2001). Make to stock or make-to-order: The decoupling point in the food processing industries. *International Journal of Production Economics, 69*(2), 297-306.

van Harmelen, F., Patel-Schneider, P. F., & Horrocks, I. (2001). *A Model-Theoretic Semantics for DAML+OIL.* Retrieved in December, 2005, from http://www.daml.org

vanNoord, G., & Gerdemann, D. (2001). Finite state transducers with predicates and identities. *Grammars, 4*(3), 263-286.

Vanwelkenheysen, J. (1998). The tender support system. *Knowledge-Based Systems, 11,* 363-372.

Vargas, C. (1995). *Modélisation du processus de conception en ingénierie des systèmes mécaniques. Mise en oeuvre basée sur la propagation de contraintes. Application à la conception d'une culasse automobile.* Unpublished PhD thesis, ENS Cachan, France.

Vlosky, R. P. (1998). Partnerships versus typical relationships between wood products distributors and their manufacturer suppliers. *Forest Products Journal, 48*(3), 27-35.

W3C (2006). *World Wide Web Consortium.* Retrieved March 23, 2006, from http://www.w3c.org

Wadhwa, S. S. (2002). Customer satisfaction and health care delivery systems: Commentary with Australian bias. *The Internet Journal of Nuclear Medicine.* Retrieved November 15, 2005, from www.ispub.com/ostia/index.php?xmlFilePath=journals/ijh/vol3n1/bias.xml

Walker, R.H., Craig-Lees,M., Hecker, R., & Francis, H. (2002). Technology-enabled service delivery: An investigation of the reasons affecting customer adoption and rejection. International *Journal of Service Industry Management, 13*(1), 91-106.

Wang, F. -H., & Shaob, H. -M. (2004). Effective personalized recommendation based on time-framed navigation clustering and association mining. *Expert Systems with Applications, 27,* 365-377.

Wang, M. (2003). Assessment of e-service quality via e-satisfaction in e-commerce globalization. *The Electronic Journal on Information Systems in Developing Countries, 11*(10), 1-4.

Warmer, J., & Kleppe, A. (2003). *The Object Constraint Language 2.0*. Addison Wesley.

Wastell, D. G., White, P., & Kawalek, P. (1994). A methodology for business process redesign: Experiences and issues. *Journal of Strategic Information Systems, 3*(1), 23-40.

Watanabe, K., Shimomura, Y., Sakao, T., Raggi, A., & Petti, L. (2004). Application of a service modeling tool to hotel industry. In *Proceedings of the Sixth International Conference on EcoBalance* (pp. 495-498).

Westphal, J. R. (2000). *Komplexitätsmanagement in der Produktionslogistik*. Institut für Wirtschaft und Verkehr, Lehrstuhl für Verkehrsbetrieblehre und Logistik, Technische Universität Dresden. Retrieved December 15, 2005, from http://www.tu-dresden.de/vkiwv/VWL/diskussion/diskp/dskp0004.pdf

Wikner, J., & Rudberg, M. (2005). Integrating production and engineering perspectives on the customer order decoupling point. *International Journal of Operations & Production Management, 25*(7), 623-641.

Wildemann, H. (1998). Komplexitätsmanagement durch Prozess- und Produktgestaltung. In D. Adam, et al., *Komplexitätsmanagement*, Schriften zur Unternehmensführung (pp. 29-45). Wiesbaden, Germany: Gabler.

Wilke, J. (2002). Using agent-based simulation to analyze supply chain value and performance. In *Proceedings of the Supply Chain World Conference and Exhibition*, New Orleans, LA.

Wind, J., & Rangaswamy, A. (2001). Customerization: The next revolution in mass customization. *Journal of Interactive Marketing, 15*(1), 13-32.

Wind, Y. (2001). The challenge of "customerization" in financial services. *Communications of the ACM, 44*(5), 39-44.

Winkler, R. (2005). *Modulare Auftragsbewirtschaftung. Methode der virtuellen Modularisierung in der automobilen kundenindividuellen Serienfertigung aus logistischer Perspektive*. Unpublished doctoral dissertation, constituent of a current doctoral project, publication in preparation, Graz University of Technology, Industrial Management and Innovations Research.

Winter, R. (2001). Mass customization and beyond - Evolution of customer centricity in financial services. In M. F. Sebaaly (Ed.), *Proceedings of the International NAISO Congress on Information Science Innovations (ISI'2001)*. ICSC Academic Press. 8 pages (CDROM) Republished in C. Rautenstrauch, R. Seelmann-Eggebert, & K. Turowski (Eds.), *Moving into mass customization - Information systems and management principles* (pp. 197-213). Berlin: Springer.

Wright, J. R., Weixelbaum, E. S., Vesonder, G. T., Brown, K. E., Palmer, S. R., Berman, J. I., & Moore, H. H. (1993). A knowledge-based configurator that supports sales, engineering, and manufacturing at AT&T network systems. *AI Magazine, 14*(3), 69-80.

WS-I (2006). Web services interoperability organization. *WS-I*. Retrieved March 23, 2006, from http://www.ws-i.org

XMI, XML Meta-data Interchange (2006). Retrieved March 23, 2006, from http://www.omg.org/technology/xml/index.htm

Yang, B., & Burns, N. (2003). Implications of postponement for the supply chain. *International Journal of Production Research, 41*(9), 2075-2090.

Yeong, B. C., Yoon, H. C., & Soung, H. K. (2005). Mining changes in customer buying behavior for collaborative recommendations. *Expert Systems with Applications, 28*, 359-369.

Yokoo, M. (2001). *Distributed constraint satisfaction*. Berlin/New York: Springer.

Yokoo, M., Durfee, E. H., Ishida, T., & Kuwabara, K. (1998). The distributed constraint satisfaction problem. *IEEE Transactions on Knowledge and Data Engineering, 10*(5), 673-685.

Yong, S. K., Yum, B. -J., Song, J., & Su, M. K. (2005). Development of a recommender system based on navigational and behavioral patterns of customers in e-commerce sites. *Expert Systems with Applications, 28*, 381-393.

Yoon, H. C., & Jae, K. K. (2004). Application of Web usage mining and product taxonomy to collaborative recommendations in e-commerce. *Expert Systems with Applications, 26*, 233-246.

Yu, B., & Skovgaard, H. J. (1998). A configuration tool to increase product competitiveness. *IEEE Intelligent Systems, 13*(4), 34-41.

Yu, E., & Mylopoulos, J. (1995). From E-R to A-R - Modelling strategic actor relationships for business process re-engineering. *International Journal of Cooperative Information Systems, 4*(2 & 3), 125-144.

Yu, L., Liu, L., & Li, X. (2005). A hybrid collaborative filtering method for multiple-interests and multiple-content recommendation in e-commerce. *Expert Systems with Applications, 28*, 67-77.

Yuan, S. -T., & Cheng, C. (2004). Ontology-based personalized couple clustering for heterogeneous product recommendation in mobile marketing. *Expert Systems with Applications, 26*, 461.

Zadeh, L. A. (1973). Outline of a new approach to the analysis of complex systems and decision processes. *IEEE Transactions on Systems, Man, and Cybernetics, SMC-3*(1), 28-44.

Zanker, M. (2002). *Distributed configuration*. PhD thesis, University Klagenfurt, Austria.

Zhang, W. R., Chen, S. S., & Bezdek, J. C. (1989). Pool2: A generic system for cognitive map development and decision analysis. *IEEE Transactions on Systems, Man, and Cybernetics, 19*(1), 31-39.

Zhang, X. Y., & Huan, G. Q. (2005). Integrated platform product development and supply chain configuration for manufacturing firm in mass customization. In T. Blecker & G. Friedrich (Eds.), *Mass customization, concepts - Tools - Realization. Proceeding of the International Mass Customization Meeting 2005 (IMCM'05). Gito, Berlin* (pp. 457-470).

Zipkin, P. (2001). The limits of mass customization. *MIT Sloan Management Review, 42*(3), 81-87.

About the Contributors

Thorsten Blecker is a full professor at the Hamburg University of Technology, Department for Business Logistics and General Management (5-11). He holds a master's degree in business administration (with honors) and a PhD (summa cum laude) from the University of Duisburg, Germany. He finished his habilitation thesis in September, 2004, at the University of Klagenfurt, Austria. Blecker is guest-editor of a special issue of *IEEE Transactions on Engineering Management* on "Mass Customization Manufacturing Systems" (forthcoming by 2007), co-editor and author of several books, for example, *"Production/Operations Management in Virtual Organizations"*, *"Enterprise without Boundaries"*, *"Competitive Strategies"*, *"Web-Based Manufacturing"* and *"Information and Management Systems for Product Customization"*. His main research interests include business logistics and supply chain management, production/operations management, industrial information systems, Internet-based production systems, mass customization manufacturing systems, strategic management, and virtual organizations.

Gerhard Friedrich is a full professor of computer science at the University Klagenfurt, Austria. He manages the Institute for Business Informatics and Application Systems and directs the Computer Science in Production, Operation and Management research group. From 1993 to 1997, he was the head of the Department for Configuration and Diagnosis Systems at Siemens Austria. Friedrich received a PhD and an MS in computer science from Vienna University of Technology, Austria, and was a guest researcher at the Stanford Research Institute and at Siemens Corporate Research. His research interests include knowledge acquisition, constraint satisfaction, configuration, planning, and diagnosis.

* * *

Pierre America received a master's degree from the University of Utrecht in 1982 and a PhD from the Free University of Amsterdam in 1989. Since he joined Philips Research in 1982, he has been working in different areas of computer science, ranging from formal aspects of parallel object-oriented programming to music processing. Over the last years, he has been working on software and system architecting approaches to deal with variability in product families, with integrating systems into larger systems, and with evolution of systems. He has been applying and validating these approaches in close cooperation with Philips Medical Systems.

José Ángel Lakunza is the design and production technologies area manager in the design and production area at Ikerlan. He has 20 years' experience working within the areas of CAD/CAM, design technologies, business processes, and so forth. He has been involved in several national and European research projects as well as industry transfer projects in the fields of CAD/CAM systems, product configurators, new product development, and business process redesign. Currently, he is involved in national research projects dealing with product models and mass customization.

Joseba Arana is a principal investigator in the design and production technologies area at Ikerlan, where he has over 20 years' experience working in and heading different departments within the areas of CAD/CAM and design technologies. Previously, he worked as an R&D engineer in the design and construction industry after studying industrial engineering at the Engineering School in Bilbao. He is involved in, and manages, several national and European research projects as well as industry transfer projects within the areas of mass customization, product configuration, product architecture, new product development, and knowledge management.

María Elejoste is an investigator in the design and production technologies area at Ikerlan, where she has over 10 years' experience working within the areas of CAD/CAM and design technologies. She manages several industry transfer projects in the fields of tailor-made CAD/CAM and product configuration systems development. Currently, she is involved in national research projects dealing with product architecture and modularity for mass customization.

Corinna Engelhardt-Nowitzki is head of the Institute for Industrial Logistics, University of Leoben, Austria. She holds a master's degree in business administration from the University of Munich, Germany, and a PhD on the topic of information logistics from the University of Leoben, Austria. Since 2003, she has been chair of industrial logistics at the University of Leoben. Her research concerns process management and supply chain management, production logistics, and knowledge logistics. Her industrial experience has touched several fields, mainly located in the electronic and microelectronic sector (for example, Siemens AG) as well as consulting, training, and coaching in the field of logistics and process management.

Alexander Felfernig is a university assistant of computer science at the University Klagenfurt. He received a PhD and MS from the University Klagenfurt, where he is a member of the Computer Science in Production, Operation, and Management research group. His main research areas include knowledge-based configuration, knowledge-based recommenders in e-commerce, psychological aspects of consumer buying behavior, model-based diagnosis with a special focus on knowledge acquisition, and approaches to test automation in knowledge-based systems development. Within the context of these research areas, he coordinated a set of industrial and research projects and has published in a number of international journals and conferences.

Manoochehr Ghiassi is a professor of information systems, a Breetwor fellow, and director of the MSIS program at Santa Clara University, Santa Clara, CA. He received a BS from Tehran University, and an MS in economics from Southern Illinois University at Carbondale. He also holds an MS in computer science and a PhD in industrial engineering, both from the University of Illinois at Urbana-Champaign. His current research interests include artificial neural network, software engineering, software testing, supply chain management, and simulation modeling. He is a member of the IEEE, and the ACM.

António Grilo holds a PhD in e-commerce from the University of Salford, UK. He lectures on project management, operations management, and information systems at the university, in master and undergraduate degrees. He also collaborates with UNINOVA Institute on research. Besides academia, he has been working in the last seven years as a management information systems consultant, particularly in e-business, e-commerce, and project management information systems. Currently he is a partner at Neobiz Consulting, a Portuguese management and information systems company.

Dieter K. Hammer is a professor for CS at the University of Groningen, and *emeritus* professor at the Eindhoven University of Technology, The Netherlands. His current research interests are software engineering and software architecture. Before his university appointment, he worked for 10 years in industry. He holds a BSc in mechanical engineering and received his MSc and PhD from the Physics Department of the Vienna University of Technology. During his professional career, he has written over 100 papers on various subjects. He has also been involved in the organization of many workshops and conferences and has provided consultancy to major industries.

Mikko Heiskala is a researcher in the Human Capital and Leadership Research Group (HCL) at the Department of Industrial Engineering and Management of Helsinki University of Technology (HUT). His main research interests are mass customization and configuration, particularly of services, modeling configurable services for configuration and design, configurators, and business and operations based on these. He has worked in the area of product configuration and modeling since the year 2000. He is currently working towards a PhD at HUT.

Mugurel Ionita is a member of the Software Engineering and Architecture Group at University of Groningen. Here, Ionita's research interests include strategy and innovation, strategic methods for system design, system architecture assessment, and service-centric system engineering. Ionita holds an MSc degree from the Politehnica University of Bucharest, and a PhD from the Eindhoven University of Technology. Currently, he follows an MBA program at the University of Groningen, to combine knowledge about business and technology.

Dietmar Jannach is a university assistant at the University Klagenfurt, Austria, where he also received his MS and PhD in computer science. His research interests are on the different aspects of building intelligent systems in e-commerce, comprising of knowledge-representation approaches, problem-solving techniques, interactive applications, as well as engineering aspects. Jannach has published numerous international journal, conference, and workshop papers in the area of interactive selling solutions and, in particular, in the domain of next-generation product configuration systems.

Ricardo Jardim-Goncalves holds a PhD degree in industrial information systems by the New University of Lisbon. He is an auxiliar professor at the New University of Lisbon, Faculty of Sciences and Technology, and a senior researcher at UNINOVA institute. He is graduated in computer science, with MSc in operational research and systems engineering. His research activities have focused on standard-based intelligent integration frameworks for interoperability, covering architectures, methodologies, and toolkits to support improved development, harmonization, and implementation of standards for data exchange in industry, from design to e-business. He has been a technical international project leader for more than 10 years, with more than 50 papers published in conferences, journals, and books. He is project leader in ISO TC184/SC4.

Jianxin Jiao is an assistant professor of systems and engineering management, School of Mechanical and Aerospace Engineering, Nanyang Technological University, Singapore. He is the convener and coordinator of Global Manufacturing and Logistics Forum at Nanyang. He received a PhD from the Department of Industrial Engineering and Engineering Management, Hong Kong University of Science and Technology. He holds a bachelor's degree in mechanical engineering from Tianjin University of Science and Technology in China, and a master's degree in mechanical engineering from Tianjin University in China. He has worked as a lecturer in the Department of Management at Tianjin University. His research interests include mass customization, design theory and methodology, reconfigurable manufacturing systems, engineering logistics, and intelligent systems.

Bill Karakostas is a senior lecturer at the School of Informatics at the City University, London. Dr. Karakostas holds a BSc (Hons) in computer engineering from the University of Patras, Greece, as well as an MPhil and a PhD from the Department of Computation at the University of Manchester Institute of Science and Technology (UMIST), England. He has been leading research projects in IS/IT for over 15 years, and he has published extensively in the areas of software engineering and IS modeling and e-commerce technologies. He is scientific advisor in IT to English and Greek companies.

Dimitris Kardaras is an assistant professor in information systems management in the Department of Business Administration, at the Athens University of Economics and Business (AUEB), Athens, Greece. He holds a BSc (Hons) in informatics and a BSc (Hons) in management both from the Athens University of Economics and Business, as well as an MSc in information systems engineering and a PhD in information systems from the Department of Computation at the University of Manchester Institute of Science and Technology (UMIST), England. Dr. Kardaras has participated in many research projects in IS/IT since 1990, and he has been teaching in IS courses as senior lecturer at South Bank University in London for seven years. He has published in the areas of IS planning, fuzzy cognitive maps, IS modeling, and e-commerce.

Gerold Kreutler is a PhD candidate and research assistant at the Department of Computer Science and Manufacturing at the University of Klagenfurt, Austria, and works within the interdisciplinary multi-year research projects "Modeling, Planning, and Assessment of Business Transformation Processes in the Area of Mass Customization" and "TECTRANS – Technology Transfer". He holds a master's degree in computer science (with Hons) and has been working in the domain of configuration systems for several years, especially in the field of online customer advisory. His main research interests are personalization of Web-based information systems, business process management, and the application of ERP systems.

Giuseppina Pagliuca has been a research assistant at the Department of Management, Statistical, Technological, and Environmental Sciences (DASTA) of the University "G. d'Annunzio", Pescara, Italy, since 1988. She received her PhD in data quality and documentation in life cycle assessment from the University "G. d'Annunzio" in 2003. Dr. Pagliuca's research interest includes implementation of LCA methodology and data quality in LCA.

Kaija-Stiina Paloheimo is an MSc and PhD student at Helsinki University of Technology Laboratory of Work Psychology and Leadership, and project manager at BIT Research Centre. Having close to 20 years of experience in various development and marketing functions of globally-operating equipment manufacturing companies within the area of medical technology, she has studied the customer interfaces and service business development of globally-operating industrial manufacturers for industrial customers, of industrial design agencies, of real estate and facility service providers, and of financial service providers. Her dissertation focuses on customer knowledge and service business development.

Thomas Ditlev Petersen holds a Master of Science in engineering and currently holds an industrial PhD scholarship. He is employed at Aalborg Industries A/S and related to Department of Production at Aalborg University. His primary research areas are product modeling, information modeling, and mass customization and product configuration in ETO companies. His industrial PhD project was initiated in the fall of 2004 and is scheduled to be finished in the summer of 2007.

Luigia Petti has been an associate professor in quality and environmental management systems, at "G. d'Annunzio" University, Pescara (Italy) since 2002. She was a researcher at the same university from 1993 to 2002 and a visiting researcher at "Carlo Bo" University, Urbino, Italy, from 1994 to 1996. Her research interests include methodology and application of environmental management tools, such as life cycle assessment (and simplified life cycle-based tools), quality function deployment for environment, and eco-labeling.

Andrea Raggi graduated in 1988 from the University of Bologna, Italy, where he studied economics and business administration. In 1989, he joined the University of Bologna as an assistant professor. During 1998-2004, he was associate professor at the Faculty of Economics, University "G. d'Annunzio", Pescara, Italy. Since 2005, he has been full professor in industrial ecology and related disciplines at the same university. In the environmental science field, he has been working on the development of environmental quality indices, the assessment of the strategic value of eco-compatible technologies, the evolution of environmental management tools, and their implementation.

Soroosh Saghiri is a PhD student in the Strategic Operations Management Centre, Norwich Business School, University of East Anglia (UEA), and also as a lecturer in operations and supply chain management at the University of Greenwich Business School. His MSc and BSc degrees are in industrial engineering. He has six years of experience in academics as well as consultancy, mainly in operations strategy, supply chain management, and business process improvement. Soroosh has publications in international journals and conferences. His main research areas are: supply chain management modeling and analysis; contemporary production management systems, which include agile manufacturing, lean production, mass customization, and quick response systems; quantitative modeling; soft computing, and fuzzy mathematical programming; and decision-making modeling and operational research approaches to production planning and control.

Tomohiko Sakao has been a guest researcher at Institute for Product Development and Machine Elements, Darmstadt University of Technology, since 2005. He received a BS, an MS, and a PhD in precision machinery engineering from the University of Tokyo (1993, 1995, and 1998, respectively). He was a researcher at Mitsubishi Research Institute, Inc., Japan, from 1998 to 2005. He has been a visiting researcher at Research into Artifacts, Center for Engineering, the University of Tokyo, Japan, since 2002. His research interests include Service Engineering, product/service customization, environmental engineering (for example, Ecodesign and Life Cycle Assessment), and intelligent machines (for example, self-maintenance machines and cellular machines).

Yoshiki Shimomura has been a professor in the Human Mechatronics Systems Course, Faculty of System Design, Tokyo Metropolitan University, since 2005. Prior to this appointment, he was an associate professor in research into artifacts, Center for Engineering, the University of Tokyo. He received his PhD in precision machinery engineering from the Graduate School of the University of Tokyo in 1997. Dr. Shimomura's research interest includes service engineering, life cycle engineering, design theory and methodology, intelligent systems, reasoning mechanism, and soft machines (self-maintenance machines and cellular machines).

Alberto Simboli is a PhD student at the Science Dept, University "G. d'Annunzio", Pescara, Italy. He has been granted a research scholarship on the subject "Evolution of Production Systems". He graduated cum laude in 2002 from the Faculty of Economics of the same university, where he studied business management and economics. He carried out a final degree thesis titled "Study and Implementation of an Integrated System for Production and Logistics". Since 2003, he has been carrying out research on cleaner technologies, DfE (design for environment), reverse logistics, and organizational innovation.

Timo Soininen is a docent at Helsinki University of Technology (HUT), Software Business and Engineering Institute (SoberIT). His research interests center on the processes and information system tools for configurable products, software, and services. He has previously worked at HUT as acting professor of information technology during 2001-2005. He has authored and co-authored close to five dozen articles published in various scientific journals, conferences, and workshops. He has also been a member of the program and organizing committees of a dozen conferences and workshops, including the annual series of Configuration Workshops since 2000, and acted as a guest editor, associate editor, or referee for various journals related to his research interests.

Cosimo Spera is the chief executive officer of Zipidy Inc., a Fulbright scholar, and a NATO and MINE fellow. He holds a PhD in operations research from Yale University and the University of Siena, Italy, and an MS in applied mathematics from the University of Siena. His current research interests include supply chain management, agent technology, adaptive and learning systems. He is a member of the INFORMS and MPS societies.

Adolfo Steiger-Garcao is a full professor at the Department of Electrical and Electronic Engineering (DEE) of the Faculty of Science and Technology of the New University of Lisbon (DEE/FCT/UNL). He is the head of the DEE/FCT/UNL, the executive director of the UNINOVA Institute, and the director of the Intelligent Robotics Centre, where he is responsible for the areas of digital systems and micro-electronics. He has more than 150 scientific publications in international journals, book chapters, and international conferences, many of them in the area of computer science and interoperable systems. He has been responsible, during the last 10 years, for more than 50 international R&D projects. He is also a scientific evaluator of national and international projects and programs.

Lic.Sc. (Tech) Juha Tiihonen is a researcher and project manager in the Product Data Management Group (PDMG) at the Department of Computer Science and Engineering of Helsinki University of Technology (HUT). His main interest is product and service configuration in its various forms, including conceptual models for configuration knowledge, modeling methods and tools, configurators, operations management aspects of business processes based on product and service configuration, long-term management of configuration knowledge, and design for configuration. He currently manages and a three-year research project on service configuration and its configurator support, and finalizes his doctoral thesis.

Jone Uribetxebarria is an investigator in the design and production area at Ikerlan, where she has over 10 years' experience working within the areas of robotics, production, and design technologies. She has been involved in several national research projects, as well as industry transfer projects in the fields of CAD/CAM systems, product configurators, production systems, and new product development methodologies. Currently, she is involved in national research projects dealing with product models and mass customization

Martín Zangitu is an investigator in the information technologies area at Ikerlan. He has 20 years' experience working within the areas of CAD/CAM, design technologies, business processes, and so forth. He has been involved in several national research projects, as well as industry transfer projects in the fields of CAD/CAM systems, product configurators, and business process redesign. Currently, he is involved in national research projects dealing with product models and mass customization.

Markus Zanker is an assistant professor of computer science at the University Klagenfurt. He received an MS as well as a MBA from the University Klagenfurt and wrote his PhD thesis on multi-site product configuration. His research interests lie in knowledge-based applications such as recommendation and interactive selling applications as well as configuration systems. Furthermore, he is currently putting a specific emphasis on knowledge acquisition and modeling of user interaction as well as on distributed problem-solving and constraint techniques.

Yiyang Zhang is a PhD candidate in School of Mechanical and Aerospace Engineering at Nanyang Technological University, Singapore. She received her BBA and MBA degrees from School of Management at Northeastern University, China (1999 and 2002, respectively). Her current research interests are customer decision-making process, product portfolio planning, and customer requirement management.

Helmut Zsifkovits is a senior lecturer at the Institute for Industrial Logistics, University of Leoben, Austria, and a member of the executive board, Bundesvereinigung Logistik Austria (Austrian Logistics Association). He holds both a master's and PhD degrees in business administration from the University of Graz, Austria, with a focus on information systems. His research is focused on logistics systems, process management, and process modeling. He is the author and editor of books and papers on project management, TQM, and executive information systems implementation. Former assignments include head of eLogistics, evolaris eBusiness Competence Center in Graz, Austria; professor of Logistics and Process Management for the FH JOANNEUM University of Applied Sciences in Kapfenberg, Austria; head of IT and Logistics for the Austrian Academy of Management; and information office manager for UBG GmbH, a DaimlerChrysler company.

Index

A

Aalborg Industries A/S (AI) 72
able-to-production (ATP) 174
abstract data type (ADT) 142
Active
  Data Objects (ADO) 116
  Server Pages (ASP) 116
advisory system 250
aggregate relationships (AND) 38
Application
  Program Interface (API) 45, 116
application
  protocols (APs) 141
artificial intelligence (AI) 222
assemble-to-order (ATO) 42, 187, 191
association rule learning method 109
Automated debugging 226
Axiomatic Design Theory 35

B

Basque industry 34
behavioral view 35
bill-of-material (BOM) 8, 191
build-to-forecast (BTF) 174
build-to-order (BTO) 64, 175

build-to-order supply chain management 64
business objects (BOs) 141
business process reengineering (BPR) 243
business strategy xii

C

CBA-CB algorithm 112
channel parameters (ChPs) 259
co-producer xiii
coefficient of variation (COV) 82
collaborative filtering (CF) 108, 109
Communications of the ACM, 40 120
Comprehensive Framework Encompassing the Main
    Conditions for Achieving Mass Customization
    78
computer-aided quality control (CAQ) 190
Computer Aided Design 34
configurable products (CP 2
configuration knowledge base (CKB) 226
constraint satisfaction problem 224
content-based filtering (CBF) 108, 109
content parameters (CoPs) 259
customer-centric production system 163
customer relation management systems (CRM) 199
customer relationship management xiii